SOCIOLOGICAL METHODOLOGY ❧ 1991 ❧

SOCIOLOGICAL METHODOLOGY 1991

VOLUME 21

EDITOR Peter V. Marsden

ADVISORY EDITORS Gerhard Arminger

Aaron Cicourel

Glenn Firebaugh

Jan Hoem

Margaret M. Marini

Ronald Schoenberg

Michael E. Sobel

Christopher Winship

An official publication by Basil Blackwell Ltd. for

THE AMERICAN SOCIOLOGICAL ASSOCIATION

WILLIAM V. D'ANTONIO, *Executive Officer*

Library of Congress Catalog Card Information
Sociological Methodology. 1969–85
San Francisco, Jossey-Bass. 15 v. illus. 24 cm. annual. (Jossey-Bass behavioral science
series)
Editor: 1969, 1970: E. F. Borgatta; 1971, 1972, 1973–74: H. L. Costner;
1975, 1976, 1977: D. R. Heise; 1978, 1979, 1980: K. F. Schuessler;
1981, 1982, 1983–84: S. Leinhardt; 1985: N. B. Tuma

Sociological Methodology. 1986–88
Washington, DC, American Sociological Association. 3 v. illus. 24 cm. annual.
Editor: 1986: N. B. Tuma; 1987, 1988: C. C. Clogg

Sociological Methodology. 1989–1991
Oxford, Basil Blackwell. 3 v. illus. 24 cm. annual.
Editor: 1989, 1990: C. C. Clogg; 1991: P. V. Marsden
"An official publication of the American Sociological Association."
1. Sociology—Methodology—Year books. I. American Sociological
Association. II. Borgatta, Edgar F., 1924– ed.

HM24.S55   301'.01'8   68-54940
                           rev.
Library of Congress   [r71h2]

British Cataloguing in Publication Data
Sociological Methodology. Vol. 21
1. Sociology. Methodology
301'.01'8

ISBN 0-631-18155-5
ISSN 0081-1750

Typeset by Huron Valley Graphics, Ann Arbor, MI
Printed by Edwards Brothers, Ann Arbor, MI

CONSULTANTS

Alan Agresti
Michael Akritas
Paul D. Allison
Gerhard Arminger
Mark P. Becker
Richard A. Berk
William T. Bielby
Kenneth A. Bollen
Edgar F. Borgatta
Ronald L. Breiger
Richard T. Campbell
Glenn R. Carroll
Herbert L. Costner
Thomas A. DiPrete
Patrick Doreian
Scott R. Eliason
Glenn Firebaugh
Gene Fisher
Neil Fligstein
Thomas Flory
John Fox
Steven Gortmaker
John Grego
David B. Grusky
David K. Guilkey
Kenneth A. Hardy
David R. Heise
Michael Hout
Guillermina Jasso
David A. Kenny
George Kephart

Gary King
Tim Futing Liao
Robert D. Mare
William M. Mason
Ross L. Matsueda
J. Miller McPherson
Robert Mislevy
N. Krishnan Namboodiri
Robert Nash Parker
Trond Petersen
Adrian Raftery
David Rauma
Ronald Schoenberg
Joseph Schwartz
James W. Shockey
Herbert L. Smith
Michael E. Sobel
John Sonquist
Aage B. Sørensen
Seymour Sudman
Judith Tanur
Jay Teachman
David Thissen
Nancy Brandon Tuma
Stanley Wasserman
Halliman H. Winsborough
Christopher Winship
Lawrence L. Wu
Yu Xie
Kazuo Yamaguchi

CONTENTS

CONTRIBUTORS

Gerhard Arminger, Department of Economics, Bergische Universität, Wuppertal

David J. Bartholomew, London School of Economics and Political Science

Richard A. Berk, Department of Sociology, University of California, Los Angeles

William T. Bielby, Department of Sociology, University of California, Santa Barbara

Hubert M. Blalock, Jr., Department of Sociology, University of Washington

Kenneth A. Bollen, Department of Sociology, University of North Carolina, Chapel Hill

David A. Freedman, Department of Statistics, University of California, Berkeley

Michael T. Hannan, Department of Sociology, Cornell University

Leeann Jolly, Department of Sociology, Ohio State University

Emily W. Kane, Department of Sociology, University of Wisconsin, Madison

Robert L. Kaufman, Department of Sociology, Ohio State University

Robert D. Mare, Department of Sociology and Center for Demography and Ecology, University of Wisconsin, Madison

William M. Mason, Department of Sociology, University of California, Los Angeles

Ross L. Matsueda, Department of Sociology, University of Wisconsin, Madison

Robert M. O'Brien, Department of Sociology, University of Oregon

Toby L. Parcel, Department of Sociology, Ohio State University

Trond Petersen, Walter A. Haas School of Business Administration, University of California, Berkeley

Karl F. Schuessler, Department of Sociology, Indiana University

Howard Schuman, Department of Sociology and Institute for Social Research, University of Michigan

Christopher Winship, Departments of Sociology and Statistics, Northwestern University

INFORMATION FOR AUTHORS

Sociological Methodology is an annual volume on methods of research in the social sciences. Sponsored by the American Sociological Association, *Sociological Methodology*'s mission is to disseminate material that advances empirical research in sociology and related disciplines. Chapters present original methodological contributions, expository statements on and illustrations of recently developed techniques, and critical discussions of research practice. *Sociological Methodology* seeks contributions that address the full range of problems confronted by empirical work in the contemporary social sciences, including conceptualization and modeling, research design, data collection, measurement, and data analysis. Work on the methodological problems involved in any approach to empirical social science is appropriate for *Sociological Methodology*.

The content of each annual volume of *Sociological Methodology* is driven by submissions initiated by authors; the volumes do not have specific annual themes. Editorial decisions regarding manuscripts submitted are based heavily on the advice of expert referees; each article submitted for consideration is read by two or more editorial consultants. Criteria for evaluation include originality, breadth of interest and applicability, and expository clarity. Discussions of implications for research practice are vital, and authors are urged to include empirical illustrations of the methods they discuss.

Authors should submit four copies of manuscripts to the Editor (see below). Manuscripts should include an informative abstract of not more than one double-spaced page, and should not identify the author within the text. Submission of a manuscript for review by *Sociological Methodology* implies that it has not been previously published and that it is not under review elsewhere.

Inquiries concerning the appropriateness of material and other aspects of editorial policies and procedures are welcome; prospective authors should direct correspondence to:

Peter V. Marsden, Editor
Sociological Methodology
Department of Sociology
Harvard University
616 William James Hall
33 Kirkland Street
Cambridge, MA 02138
Electronic mail address:
SOCMETH@HARVUNXT.BITNET

PROLOGUE

The chapters in this twenty-first volume of *Sociological Methodology* introduce novel approaches to social science research problems, refine previous ones, and reevaluate research practices that have become conventional. Most contributors suggest concrete steps that practicing researchers can take to strengthen the conclusions they draw from data. The volume begins with an outstanding exemplar of the integration of theory and research. Succeeding chapters present innovations in sampling designs, measurement methods, and techniques for data analysis. The closing section focuses attention on the interrelationships among theoretical models, research designs, and approaches to extracting causal inferences.

In his chapter on theoretical and methodological issues in the study of organizational evolution, Michael Hannan's substantive concern is with legitimation processes and how they influence the creation and dissolution of organizations. His modeling efforts translate theoretical claims about unobservable processes of legitimation and competition into researchable hypotheses about the dependence of creation and dissolution rates on the density (number of organizations) of an organizational population. Hannan's chapter goes on to discuss observation plans and the specification of stochastic models for data analysis; some points of special interest are its use of different statistical models for event counts—Poisson and negative binomial regression—and its discussion of the intrinsic difficulty of choosing between different parametric specifications of the legitimation process, given the nature of that process and the data available.

Chapter 2, by Toby Parcel, Robert Kaufman, and Leeann Jolly, illustrates the use of multiplicity sampling methods for obtaining random samples of organizations and other aggregates of which individuals are members. This approach, also known as hypernetwork sampling, generates probability-proportional-to-size samples of aggregate units by asking individuals in random probability samples about their affiliations. This individual-based approach to sampling aggregates is of special value when sampling frames for aggregate units are unavailable or known to be flawed. Parcel and colleagues show that the approach can be used for multilevel studies—in their case, of individuals, work units, and work establishments. They provide a valuable review of other approaches to assembling data on organizations and a detailed report on the conduct and results of their pilot study that used the multiplicity sampling technique.

Chapters 3 through 5 deal, in different ways, with problems of measurement. Emily Kane and Howard Schuman study what is, in essence, a problem of validity: the assumption that answers to open-ended questions in surveys reflect respondents' relatively intense concerns. Kane and Schuman suggest the alternative view that under typical interview conditions, survey respondents are likely to provide answers that reflect current awareness rather than concern. Issues that have been matters of media attention or public debate at the time of an interview will be salient and cognitively accessible to respondents and may be mentioned frequently in response to open-ended survey queries. Kane and Schuman compare responses to open and closed questions in Samuel Stouffer's classic study, *Communism, Conformity, and Civil Liberties.* Their new analyses of these data show that mentions of Communism in response to open-ended questions about worries and concerns did not necessarily measure intensity of concern about Communism. This finding does not lead Kane and Schuman to a general conclusion about the relative merits of open and closed questions; it does remind survey analysts of the necessity to consider carefully the context of an interview situation when interpreting data.

Many chapters in previous volumes of *Sociological Methodology* have applied statistical methods to the assessment of the reliability of measures; see, for example, the chapter by David Heise and George Bohrnstedt in *Sociological Methodology 1970,* or that by Duane Alwin and David Jackson in *Sociological Methodology 1980.*

Much of this work has concentrated on factor-analytic and covariance structure methods for assessing the reliability of multiple, continuous measures of unobserved variables. In Chapter 4, David Bartholomew and Karl Schuessler develop a reliability coefficient for scales formed from dichotomous items, assuming that a latent trait (logit-probit) model is used to score the items. They present methods of estimating this coefficient and demonstrate that the magnitude of the coefficient varies with the number of items in a scale as well as with the degree to which items are related to latent true scores. Numerous examples illustrate the use and the properties of this reliability coefficient.

Robert O'Brien's chapter studies the effect of measurement error on the correlations and covariances of aggregate-level measures. The measures that O'Brien studies are mean ratings of aggregates by raters (respondents), or means of variables that characterize elements that compose an aggregate. Such measures are often obtained in multilevel studies, where several lower-level elements are nested within each aggregate unit; the number of elements may vary across aggregates. For example, one might measure a property of a work organization using the mean response to a survey item by a sample of the organization's employees. (Note that such a design differs from that used by Parcel et al., in which there normally would be only one lower-level element [individual respondent] for each higher-level unit [work group or organization].) Aggregate measures are also obtained from "crossed" designs in that each of several aggregates is scored by each member of a panel of raters. Aggregate measures will be unreliable to the extent that the responses of potential raters (or characteristics of elements that might be sampled in obtaining the measures) vary within an aggregate. Further, measures of relationship involving aggregate variables must be adjusted for joint sampling: The correlation and covariance between two aggregate-level scores may be inflated or deflated when both scores are based on data that come from the same elements (e.g. employees, raters); the problems posed by joint sampling parallel, in a way, those presented by correlated measurement error. Chapter 5 shows how techniques based on a psychometric approach known as generalizability theory can be used to address these problems. Reliability estimates for aggregate measures are developed using components of variance. O'Brien next shows how to adjust correlations and covariances of aggregate-level measures for unreliability and joint sampling, in a manner analogous to the correction for attenuation from classical test theory. The approach outlined in Chapter 5 should be of very wide applicability as sociologists continue to develop multilevel data bases.

Chapters 6 and 7 address different problems that arise in the study of simultaneous (nonrecursive) structural equation models. William Bielby and Ross Matsueda note that estimates of reciprocal effects from such models often have quite high sampling variability, which makes it difficult for researchers to draw firm conclusions about the relationships of greatest concern to them. Chapter 6 suggests that it is useful to view this problem as one of the adequacy of statistical power—the capacity of statistical tests to reject false null hypotheses. Bielby and Matsueda demonstrate that the power of tests associated with reciprocal effects depends on various features of a nonrecursive model—its number of overidentifying restrictions, the quality of its instrumental variables, and the extent to which its disturbance terms covary. The power of tests for detecting nonzero effects of endogenous variables or for detecting asymmetries of such effects may be quite limited—even when the specification of a model meets formal criteria for identification, a sample is reasonably large, and exogenous variables are modestly correlated. Assessing the power of a test using the approach outlined in this chapter can help a researcher to judge whether reciprocal effects are genuinely absent or symmetric, or whether failure to reject a null hypothesis might instead reflect insufficient statistical power.

Chapter 7, by Robert Mare and Christopher Winship, is concerned with the estimation of nonrecursive models for systems of discrete variables, as distinct from the continuous variables with which Bielby and Matsueda's presentation is concerned. Previous discussions of such models (for example, Stephen Brier's chapter in *Sociological Methodology 1979*) have concluded either that logit and loglinear techniques for the analysis of cross-classified data cannot separate the causal or "structural" effects of endogenous variables on one another from their partial (noncausal) association, or that they require the structural effects of endogenous variables on each other to be equal. Mare and Winship demonstrate, however, that it is possible to estimate nonrecursive loglinear models that are fully analogous to linear simultaneous equation models. They accomplish this by making use of recently developed techniques for studying cross-classifictions with partially observed variables. Mare and Winship argue that their loglinear approach is preferable to an approach based on multivariate probit analysis because they avoid the assumption that discrete variables are always realizations of latent, normally distributed continuous variables.

During the 1980s, there was substantial methodological work on criticism, or the diagnosis of violations of assumptions in fitted statistical models; see, for example, the chapter by Dennis Cook and Sanford Weisberg in *Sociological Methodology 1982*. Most of this work is concerned with regression models for observed variables; it introduces graphical and statistical diagnostic methods for identifying cases that are outliers or that exert high influence on a fitted regression surface. The location of such cases may point to errors of measurement or data transcription; it may suggest transformations of variables or other changes in functional form. There has, however, been very little work on diagnostics for models that involve latent variables, such as factor analytic or covariance structure models. In Chapter 8, Kenneth Bollen and Gerhard Arminger define residuals for models with continuous latent variables and continuous indicators. Their formulations show how residuals can be defined for different methods of estimating factor scores (values of latent variables for specific cases) from observed data. Bollen and Arminger develop measures of the variability of these residuals and then propose large-sample statistics for the identification of outlier cases. Their simulation results show that a naive standardization of residuals performs inadequately, but that an alternative standardization is a helpful guide to outliers, even in relatively small ($N = 60–100$) samples.

Trond Petersen's Chapter 9 is about how imprecise measurement of the time at which events occur affects the results of event-history or hazard-rate analyses. He shows that estimators of rates that assume exact measures of time are biased if data tell only the interval of time in which an event took place and a researcher assumes that the actual timing is at the end of the interval. Petersen refers to this problem as time-aggregation bias. His chapter demonstrates that the extent of such bias grows as the interval of time within which the event took place becomes wider and as the true rate of the occurence of events becomes higher. Having identified the problem, Petersen then turns attention to the practical question of how a researcher should assign a time within the interval in order to minimize the bias. His analysis suggests that the intuitive solution of assigning the midpoint of the interval serves this purpose well, at least for the specific models considered in this chapter.

Chapters 10 through 14 continue the discussion of issues of causal inference from nonexperimental data that has taken place in recent volumes of *Sociological Methodology,* particularly those that appeared in 1987 and 1988. David Freedman's essay "Statistical Models and Shoe Leather" points to the inseparability of theoretical models, research designs, and data analysis, and argues that there are severe limits to the capacity of strictly statistical tools to support causal inferences. Freedman tells much of his story by example; in particular, he describes John Snow's research on the causes of cholera as an example of a convincing causal inference built on nonexperimental information. Freedman asserts that Snow's success came about because his model of cholera causation implied many observable outcomes and because he devoted great effort to collecting appropriate data.

Freedman's discussion stresses the need for substantive models that justify the functional forms assumed in statistical models, as well as the strengths of quasi-experimental designs. He observes that many causal inferences rest only on the results of statistical tests of null hypotheses and suggests that analysts will obtain more convincing inferences if findings are replicated and cross-validated in tests on multiple data sets. He further argues that efforts to extract convincing inferences from nonexperimental data using statistical methods must give far more attention to the formulation of models and the accuracy of assumptions than is typical in contemporary quantitative research in the social sciences. Moreover, in Freedman's view there are limitations in the extent to which "technical fixes" can compensate for deficiencies in research design, the availability of data, or measurement.

Freedman's essay raises basic questions about much current research practice. The succeeding chapters provide reflections on Freedman's position by Richard Berk and William Mason, recent Chairs of the Section on Methodology of the American Sociological Association, and by Hubert M. Blalock, Jr., one of the intellectual leaders of the effort to develop methodology for drawing causal inferences on the basis of nonexperimental data. Berk concentrates on recommendations for improving the conduct of research, arguing for increased use of cross-validation and for matching scientific aspirations to both the state of substantive knowledge and the capacity of data sets. Blalock contends that analysts long have been aware of some of the issues that Freedman raises, and he claims that any piece of research necessarily involves untested assumptions. He asks why there has been little cumulative progress on the development of models through an iterative process of questioning assumptions, collecting new data, and reexamining prior conclusions; he suggests that this has to do both with the nature of contemporary professional training and with the institutional organization of sociology as a discipline. Mason, while concurring in large part with Freedman, also stresses the need for strengthening graduate training and calls for closer collaboration between social scientists and statisticians. His essay identifies a number of unresolved statistical issues of special interest to social scientists. *Sociological Methodology 1991* concludes with Freedman's brief response to the three commentaries.

ACKNOWLEDGEMENTS

This is the first volume of *Sociological Methodology* that I am privileged to have the opportunity to edit, and it is my hope that readers will learn as much from reading it as I have in the course of assembling it. As is typical in such collective enterprises I have numerous debts to acknowledge. I am especially grateful to the 61 editorial consultants who have reviewed one or more of the manuscripts considered for this volume; more than anything else, the selection of the material presented here was based on the advice of these scholars. Their freely provided critiques are detailed, thoughtful, and almost uniformly constructive; their commentaries have strengthened substantially several of the presentations that appear here. I also wish to thank my predecessor as editor of *Sociological Methodology,* Clifford Clogg, who turned the publication over to me in excellent condition, initiated the review of some of the chapters that appear here, and was generous with his time and advice during the editorial transition.

Several people have collaborated with me in developing this volume. Sandra Leonard and Suzanne Washington of the Department of Sociology at Harvard University have aided me in manuscript processing and office operations. Ann Kremers has continued to give thorough, quality attention to copyediting the manuscripts. And Colleen Doyle of Basil Blackwell, Ltd., has efficiently managed the production of the volume and has patiently but firmly ridden herd on the rest of us to see that it appears in a timely fashion. Finally, I am delighted to acknowledge the continuing financial support of the American Sociological Association for *Sociological Methodology,* and the material contributions of Harvard University to the operations of the editorial offices.

Peter V. Marsden
Harvard University
November, 1990

THEORETICAL AND METHODOLOGICAL ISSUES IN ANALYSIS OF DENSITY-DEPENDENT LEGITIMATION IN ORGANIZATIONAL EVOLUTION

Michael T. Hannan*

This paper examines theoretical and methodological issues that arise in research on density dependence in organizational founding processes. It proposes and evaluates new models of density dependence. The models vary the specification of the legitimation process used in prior research on founding rates in organizational populations. That research is based on a generalized Yule model. This model assumes that increasing density has its maximal impact on legitimation when density is near zero, that is, at the onset of an organizational population's growth.

One of the proposed models is only a slight extension of the generalized Yule model; it adds a "constant source" (a nonzero founding rate at zero density). The other two models differ qualitatively;

An earlier version of this paper was presented in a symposium at the University of Washington, Seattle, in honor of Hubert M. Blalock, Jr. It is a pleasure to acknowledge my great intellectual debt to Tad Blalock. The research reported here was supported by National Science Foundation grants SES-8809006 and SES-9008493. It is part of a collaborative project with Glenn Carroll on legitimation and competition in the evolution of organizational populations. I thank David Barron for excellent technical assistance and Jane Banaszak-Holl, David Barron, Glenn Carroll, Miller McPherson, Susan Olzak, James Ranger-Moore, David Weakliem, and two reviewers for helpful comments on earlier drafts.
*Cornell University

they assume an S-shaped relationship between density and legitimation. In other words, they assume that density has its maximal impact on legitimation at some intermediate level of density. The new models are versions of the well-known logistic and Gompertz models but with a twist. Instead of representing the growth of a phenomenon—legitimation here—in *time,* as is usual (see, for example Hamblin, Jacobsen, and Miller 1973; Tuma and Hannan 1984), the proposed models represent growth in legitimation as a function of *density.*

In addition to proposing new formulations of the legitimation process, this paper treats methodological issues that arise in efforts to estimate models of founding processes with commonly available archival data. This relatively unconventional coupling of theoretical and methodological themes reflects a conviction that explaining sociological processes involves explicit attention to correspondence between general theory and models of particular instances of the processes implied by the theory, models of processes, stochastic representations, estimators, observation plans, and data.[1] The general methodological issues treated presumably have implications for efforts to test broad classes of sociological theories.

The research reported here comes from a research program that seeks to make such connections explicit in research on organizational ecology. The substantive import of the new models and of empirical estimates of their parameters can best be appreciated if the full chain of inference is considered. For this reason, this paper (1) sketches the general theory that motivates the models of founding processes, (2) compares several parametric models of founding processes, (3) relates the models to stochastic models of arrival processes, (4) motivates use of negative binomial regression models applied to observation plans that produce yearly counts of foundings, and (5) presents and interprets empirical estimates of four models of foundings of American national labor unions.

1. THEORETICAL BACKGROUND

The problem of understanding the effects of density on founding rates in organizational populations arises from developments in

[1]Few sociological theorists and methodologists consider all of these links. The most forceful proponents of the strategy of making all the connections explicit are Blalock (1968, 1969, 1989) and Coleman (1964, 1968, 1989).

population ecology theories of organizations. These macrosociological theories of organizations build on general ecological and evolutionary models of change. Their goal is to understand the forces that shape organizational structures over long time spans. This theoretical approach makes two major departures from mainstream sociological theories of organization: It takes as a unit of analysis the population of organizations, and it emphasizes selection rather than adaptation. The population perspective concentrates on the sources of variability and homogeneity of organizational forms. It considers the rise of new forms and the demise or transformation of existing forms. In doing so, this approach pays considerable attention to population dynamics, especially the processes of competition among diverse organizations for limited resources such as organizers, members, and capital.

The initial phases of theory and research on the population ecology of organizations have focused mainly on *numerical* features of the world of organizations. In their earliest statements of the approach, Hannan and Freeman (1977) asked, Why are there so many kinds of organizations? This is a natural and important question for sociology because organizations can in principle grow without limit. Under what conditions will one or a few organizations expand to take on many activities in society? When will the growth of organizations be constrained so that none grows really large and many kinds proliferate? Answering these questions involves considering the impacts of both external environments and internal population dynamics.[2] This paper concentrates on the effect of internal population dynamics (given external constraints) on the growth of organizational populations.

Theory and research on internal population dynamics and population growth have come to focus on *density dependence* in vital rates of organizational populations: rates of founding and mortality (of various forms).[3] This paper considers only founding rates. The

[2]Aldrich and Marsden (1988), Freeman and Hannan (1989), and Singh and Lumsden (1990) provide recent assessments of theory and research on the population ecology of organizations.

[3]Organizational density is the number of organizations in a population. The size of the population is implicit in its spatial and temporal definition and in the structure of covariates used to represent the environment. The parameters of the models discussed in this paper vary with the specifications of the population. An interesting analysis by Carroll and Wade (1991) contrasts esti-

same theory and models apply to mortality as well. However, analysis of mortality is more complicated in that it must consider processes of aging and individual characteristics of organizations in addition to the variables considered here (see Hannan and Freeman 1989). Numerous recent studies have used variations on the models discussed here to investigate density dependence in rates of organizational mortality. See, for instance, Hannan and Freeman (1988), Carroll and Hannan (1989a, 1989b), Delacroix, Swaminathan, and Solt (1989), and Barnett and Amburgey (1990).

Prior research on density dependence in organizational founding rates uses a theory and a parametric model proposed by Hannan (1986, 1989b). The theory claims that the founding rate of an organizational population depends on legitimation and competition. It postulates that the founding rate at historical time t, denoted by $\lambda(t)$, is proportional to the legitimation (L) of the population at that time and inversely proportional to the intensity of competition (C) within the population at that time. That is,

$$\lambda(t) = a_t \frac{L_t}{C_t}. \tag{1}$$

Here, a_t represents a function that summarizes the impacts of time-varying environmental conditions.

The theory also holds that levels of legitimation and competition are functions of the number of organizations in the population— that is, density. The model, discussed in the next section, consists of parametric representations of the dependence of legitimation and competition on density. In this section we discuss the theoretical motivation for the model and the parametric specifications.[4]

1.1. Competition and Density

The concept of niche provides a general way to express effects of environmental variations and competition on the growth rates of organizational populations. Niche theory in population biology began to take its modern form when Hutchinson (1957) proposed an

mates of parameters for populations of brewing firms defined at the level of the city, state, region, and nation.
    [4]An extended discussion of the issues treated in this section can be found in Hannan and Carroll (1991).

abstract geometric treatment of the niche. He defined the fundamental niche of a population as the hypervolume formed by the set of points for which the population's growth rate (fitness) is nonnegative. In other words, the fundamental niche consists of the set of all environmental conditions in which the population can grow or at least sustain its numbers. By extension, the fundamental niche of an organizational form consists of the social, economic, and political conditions required to sustain the functioning of organizations that embody the form.

The geometric conception of the niche facilitates definition of the *intersection* of fundamental niches of pairs of populations. If two populations rely on completely different kinds of resources and depend on different kinds of social and political institutions, then their fundamental niches do not intersect. Otherwise, they do intersect, and it makes sense to measure their similarity in terms of the degree of intersection (or overlap, when only one or two environmental dimensions are considered). The concept of intersection of fundamental niches leads naturally to a definition of *potential competition:* The potential for two populations to compete is proportional to the intersection of their fundamental niches. (This is potential competition because the populations must exist in the same systems to actually compete.) It follows that two populations compete if and only if their fundamental niches intersect. The implied equivalence of niche intersection and competition has played a crucial role in allowing ecologists to relate naturalistic observations on realized niches to dynamic models of population growth and expansion. Hannan and Freeman (1977, 1989) argue that such equivalence can play a similarly central role in empirical analysis and theoretical analysis of organizational dynamics.

When populations with intersecting fundamental niches inhabit the same system, potential competition is converted into actual competition. Under such conditions, the expansion of one population changes the conditions of existence of the others. In the case of competition, the presence of the competitor reduces the set (range) of environments in which the other populations can sustain themselves. Hutchinson coined the term *realized niche* to denote the restricted set of environments in which growth rates are positive in the presence of competitors (a subset of the fundamental niche). Except in the highly unusual case in which a population exists in isolation from all competitors, what can be observed in any concrete setting are realized niches.

Observing competition directly usually proves to be difficult because competitive influences are often indirect and diffuse. Hence, empirically minded analysts look for ways to study competition indirectly. One way is by exploiting the relationship between niche intersection and competition implied by classic competition theory. Population ecologists typically rely on the close relationship between competition theory and niche theory to obtain indirect estimates of competition from analysis of the effects of densities of interacting populations on changes in their realized niches (defined in terms of observed utilization of resources). The theoretical program that motivates this paper follows a similar approach. It focuses on the effects of organizational density on the intensity of competition.

Concentrating on the relationship between density and competition makes sense because the intensity of competition depends both on the degree of intersection of fundamental niches and the numbers of competitors involved. Even when two populations in the same system have intersecting fundamental niches, they presumably do not compete intensely if their numbers are very small (relative to the abundance of resources). Numbers (density) and resource abundance interact in affecting the intensity of competition. Mathematical models of ecological competition represent abundance in a scalar "carrying capacity" of the environment for a population. This term refers to the numbers that can be sustained in a particular environment in isolation from other populations (that is, in the absence of competition and facilitation). A useful way to formalize the concept of competition builds on the idea that the presence of a competitor in the system lowers the carrying capacity for the focal population. Because the intensity of competition depends on the numbers of actors in the competing population, models of competition commonly parameterize the effect of adding a member to the competing population on the growth rate of a focal population. The parameters that relate the density of the competitor to the growth rate are called competition coefficients.[5]

[5]MacArthur (1972) and Hutchinson (1978) provide insightful treatments of mathematical models of ecological competition, and Kingsland (1985) provides a fascinating intellectual history of the development of the models.

The research reported here concentrates on *intrapopulation* competition. This focus greatly simplifies the problem of identifying competition because one can safely assume that members of the same population have (very nearly) the same fundamental niche.[6] It follows that members of a population compete in the sense that the life chances of any one member depend on the presence of other members.

According to the theory, adding an organization to the population has only a slight effect on the frequency and strength of competitive interactions when density is low relative to abundance of resources. But when density is high, adding an organization strongly increases competition. In other words, the qualitative implication is that *competition increases with density at an increasing rate.*

1.2. *Legitimation and Density*

The literature on organizational sociology abounds with conceptualizations of institutionalization and legitimation. The richest vein of institutional theory appears to be one developed by John Meyer and collaborators (Meyer and Rowan 1977; Meyer and Scott 1983). These sociologists have led the way in developing the image of the institutional environment of modern organizations as largely cognitive and normative. In this view, the institutional environment consists largely of agreed-upon categories and normative prescriptions. Institutional norms are "rationalized and impersonal prescriptions that identify various social purposes as technical ones and specify in a rulelike way the appropriate means to pursue these technical purposes rationally" (Meyer and Rowan 1977, pp. 341–42). Such broad orienting institutional rules are supplemented by myriad specific norms that prescribe organizational structures appropriate in particular realms of activity—for example, schooling, medical care, and manufacturing.

What, then, does it mean for an organizational form to be institutionalized or legitimated? The most obvious answer—though not necessarily the most important one—is that an organizational form is legitimated to the extent to which its structure and routines

---

[6]The validity of this assumption depends, of course, on the precision with which boundaries of populations are marked.

follow the dictates of the prevailing institutional rules. In this sense, institutionalization means conformity with some set of rules, what DiMaggio and Powell (1983) termed institutional isomorphism. A second meaning holds that an organizational form is institutionalized or legitimated to the extent that it has a taken-for-granted character (Meyer and Rowan 1977; Meyer and Scott 1983). A form is legitimated in this sense when no question arises in the minds of actors that it serves as the natural way to effect some kind of collective action.

These two meanings of the concept of legitimation are not necessarily congruent. They diverge most clearly in cases in which some institutional rules are codified and promulgated as laws. What a society's laws endorse and prohibit may not agree with what its members take for granted. For instance, even though most forms of gambling are widely illegal in the U.S., many organizations in the gambling business, such as those operating numbers rackets and football pools, are taken for granted. Indeed, they also frequently have high institutional standing in the eyes of law-enforcement agencies because of highly formalized arrangements of payoffs. Which matters more: the laws or the conceptions and actions of consumers, police, and other key actors? The answer depends, no doubt, on the problem.

The idea of legitimation as taken-for-grantedness turns out to be more useful for the research problem considered here because it has an obvious link with density. So, without implying that other forms of legitimation are irrelevant, legitimation is used here to refer to taken-for-grantedness. In particular, legitimation does not mean formal legality of an organizational form. Indeed there is no obvious reason why the arguments cannot be applied to organizations involved in illegal activities such as prostitution, gambling, and price fixing.

How does the legitimation of an organizational form depend on its density? From the perspective of legitimation as taken-for-grantedness, it seems clear that extreme rarity of a form poses serious problems of legitimation. If almost no instances of a form exist, it can hardly be taken as the natural way to achieve some collective end. On the other hand, once a form becomes common, it seems unlikely that increases in numbers will have a great effect on its institutional standing. In other words, the conception of legitimation as taken-for-grantedness suggests that legitimation reacts to variations in density in the lower range but that something like a ceiling effect applies to the relationship. That is, *legitimation in the sense of taken-for-grantedness increases with density at a decreasing rate.*

2. A GENERALIZED YULE MODEL

The next step involves specifying particular substantive models that are consistent with the general arguments and that facilitate empirical analysis. We begin with the original model proposed by Hannan (1986) and used in most subsequent empirical research.

The first of the qualitative arguments about density dependence in the previous section holds that competition (C) increases with density (N) at an increasing rate:

$$\frac{dC}{dN} > 0 \quad \text{and} \quad \frac{dC^2}{d^2N} > 0.$$

Many parametric specifications can be consistent with these inequalities (depending on signs of parameters). This substantive model used one with a single parameter (other than a scaling factor)—an exponential relation between competition and the square of density:

$$C(t) = c_t \exp(\beta N_t^2), \qquad \beta > 0, \tag{2}$$

where c_t represents the effects of factors other than density that affect levels of competition. Choice of an exponential relationship rather than a simple linear relationship between competition and the square of density reflects the definition of rate as nonnegative. As far as can be determined from the research discussed below, this choice of specification does a reasonably good job of representing density dependence in the vital rates.

One possible motivation for the specification in (2) comes from considering the net of possible ties among actors in a population.[7] Suppose that the level of (indirect) competitive pressure is proportional to the number of pairs that can be formed: $\binom{N}{2} = \frac{N^2}{2} - \frac{N}{2}$. As a population grows, the squared term dominates such that the number of pairs is approximately $N^2/2$. Thus, the specification in (2) can be

[7]This interpretation has been suggested by Ronald Breiger and John Padgett (personnel communications).

considered an approximation of a model in which the strength of intrapopulation competition is proportional to the number of possible pairwise interactions (with the accuracy of the approximation improving as density increases, meaning that N^2 dominates N). This interpretation deserves attention because it can serve as a point of departure for integrating ecological and network conceptions of interaction and competition.

The second qualitative argument holds that legitimation increases with density at a decreasing rate:

$$\frac{dL}{dN} > 0 \quad \text{and} \quad \frac{dL^2}{d^2N} < 0.$$

Again, there are many models that can fit this pattern. The lack of any empirical information about the relationship and a preference for simple models over more complicated ones suggested a particularly simple assumption: Legitimation as taken-for-grantedness increases with density according to a power law:

$$L(t) = l_t N_t^\alpha, \qquad 0 < \alpha < 1, \tag{3}$$

where l_t represents the impacts of other time-varying factors. The inequality constraints in (3) ensure that the level of legitimation increases with density at a decreasing rate, in agreement with the qualitative argument.

The pair of assumptions about density dependence in competition and legitimation, equations (2) and (3), together with the basic model for the founding rate, equation (1), implies a parametric relationship between density and the founding rate. This set of assumptions has the particular advantage of forming a clear bridge from the general theory to empirical estimation. Inserting equations (2) and (3) into equation (1) yields an *estimable* model of density dependence in founding rates:

$$\lambda(t) = \kappa_\lambda(t)N_t^\alpha \exp(-\beta N_t^2) = \kappa_\lambda(t)N_t^\alpha \exp(\gamma N_t^2), \qquad \gamma = -\beta, \tag{4}$$

where $\kappa_\lambda(t) = a_t l_t / c_t$. (The signs of the second-order effect of density are switched from $-\beta$ to γ to simplify presentation of empirical results.) The key substantive hypotheses are

$$\alpha > 0, \qquad \gamma < 0.$$

This model implies that legitimation processes dominate at low density but that competition processes dominate at high density.

That is, *density has a nonmonotonic effect on the founding rate*. The founding rate rises as density increases until N reaches $N^* = \sqrt{\alpha/2\beta}$. From that point on, the founding rate falls with increasing density. This feature of the model distinguishes it from more conventional models of population growth.

The model in (4) has been called a generalized Yule (GY) model. It is a generalization of a Yule process in the sense that setting $\alpha = 1$ and $\beta = 0$ produces the classical Yule model of a birth process (Yule 1924; see Karlin and Taylor 1975).

2.1. *A Log-Quadratic Approximation*

Some research on nonmonotonic density dependence in organizational founding processes has used a log-quadratic approximation to the GY model.[8] This is a model in which the founding rate is a log-quadratic function of density:

$$\lambda(t) = l_t \exp(aN_t + bN_t^2), \qquad a > 0, b < 0. \tag{5}$$

Some researchers have estimated both the GY model and its approximation and have found that the approximation fits better than the original model. Consequently, it might seem natural to consider the specification in (5) as a rival model.

As Carroll and Hannan (1989a) explain, the approximation can give rise to similar paths of density dependence in the founding rate but does not have as straightforward a theoretical interpretation as the GY model. In particular, the representation in (5) does not follow from the assumption that legitimation increases with density at a decreasing rate.[9] Because the log-quadratic specification does

---

[8] This variation on the model entered the literature when Hannan and Freeman (1988) could not get maximum likelihood estimates of the GY model to converge in estimating mortality rates of national labor unions. They shifted to an alternative specification whose parameters have a similar qualitative interpretation and for which they could obtain stable empirical estimates.

[9] Carroll and Hannan (1989a) discuss two possible links between equation (5) and density-dependent legitimation. The log-quadratic representation in (5) implies either that legitimation is a positive exponential function of density, increasing with density at an increasing rate, or that legitimation is a log-quadratic function of density, increasing with density but eventually falling with increasing density beyond some point. Neither assumption appears to fit the theoretical arguments of the previous section. For this reason, the log-quadratic formulation is probably best viewed as a somewhat *ad hoc* approximation to the GY model.

not fit the theory and because it does not fit as well as the GY model with the data analyzed below, it is not considered further, except to note that it has been used in some of the empirical research on the subject of interest here.[10]

3. RESULTS OF PRIOR RESEARCH

There has been much research on the GY model (and the log-quadratic approximation) of nonmonotonic density dependence in founding rates during the past three years. Hannan and Freeman (1987) analyzed founding rates with data on national labor unions in the U.S. over the entire history of the population, 1836–1985. Their findings strongly support the hypothesis of nonmonotonic density dependence. Barnett and Carroll (1987) analyzed rates of founding of independent local telephone companies in several Iowa counties in the early history of this industry (1900–1917) and obtained similar qualitative results (with the log-quadratic approximation). So too did studies of foundings of brewing firms in the U.S. from 1634 to 1988 (Carroll and Swaminathan 1989) and in Germany from 1900 to 1988 (Carroll et al. 1989). Carroll and Hannan (1989a) analyzed foundings in populations of newspapers in nine areas: Argentina (1801–1900), Ireland (1801–1975), and seven metropolitan areas in the U.S. (1801–1975). They found the predicted pattern of first-order and second-order effects of density for all nine populations. However, these effects were statistically significant for only six populations, including the three largest. Finally, Olzak and West's (1990) study of American ethnic newspapers, Lomi and Freeman's (1990) study of Italian cooperatives in several industries, and Ranger-Moore, Banaszak-Holl, and Hannan's (1989) study of banks in Manhattan (1792–1980) and life insurance firms in the U.S. (1760–1937) also found the predicted pattern of effects.

A pair of analyses of founding rates of voluntary social service organizations (VSSOs) in Toronto in 1970–1982 found mixed support for the hypothesis of nonmonotonic density dependence. Tucker et al. (1988) found that the predicted pattern of density dependence holds for the full population only when public funding is increasing. However, when Tucker, Singh, and Meinhard (1990) considered

[10]Detailed comparison of fits of GY models and log-quadratic models for diverse empirical populations is the subject of current research with Glenn Carroll.

founding rates of specialist and generalist VSSOs separately, the findings supported the model. The Toronto study is limited in that it examined only a small slice of the population's history.[11]

Studies of diverse organizational populations, especially populations analyzed over long historical periods, offer strong support for the model. Singh and Lumsden (1990) provide a similar assessment of the evidence. So it appears that we have a strong empirical regularity—nonmonotonicity in density dependence in founding rates—and a theory and model that can explain it. The strength of the regularity provides motivation for investigating the structure of the model in more detail.

4. REFORMULATIONS OF THE LEGITIMATION FUNCTION

Most of the research on this subject has given more emphasis to the qualitative pattern of nonmonotonic density dependence than to the details of model specification. However, given the seemingly strong regularity in the form of density dependence, it seems worthwhile to scrutinize the model that has generated this research and to address the power of available data to discriminate among plausible competing models. Numerous parametric models of the relationship of legitimation and competition to density other than those in the generalized Yule model are consistent with the qualitative implications of the theoretical argument in section 1. Moreover, there are other ways of deriving nonmonotonic relationships between vital rates and density. This paper considers three plausible alternatives to the original GY specification.

[11]Three studies have estimated the model with data on *entries* of firms into an industry or local market. The results are mixed. Mitchell's (1987) study of rates of entry into the medical diagnostic imaging industry (1959–1986) supports the model. Wholey, Christianson, and Sanchez (1990) analyzed entry of HMOs into metropolitan statistical areas in the U.S. over the history of the population (1976–1988). In this case, entries into local markets include founding of local HMOs as well as creation of local organizations by national or regional firms in the HMO business. The results strongly support the model of nonmonotonic density dependence in the entry rate. But Hannan and Freeman (1989) found that density dependence in the rate of entry into the semiconductor industry was monotonic. Processes of entry into an industry are likely to differ from founding processes because entry includes foundings and adaptive changes of firms that operated in other industries. Given this difference, it is not clear what to make of the failure of the model to explain entries into the semiconductor industry.

4.1. *Adding a Source to the Generalized Yule Model*

The GY model has a potential disadvantage that has not been addressed in prior research on founding rates. The model implies that the founding rate is zero at zero density: There can be no foundings in a population whose density has shrunk to zero (as has happened several times in the early history of the population of American national labor unions, the subject of the empirical analysis below). This is a potential problem for two reasons. First, it runs counter to the observed facts: Foundings do occur in organizational populations with zero density. Second, the method of estimation used here (maximum likelihood [ML] estimation of negative binomial models) breaks down when density is zero because the likelihood is zero when density is zero.

Previous analyses of the GY model have used an *ad hoc* fix to this problem, replacing N with $N + c$, with c close to zero. For instance, Hannan and Freeman (1987) chose $c = .01$. With this modification, the founding rate is positive but small at zero density (as long as c is close to zero), and ML analysis can be performed.[12] But this kind of fix does not deal with a related problem. The model appears to be sensitive to the presence of observation of zero density because the distance (in terms of the model) between zero and one is so great. In other words, estimates of the model are likely to give great weight to observations with zero density. When there are many such observations, excluding them appears to cause large changes in estimates of α. This is not the case with the log-quadratic approximation or with the models proposed here.

If the GY model is to be used, the problem of the behavior of the model at zero density should be handled in another way. Perhaps the most straightforward modification is to add a constant, s, to the model:

$$\lambda(t) = e^s + \kappa_\lambda(t)N_t^\alpha \exp(-\beta N_t^2).$$ (6)

The constant, s, allows the founding rate to be positive even when density is zero.[13] Comparisons of estimates of GY models with and

[12]It is possible to estimate c directly using the method of maximum likelihood. This strategy has not proved to be useful with the model and data considered in this paper. More precisely, the estimates of c turn out to be very unstable.

[13]The loglinear relation between the constant and the rate is a convenience that constrains the rate to be nonnegative.

without the additive constant suggest that adding the constant greatly reduces the weight given to the observations with zero density.

Adding a constant to a model of density-dependent growth has many antecedents in the modeling of population growth, epidemics, and other processes whose rate of increase is some function of prevalence. In models of population growth, the constant represents immigration (see, for instance, Karlin and Taylor 1975, p. 195). In models of diffusion of innovations, the constant represents the effect of a constant source operating independently of interactions among members of a population (see, for instance, Bartholomew 1973; Coleman 1964). In the present context, the constant refers to a constant source of attempts at founding. Thus, the model in (6) is called a GY model with an additive constant (or source).

4.2. *A Logistic Model*

The GY specification with $0 < \alpha < 1$ (with or without an additive constant) implies that the biggest impact of growing density on legitimation occurs in tiny populations. This may not be sociologically realistic. Instead, perhaps there is a "threshold" of density below which a population virtually escapes notice, meaning that increases in density below the threshold do not create taken-for-grantedness. Once the threshold is passed, increases in density might have strong impacts on legitimation over some range. But ultimately, the impact of growing density ought to decline at high density, as the original model assumes. Such a reconceptualization suggests adoption of models of legitimation that have S-shaped growth paths, such as the logistic and Gompertz models.

As noted at the outset, the standard logistic model of population growth (and the Gompertz model) represents growth in some phenomenon in time; it is a particular model for the time derivative of some phenomenon. But there is nothing essential in the choice of time as the metric in logistic growth. In particular, the logic of the model does not prevent one from representing growth in legitimation as a logistic function of density:

$$\frac{dL}{dN} = \alpha L \left(1 - \frac{L}{L^*} \right).$$

Here L^* denotes the ceiling on legitimation, the maximum level of legitimation that an organizational form can achieve in a given socio-cultural environment. This specification conforms to the view that legitimation grows slowly with density in the early history of a population, when legitimation is low. Then at some point, it grows rapidly and finally slows as the upper limit is approached. The growth path of legitimation implied by this process is an S-shaped function of density. As density rises from zero, legitimation grows according to the (integral) function:

$$L = \frac{L^*}{1 + \left(\frac{L^*}{L_0} - 1\right) e^{-\alpha N}}. \tag{7}$$

The hypotheses are α, L_0, $L^* > 0$.

4.3. A Gompertz Model

The logistic model imposes the constraint that the growth path of legitimation be symmetric around the point of maximum growth rate, that is, that the S-shaped path be exactly symmetric. Because this requirement seems stronger than the qualitative reasoning demands, we also consider the Gompertz model, which is roughly similar but does not incorporate the symmetry restriction.

The Gompertz model can be derived as a consequence of time dependence in the growth rate of a compound growth process (Tuma and Hannan 1984, pp. 471–76). In the case under consideration, the compound growth process is one in which legitimation and the growth rate in legitimation are expressed as functions of density rather than time:

$$\frac{dL}{dN} = \rho(N)L. \tag{8}$$

Suppose that the change in the growth rate with density is negatively proportional to the growth rate:

$$\frac{d\rho(N)}{dN} = -\alpha\rho(N).$$

Solving this differential equation (subject to the initial condition $r(0) = r_0$) gives

$$\rho(N) = \rho_0 e^{-\alpha N}. \tag{9}$$

In other words, the Gompertz model builds on the assumption that the growth rate in legitimation declines exponentially with density. Finally, substitute the integral equation for the growth rate (9) into the compound growth process (8). This gives the Gompertz model in density:

$$\frac{dL}{dN} = \rho_0 e^{-\alpha N} L.$$

Solving this differential equation (subject to initial condition $L(0) = L_0$) yields

$$L(N) = L_0 \exp(c[1 - e^{-\alpha N}]), \qquad c = \rho_0/\alpha. \qquad (10)$$

The hypotheses are $\alpha, c > 0$.

It is also possible to incorporate a constant source into the logistic and Gompertz models. This paper does not report estimates of such models because they turned out to be very difficult to estimate. More specifically, the iterative ML programs rarely succeeded in obtaining convergent estimates.

5. EMPIRICAL SPECIFICATIONS

The remainder of the paper describes how we estimate the four models of legitimation and competition in founding rates. To clarify presentation, we restate the four models in the exact form in which they are estimated. This section merely records these forms to facilitate understanding of the empirical results.

The GY model estimated below has the form given in (4) but with a slight reparameterization and with a regression structure for the effects of environmental covariates and period effects:

$$\lambda(t) = N_t^\alpha \exp(\gamma N_t^2 + x_t'\pi), \qquad \gamma = -\beta. \qquad (11)$$

Here, x_t is a vector of time-varying covariates, and π is a vector of regression coefficients (and a constant). The hypotheses of theoretical interest are $0 < \alpha < 1$ and $\gamma < 0$.

The GY model with an additive constant is simply

$$\lambda(t) = e^s + N_t^\alpha \exp(\gamma N_t^2 + x_t'\pi). \qquad (12)$$

The hypotheses of theoretical interest are the same as those indicated for the GY model.

The empirical model of density-dependent legitimation and competition is formed by combining the assumption about the relationship of competition and density, in (2), with the logistic specification of the legitimation process:

$$\lambda(t) = \left(\frac{L^*}{1 + \left[\frac{L^*}{L_0} - 1\right]e^{-\alpha N_t}} \right) \exp(\gamma N_t^2 + x_t'\pi), \qquad (13)$$

where L^* is a multiplicative "constant." We had difficulty obtaining convergent estimates of the model when we also included a constant in π. So in implementing this model empirically, we do not include a constant term; there is no π_0 term. The hypotheses of theoretical interest are $\alpha > 0$ and $\gamma < 0$. We compute empirical estimates of this model by treating L^* and L_0 as constants to be estimated from the data. The ceiling on legitimation presumably depends on various properties of the match between the organizational form and the social structure. The analysis reported below treats the ceiling as unobserved but potentially estimable; it assumes further that L^* is a constant.

For ease of comparison of estimates with the logistic model and for ease of estimation, we rewrite the Gompertz model of density-dependent legitimation in (10) as

$$L(N) = e^c L_0 \exp(-ce^{-\alpha N}).$$

The ceiling on legitimation (as N goes to infinity) is

$$L^* = e^c L_0. \qquad (14)$$

Therefore, the model can be expressed as

$$L(N) = L^* \exp(-ce^{-\alpha N}). \qquad (15)$$

Combining equation (14) with the standard model of density-dependent competition yields a model for founding rates:

$$\lambda(t) = L^* \exp(-ce^{-\alpha N_t}) \exp(\gamma N_t^2 + x_t'\pi). \qquad (16)$$

The hypotheses of theoretical interest are $\alpha > 0$ and $\gamma < 0$. When estimating models with the form of (16), we recover estimates of L_0 by using the definition of L^* in (14) in conjunction with estimates of c. As with the logistic, we do not include a constant term (π_0) in the vector of regression coefficients (π) because L^* plays the role of the multiplicative constant in the model.

6. STOCHASTIC MODELS FOR ORGANIZATIONAL FOUNDING RATES

The next step in the research process is to relate the substantive models of founding rates to specific stochastic models that can be estimated from available data. Among other things, this means providing a precise definition of the founding rate, $\lambda(t)$.

6.1. *Definition of the Founding Rate*

Defining the rate requires clear specification of the unit of analysis, which has been an issue of confusion in some research on founding rates. For understandable reasons, organizational analysts customarily take the individual organization as the unit of observation and analysis in research. But in analysis of organizational foundings, the unit of observation must be something other than the set of individual organizations whose appearances are recorded. The most telling argument about the appropriate unit of analysis in this case is that "nonevents," the conditions under which the founding rate falls and no new organizations appear, figure just as importantly in understanding the process of founding as observed foundings. Because nonevents cannot be associated with particular organizations, it follows that the unit of analysis cannot be the individual organization. Rather the *population* itself experiences the foundings. Detailed information on foundings tell when increments to the population occur.

An organizational founding process can usefully be considered as an instance of an *arrival process* for the population (Hannan 1989a). A type of point process, an arrival process characterizes the stochastic behavior of the flow of arrivals to some system, such as a queue or a population. Let the cumulative number of foundings by time t be represented by the random variable $Y(t)$, and let the time of the ith founding be represented by T_i. The stochastic process of interest, the founding process, is $\{Y(t) \mid t \geq 0\}$, with state space equal to $\{0,1,2, \ldots\}$. The *founding rate,* the rate of arrival at state $y + 1$ at (just after) time t, can be defined as

$$\lambda_y(t) = \lim_{\Delta t \downarrow 0} \frac{\Pr\{Y(t + \Delta t) - Y(t) = 1 \mid Y(t) = y\}}{\Delta t}.$$

An equivalent definition of the founding rate uses the distribution of interarrival times. Let U_y denote a random variable that tells the *interarrival time,* the waiting time between the yth and $(y + 1)$th founding: $U_y = T_{y+1} - T_y$. The density of interarrival times is given by

$$f(u_y) = \lim_{\Delta u \downarrow 0} \frac{\Pr\{U_y \leq u_y + \Delta u \mid u_y < U_y\}}{\Delta u}.$$

The survivor function, the probability that an interarrival time exceeds any chosen value, is

$$G(u) = \Pr\{U > u\}.$$

Using the definition of conditional probability, we can define the founding rate as the ratio of the density to the survivor function:

$$\lambda_y(u) = \lim_{\Delta u \downarrow 0} \frac{\Pr\{U_y \leq u_y + \Delta u \mid U_y > u_y\}}{\Pr\{U_y > u_y\}\Delta u} = \frac{f(u_y)}{G(u_y)}.$$

6.2. Observation Plans and Stochastic Models

Ideal observation plans for studying founding processes obtain information on the exact time (to the day) of all foundings in a population. When the archival records provide such detail, the most efficient use of the data is standard event history analysis (or hazard analysis) of the interarrival times (Hannan 1989a; Olzak 1989). Although some archives provide complete detail and exact dates of foundings, published studies of founding processes have used data that contain only yearly counts of foundings or a mixture of exact dates of foundings for some cases and years of foundings for others. The data used in the analysis reported below contain exact times of foundings (to the month or month and day) for roughly half of the events and years of foundings for the rest. Here we adopt the conservative position of ignoring the exact detail for some events and aggregating all data to produce yearly counts. Many other published studies have used data that contain only yearly counts.

What implications does such temporal aggregation have for modeling and analysis? Many social scientists believe that the observation plan determines the form of the stochastic model. In this case, this means considering yearly counts as counts in discrete time and concluding that the appropriate stochastic models must therefore have a discrete-time parameterization. The view taken here is that the form of the stochastic model should be determined by the actual structure of events under study. Complete or partial data on exact timing of foundings show that foundings occur at any time of the year. Therefore, in the interest of realism, we should use a *continuous-time* stochastic model for this phenomenon. For the problem under study, there is no difficulty—indeed there is no added complexity—in using yearly counts to estimate underlying continuous-time stochastic models such as the Poisson models discussed next, as Coleman (1964) has shown.

6.3. *The Poisson Process*

The natural baseline model for arrival processes in continuous time is the Poisson process. This model assumes that the rate of arrival does not depend on the history of previous arrivals, including the number of previous arrivals and time of the last arrival. If the rate at which organizations enter a population follows a Poisson process, the rate of arriving at state $y + 1$ at (just after) time t is a constant. That is, $\lambda_y(t) = \lambda$ under the assumptions of a Poisson process. A basic result on Poisson processes holds that the distribution of interarrival time is exponential:

$$f(u) = \lambda e^{-\lambda u},$$

and

$$G(u) = e^{-\lambda u}.$$

According to the arguments of the previous sections, the founding rate depends on density (according to one of the four parametric models in section 5) and a vector of time-varying covariates. The empirical analysis treats processes whose rates have a general regression structure:

$$\lambda(t) = \lambda(N_t, \mathbf{x}_t) = \varphi(N_t)\exp(\mathbf{x}_t'\boldsymbol{\pi}),$$

where $\varphi(N_t)$ is one of the four parametric models of density dependence in section 5. It is important to note that this general specification assumes that time variation in the founding rate reflects only time variation in the density and in the measured covariates. It implies that the rate is the same in all periods in which density and the

covariates have the same values. Put differently, there is no disturbance term in the equation relating the rate to density and the covariates. (We relax this restriction below.)

When exact dates of foundings (arrivals, more generally) are
known, the optimal procedure for estimating the founding rate and
parameters of regression specifications of the founding rate is to use
the interfounding times (U) along with the density and survivor function of the Poisson model. Such estimation involves standard methods of event history analysis, as noted above.[14]

But suppose there is temporal aggregation in the dates, that
all that is observed are counts of foundings within predetermined
intervals. One can still use the continuous-time Poisson model (or
other continuous-time models) by deriving the probability law that
governs the distribution of events within intervals from the underlying model.[15] This happens to be a particularly simple problem in the
case of the Poisson process. If the flow of arrivals in continuous time
follows a Poisson process, then the number of arrivals in an interval
of constant width is governed by the probability law:

$$\Pr(Y = y \mid \mathbf{x}_t) = \frac{e^{-\lambda}\lambda^y}{y!}$$
$$= \frac{\exp\Big(-\varphi(N_t)\exp[\mathbf{x}_t'\boldsymbol{\pi}]\Big)\Big(\varphi(N_t)\exp[\mathbf{x}_t'\boldsymbol{\pi}]\Big)^y}{y!}. \tag{17}$$

Well-known implications of the Poisson process are that the expected
number of events in a unit interval equals the rate and that the
variance of the number of events also equals the rate. Given that the
data on foundings provide yearly counts, we treat a year as the unit

---

[14]Some published analyses of founding processes have used event history
methods even when data on timing of foundings were not available. Researchers
have allocated events uniformly within years (simply dividing the number of
days by the number of observed events to yield a constant interfounding time for
the year) and have estimated models using the resulting interfounding times
(see, for example, Carroll and Hannan 1989*a;* Wholey et al. 1990). Hannan and
Freeman (1987) allocated the events with unknown month within years randomly and then analyzed interfounding times. But in a parallel analysis, Hannan
and Freeman (1989) ignored the partial data on exact timing and analyzed yearly
counts. The results of the two analyses agree fairly closely.

[15]Some previous research on founding processes has used conventional
time series analysis without correcting for the nonnegativity of counts or for the
discontinuous nature of count data (see, for example, Tucker et al. 1988).

interval and use the probability law in (17) to analyze the flow of foundings over years.

In estimating models from yearly counts of foundings, we exclude the observation for a population's first year because it has a peculiar status. By definition, a population's first year is the first *positive* value in a time series of counts of yearly foundings. In other words, the first year of a population's history is constrained by definition to have a positive number of foundings. No other year is so constrained; each subsequent year can have zero foundings or some positive number of foundings. The first year's count and subsequent years' counts cannot be assumed to be realizations of the same (unconstrained) probability mechanism. For this reason, it makes sense to condition on the appearance of a population in a particular year by beginning the record in that year and analyzing the flow of foundings in all subsequent years.

6.4. *Negative Binomial Models*

Biostatisticians have long questioned the applicability of Poisson processes to the flow of events because empirical research seldom finds that the mean equals the variance, even approximately, as the Poisson process implies. Instead, it has been common to find the condition called *over-dispersion,* in which the variance of event counts exceeds the mean, often by a considerable margin. Such a result can arise for a number of different reasons, including unobserved heterogeneity and time dependence.[16]

It has often proved useful in prior research to regard the Poisson model as a special case of a negative binomial model. The seemingly most-common representation, begun by Greenwood and Yule (1920), assumes that a Poisson process is at work but that it is disturbed by a multiplicative error process:

$$\lambda_t = \exp(x'_t \pi)\epsilon_t, \tag{18}$$

where ϵ_t is uncorrelated over units at risk (time periods, regions, and so forth, depending on the application). Then the probability law for the event counts, now a mixture of Poisson processes, becomes

[16]Johnson and Kotz (1969) provide a useful historical account of the development of this model and of the range of applications. See also McCullagh and Nelder (1989) and Cameron and Trivedi (1986).

$$\Pr(Y_t = y \mid \mathbf{x}_t) = \int \frac{\exp(\exp[-\mathbf{x}_t'\boldsymbol{\pi}]\epsilon_t)(\exp[\mathbf{x}_t'\boldsymbol{\pi}]\epsilon_t)^{y_t}}{y_t!} g(\epsilon_t) d\epsilon_t. \quad (19)$$

The negative binomial model follows from the assumption that the unobservable has a gamma distribution. That is, $g(\epsilon_t) \sim \Gamma(\phi_t, \nu_t)$.[17] In this case, $E(\lambda_t) = \phi_t$ and $Var(\lambda_t) = \phi_t^2/\nu_t$. As is usual in such a setup, one "integrates out" the unobservable in (19) to obtain an estimable model. In the present case, this procedure yields a version of the negative binomial model:

$$\Pr(Y_t = y \mid \mathbf{x}_t) = \frac{\Gamma(y_t + \nu_t)}{\Gamma(y_t + 1)\Gamma(\nu_t)} \left(\frac{\nu_t}{\nu_t + \phi_t} \right)^{\nu_t} \left(\frac{\phi_t}{\nu_t + \phi_t} \right)^{y_t}, \quad (20)$$

with

$$E(Y_t) = \phi_t \quad \text{and} \quad Var(Y_t) = \phi_t + \frac{1}{\nu_t}\phi_t^2.$$

To maintain the parallel with the Poisson regression model, we again specify that the mean of the process is a loglinear function of the covariates:

$$E(Y_t) = \phi_t = \exp(\mathbf{x}_t'\boldsymbol{\pi}).$$

Unlike the case of the Poisson process, the variance does not necessarily equal the mean. This model can accommodate over-dispersion.

In empirical analysis, we have tried two relationships between the mean and the variance (two choices of ν). Each is a special case of a general framework:

$$\nu_t = \frac{1}{\omega} \left(\exp[\mathbf{x}_t'\boldsymbol{\pi}] \right)^k = \frac{1}{\omega} E^k(Y_t),$$

where k is an arbitrary constant and ω is an *over-dispersion parameter*. Following McCullagh and Nelder (1989) (see also Cameron and Trivedi 1986), we use two choices of k. The first, $k = 1$, causes the variance of the expected count to be proportional to the expected count:

---

[17]The parameterization used here assumes the so-called index parameterization of the gamma function (see McCullagh and Nelder 1989):

$$\Gamma(\phi_t, \nu_t) = \frac{1}{\Gamma(\nu_t)} \left(\frac{\nu_t \lambda_t}{\phi_t} \right)^{\nu_t} \exp \left(\frac{-\nu_t \lambda_t}{\phi_t} \right) \frac{1}{\lambda_t}.$$

$$\text{Var}(Y_t) = (1 + \omega)\text{E}(Y_t). \qquad (21)$$

In other words, this specification assumes a constant coefficient of variation (ratio of the variance to the mean). The second, $k = 0$, results in quadratic dependence:

$$\text{Var}(Y_t) = \text{E}(Y_t)(1 + \omega\text{E}[Y_t]). \qquad (22)$$

This specification assumes that the coefficient of variation increases linearly with the mean. In either case, setting $\omega = 0$ reduces the model to a Poisson process. Thus, we can form likelihood-ratio tests of the Poisson process versus the negative binomial.[18]

An alternative derivation assumes that there is "contagion" in the process over time within intervals studied (within years in this case). This means that the occurrence of an event affects the rate of subsequent occurrences, that the occurrences are not independent within time intervals. Positive contagion leads to over-dispersion.[19]

Either interpretation fits the present application. Founding rates may well fluctuate randomly over time, net of the effects of the variables used as covariates, because of unmeasured changes in environments.[20] Previous research has generally found that counts of foundings in the prior year have significant positive effects on the founding rate—a form of contagion between years. There is no reason to suspect that such contagion does not also operate *within* years, such that the occurrence of one or more foundings early in a year increases the rate for the rest of the year. This would be an instance of unobserved contagion in the process. The available data do not

[18]King's (1990) COUNT program for ML estimation of the specification in (21) is an applications module in GAUSS (Aptech Systems Inc. 1990). A program for ML estimation of the specification in (22) is included in LIMDEP (Greene 1988) and has also been programmed in GAUSS by David Barron.

[19]More precisely, the negative binomial can be derived as a limiting distribution of an Eggenberger-Pólya urn scheme in which the probability of an event depends on the previous number of events (see Johnson and Kotz 1969; pp. 124–25).

[20]A potentially important extension of regression specifications of negative binomial models by Zeger (1988) involves quasi-likelihood estimation of models with general forms of autocorrelation in the unobservable in (29). Barron (1990) has implemented Zeger's proposed estimator using a first-order autoregressive structure. Barron (1990) and Barron and Hannan (1990) find that estimates of the GY model for the data on national labor unions used below (and for a number of other populations) are quite robust with respect to this form of autocorrelation.

permit us to choose between alternative sources of over-dispersion. The analyses reported here simply control for over-dispersion with the pair of specifications of the negative binomial introduced above so that estimated standard errors are not understated.

7. DATA ON FOUNDINGS OF NATIONAL LABOR UNIONS

This paper presents reanalyses of data on foundings of national labor unions. Hannan and collaborators collected data on *national* labor unions, unions that organized in more than one state (Hannan 1980, 1988b).[21] They tried to collect information about every national labor union that has existed, however briefly, in the U.S. First, they compiled the lists of names (with starting dates) contained in reports published in various years that claimed exhaustive coverage of the population of unions. They found relatively complete data on 621 unions. The outcome of interest in the present analysis is *founding*, defined as the formation of a national union by the joint decision of several locals or by some unorganized group of workers. Of the 621 unions, 479 began with a founding.[22] Plots of yearly counts of foundings can be found in Hannan and Freeman (1987, 1989).

The key covariate is density. This is defined as the number of unions in existence on December 31 of the year before the observation. Density ranges from 0 to 211 over the 150-year history. Fourteen years had zero density. Once density began to grow substantially away from zero, growth to the maximum was very rapid (as has been observed in numerous other organizational populations). Figure 1 plots the evolution of density over the history of this population. Such a growth pattern means that the distribution of observed density is quite unusual. We normally expect observations to be clustered in the center of a distribution and the tails to be thin, but the pattern is reversed for density of American labor unions. Because the population spent much time at low density and at relatively high

[21]These data are available from the Data Archive of the Cornell Institute of Social and Economic Research, Cornell University, Ithaca, NY 14853.

[22]The rest began as the result of secessions of factions from existing unions, mergers of existing unions, or the transformation of a professional association into a labor union.

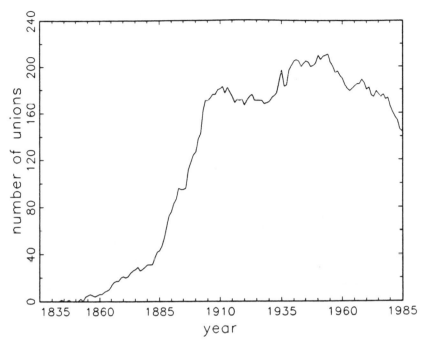

FIGURE 1. Density of national labor unions, by year, 1836–1985.

density and relatively little time in making the transition between them, observations are relatively sparse in the center of the distribution, as can be seen in Figure 2. We discuss the implications of this pattern for estimation below.

The length of the period of study greatly limits the measures of environmental conditions that can be used without excluding information on the founding process. Hannan and Freeman (1987, 1989) explored the effects of numerous measures of general economic conditions, such as an index that identifies years of economic crisis and depression, the real wage of common laborers, business failures, gross national product per capita, and so forth. They used data on immigration and dummy variables that distinguish years of so-called employer offensives and wars. Most of these variables failed to have any systematic or sizeable effect on the union founding rate when period effects and the measures discussed below were included in the model.

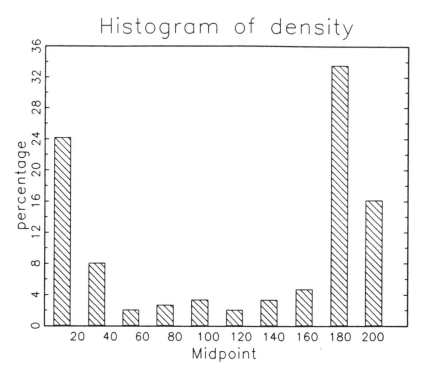

FIGURE 2. Histogram of yearly observations on union density.

Based on previous research, economic depression is the only measure of economic conditions included in the analyses reported below. In addition, the models allow rates of founding to vary among five historic periods. The periods are defined with dummy variables coded 1 for the year in which a period begins and all subsequent years and coded 0 for all years preceding the beginning of the period. The coefficients for periods therefore represent the ratio of the (adjusted) log-founding rate in a period relative to that in the previous period. The first period begins in 1837, the year following the foundings of the first national unions. The second starts in 1886, the year in which the American Federation of Labor (AFL) was founded. The third period begins in 1932 with the New Deal, and the fourth period begins in 1947, when the Taft-Hartley Act rescinded some New Deal protections for union organizing. The fifth period begins in 1955, when the AFL merged with the Congress of Industrial Organizations (CIO).

8. RESULTS

Table 1 reports estimates of the four models. The parameter estimates reported are ML estimates of parameters of negative binomial regression models fitted to the time-series data on yearly counts of foundings. In every case it turned out that the negative binomial models fit significantly better than analogous Poisson models. For instance, in the case of the generalized Yule model, a likelihood-ratio test statistic of the negative binomial model (with specification (22)) against the Poisson model is 33.1 with 1 degree of freedom, which is significant at the 0.001 level. The other specifications of the legitimation process produce similar results. We can reject decisively the null hypothesis that the conditional variance of the yearly count of foundings equals the conditional mean. More simply, there is significant over-dispersion in these data even after the effects of covariates have been taken into account. As we noted above, such over-dispersion may reflect either unobserved heterogeneity due to the effects of omitted causal factors that vary over years or contagion within years.

For each of the four models, the specification in which the coefficient of variation is a linear function of the mean of the Poisson process (that is, the specification in (22)) fits better than the more common specification in which the coefficient of variation is constant (21). The estimates in Table 1 come from models that use the better-fitting specification. The result that the coefficient of variation increases with the mean seems to be consistent with the view that the over-dispersion is due to contagion. But we have not been able to derive this result formally. Moreover, an interpretation of the result in terms of unobserved heterogeneity can surely be contrived. So we do not forward an interpretation of the result.

8.1. *Generalized Yule Models*

Column 1 of Table 1 contains estimates of the original GY model in (11). The results agree with the hypotheses. The estimated first-order effect of density, $\hat{\alpha}$, is positive as predicted and statistically significant.[23] The fact that $0 < \hat{\alpha} < 1$ means that legitimation in-

[23]Here and elsewhere we use the 0.05 level and one-tailed tests to evaluate the (directional) hypotheses concerning parameters of the specifications of density dependence in the founding rate. We do not indicate significance of the effects of other covariates.

TABLE 1

Maximum Likelihood Estimates of Negative Binomial Regression Models
of Founding Rates of National Labor Unions
(Asymptotic Standard Errors in Parentheses)

Variable	Parameter	GY Models		Logistic Model	Gompertz Model
		(1)	(2)	(3)	(4)
Multiplicative constant	π_0	−.534 (.289)	−2.68 (.841)		
N	α	.431* (.089)	1.056* (.233)	.074* (.017)	.033* (.013)
$N^2/1{,}000$	$\gamma \times 1{,}000$	−.036* (.015)	−.070* (.019)	−.045* (.016)	−.033* (.017)
(Source)	s		−1.23* (.510)		
(Initial legitimation)	L_0			.415* (.123)	
(Ceiling on legitimation)	L^*			6.98* (2.22)	8.59* (4.44)
(Gompertz parameterization	c				3.17* (.477)
Founding s_{t-1}		.077 (.018)	.060 (.019)	.055 (.019)	.055 (.019)
Depression		.262 (.156)	.216 (.167)	.215 (.151)	.196 (.153)
Period 2 (1886–1985)		.352 (.392)	.290 (.401)	.460 (.383)	.345 (.403)
Period 3 (1932–1985)		.215 (.265)	.509 (.282)	.426 (.263)	.449 (.269)
Period 4 (1947–1985)		.151 (.345)	.149 (.361)	.113 (.331)	.112 (.331)
Period 5 (1955–1985)		−1.09 (.357)	−1.57 (.441)	−1.29 (.356)	−1.32 (.362)
(Overdispersion)	ω	.224 (.066)	.184 (.059)	.189 (.060)	.187 (.060)
Number of cases		149	149	149	149
log $\mathcal{L}$		−288.32	−282.03	−283.97	−283.33

Note: The reference period runs from 1837 to 1985.
*$p < .05$ (one-tailed test).

creases with density at a decreasing rate. The prediction about the second-order effect of density is also confirmed. That is, $\hat{\gamma}$ is negative, as predicted, and statistically significant. This result is consistent with the view that the intensity of competition increases with density at an increasing rate (since $\gamma = -\beta$) and that competition, in turn, depresses founding rates.

According to the qualitative argument, the relationship between density and the founding rate is nonmonotonic over the observed range of density. If so, the maximum falls within the observed range. This turns out to be the case for national labor unions. The observed range of density is [0,211]. The maximum implied by the estimates in column 1 is $N = 77$, reasonably close to the center of the empirical range. The estimates imply that the founding rate at this level of density is 3.1 times that at zero density. In other words, density-dependent legitimation has increased the founding rate roughly three-fold at the point at which competitive pressures begin to dominate. At the observed maximum of density (211), the implied rate is 1.2 times the rate at zero density. In other words, density-dependent competition has driven the rate down by roughly 60 percent from its peak. Both legitimation and competition processes appear to have operated strongly in the evolution of density in the population of national labor unions, according to the estimates of the GY model.

How do the other models compare with the (original) GY model? We answer this question by focusing next on the model that is closest to the original—the one in (12), which adds a source (an additive constant), denoted by s, to the GY model in column 1. Column 2 of Table 1 contains the estimates of the extended model. The seemingly slight change in the specification makes a big difference in the results. First, allowing the founding rate to be (substantially) greater than zero improves the fit of the model considerably. Since the original GY model in column 1 is a constrained version of the GY model with additive constant in column 2, a standard result holds that -2 times the difference in log-likelihoods of the models is distributed asymptotically as chi square with degrees of freedom equal to the number of constraints (1 in this case). This statistic equals 16.27, which is highly significant.

Second, including an additive constant changes the estimates of relevant parameters (α, γ, and π_0) considerably. It increases $\hat{\alpha}$

from 0.43 in column 1 to 1.06 in column 2. The latter result implies that the founding rate increases with density at a slightly increasing rate (counter to the hypothesis). But given the size of the standard error, we cannot have much confidence that α exceeds unity in the extended model. Indeed, the result in column 2 suggests that a *pure* Yule process (that is, where $\alpha = 1$) is operating. In other words, when an additive constant is included in the model, legitimation appears to be simply *proportional* to density.

Why the big change in $\hat{\alpha}$ when a source is added to the model? It appears that this result reflects the sensitivity of the GY model to the presence of observations with zero density. Recall that this is the case for 14 of 150 years in these data. To get a rough idea of such sensitivity, we also tried estimating the original GY model after excluding the 14 observations with density equal to zero. It turns out that $\hat{\alpha} = 0.94$ in this re-estimation, close to the estimate of the model with additive constant in column 2.

The change in the magnitude of the first-order effect of density needs to be considered in the context of the magnitudes of the multiplicative constants (π_0). When we compare results in columns 1 and 2 of Table 1, we see that adding a source to the model decreased $\hat{\pi}_0$ enormously. The estimated legitimation functions are

$$e^{\hat{\pi}_0} N_t^{\hat{\alpha}} = 0.59 \, N_t^{0.43}$$

for the plain GY model and

$$e^{\hat{s}} + e^{\hat{\pi}_0} N_t^{\hat{\alpha}} = 0.29 + 0.07 \, N_t^{1.06}$$

for the GY model with a constant source. The very much smaller multiplicative constant for the extended model means that this model predicts lower founding rates at low density than the plain GY model (Figure 3). But as density increases, these functions cross (at about $N = 25$), and from this point, the legitimation function of the extended model exceeds that of the GY model. But the important point, for understanding the qualitative implications of the models, is that adding a constant source actually decreases the predicted rate at low density.

Adding the source to the GY model also has a big impact on the second-order effect of density: The $\hat{\gamma}$ in column 2 is twice as large (in absolute value) as the $\hat{\gamma}$ in column 1. This result is not surprising in view of the change in the first-order effect discussed above. A more powerful second-order effect is needed to keep the founding

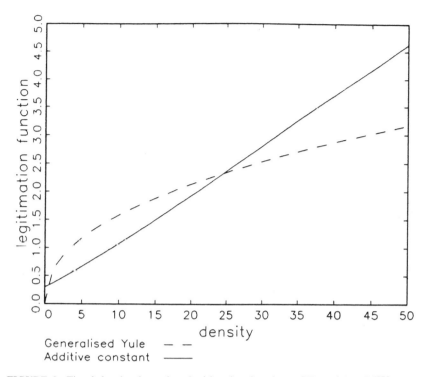

FIGURE 3. Fitted density-dependent legitimation functions: GY model and GY model with constant source.

rate down (within the range of the observations) when the first-order effect is so large.

Figure 4 shows the results of the combined action of the estimated legitimation and competition processes for the GY model and its extension. Note that the predicted rate under a GY model rises more rapidly and flattens out at a much lower level. Whereas the estimates of the extended model imply that the rate at its maximum is five times higher than the rate at zero density, estimates of the GY model imply only a three-fold rise in the rate.

8.2. *Logistic and Gompertz Models*

Next we consider the results of using models that specify that legitimation is an *S*-shaped function of density, namely the logistic model in (13) and the Gompertz model in (16). Both models repre-

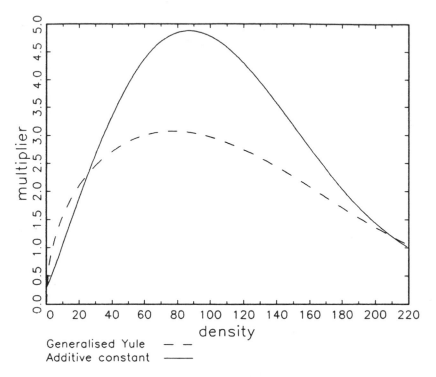

FIGURE 4. Estimated effects of density on the founding rate of national labor unions: GY model and GY model with constant source.

sent the growth of legitimation as a function of density in terms of three parameters: L_0, the level of legitimation at zero density (the floor on the process), L^*, the maximum level of legitimation (the ceiling on the process), and α, the rate at which legitimation increases from floor to ceiling as density increases.

Columns 3 and 4 of Table 1 report ML estimates of negative binomial regression specifications of these alternative models. The log-likelihoods are -284.0 for the logistic model and -283.3 for the Gompertz model, compared with -288.3 for the GY model (column 1) and -282.03 for the GY model with additive constant (column 2). The GY model (with or without an additive constant) is not a special case of either of the more complicated models. So one cannot construct likelihood-ratio tests for the pairs of models. Model fits, as judged by log-likelihoods, are very close for the GY model with additive constant, the logistic model, and the Gompertz model (all of which have the same number of parameters). Each of the trio fits noticeably better than the original GY model.

The logistic and Gompertz models yield similar estimates of the ceiling on legitimation, L^*: 7.0 for the logistic model and 8.6 for the Gompertz model. Estimates of floor levels, L_0, also agree closely. For the logistic model the estimate of L_0 in Table 1 is 0.41. To obtain an estimate of L_0 for the Gompertz model, we use the relation $L^* = e^c L_0$ (compare (14)) with estimates of L^* and c: $\hat{L}_0 = 8.59/e^{3.17} = 0.36$. Estimates of both models indicate that legitimation begins close to zero and rises greatly as density rises. The ratio of the ceiling level of legitimation to the floor is 17 according to the estimates of the logistic model and 24 according to the estimates of the Gompertz model.

The estimates of the first-order effects of density ($\hat{\alpha}$) are positive and significant with each model. The second-order effects ($\hat{\gamma}$) are negative and significant in each case. The second-order effect has the same interpretation as in the GY model. Changing the legitimation function has only modest effects on the magnitudes of the competitive effects.

The first-order effects of density in columns 3 and 4 are not directly comparable to those for the GY models in columns 1 and 2. What do these estimates ($\hat{\alpha} = 0.074$ for the logistic model and $\hat{\alpha} = 0.033$ for the Gompertz model) imply substantively? Figure 5 shows the relationship between legitimation and density implied by the estimates. The GY model implies that legitimation rises quite rapidly as density rises in its lower range and keeps rising gradually over the entire observed range (Figure 3). The logistic and Gompertz models imply that legitimation rises slowly with increasing density when density is very small, then rises very rapidly when density is in the range of 20 to 60, and then slows rapidly as density approaches 80 (for the logistic model) or 100 (for the Gompertz model). The level of density at which legitimation rises most rapidly with increasing density is $N = 38$ for the logistic model and $N = 35$ for the Gompertz model, according to these estimates. Considering the actual historical path of density reveals that it took roughly 50 years for this level of density to be reached in the population of national unions (which began in 1836). In substantive terms, the logistic and Gompertz models imply that the strongest effects of density on legitimation occurred much later in the historical process, and the GY model implies that the strongest effects occurred at the beginning of the population's history.

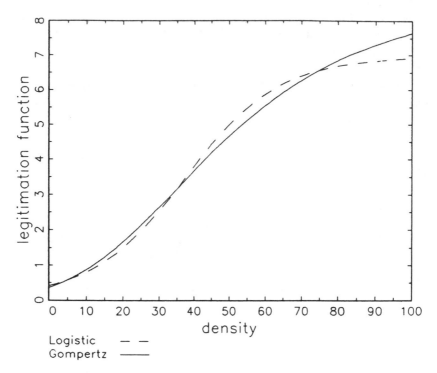

FIGURE 5. Fitted density-dependent legitimation functions: logistic model and Gompertz model.

Figure 6 plots the estimated relationship between density and the founding rate of labor unions for each of the logistic and Gompertz models. This figure shows the combined effects of legitimation and competition on the founding rate. Estimates of both models agree about the basic shape of the relationship: Both imply that the founding rate increases about five-fold as density increases and then drops close to its initial level as density reaches its observed maximum. The actual paths of growth and decline in the rate with density of logistic and Gompertz models (Figure 6) agree closely.[24] Comparison with Figure 4 reveals that the implications of the logistic and Gompertz models differ noticeably from the implications of the GY model. The former locates the range of high founding rates in a much narrower band of the range of variation in density. But the implications of the models

[24]Note that the estimate of the "source" in the extended GY model in column 2 also agrees closely with the estimates of L_0, since $e^{1.23} = 0.29$.

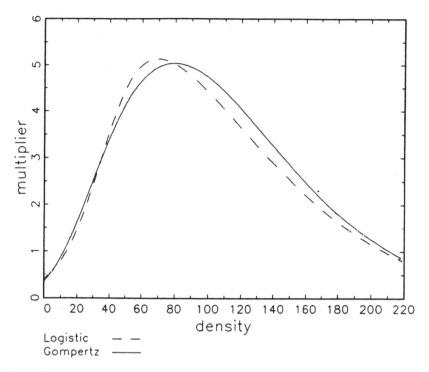

FIGURE 6. Estimated effects of density on the founding rate of national labor unions, logistic and Gompertz models.

with *S*-shaped growth paths do not differ much from the implications of the GY model with an additive constant.

9. DISCUSSION

The results of this analysis have both substantive and methodological implications. Perhaps the most important substantive implication is that nonmonotonicity in the estimated effect of density on founding rates is relatively insensitive to details of model specification. Four variations on the form of density-dependent legitimation (the form of the first-order effect of density) and a change in the stochastic specification (negative binomial models) lead to the same broad conclusion. The founding rate rises sharply with increasing density in the lower range and then declines with increasing density beyond some critical value. The robustness of the pattern over specifications for the population of unions (and over populations in other studies) supports the theoretical claims about legitimation, competition, and density dependence.

The results reported here suggest that we can improve on the original specification of the legitimation function—the generalized Yule model. Estimates of three alternative specifications suggest that the impact of density in founding rates is not strongest close to zero density, as the GY model holds. Moreover, these alternatives imply that the legitimation effect is much stronger over the relevant range of density than the estimates of the GY model imply. So the choice between the GY model and the alternatives makes a substantive difference, albeit a subtle one.

What about choice among the three alternative models of legitimation? One, the extension of the GY model with a constant source, leads to the result that legitimation is simply proportional to density. The other two, the logistic and Gompertz models, are constrained to have S-shaped growth paths. The three models have the same number of parameters and fit the data roughly equally well. Moreover, the relationships between density and legitimation implied by empirical estimates of their parameters are quite close (Figures 3 and 5). These paths differ only in the mid-range, the region in which the logistic and Gompertz models have their points of inflection. But this is the region in which data are sparse (Figure 2), making it hard to choose among the three models with the present data.

An obvious next order of business is to compare the fits of these models to data that are not so sparse in the mid-range of density. However, we need to recognize that the theory underlying this research implies that such sparsity is endemic to the phenomenon. The theory holds that founding rates rise and that mortality rates fall in the mid-range of density because of the effects of density-dependent legitimation. Growth in density is most rapid in the mid-range because density rises when the founding rate is high and the mortality rate is low. So populations tend to traverse the mid-range of density quickly, producing few years of observation in this range. Thus, it may be inherently difficult to distinguish sharply among models whose main differences concern behavior in the mid-range of density.

Finally, this research finds a strong advantage to using negative binomial regression models in place of more common Poisson regression models to analyze yearly time series of counts of foundings. The degree of over-dispersion in these data (net of the effects of covariates) is high, and negative binomial models fit much better than the Poisson models that build on the assumption that the variance of the series equals the mean. Choosing between these specifications usually makes a noticeable difference in the estimates of regression parameters with the present data. In other words, shifting to the negative binomial model not only improves the fit but also affects substantive conclusions. In addition, the specification of the relationship between the variance and the mean of the distribution of the unobservable also makes a difference. In this research the uncommon specification in which the variance is a quadratic function of the mean fits these data better than the usual specification in which this relationship is linear.

REFERENCES

Aldrich, Howard E., and Peter V. Marsden. 1988. "Environments and Organizations." Pp. 361–92 in *Handbook of Sociology,* edited by Neil J. Smelser. Beverly Hills: Sage.

Aptech Systems Inc. 1990. *GAUSS Applications Modules.* Kent, WA: Aptech Systems Inc.

Barnett, William P., and Terry L. Amburgey. 1990. "Do Larger Organizations Generate Stronger Competition?" Pp. 78–102 in *Organizational Evolution: New Directions,* edited by Jitendra V. Singh. Beverly Hills: Sage.

Barnett, William P., and Glenn R. Carroll. 1987. "Competition and Commensalism Among Early Telephone Companies." *Administrative Science Quarterly* 30: 400–21.

Barron, David N. 1990. *Analysis of Count Data: Over-Dispersion and Auto-correlation.* M.S. thesis, Cornell University.

Barron, David N., and Michael T. Hannan. 1990. "Assessing Autocorrelation in Models of Organizational Founding Rates: Quasi-likelihood Estimation." Technical Report 90-10. Ithaca: Cornell University, Department of Sociology.

Bartholomew, D. J. 1973. *Stochastic Models for Social Processes.* 2d ed. New York: Wiley.

Blalock, Hubert M., Jr. 1968. "Theory Building and Casual Inferences." Pp. 155–98 in *Methodology in Social Research,* edited by Hubert M. Blalock, Jr., and Ann Blalock. New York: McGraw-Hill.

———. 1969. *Theory Construction: From Verbal to Mathematical Formulations.* Englewood Cliffs, N.J.: Prentice-Hall.

———. 1989. "The Real and Unrealized Contributions of Quantitative Sociology." *American Sociological Review* 54: 447–60.

Cameron, A. Colin, and Pravin K. Trivedi. 1986. "Economic Models Based on Count Data." *Journal of Applied Economics* 1: 29–53.

Carroll, Glenn R., and Michael T. Hannan. 1989a. "Density Dependence in the Evolution of Newspaper Populations." *American Sociological Review* 54: 524–41.

——— 1989b. "Density Delay in the Evolution of Organizational Populations: A Model and Five Empirical Tests." *Administrative Science Quarterly* 34: 411–30.

Carroll, Glenn R., Peter Preisendorfer, Anand Swaminathan, and Gabriel Wiedenmayer. 1989. "Brewery and Brauerei: The Comparative Organizational Ecology of American and German Brewing Industries." Technical Report OBIR-34. Berkeley: University of California, Center for Research in Management.

Carroll, Glenn R., and Anand Swaminathan. 1989. "Density Dependent Evolution in the American Brewing Industry from 1633 to 1988." Technical Report OBIR-35. Berkeley: University of California, Center for Research in Management.

Carroll, Glenn R., and James B. Wade. 1991. "Density Dependence in the Evolution of the American Brewing Industry Across Different Levels of Analysis." *Social Science Research,* forthcoming.

Coleman, James S. 1964. *Introduction to Mathematical Sociology.* New York: Free Press.

——— 1968. "The Mathematical Study of Change." Pp. 428–78 in *Methodology in Social Research,* edited by Hubert M. Blalock, Jr., and Ann Blalock. New York: McGraw-Hill.

——— 1989. *Foundations of Social Theory.* Cambridge, MA: Belknap.

Delacroix, Jacques, Anand Swaminathan, and Michael E. Solt. 1989. "Density Dependence Versus Population Dynamics: An Ecological Study of Failings in the California Wine Industry." *American Sociological Review* 54: 245–62.

DiMaggio, Paul J., and Walter W. Powell. 1983. "The Iron Cage Revisited: Institutional Isomorphism and Collective Rationality in Organizational Fields." *American Sociological Review* 48: 147–60.

Freeman, John, and Michael T. Hannan. 1989. "Setting the Record Straight on Organizational Ecology: Rebuttal to Young." *American Journal of Sociology* 95: 425–39.

Greene, William. 1988. *LIMDEP Version 5 Manual.* Unpublished manuscript. New York University.

Greenwood, M., and G. U. Yule. 1920. "An Enquiry into the Nature of Frequency Distributions of Multiple Happenings, With Particular References to the Occurrence of Multiple Attacks of Disease or Repeated Accidents." *Journal of the Royal Statistical Society,* ser. A, 83: 255–79.

Hamblin, R. L., R. B. Jacobsen, and J. L. L. Miller. 1973. *A Mathematical Theory of Social Change.* New York: Wiley.

Hannan, Michael T. 1980. "The Ecology of National Labor Unions: Theory and Research Design." Technical Report No. 1, Stanford: Stanford University, Organization Studies Section, Institute for Mathematical Studies in the Social Sciences.

——— 1986. "Competitive and Institutional Processes in Organizational Ecology." Technical Report 86-13. Ithaca: Cornell University, Department of Sociology.

———— 1988. "Documentation of Public-Use Data Set: Ecology of Labor Unions Study." Technical Report 88-2. Ithaca: Cornell University, Department of Sociology.

———— 1989a. "Macrosociological Applications of Event-History Analysis: State Transitions and Event Recurrences." *Quantity and Quality* 23: 351–83.

———— 1989b. "Competitive and Institutional Processes in Organizational Ecology." Pp. 388–402 in *Sociological Theories in Progress: New Formulations,* edited by Joseph Berger, Morris Zelditch, Jr., and Bo Andersen. Newbury Park, CA: Sage.

Hannan, Michael T., and Glenn R. Carroll. 1991. "Competition, Legitimation, and Organizational Change." Oxford: Oxford University Press, forthcoming.

Hannan, Michael T., and John Freeman. 1977. "The Population Ecology of Organizations." *American Journal of Sociology* 82: 929–64.

———— 1987. "The Ecology of Organizational Founding: American Labor Unions, 1836–1985." *American Journal of Sociology* 92: 910–43.

———— 1988. "The Ecology of Organizational Mortality: American Labor Unions, 1836–1985." *American Journal of Sociology* 94: 25–52.

———— 1989. *Organizational Ecology.* Cambridge, MA: Harvard University Press.

Hutchinson, G. Evelyn. 1957. "Concluding Remarks." *Cold Spring Harbor Symposium on Quantitative Biology* 22: 415–27.

———— 1978. *An Introduction to Population Ecology.* New Haven: Yale University Press.

Johnson, Norman L., and Samuel Kotz. 1969. *Distributions in Statistics: Discrete Distributions.* Boston: Houghton Mifflin.

Karlin, Samuel, and Howard M. Taylor. 1975. *A First Course in Stochastic Processes.* 2d ed. New York: Academic Press.

King, Gary. 1990. "COUNT: A Program for Estimating Event Count and Duration Regressions." Unpublished manuscript. Department of Government, Harvard University.

Kingsland, Sharon E. 1985. *Modeling Nature: Episodes in the History of Population Biology.* Chicago: University of Chicago Press.

Lomi, Alessandro, and John Freeman. 1990. "An Ecological Study of Founding of Cooperative Organizations in Italy From 1963 to 1987: Some Preliminary Results." Working Paper 90-06. Ithaca: Cornell University, Johnson Graduate School of Management.

MacArthur, Robert H. 1972. *Geographical Ecology: Patterns in the Distributions of Species.* Princeton: Princeton University Press.

McCullagh, P., and J. Nelder. 1989. *Generalized Linear Models.* 2d ed. London: Chapman and Hall.

Meyer, John W., and Brian Rowan. 1977. "Institutionalized Organizations: Formal Structure as Myth and Ceremony." *American Journal of Sociology* 83: 340–63.

Meyer, John W., and W. Richard Scott. 1983. *Organizational Environments: Ritual and Rationality.* Beverly Hills: Sage.

Mitchell, Will 1987. "Dynamic Tension: Theoretical and Empirical Analyses of Entry Into Emerging Industries." Paper presented at the Stanford Asilomar Conference on Organizations.

Olzak, Susan. 1989. "Analysis of Events in Studies of Collective Action." *Annual Review of Sociology* 15: 119–41.

Olzak, Susan, and Elizabeth West. 1990. "Ethnic Conflicts and the Resilience of Ethnic Newspapers." Technical Report 90-8. Ithaca: Cornell University, Department of Sociology.

Ranger-Moore, James, Jane Banaszak-Holl, and Michael T. Hannan. 1989. "Effects of Density and Environmental Conditions on Founding Rates of Financial Institutions." Technical Report 89-3. Ithaca: Cornell University, Department of Sociology.

Singh, Jitendra V., and Charles J. Lumsden. 1990. "Theory and Research in Organizational Ecology." *Annual Review of Sociology* 16:161–95.

Tucker, David J., Jitendra V. Singh, and Agnes G. Meinhard. 1990. "Organizational Form, Population Dynamics, and Institutional Change: A Study of Founding Patterns of Voluntary Associations." *Academy of Management Journal* 33: 151–78.

Tucker, David J., Jitendra Singh, Agnes G. Meinard, and Robert J. House. 1988. "Ecological and Institutional Sources of Change in Organizational Populations." Pp. 127–52 in *Ecological Models of Organizations,* edited by Glenn R. Carroll. Cambridge, MA: Ballinger.

Tuma, Nancy Brandon, and Michael T. Hannan. 1984. *Social Dynamics: Models and Methods.* New York: Academic Press.

Wholey, Douglas R., Jon B. Christianson, and Susan M. Sanchez. 1990. "The Diffusion of Health Maintenance Organizations: Density, Competitive, and Institutional Determinants of Entry." Unpublished manuscript.

Yule, G. Udny. 1924. "A Mathematical Theory of Evolution, Based on the Conclusions of Dr. J. C. Willis, F.R.S." *Philosophical Transactions of the Royal Society, London,* ser. B, 213: 21–87.

Zeger, Scott L. 1988. "A Regression Model for Time Series of Counts." *Biometrika* 75: 621–29.

2

GOING UP THE LADDER: MULTIPLICITY SAMPLING TO CREATE LINKED MACRO-TO-MICRO ORGANIZATIONAL SAMPLES

*Toby L. Parcel**
*Robert L. Kaufman**
*Leeann Jolly**

We argue that researchers should use representative samples to address many issues and that long-standing interest in the connections between macrolevel and microlevel processes is also central to organizational analysis. Our literature review suggests that designs that link organizations to suborganizational units or members have deficiencies involving atypicalness of cases studied or inadequate and unreliable data on organizations derived from more representative samples of individuals. Instead we

The research reported in this paper was supported by National Science Foundation grant SES-8706529. It was also supported by the Committee on Urban Affairs, the Urban Assistance Program, the College of Social and Behavioral Sciences, the Office for Research and Graduate Studies, and the Graduate School of the Ohio State University. We thank Kevin Leicht for major contributions to data production in the third phase of the research, Michael Wallace for major contributions to data production in all phases of the research, and William Form for support throughout the project. Three anonymous reviewers and Peter Marsden provided helpful comments. Any remaining errors are our own. Earlier summaries of these findings were presented to the National Science Foundation in May 1988 and at the 1988 Annual Meetings of the American Sociological Association, Atlanta.
*Ohio State University

advocate using a form of multiplicity sampling in which the probability of an organization's inclusion in the sample is proportional to the number of workers it employs. To illustrate this design, we use data from a study of the impact of technology and technological change on workers and their work outcomes. In our study, we first obtained a representative sample of workers, who provided data on their current or most recent places of employment. We then interviewed informants within those organizations to obtain organizational data. We demonstrate that our sample of establishments does not differ significantly in size or industrial affiliation from the distributions reported in archival data when the survey data are provided by the CEOs of the establishments but that workers and managers are less reliable sources of these data. We discuss the limitations of this design, as well as its potential to inform a number of issues critical to organizational analysis and macro-to-micro relationships.

1. INTRODUCTION

The area of organizational theory has long been considered at the core of sociology. Recent developments have shown its value and vitality within the specialty, e.g., by engendering lively debates regarding the population ecology approach. It has also been a source of cross-fertilization, spreading ideas and insights into other specialties within sociology; Baron's (1984) summary of the relationship between organizational and stratification research is a case in point. Sociological perspectives on organizations also influence other disciplines.

Despite such developments, a fundamental methodological issue in this area has yet to be satisfactorily resolved: How do we select organizations for empirical study? An axiom in virtually all specialties in sociology is that researchers should strive for generalizability or representativeness in their selection of cases to be studied. This leads to a preference for representative samples of broadly defined populations. In this paper we present a valid, feasible, and cost-effective method for deriving such samples of organizations. We also report on the results of a demonstration project that provide evidence of the method's validity.

What is striking about the empirical research on organizations is that studies rarely use "typical" samples, let alone broadly defined representative samples in sociology and related disciplines. Zucker (1988) surveyed articles on organizations published in 1986–1987 in the leading social science journals and the organizational data sets available from the International Consortium for Political and Social Research (ICPSR) and classified them according to the type of sample-selection procedure used when the unit of analysis was organizational. She found that the *least* common method of case selection was random sampling (10 percent). The most common case-selection method was convenience sampling (33 percent), closely followed by stratified nonrandom sampling (31 percent) and by dense or universe sampling (15 percent) of very narrowly defined populations (e.g., all hospitals in a single metropolitan area). An earlier survey by Drabek et al. (1982) found very similar percentages across these categories; thus, the problem is longstanding.

The predominant use of atypical samples severely restricts the cumulation of knowledge about organizations and organizational processes (Freeman 1986). This has led some researchers to recommend the development of a nationally representative organizational data base. In a volume published by the National Academy of Sciences, Gerstein et al. (1988) recommend that a major priority for social science research be the development of such data bases. The National Science Foundation has sponsored pilot studies and conferences to grapple with the design issues. The demonstration project we describe in this chapter was one of these studies.

Concurrently, sociologists have become increasingly concerned with the connections between macrolevel and microlevel processes. Indeed, "Macro and Micro Interrelationships" was a major theme of the 1989 Annual Meetings of the American Sociological Association. A variety of critical and interesting macro-micro issues could be answered with multilevel data sets. For example, our own interest in the design of a sampling method that links macro organizational data with micro individual data developed in the context of a substantive interest in the link between macrolevel and microlevel processes of technological change in the workplace (see Form et al. 1988 for more details). Such a design is also relevant to debates on the level at which labor market processes should be conceptualized and studied (Baron and Bielby 1984; Hodson 1984). While our substantive interests provided the motivation and focus for our demonstration project, the design we propose is very general and easily adapts to a variety of substantive questions.

The use of such linked macro-micro data bases, however, must await the demonstration of scientifically valid, feasible, and cost-effective methods of generating representative samples of organizations linked to representative samples at lower levels. In the next section, we evaluate the strengths and weaknesses of past research design options. We then offer a theoretical solution to the limitations of past designs: a form of multiplicity sampling. Multiplicity sampling has been used in the study of multilevel organizational processes (McPherson and Smith-Lovin 1986, 1987), but we show how it can be used in the study of work organizations. In particular, we provide evidence from a pilot project to support our claims of validity and feasibility. We conclude by discussing the implications of our method for future research.

2. EVALUATING PAST RESEARCH DESIGNS

Research on a variety of substantive topics has used different designs to collect data that link organizations to their lower-level components: e.g., suborganizational units or individual members. These designs can be classified into three different categories: (1) case studies and other nonrandom samples of organizations, (2) random and dense samples of narrowly defined populations of organizations, and (3) random samples of individuals with archival data on organizations.

2.1. *Case Studies and Other Nonrandom Samples of Organizations*

At its best, a case study is an in-depth examination of the interplay between organizational structure, informal groups, and individuals. Convenience samples, also included in this category, differ from case studies only insofar as they include a wider range of cases, often, but not always, selected to provide contexts that contrast in interesting ways. Some variations of convenience sampling stratify the population by key characteristics, e.g., by industry and size. The most useful of such studies are those that systematically compare case settings (Horowitz and Herrenstadt 1966; Blauner 1964; Burns and Stalker 1966; Perrow 1984). Many studies, instead of considering the organizations in which changes occur, concentrate on a few occupations or industries (Stone 1974; Glenn and Feldberg 1977; Carter 1984; Levy, Bowes, and Jondrow 1984; Noble 1984; Cornfield 1987).

Moreover, all case studies and nonrandom samples share a fundamental weakness: However ingeniously designed, their results cannot be generalized much beyond the specific settings (e.g., Wilson 1985).

2.2. *Random and Dense Samples of Narrowly Defined Populations of Organizations*

In such designs a set of criteria is used to delimit the population of interest to a small subset (sometimes as narrow as a single industry or specific type of organization in a geographic region) and organizations are then randomly sampled for study. One common variation is to take dense samples (a high proportion of cases relative to the size of the population) or even universe samples to assure that the results can be generalized back to the population. By intensively sampling members of each selected organization, such designs create data sets that link organizational-level and individual-level data. An exemplar of this approach is the Indianapolis-Tokyo Work Commitment Project (Lincoln and Kalleberg 1985, 1990). In this study about 50 firms were selected in both the U.S. and Japan by function (limited to manufacturing in seven industries) and organization size. Questionnaires were then distributed to production workers and managers at various echelons in the firms. In addition, key informants, such as the chief executive officer (CEO) and the personnel manager, were interviewed. Mail-back questionnaires were also distributed to gather other detailed information about the firms and their employment policies.

This strategy has both advantages and limitations. A clear advantage is that it produces data on multiple respondents/informants per organization. Obtaining approval at the start of the study from top managers allows recovery of data from multiple executive informants, thus making possible some checks on reliability. It also allows access to a large number of employees, thus creating sufficient cross-person variation to make contextual analyses of firm effects meaningful. However, the samples still lack representativeness. Even though Lincoln and Kalleberg (1990) collected data from over 4,000 respondents in each country, given the original narrow definition of the population of organizations considered, their findings cannot be generalized to the entire occupational and industrial structure. Thus, although this type of design can provide rich organizational data that can be generalized back to the seven industries from which the firms were sampled, it is not broadly representative at the individual level or the organizational level. Other studies use similar designs (e.g. Cacioppe and Mock 1984).

2.3. *Random Samples of Individuals with Archival Data*

This design option allows the construction of a multilevel data set in which the probability of an organization's selection is proportional to its size. This design has the features we advocate. However, in its typical implementations, data-production decisions have frequently limited the usefulness of the resulting information. A rudimentary form of this option is the *random household design,* in which respondents are asked to provide a limited set of information about the establishment in which they work. This strategy was used, for example, in two versions of the Quality of Employment Survey in the 1970s and has been used to demonstrate the importance of organizational characteristics in stratification research (Stolzenberg 1978; Kalleberg, Wallace, and Althauser 1981). Mueller et al.'s (1969) benchmark study of technological change also used a random household design to solicit workers' views and reactions about technological changes in their jobs. While this study has rich individual-level data from a representative sample of the labor force, little organizational data were retrieved. Much of the data about the impact of technology were highly subjective opinions. Thus, the findings regarding technological change must be considered speculative.

Although this design initially appeared fruitful, it has several limitations. The first is the respondents' limited range of knowledge about the organization. Some critical aspects of organizational form and environment—e.g., market share, profit rates, capital intensity, relations with suppliers and customers, linkages with the state—are beyond the reach of this approach. Second, individual reports of organizational variables are highly subjective and often inaccurate. Even reports of numbers of employees are likely to be erroneous when establishments are very large, geographically dispersed, or subsidiaries of larger corporations. While Bagozzi and Phillips (1982) and Phillips (1981) demonstrate how unreliability can be detected and removed in models of organizational processes using multiple informants, all their informants could in theory be expected to produce valid data on questions posed to them. We argue more broadly that there is considerable information about work organizations that many organizational respondents do not have, a problem multiple-indicator models cannot adequately address.

A second, related strategy overcomes some of these limitations by mapping *archival data* on the industry or firm onto a representative sample of workers. Mapping *industry*-level archival data onto individual data sets provided important extensions of the economic segmentation literature (see Kalleberg et al. 1981; Parcel and Mueller 1983; Tolbert, Horan, and Beck 1980), but Hodson (1983, 1984) was the first to demonstrate the utility of mapping *organizational*-level data onto such files. Hodson's approach produces reliable, "objective" data on organizations, sidestepping the problems of individual reports of organizational characteristics. However, this design has three drawbacks that are endemic to archival methods (see Hodson 1983, chap. 4). First, many organizations are not listed in archival data sources, so the proportion of missing data is high. Second, the incidence of missing data is negatively associated with establishment size, creating samples biased towards larger organizations. Third, while many important concepts can be measured using archival data (scale, profitability, foreign involvement, subsidiary status, and capital intensity), other important concepts cannot (e.g., market scope, market power, technology, and internal organizational structure), and the reliability and accuracy of the archival data are not known. These limitations are particularly critical, since our goal is to produce data across organizations that are representative of the entire population of work establishments.

In short, all these methods have limitations with respect to the organizational data they produce. In general, designs that use the organization to define the population provide rich detail and measure a wide range of characteristics (e.g., Lincoln and Kalleberg 1990), but they do so at the cost of generalizability and representativeness of a broad range of organizations. Studies that use conventional household designs in which respondents define the population and are used as key informants (Mueller et al. 1969) or archival organizational data (Hodson 1983) have the opposite defect. These designs greatly restrict the range of organizational characteristics that can be measured across a broadly representative variety of organizations. We seek a design that overcomes these limitations while retaining the merits of both household and organizationally based designs. At the same time, we want to explore further the utility of archival sources for organizational variables.

3. SAMPLING ORGANIZATIONS USING A HOUSEHOLD SAMPLING FRAME

Because our demonstration project was designed to produce data to assess the impact of technological change on workers and work organization, we made a number of decisions that influenced the particular form of the design that sampled organizations using a household sampling frame. We first sketch two particular decisions we made within the context of both our substantive agenda and feasibility and describe the resulting design we used. We then describe how the design can be modified to address other substantive problems with no loss of generality.

First, we decided to study not only workers and characteristics of their organizations but also characteristics of their immediate work units, such as departments or divisions. While we faced a dilemma in the definition of work unit, respondents related to this concept easily when responding to the questions noted in Table 1. Substantively, we reasoned that the department or its equivalent is a critical context for understanding technological change. Within an organization, technological change may proceed at different rates in different units, and worker reaction to change may vary by unit. Data regarding the organization as a whole, without measures of unit characteristics to act as intervening variables, was deemed potentially too global to influence individual workers. Second, we struggled with the problem of defining an organization and settled on the strategy of using the work establishment as the operational definition. We define an establishment as a physical location with an identifiable address where work is performed. We reasoned that while parent companies affect constituent establishments, we needed to understand how technology was being implemented in the workplace before studying the role of the larger organizational context. We also produced data on the status of each establishment relative to parent companies so that we could more fully understand the implications of this decision.

The *three-stage hierarchical design* that we have developed integrates the best features of both household and organizationally based designs. It generates rich data at three levels: the establishment, the subestablishment unit, and the members. Moreover, the data at each level are representative (with weights) of that unit/level of analysis in the population as a whole. Thus, the design ensures representativeness while it also provides organizational-level data. It guarantees that almost every respondent is matched with unique organizational data, thus maximizing the potential explanatory power of organizational variables. Further, it offers the potential for linking relevant archival data on organizations to each case.

The underlying problem that has led so much of past research to use nonrepresentative or narrowly representative samples is the difficulty of establishing a good, broadly defined sampling frame of organizations so that a random sample can be drawn. For example, Kalleberg et al. (forthcoming) have shown that various compiled lists of organizations (i.e., Dun and Bradstreet files, Employment Security Commission Unemployment Insurance listings, and the telephone directory) provide poor coverage of the population of organizations. Even a walking census of a small geographic region (a county) has substantial coverage problems. Our solution is based on the fact that all organizations consist of people, that people can be randomly sampled, and that the organizations to which they belong can be identified. This method of drawing a sample of organizations has been used to follow supervisory chains in organizations (Spaeth 1985) and to study voluntary organizations (McPherson 1982, 1983). Villemez and Bridges (1988) and Bridges and Villemez (1986) use this strategy to study the effects of organizational size on individual outcomes and informal hiring in the labor market. While the sample of identified organizations is not a simple random sample, it is a multiplicity random sample, in which probabilities of selection can be readily calculated, and, hence, weights can be used to make the sample representative.

In the first stage of the design, we use a random household survey akin to the conventional household design. Respondents, whom we label the target members, must constitute a representative sample of the population of interest, be it a particular geographic region or the entire nation. For example, if the oranizational population of interest is work organizations, then the first-stage sampling frame should be limited to individuals in the labor force. In addition to providing information relevant to a study's substantive focus, members are also asked to provide the name and address of their establishment, the name of their unit, the name of their unit head, and a contact phone number. These data are useful for the two subsequent stages of the design: gathering relevant unit and establishment data. However, not all of these data are absolutely essential. With just the organization's name, you can frequently find the remaining information.

The second stage of the design requires an interview with the unit heads identified by the target members. As before, unit heads are used not only to provide data about relevant substantive concerns but also to provide the name and contact number of the CEO or the administrator in charge of the establishment. The number of members in the unit must also be determined so that the proper weight can be calculated (discussed below) and the units made representative of the population of units. This stage of the design provides a weighted-representative sample of unit-level information and contextual unit-level data that can be mapped onto the target member data base.

Finally, in the third stage of the design, establishment-level data are collected from the CEO or the top administrator. From a design point of view, only one piece of data is essential at this stage: the number of members of the establishment. This determines the appropriate weight for the establishment. Obviously, however, a wide variety of organizational data can be obtained in the interview. These establishment-level data can be used to analyze organizational processes and issues, but they also provide contextual data that can be used in analyses of issues at the two lower levels.

The representativeness of the target members is assured by the proper use of random sampling methods in the first stage of the design. We claimed above that the other two stages also provide representative data on work units and establishments if they are properly weighted. The basis for our claim is the application of the principles of multiplicity sampling (Sudman, Sirken and Cowan 1988). When there are multiple, independent paths that can each cause a population member I to be included in a sample, the probability of selection for included members is the sum of the probability of each path:

$$\text{Pr(select } I) = \sum_j \text{Pr(path}_j). \tag{1}$$

The sample weight that makes each sample member representative of the population is then inversely proportional to the probability of selection of member I and should be normed by the mean of sample weights to reproduce the sample size:

$$\text{weight for } I = \frac{1/\text{Pr(select } I)}{(\sum_M 1/\text{Pr(select } M))/N}, \tag{2}$$

where N is the number of members included in the sample. If the probabilities of selecting each path to each population member are equal, then the above formulas simplify to depend on the number of paths to each population member:

$$\text{Pr(select } I) = NP_I \times \text{Pr(path)}, \tag{3}$$

$$\text{weight for } I = \frac{1/NP_I}{(\sum_M 1/NP_M)/N}, \tag{4}$$

where NP_I is the number of paths to member I.

The design described above conforms to those assumptions as long as the first-stage target members are selected with equal probability. In the case of the second-stage units, the number of paths is simply the number of members of the particular unit in an establishment. And for the third-stage establishments, the number of paths is simply the number of members of the establishment. These data can be used in conjunction with equation (4) to construct weights for analyses at the unit and establishment levels.

The effects of using this design with weighted estimation procedures on the sampling variance of either simple statistics (e.g., means) or complex statistics (e.g., regression coefficients) is not invariant across population characteristics and alternative designs and thus cannot be simply specified (Cochran 1953, p. 211; Cassel, Särndal, and Wretman 1977, p. 161; Nathan and Holt 1980, pp. 383–84). The discussion below presumes that the first stage of the sample was drawn using simple random sampling or an equivalent design (e.g., stratified random sampling). The use of more complex designs at the first stage is possible as long as the target members are selected with equal probability, but this increases the sampling variance of the design.

In the case of simple statistics, the relative efficiency of such a design can be specified when the variance of the population characteristic is a power function of the size of the unit: $V(Y) = \sigma^2 \times size^p$. For values of p greater than 1.0, this design using weighted estimation is more efficient than simple random sampling (srs), whereas for values of p less than 1.0, this procedure is less efficient (Cassel et al. 1977, p. 161). As Sudman (1976, p. 115) notes, when sampling institutions, larger units usually have greater variance, suggesting that p is usually greater than 1.0. Thus, we can generally expect this design with weighted estimation to efficiently estimate simple statistics. Moreover, it is important to note that unweighted simple statistics calculated for the sample generated by this design are biased.

The sampling variance of regression coefficients is more complicated. From Nathan and Holt's (1980, p. 384) formula for the variance of a weighted bivariate regression coefficient for this design, it is clear that this sampling variance can be either larger or smaller than the sampling variance for the srs unweighted OLS estimator. If there is a zero partial correlation in the population between the dependent variable and size (partialling on the independent variable), then the sampling variance for this weighted OLS estimator is less than or equal to the sampling variance for the srs unweighted OLS estimator. However, this condition seems unlikely to hold for a wide range of establishment characteristics. Results from Nathan and Holt's computer simulation suggest that using this weighted OLS estimator in such cases may not create substantial loss in efficiency. They find that the sampling variance of a weighted OLS estimator is "relatively insensitive to the sampling design" (1980, p. 385). There is less than a 6 percent loss in efficiency when there is a modest partial correlation between the dependent variable and size. It should be noted that using an unweighted OLS estimator for the sample generated by this design is not a viable alternative, since it is biased and inconsistent.

This design has three potential disadvantages: (1) securing three complete interviews to complete a single case is labor intensive and costly, (2) there is the possibility of lower response rates at the unit and establishment levels, and (3) there are some limitations on the amount and type of organizational data that can be gathered, even though this design permits the collection of more such data than most designs. On the other hand, this design can generate rich data at multiple organizational levels *and* provide representative samples, not only of members but also, with weights, of establishments and units.

This design will not be implemented in its fullest form for all target members. For example, in the study of work organizations, the department-level and establishment-level stages of the design would be dropped for the self-employed target worker because the department and establishment levels are coincident with the worker. In addition, because of the elaborate chains of authority in government organizations, the inclusion of government employees as target members may require additional consideration. The boundaries of governmental establishments are more amorphous than in the private sector, and the operational definition of a CEO must be thought through. However, since we defined the establishment as the work site about which the questions are asked, this problem is ameliorated; most governmental work sites have identifiable CEOs.

Depending on the particular substantive agenda, this design can be modified without loss of generality. For example, it may not be necessary to interview unit managers before interviewing CEOs. While it may be convenient to obtain a CEO's name and phone number from a department-level manager, for example, this information can often also be obtained from a receptionist or from written documents. In small organizations, target workers can provide this information. Such two-stage designs retain the multiplicity nature of the organizational sample.

Alternatively, it may be necessary to interview more layers within the organization, i.e., more rungs on the ladder. Spaeth's (1985) studies of organizational authority hierarchies are a case in point. He interviewed every rung on the supervisory ladder until he either reached the top or was refused access and could not obtain information to locate the remaining informants. In this case, each respondent can be assigned a weight based on the number of members in the respective units. Obviously, the multiplicity nature of the sample is maintained. Another variation on this latter model might be to extend the design an additional stage to include an interview with the parent organization for those establishments that are not autonomous. This might necessitate interviews on four rungs of the organizational ladder: worker, supervisor, establishment CEO, and corporate CEO. Other investigations may find it appropriate to interview more than one informant at certain levels. Questions about who speaks for the organization and whether CEOs can provide adequate technical or personnel information might be resolved by interviewing top executives in addition to the CEO. Investigators studying the effects of organizational characteristics on workers and their spouses might opt for interviews of the target worker and spouse, followed by organizational interviews as appropriate. Again, the multiplicity nature of the sample is maintained with reference to both workers and spouses.

4. RESULTS FROM A DEMONSTRATION PROJECT

Our demonstration project developed out of a substantive interest in the study of individual, departmental, enterprise, and extra-enterprise effects of technology and technological change (see Form et al. 1988 for details). As Zucker (1988) has demonstrated in general for organizational research, past studies on the effects of technology and technological change in organizations have been limited in their representativeness and scope. The design described above was specifically intended to overcome these limitations.

Given our substantive issue, we defined the organizational population of interest as work establishments in the Columbus, Ohio, metropolitan area. Columbus was selected for convenience, but data from *County Business Patterns* (U.S. Bureau of the Census 1989, Table 2) suggest that average establishment size in Franklin County in 1987 (18.95) was comparable to that in Dallas (18.41), Cook (18.93), Cuyahoga (Cleveland) (18.31), and Hamilton (Cincinnati) (19.99) Counties. Franklin County ranks 27th out of 175 in number of establishments listed in *County Business Patterns* (U.S. Bureau of the Census 1989, Table 2). Inspection of data for those counties with numbers of establishments *similar* to Franklin County suggests lower average establishment sizes in the fastest growing counties (e.g., San Diego County's ratio is 13.15) owing to high numbers of establishments with 1–4 and 5–9 employees. Comparing

Franklin County to those with the *greatest* numbers of establishments suggests higher average sizes in more established urban areas (e.g., New York County's average size is 20.40).

Our design involved "going up the ladder" from workers to their departments and supervisors to the CEOs of their local establishments. First, we conducted telephone interviews with a sample of 228 workers in the Columbus area to obtain information about their establishment (name, location, industry) and their supervisor (name, phone, number, and department name). The sample was derived via random-digit dialing. At this stage we also collected a host of information about workers' jobs, work organization, use of technology, and adaptation to technological change. Second, we contacted by phone the 207 departmental supervisors who could be identified to obtain the name and phone number of the establishment's CEO and to capture information on work and technology relevant to departmental units. Third, we attempted interviews with the CEOs of the 184 unique establishments identified in the sample of 204 establishments.[1] We collected data from the CEOs on the organizational and technological characteristics of the enterprise and its environment, recent changes in technology and organization in response to pressures from the organizational environment, the strategy of implementing these changes, and so on. As we discuss in detail below, the success of this design can be assessed in terms of two criteria: (1) how practical and successful the design is in creating a sample of establishments with data on establishments linked to data on individuals, and (2) whether or not the sample of establishments is representative of the population of establishments.

Table 1 presents some of the questions used to operationalize key aspects of the design. To obtain supervisor information from the worker, at the end of the interview we asked for the supervisor's name for another study. We asked similar questions to obtain CEO information from supervisors. As noted above, while it was difficult to define what we meant by work unit because establishments refer to internal divisions differently, respondents answered the relevant questions easily. Regarding multiple jobs, we asked workers if they held more than

[1]Not all of the third-stage respondents were the local establishment's CEO. Although local CEOs were extremely cooperative, 13 percent of the completed interviews were with respondents who were knowledgeable senior executives to whom we were referred by the CEO.

TABLE 1
Strategies Used to Operationalize Key Aspects of the Design

1. Obtaining the supervisor's name from the target worker
   Questions:

   We would like to talk to people at other levels in your organization for a
   future study. We will ask them questions like those we have asked you.
   Your answers will be kept confidential. Nobody outside of study personnel will EVER see your answers.

   Would you please tell me the name of your supervisor?

   What is his or her telephone number at work?

   Note:

   Analogous questions about the former supervisor were asked if the respondent was currently unemployed but reported a former employer.

   These were the very last questions asked in the target-worker interview
   before thanking the respondent for his/her cooperation.

2. Obtaining the CEO's name from the supervisor
   Questions:

   We would like to talk to people at other levels in your organization for a
   future study. We will ask them questions like those we have asked you.

   Could you please tell me the name of the person who is the top manage-
   rial person at the location of (the physical location) where you work?

   What is his or her phone number at work?

   Is that person the top supervisory person (at the physical location where
   you work)?

   Note:

   These were the very last questions asked in the supervisor/manager interview before thanking the respondent for his/her cooperation.

3. Defining work-unit boundaries
   Questions:

   Is the place where you work divided into two or more work units, like
   sections, departments, or divisions?

   If yes,

   Are those work units called sections, departments, or what?

   What is the name of the (section, department, etc.) you work in?

4. Handling people with multiple jobs
   Questions:

   Do you work for just one employer or for more than one employer?
   What is your job title?
   What is the job title for your PRIMARY job?
   What is the job title for your second job?

Please tell me some more about your PRIMARY job.
What are your MAIN duties on the job; that is, what kinds of work do
you do? (Well, in general, what kind of work do you do?)

5. Deriving information on industry affiliation
   Question:
   What kind of business or industry do you work in; that is, what kind of
   product is made or what service is given?

---

one job and to respond to questions regarding job activities in terms of their primary job. This strategy may underrepresent establishments in industries that rely heavily on part-time employment, where the part-time jobs represent workers' second jobs. As we later show, however, in our study such underrepresentation did not occur. Both occupation and industry were coded using U.S. Census procedures from the respondents' descriptions of job activities and type of product/service produced.

Table 2 shows the response rates for the three levels of respondents in the study. The somewhat low response rate at the worker level can be attributed to the use of nonprofessional interviewers for this wave of data production; their response rates improved as the survey progressed. Professional interviewers were used for the two remaining waves and achieved much higher response rates. At the CEO level, most of the interviews were completed via phone. We targeted those CEOs for whom repeated call backs resulted in neither completed interviews nor referrals to other informants for additional effort.[2] This strategy resulted in an additional seven interviews, thus bringing the CEO response rate to 78 percent. By way of comparison, Spaeth (1989), who used students to interview eligible respondents at the worker level, reports a response rate of 75 percent but only a 52 percent response rate including eligible respondents plus those whose eligibility was unknown in the denominator. Using professional interviewers in subsequent stages yielded response rates of 84.2 percent and 76.3 percent for the second and third stages, respectively.

[2]Project principal investigators called each and stressed the importance of the study and the potential usefulness of the report on technological change in Columbus based on the survey results, which they were told they would receive if they participated in the study. We offered them the opportunity to respond to written questionnaires or to be interviewed in person, in addition to the opportunity to be interviewed by telephone at any convenient time.

TABLE 2

Disposition of Cases and Response Rates for Each Level of Interviewing

	Number of Cases	Response Rate[a]
Level 1: Workers		67%
Households contacted	413	
Ineligible households	72	
Refusals	114	
Interviews	227	
Level 2: Supervisors		85%
Duplicate supervisors[b]	1	
Supervisors not identifiable	20	
No second level, supervisor is CEO contacted for third level	55	
Supervisors contacted	151	
Supervisor refusals	23	
Successful interviews	128	
Level 3: CEOs		78%
Duplicate CEOs[c]	23	
CEO not identifiable	1	
CEOs contacted	184	
CEO refusals	40	
CEO interviews	144	

[a]The response rate is defined as (number of interviews) ÷ (number of interviews + number of refusals).

[b]These are cases from the first level that share the same supervisor. Only one contact was necessary.

[c]These are cases from the first level or second level that share the same CEO. Only one contact was necessary.

Figure 1 shows the routes by which we completed cases across levels of our design. The first three routes are those that required no information other than that obtained in the interviews and represent the three possible combinations of levels of relevant interviews. In route 1a, the standard situation, the worker, appropriate supervisor, and CEO were identified and interviewed without any additional intervening steps. In route 1b, the worker is in an establishment in which there is no supervisor other than the CEO. Either the establishment is large and the worker is at a high enough level to work directly below the CEO, or the establishment is small and there are

Route	Diagram		
1a	Worker	Supervisor	CEO
1b	Worker		CEO
1c	Worker/ CEO		Worker/ CEO
2a	Worker	Supervisor ↓ Supervisor? ↓ • • ↓ Supervisor	CEO
2b	Worker	Supervisor	CEO? ↓ CEO? ↓ • • ↓ CEO
2c	Worker	Supervisor? ↓ Supervisor? ↓ • ↓ Supervisor	CEO? ↓ CEO? ↓ • • ↓ CEO
3	Worker	CEO/ Supervisor	CEO/ Supervisor
4	Worker ? ?	Supervisor ?	CEO

FIGURE 1. Diagrams of routes to completed cases across levels with initial-worker random-sampling design. The route numbers are described in Table 4. The question marks indicate that the specified contact referred interviewers to another person in the organization or that information from outside the interview was needed to identify the next respondent.

just two levels: workers and CEO. In route 1c, the initial respondent is both worker and CEO but because of initial resource limitations had to be interviewed twice. Assuming adequate resources, computerized telephone interviewing systems would permit appending CEO questions onto the original worker-level interview when appropriate.

In the second set of routes, there were referrals at only the supervisor level (route 2a), only the CEO level (route 2b), or both the supervisor and CEO levels (route 2c). While some referrals were made by the contacted person, some of the referrals occurred because we screened for proper managers rather than nominal supervisors at the second stage and requested referrals if the contacted person was not a proper manager (Wright 1978). We believed that those who merely supervised the work activities of others but had minimal authority over them might be underinformed about technological change within the establishment. We defined a proper manager as the top supervisory person in the department (section, work unit, etc.) of the establishment. But we asked the target workers for their immediate supervisors, since we believed that they knew this information better than they knew the names of top supervisory personnel.

The third route occurred if the CEO was interviewed as a supervisor first and reinterviewed as a CEO if he/she was also the CEO of the establishment. Again, given adequate resources, only one interview would be necessary. Finally, the fourth route comprises those cases in which additional information, other than that obtained in prior interviews, had to be obtained to complete the case at the supervisor or CEO levels. For example, in a few cases the CEO was not the person the manager indicated, or an establishment's address was incomplete.

Table 3 delineates these patterns as well as the causes of incomplete cases in detail and indicates the frequency with which each occurred. There are separate counts and percentages for target workers versus CEOs, since multiple target workers might come from the same establishment. For example, the first row of the table shows that we successfully completed 163 cases across 144 different establishments. Further down the data suggest that for 51 cases across 44 establishments, we needed referrals to complete the case. We were able to positively identify 184 of the 204 establishments represented in the sample.

TABLE 3

Routes to Contacted Cases Across Levels with Initial-Worker Random-Sampling Design

	Worker Level		CEO Level	
	N[a]	Percentage	N[a]	Percentage
A. Routes to Completed Cases[b]	163	71%	144	71%
1. No referrals or refusals, correct identification of subsequent contacts	35	15%	35	17%
a. Interviews needed at all three levels	22	10%	22	11%
b. Interviews needed at only two levels	10	4%	10	5%
c. Interview needed at only first level	3	1%	3	1%
2. Referrals needed to complete case	51	22%	44	22%
a. Referrals at level 2, but not level 3	14	6%	13	6%
b. Referrals at level 3, but not level 2	20	9%	16	9%
c. One or more referrals at levels 2 and 3	17	7%	15	7%
3. CEO interviewed as supervisor and reinterviewed as CEO	5	2%	5	2%
4. Incorrect information or lack of information, outside information used to complete case	72	32%	60	29%
B. Routes to Incomplete Cases	65	29%	60	29%
5. Refusal at CEO level, no referral	37	10%	32	16%
6. CEO interviewed as supervisor and refused interview as CEO	4	1%	4	2%
7. Firm death before completion	3	1%	3	1%
8. Insufficient data to identify establishment	21	9%	21	10%
Total	228	100%	204	100%

[a] These numbers differ, since an interview at the CEO level may complete several cases at the worker level because multiple workers are in the same establishment.

[b] See Figure 1 for diagrams of routes for completions.

Overall, we were able to complete cases for 71 percent of our sample. For a minority of cases, 15 percent of the target workers, we completed data at all relevant levels *and* required no information other than that provided by the respondents. A second set of completed cases, 22 percent, required referrals to persons other than those originally named in a lower-stage interview. Most of these involved referrals at only one level, but about one-third of the referrals occurred at both the supervisor and the CEO levels. In about half of the referrals at the CEO level, the person contacted was not the CEO because of misinformation from supervisors. In the other half, the CEO refused but referred us to another informant.

In a full 32 percent of the cases we had incomplete information from either the initial interview or the supervisor interview, or both, and we used outside information to complete the case. Most of the cases in which outside information was needed involved interviews at the supervisor level in which target workers had given incomplete responses to questions about establishment name and location. Often the solution involved merely looking up the phone number in the telephone directory. In other cases it was necessary to call the establishment and ask if they had a department that dealt with a particular function and, if so, who the head of the department was. Incomplete names of establishments were searched with both telephone and City Business Directories; partial identifications of establishments were searched with reference to the establishment's industry and street address. By the time the CEO level had been reached, there was little additional work of this sort to be completed. However, some supervisors refused to divulge the names of their CEOs. This occurred in 12 percent of the cases, and in these instances, we telephoned the establishments to obtain this information.

Among the incomplete cases (29 percent of our sample), the most common cause of incompletion was refusal at the CEO level, including a few CEOs who had participated at the second stage as supervisors but refused to be reinterviewed as CEOs.[3] For 11 percent

---

[3]In the second wave of interviews, we did not screen supervisors at the beginning of the interview to determine if they were also CEOs. We asked who the CEO was at the end of the supervisor interview. As a result of this oversight, a few supervisors indicated that they were CEOs. In such cases we attempted reinterviews using the CEO questionnaire.

of the target-worker cases (but 18 percent of the CEO-level cases), the CEO refused to participate with no referrals. The second most common cause was insufficient information to positively identify the establishment or the CEO. For 9 percent of the target workers (10 percent of the establishments) we could not complete the case because of insufficient information. Given that Spaeth (1989) has reported an identification rate of 99 percent using professional interviewers, we assume that given adequate resources, this difficulty could be minimized. Only 1 percent of our establishments ceased operation before we could follow them up to the CEO level. There was usually a gap of a number of months between the worker and CEO interviews.[4] If, however, many establishments do not exist long enough to have phone numbers and addresses, then our sample represents the more successful establishments, those that are at a more advanced stage of the life course. The time gap did allow for turnover at both the supervisor and CEO levels. This turnover necessitated additional telephoning to obtain names and phone numbers of the new incumbents of these positions.

We now turn to the properties of the sample we generated. It is critical that we demonstrate that our sample is representative. Of course, Franklin County was selected for convenience and is not representative of all counties. For the purposes of demonstrating the usefulness of this design, this restriction should not matter, since the site is indifferent to the probability nature of the sampling procedures. However, a different county (or set of counties) might dictate differing or additional strategies of data production to actually generate a sample with the needed properties. Franklin County contains a

---

[4]We began interviewing target workers in April 1987 and continued through August 1987. We began interviewing supervisors in June 1987 and concluded in November 1987. We began interviewing CEOs in October 1987 and nearly completed interviewing by July 1988. A few more CEOs were interviewed in the late summer of 1988. The mean time interval between target worker and supervisor interviews was 3.2 months, ranging from one day to 6.8 months; the mean interval between supervisor and CEO interviews was 6.7 months, ranging from 1.2 months to 16.8 months; the mean interval between target worker and CEO interviews was 9.9 months, ranging from 5.1 months to 20.2 months. A large part of this overall time lag was a function of the fact that we were completing and pretesting the second and third questionnaires during data collection. The bulk of the interviewing was completed at the target worker and supervisor levels before supervisor and CEO interviews, respectively, were initiated. Simultaneous interviewing would reduce these time lags considerably.

high proportion of service and government establishments but a lower proportion of manufacturing establishments than many older, larger, urban areas. If there are differing response rates of establishments across industries, or if differing strategies are needed to produce data on establishments of differing types, then researchers using a different county or set of counties would have to take this into account in their data-production procedures. While any sample of counties will have establishments representing a diversity of industries, the frequency with which researchers encounter certain data-production difficulties may vary with the sample's industrial distribution, assuming that these difficulties are associated with industry. Samples from counties with larger establishment sizes may yield samples more tightly clustered across establishments than samples from counties with smaller establishments. While the degree of difference is likely minor, the former type of sample enhances the chances of separating out worker and establishment effects (see the discussion in section 5).

Tables 4 and 5 allow us to address the issue of sample representativeness, within the context of the study of Franklin County. Data from the *County Business Patterns* for 1986 (U.S. Bureau of the Census 1987) provide a limited amount of information on establishments by county in the U.S. and thus serve as a useful basis for comparison with the establishment-level data we generated in this survey. Table 4 provides a comparison of the distribution of establishments by major industry group in Franklin County, with the industries as reported by the CEOs, supervisors, and workers in our sample. At each level the respondent answered the standard U.S. Census question and a trained coder coded the responses into detailed (three-digit) industry categories. These categories were aggregated into single-digit categories for the purposes of this comparison. Table 5 provides a comparison of the distribution of establishments by size categories in Franklin County, with the establishment sizes as reported by the CEOs, supervisors, and workers in our sample. The Franklin County data were compiled from the *County Business Patterns* for 1986 (U.S. Bureau of the Census 1987, Table 2). Franklin County is almost identical to the geographic area that defined our sample. Case weights for each comparison were calculated using the establishment size reported by the respondent at each level (worker, supervisor, CEO). In each case we performed a chi-square test

TABLE 4

Industry Distribution Comparisons of Level of Respondent Reports to Franklin County Business Patterns

Major Industry	County Business Pattern Percentage	CEO Weighted Percentage	Supervisor Weighted Percentage	Worker Weighted Percentage	Composite Weighted Percentage
Agriculture	1.25	4.34*	0.87	11.28*	9.93*
Mining	0.33	0.00	0.00	0.00	0.00
Construction	7.88	1.45*	3.78	4.94	4.37
Nondurable manu-facturing	2.21	2.84	3.51	5.01*	1.90
Durable manufac-turing	2.61	1.57	1.16	1.57	1.17
Transport	2.92	0.61	0.40	3.37	0.38
Wholesale	8.87	6.70	4.90	2.06*	4.26
Retail	24.62	19.26	27.12	15.12*	18.05
Finance	12.70	17.66	16.71	17.14	15.25
Business service	9.53	7.72	10.70	10.90	10.80
Professional service	21.46	32.92*	25.34	22.55	27.22
Personal service	5.63	4.90	5.50	6.05	6.66
Unweighted N	22,072	139	135	187	186
Adjusted χ^2		11.64	5.25	54.60	46.13
Estimated λ		3.09	2.69	3.31	2.90
df		11	11	11	11
Significance level		ns	ns	$p<.001$	$p<.001$

Note: λ is the adjustment factor used to correct the χ^2 statistic for the use of weighted data from a non-srs design (see footnote 5).

*Standardized cell residual significant at $p < .05$ (see footnote 6).

(adjusted for sampling design effects)[5] to evaluate whether there was a statistically significant difference between the distributions from

[5]Rao and Scott (1981) proposed a procedure for adjusting a goodness-of-fit chi-square statistic when the sample cell counts are estimated using weighted data from a non-srs design. The initial chi-square value is divided by an adjustment factor $\hat{\lambda} = (\Sigma_i V(p_i)/p_i) / (I-1)$, where p_i is the weighted sample proportion in cell i, $V(p_i)$ is the estimated variance of p_i, and I is the number of cells. According to Nathan (1988, p. 260), a variety of empirical studies show that this adjustment procedure achieves "a close approximation to nominal levels of significance." $V(p_i)$ was estimated according to Sen (1988, p. 314), which applies to sampling with replacement, since developing exact theory for non-srs designs using sampling without replacement is complicated (Sen 1988, pp. 314–16). Consequently, the data presented in Tables 4 and 5 include each establishment as many times as it appears in the sample. We thank one of the reviewers for suggesting the use of an adjustment procedure.

the archival and the survey data, using the archival data as the expected distribution.

We found that the distribution of the industries in our sample as reported by the CEOs was not statistically significantly different from the data reported in *County Business Patterns*. Despite this overall nonstatistically significant result, three cells diverge substantially[6] from their expected values: CEOs report that there are more establishments in both agriculture and professional services but fewer in construction than expected on the basis of archival data. The distribution using the supervisor responses is also not significantly different from the archival data, and none of the cells shows a substantial difference from its expected value. Interestingly, there are noticeable differences between the industrial identification distributions for CEOs and supervisors. CEOs are more likely than supervisors to identify their establishments as agricultural and professional service and less likely to identify them as construction and retail. However, the worker distribution is significantly different from the archival data, which suggests that workers may be the worst informants about industry affiliation. Workers overestimate the frequency with which their establishments are in agriculture and nondurable manufacturing but underestimate the frequency of affiliation with both wholesale and retail trade. Interestingly, there are noticeable differences between the industrial identification distributions for workers and supervisors. Workers are more likely than supervisors to identify their establishments as in agriculture and in transportation and less likely than supervisors to identify their establishments as retail sales. We also considered the possibility of creating a hierarchical composite measure that minimizes missing information and uses the best available information (i.e., that available from the highest-level respondent). The composite measure uses CEO information if available, supervisor data only if the CEO data is missing, and worker data only if both the CEO and supervisor data are missing. This composite also fails to reproduce the archival distribution, but

---

[6]Conclusions about cell differences comparing observed and archival data are drawn from an examination of the standardized cell residuals (calculated as components of the adjusted chi-square) using the criterion suggested by Bishop, Fienberg, and Holland (1975, p. 137). It is a Bonferroni adjustment of the chi-square critical value for the effects of multiple comparisons.

again there is only one category (agriculture) that shows a significant divergence.[7]

Table 5 repeats this exercise for size of the establishment.[8] In Franklin County, fully 49 percent of the establishments have between one and four employees, and 70 percent have fewer than ten employees.[9] We again find that there is no significant difference between the archival distribution and the overall distribution generated by the CEO interviews. However, one cell is (barely) significantly different in this comparison; the 5–9 size category is significantly larger in the CEO report than in the archival data.[10] In contrast to the industrial distribution results, both the supervisor- and the worker-reported size distributions are significantly different from the archival data. The supervisors substantially underreport that their establishment falls in the 1–4 size category and overreport the 5–9 size category. While the workers also substantially overreport that their establishments are in the 5–9 size category, they underreport the 10–19 and 20–49 size categories. There are simple but interesting patterns in the differences between the size distributions reported by the supervisors and those

[7]In some cases the composite distribution has percentages that are not bounded by the range of percentages for the three separate distributions. This occurs because the weights for the composite distribution are also derived hierarchically using the best available data.

[8]The size distributions reported for our data were calculated using the same population definition used by the *County Business Pattern* report. Namely, it excludes government employees, railroad employees, and self-employed persons.

[9]While these figures may appear extreme, they are similar to those reported by Granovetter (1984), who argued for the importance of studying small establishments. He found that 23.2 percent of workers in 1981 were employed in establishments with less than 20 employees (Granovetter 1984, p. 327). Our estimate from the *County Business Pattern* data indicate that in Franklin County, about 25.1 percent of workers in 1986 were employed in establishments with fewer than 20 employees. The critical comparison, of course, is between the archival and survey data.

[10]This might have occurred because of the tendency for digit preference in self-reporting. Self-reported age distributions, for example, tend to be "lumpy" around five-year age markers (20, 25, 30, etc.) (Shryock and Siegel 1976, p. 115). An employment-size response of 5 might be such a common approximation. Also, there might have been growth in the smallest companies between the time of initial contact with the target workers and the interview of the CEOs, causing some cases to cross the narrow size category boundary and to create an overestimate of the 5–9 size category.

TABLE 5

Employment Size Distribution Comparisons of Level of Respondent Reports to
Franklin County Business Patterns

Size Category	County Business Pattern Percentage	CEO Weighted Percentage	Supervisor Weighted Percentage	Worker Weighted Percentage	Composite Weighted Percentage
1–4	49.20	45.32	26.56*	45.27	44.29
5–9	20.31	32.02*	43.22*	37.09*	36.14*
10–19	13.95	10.78	12.09	6.55*	8.63*
20–49	10.12	6.46	10.96	6.14*	5.80*
50–99	3.61	1.87	2.81	2.31	2.05
100–249	1.96	2.22	2.88	1.65	2.07
250–499	0.50	0.72	0.88	0.60	0.59
500–999	0.22	0.35	0.31	0.23	0.24
1,000+	0.13	0.26	0.29	0.16	0.18
Unweighted N	22,072	139	136	186	192
Adjusted χ^2		9.87	32.31	31.25	33.45
Estimated λ		1.45	1.59	1.21	1.27
df		8	8	8	8
Significance level		ns	$p<.001$	$p<.001$	$p<.001$

Note: λ is the adjustment factor used to correct the χ^2 statistic for the use of weighted data from a non-srs design (see footnote 5).
*Standardized cell residual significant at $p < .05$ (see footnote 6).

reported by both the workers and the CEOs. The supervisors are less likely than either the workers or the CEOs to report working in the smallest (1–4 person) establishments but more likely to report working in all larger establishments. The hierarchical composite utilizing reports on size from CEOs, supervisors, and workers also fails to adequately represent the archival data. It shows the same pattern of substantial cell divergences as the worker distribution.

5. SUMMARY AND CONCLUSIONS

Our demonstration project suggests that it is quite possible to "go up the ladder" from worker to supervisor to CEO and get quite acceptable response rates and thus produce a sample of establishments with probabilities proportional to size. While we have indicated a number of practical problems that had to be overcome, none of them is insurmountable, and future research using this design should be able to avoid many of them. Assuming use of a professional survey research organization at each stage, the data could be generated relatively quickly, relatively few cases would require access to information other than that gained from prior interviews, and very few cases would result in a failure to identify the establishment. Moreover, those cases that necessitated referrals could be completed expeditiously by a professional team. Spaeth's (1989) summary of a study in Illinois provides additional evidence that this type of design yields establishment samples with desirable properties.

Our results provide strong evidence for our claim that our design does produce a sample that is representative of the population of establishments. Using the data collected at the establishment (CEO) level does in fact reproduce the overall distributions of two key establishment characteristics in the population: industry and size. While we have been able to evaluate this claim for only these two establishment characteristics, if a broader range of establishment data were available in archives, there would be no motivation to construct a national organizational data base.

These data also bear on a central question in organizational theory: Who speaks for the organization? Some have argued that the organization is not an objective reality but rather a subjective one. Under the subjective model, the information obtained about the organization may legitimately vary, depending on the informant. Studying the differences among informants' responses to common questions provides important insights into organizational functioning, regardless of what the objective truth may be. Our findings suggest that workers cannot report accurately on either the size of the organization or its industrial affiliation but that CEOs produce reliable information on both. That supervisors produce reliable information on industry but not size is compatible with the notion that supervisors are inadequate sources for detailed, objective information but suitable sources for more general organizational data. Certainly there may be areas of objective knowledge about the organization that the CEO does not have; in these areas, personnel and operations managers will yield better data. It may be, however, that for basic organizational information that has a detailed, objective referent, the CEO is the best source. In general, using this design to produce meaningful data for research depends on careful consideration of who is competent to answer respective questions. Of course, the probability nature of the samples is indifferent to these decisions.

While we initiated this project to study the effect of technology on workers and work organization, we completed the third stage of data production with funding from the National Science Foundation's Organizational Data Base Initiative Pilot Projects. We participated in NSF-sponsored discussions about the best way to derive a national sample of organizations, in which the strategy we describe in this paper was explicitly compared with list-based strategies (Kalleberg et al., forthcoming; Reynolds et al. 1988). If the goal is to construct a nationally representative sample of organizations, we believe our strategy is superior to list-based strategies for several reasons. First, Kalleberg et al. document that the methods that they investigated failed to yield exhaustive lists; thus, none of their methods can be demonstrated to yield a representative sample of organizations. The methods they used are expensive, both in personnel time and in acquisition costs. Some data can be obtained only with state governmental permission. And their study was restricted to one county. The costs and labors of negotiations with multiple governmental jurisdictions would be enormous in a national sample. Even if a suitable sample could be constructed with a list-based strategy, it would not produce research comparable to what we have described here. Additional resources would still be required to derive data from the selected organizations.

In contrast, our strategy yields a representative sample. It utilizes the vast store of knowledge that researchers from several disciplines have accumulated on surveying individuals as the basis for surveying establishments. Thus, the cost of deriving the initial list of establishments to contact is the cost of surveying the individuals needed to produce the list. Similarly, the survey methods (e.g., clustered and stratified sampling, random-digit dialing) needed to derive that list are precisely those needed to survey the respective sample of individuals and thus are also known entities. Building on this substantial foundation of knowledge reduces the uncertainty of such a major project. A critic might wonder whether such a multiplicity sample would be worth the investment if the scope of his/her investigation were going to be geographically limited. Our view is that the resources needed to construct a local telephone sample of workers are modest and pay big dividends in representativeness of the establishment sample that can be derived from it.

Another way to see the advantages of the design we propose is to consider the success of constructing such a sample by "going down the ladder." Assuming one could obtain a representative sample of organizations from a list, the likelihood of obtaining a probability sample of workers within these organizations is near zero. Organizations are notoriously finicky about releasing names of organizational members, and even if they were not, constructing probability samples within each would be very impractical.[11]

The method is flexible in that layers of interviews can be added or eliminated depending on the substantive purpose of the project. In its simplest form, the design requires two interviews: one with a target member and one with an informant within the establishment. Based on the data we have produced, we recommend that for most establishment data, the CEO is the most reliable informant. We have argued that the design can be augmented to include interviews with additional organizational informants for more specialized information (e.g., personnel or operations managers), for detail regarding work organization within individual departments (e.g., depart-

[11]Work by McPherson (1982) and McPherson and Smith-Lovin (1986, 1987) illustrates a strategy that contrasts with ours both on the feasibility of "going down the ladder" and on the dimension of obtaining multiple respondents per organization. They generated representative samples of respondents in ten Nebraska communities and asked respondents for exhaustive lists of their voluntary associations. They then interviewed the leaders of a sample of these associations and obtained permission to briefly survey organizational members at group meetings. This strategy not only produces a representative sample of organizations but also allows each organization to be represented with multiple members, which is useful in separating organizational effects from individual effects. Of course, this strategy would be far more difficult to pursue with work establishments because of their reluctance to divulge their personnel rosters. In addition, Nebraska was chosen as the site for the study because of its history of cooperation with studies of voluntary associations. This does not suggest that the findings generated from their project are nonrepresentative, but it does suggest caution regarding assumptions of cooperation from organizations in divulging membership or personnel lists. In addition, while voluntary associations have readily available membership lists amenable to systematic or simple random sampling, the challenges inherent in constructing efficient sampling frames across organizations varying widely in size and organizational structure are likely insurmountable, especially if the geographic scope of the study is very wide. At the very least, the costs would be prohibitive.

ment managers), or for information regarding the authority structure of the establishment (see Spaeth 1985). We have also speculated that the design might be useful to study the relationship between organization structure/policies and family outcomes and that such information might necessitate interviewing both spouses at the target-worker level and at least one organizational informant for one spouse.

The method also provides an important advantage for future testing of organizational theory. It provides the opportunity to evaluate theories with a broad representative sample of establishments and to critically evaluate some of the findings that have been produced with more narrowly constructed samples. A data set with an adequate number of cases would allow for more systematic testing of interactive effects than is possible with smaller, narrowly focused samples. For example, Leicht, Parcel, and Kaufman (1989) demonstrate that the relationship between establishment size and formalization is weaker with the sample described in this chapter than with those reported in other studies (e.g., Lincoln and Kalleberg 1985; Yasai-Ardekani 1989), each of which used a more narrowly focused sample. Possibly other findings basic to organizational functioning would be revised given the type of testing we propose.

Two additional types of investigations become possible with this design. First, contextual analyses of establishment attributes on individual worker outcomes are possible, provided the surveys maintain the identification of respondents with their respective establishments. This caveat is added because it would be possible to use the multiplicity nature of this sampling design without maintaining these connections. Such a procedure would produce a multiplicity sample of establishments but destroy the possibility of contextual analysis of individual outcomes, i.e., destroy the micro-to-macro links. If these links are preserved, contextual analyses could suggest how individual outcomes (e.g., earnings, career progression, job satisfaction) are influenced by establishment attributes. While there is a rich tradition of this type of analysis within sociology generally, our literature review suggests that such studies are relatively rare in the organizational literature. We acknowledge, however, that our design is potentially more limited in its ability to separate worker from establishment effects than a design that includes many workers per establishment (e.g., Lincoln and Kalleberg 1985, 1990), because there are probability limits on the number of workers employed in one establishment that will fall into the sample, thus confounding person and establishment variation. Still, the potential for useful contextual analyses remains given good cross-person and cross-establishment variation in relevant variables, assuming that social selection does not operate to perfectly match worker and establishment characteristics.

Second, the establishment of such a data base allows us to study organizational change by following these establishments over time. This panel study would require recontacting the establishments periodically, as is done in panel studies of individuals and families. Such data would yield important information about organizational deaths. If the sample could be refreshed over time, researchers could study the dynamics of organizational change with a sample that remained representative. One strategy for sample replenishment is the technique used by the Current Population Survey (CPS) (U.S. Bureau of Labor Statistics 1982). In this technique, CPS respondents are divided into eight systematic subsamples (rotation groups). A given rotation group is interviewed for four consecutive months in one year, is absent for the next eight months, and returns for the same four calendar months in the following year. In this strategy, 75 percent of the sample segments are common from month to month, and 50 percent are common across years, thus reducing discontinuity while also reducing the burden of continued inquiry for any group of respondents (U.S. Bureau of Labor Statistics 1982, p. 6). Given the likelihood that an organizational data base would produce data only once every year or two, the establishments attached to individuals might be divided into a smaller number of rotation groups and remain in the sample for more extended periods of time to assure continuity. Small numbers of individual workers would have to be interviewed periodically to compensate for workers who leave the labor force because of death or retirement and to represent workers entering the labor force, likely into establishments different from those experiencing departures.

We have emphasized the advantages of this sampling design in creating samples linked across micro and macro levels of social organization. We have also argued for the design's ability to incorporate data from multiple organizational respondents to assess issues of reliability and its ability to add another layer of *firm* data above that on *establishments,* depending on the purpose of the investigation.

At the same time, however, this design is not a "magic cure."

It does not produce data that resolves all questions of organizational theory, since there are critical issues in organizational theory for which the design should not be used. For example, theory aimed at understanding interorganizational linkages could not be adequately tested without a sample of establishments linked to each other, something this design does not produce. So while our design excels at producing probability samples of workers contextualized within a representative sample of establishments, it cannot produce detailed information about the network of interorganizational linkages relevant to questions of interorganizational environment. As a caveat, we note that we did ask CEOs about their perceptions of intraindustry competition and organization, but their responses do not constitute objective data on interorganizational environments. In addition, the design is obviously not suited to investigations of particular organizational niches, e.g., as in the organizational ecology perspective, because the sample is by definition dispersed across niches in a representative fashion. In sum, sampling must be designed to address particular theoretical concerns, and the design we have advocated here, while of broad applicability, will leave unanswered several central questions in organizational theory.

In May 1988, NSF's Ad Hoc Organizational Data Base Initiative Advisory Panel recommended that the Initiative use a population-based design such as we have described. In addition, we are encouraged that NSF is continuing to devote resources to assessing the feasibility of constructing a nationally representative sample of establishments. We hope that this paper demonstrates the advantages and feasibility of this enterprise and encourages researchers to support such a venture. We also hope that this paper helps those organizational researchers who are interested in using multiplicity samples in their own work.

REFERENCES

Bagozzi, Richard P., and Lynn W. Phillips. 1982. "Representing and Testing Organizational Theories: A Holistic Construal." *Administrative Science Quarterly* 27:459–89.

Baron, James N. 1984. "Organizational Perspectives on Stratification." Pp. 37–69 in *Annual Review of Sociology,* edited by Ralph H. Turner and James F. Short, Jr. Palo Alto: Annual Reviews Inc.

Baron, James N., and William T. Bielby. 1984. "The Organization of Work in a Segmented Economy." *American Sociological Review* 49:454–73.

Bishop, Yvonne M.M., Stephen E. Fienberg, and Paul W. Holland. 1975. *Discrete Multivariate Analysis: Theory and Practice*. Cambridge, MA: MIT Press.

Blauner, Robert. 1964. *Alienation and Freedom: The Factory Worker and His Industry*. Chicago: University of Chicago Press.

Bridges, William P., and Wayne J. Villemez. 1986. "Informal Hiring and Income in the Labor Market." *American Sociological Review* 51:574–82.

Burns, Thomas, and G. M. Stalker. 1966. *The Management of Innovation*. London: Tavistock.

Cacioppe, R., and P. Mock. 1984. "A Comparison of the Quality of Work Experience in Government and Private Organizations." *Human Relations* 37:923–40.

Carter, Nancy M. 1984. "Computerization as a Predominate Technology: Its Influence on the Structure of Newspaper Organizations." *Academy of Management Journal* 27:247–70.

Cassel, Claes-Magnus, Carl-Erik Särndal, and Jan Håkan Wretman. 1977. *Foundations of Inference in Survey Sampling*. New York: Wiley.

Cochran, William G. 1953. *Sampling Techniques*. New York: Wiley.

Cornfield, Daniel B., ed. 1987. *Workers, Managers, and Technological Change: Emerging Patterns of Labor Relations*. New York: Plenum.

Drabek, Thomas E., Rita Braito, Cynthia C. Cook, James R. Powell, and David Rogers. 1982. "Selecting Samples of Organizations: Central Issues and Emergent Trends." *Pacific Sociological Review* 25:377–400.

Form, William, Robert L. Kaufman, Toby L. Parcel, and Michael Wallace. 1988. "The Impact of Technology on Work Organization and Work Outcomes: A Conceptual Framework and Sketch of a Research Agendum." Pp. 303–28 in *Industries, Firms, and Jobs: Sociological and Economic Approaches,* edited by George Farkas and Paula England. New York: Plenum.

Freeman, John. 1986. "Data Quality and the Development of Organizational Social Science: An Editorial Essay." *Administrative Science Quarterly* 31:298–303.

Gerstein, Dean R., R. Duncan Luce, Neil J. Smelser, and Sonja Sperlich. 1988. *The Behavioral and Social Sciences: Achievements and Opportunities*. Washington, DC: National Academy Press.

Glenn, Evelyn, and Roslyn L. Feldberg. 1977. "Degraded and Deskilled: The Proletarianization of Clerical Work." *Social Problems* 25:52–64.

Granovetter, Mark. 1984. "Small is Bountiful: Labor Markets and Establishment Size." *American Sociological Review* 49:323–34.

Hodson, Randy. 1983. *Workers' Earnings and Corporate Economic Structure*. New York: Academic Press.

———. 1984. "The Measurement of Economic Segmentation." *American Sociological Review* 49:335–48.

Horowitz, Morris, and Irwin Herrenstadt. 1966. "Change in the Skill Requirements of Occupations in Selected Industries." Pp. 227–87 in *The Employment Impact of Technological Change, Technology and The American Economy,* vol. 2. *National Commission on Technology, Automation, and Economic Progress*. Washington, DC: U.S. Government Printing Office.

Kalleberg, Arne L., Peter V. Marsden, Howard E. Aldrich, and James W. Cassell. Forthcoming. "Comparing Organizational Sampling Frames." *Administrative Science Quarterly* 35:658–88.

Kalleberg, Arne L., Michael Wallace, and Robert P. Althauser. 1981. "Economic Segmentation, Worker Power, and Income Inequality." *American Journal of Sociology* 87:651–83.

Leicht, Kevin T., Toby L. Parcel, and Robert L. Kaufman. 1989. "Organizational Type and Organizational Measurement: A Unified Approach." Unpublished manuscript.

Levy, Robert A., Marianne Bowes, and James M. Jondrow. 1984. "Technical Advance and Other Sources of Employment Change in Basic Industry." Chapter 3 in *American Jobs and the Changing Industrial Base*, edited by Eileen L. Collins and Lucretia Dewey Tanner. Cambridge, MA: Ballinger.

Lincoln, James R., and Arne L. Kalleberg. 1985. "Work Organization and Workforce Commitment: A Study of Plants and Employees in the U.S. and Japan." *American Sociological Review* 50:738–60.

––––––. 1990. *Culture, Control, and Commitment: A Study of Work Organizations and Work Attitudes in the United States and Japan.* Cambridge: Cambridge University Press.

McPherson, J. Miller. 1982. "Hypernetwork Sampling: Duality and Differentiation Among Voluntary Associations." *Social Networks* 3:225–49.

––––––. 1983. "The Size of Voluntary Organizations." *Social Forces* 61:1044–64.

McPherson, J. Miller, and Lynn Smith-Lovin. 1986. "Sex Segregation in Voluntary Associations." *American Sociological Review* 51:61–79.

––––––. 1987. "Homophily in Voluntary Organizations: Status Distance and the Composition of Face-to-Face Groups." *American Sociological Review* 52: 370–79.

Mueller, Eva, Judith Hybels, Jay Schmiedeskamp, John Sonquist, and Charles Staelin. 1969. *Technological Advance in an Expanding Economy: Its Impact on a Cross-Section of the Labor Force.* Ann Arbor: University of Michigan, Survey Research Center.

Nathan, Gad. 1988. "Inference Based on Data from Complex Sample Designs." Pp. 247–66 in *Handbook of Statistics.* Vol. 6, *Sampling,* edited by P. R. Krishnaiah and C. R. Rao. New York: North-Holland.

Nathan, Gad, and D. Holt. 1980. "The Effect of Survey Design on Regression Analysis." *Journal of the Royal Statistical Society,* ser. B, 42:377–86.

Noble, David F. 1984. *Forces of Production: A Social History of Industrial Automation.* New York: Knopf.

Parcel, Toby L., and Charles W. Mueller. 1983. *Ascription and Labor Markets: Race and Sex Differences in Earnings.* New York: Academic Press.

Perrow, Charles. 1984. *Normal Accidents: Living With High Risks.* New York: Basic Books.

Phillips, Lynn W. 1981. "Assessing Measurement Error in Key Informant Reports: A Methodological Note on Organizational Analysis in Marketing." *Journal of Marketing Research* 18:395–415.

Rao, J. N. K., and A. J. Scott. 1981. "The Analysis of Categorical Data from

Complex Sample Surveys: Chi-Squared Tests for Goodness of Fit and Independence in Two-Way Tables." *Journal of the American Statistical Association* 76:221–30.

Reynolds, Paul D., David Knoke, Naomi Kaufman, and Brenda Miller. 1988. "Reliability of Organizational Measures: Estimates Based on a Sample of Urban Organizations." Presentation given at The National Science Foundation, May 1988.

Sen, Pranab Kumar. 1988. "Asymptotics in Finite Population Sampling." Pp. 291–331 in *Handbook of Statistics*. Vol. 6, *Sampling,* edited by P. R. Krishnaiah and C. R. Rao. New York: North-Holland.

Shryock, Henry S., and Jacob S. Siegel. 1976. *The Methods and Materials of Demography.* Condensed ed. New York: Academic Press.

Spaeth, Joe L. 1985. "Job Power and Earnings." *American Sociological Review* 50:603–17.

———. 1989. "Probability Sampling of Work Organizations." Unpublished manuscript.

Stolzenberg, Ross M. 1978. "Bringing the Boss Back In: Employer Size, Employee Schooling, and Socioeconomic Achievement." *American Sociological Review* 43:813–28.

Stone, Katherine. 1974. "The Origins of Job Structure in the Steel Industry." *Review of Radical Political Economics* 6:113–73.

Sudman, Seymour. 1976. *Applied Sampling.* New York: Academic Press.

Sudman, Seymour, Monroe Sirken, and Charles D. Cowan. 1988. "Sampling Rare and Elusive Populations." *Science* 240:991–96.

Tolbert, Charles M., Patrick M. Horan, and E. M. Beck. 1980. "The Structure of Economic Segmentation: A Dual Economy Approach." *American Journal of Sociology* 85:1095–1116.

U.S. Bureau of Labor Statistics. 1982. *Handbook of Methods,* vol. 1., Bulletin 2134-1. Washington, DC: U.S. Government Printing Office.

U.S. Bureau of the Census. 1987. *County Business Patterns, 1986, Ohio.* Washington, DC: U.S. Government Printing Office.

———. 1989. *County Business Patterns, 1987, The United States.* Washington, DC: U.S. Government Printing Office.

Villemez, Wayne J., and William P. Bridges. 1988. "When Bigger is Better: Differences in the Individual-Level Effect of Firm and Establishment Size." *American Sociological Review* 53:237–55.

Wilson, E. 1985. "What Counts in the Death or Transformation of an Organization?" *Social Forces* 64:259–80.

Wright, Erik O. 1978. "Race, Class and Income Inequality." *American Journal of Sociology* 83:1368–97.

Yasai-Ardekani, Masoud. 1989. "Effects of Environmental Scarcity and Munificence on the Relationship of Context to Organizational Structure." *Academy of Management Journal* 32:131–56.

Zucker, Lynne G. 1988. "Guidebook to Organizational Data." Paper presented at the Annual Meetings of the American Sociological Association, Atlanta.

3

OPEN SURVEY QUESTIONS AS MEASURES OF PERSONAL CONCERN WITH ISSUES: A REANALYSIS OF STOUFFER'S *COMMUNISM, CONFORMITY, AND CIVIL LIBERTIES*

*Emily W. Kane**
Howard Schuman†

Answers to open survey questions, because they represent a respondent's own words rather than a choice among preformulated responses, are often assumed to reflect concern over or involvement in an issue mentioned spontaneously. Stouffer (1955) makes such an assumption in his classic book, Communism, Conformity, and Civil Liberties, *which includes both open and closed questions about the same attitude objects. The open questions are intended to assess "the depth and intensity of opinions" expressed. We reanalyze Stouffer's data and show that his assumption about answers to open questions cannot be sustained, at least with respect to the main issues that concerned the author and his readers and that continue to concern us today. However, some indirect evidence supports a modification of the assumption in the case of issues that are not the focus of media attention.*

This research was supported by NSF grant 8713633. Authorship is equal.
*University of Wisconsin, Madison
†University of Michigan

1. INTRODUCTION

When people answer open questions about their worries or concerns, they must make use of what comes to mind—in Tversky and Kahneman's (1982) terminology, what is available to them. Some social scientists assume that availability usually reflects what is most important to respondents (Scott 1968; Schuman, Ludwig, and Krosnick 1986). This assumption can be extrapolated from extreme non-survey examples, such as the images of food that overwhelm people who are starved (Levi 1959), or the preoccupations of individuals who have fallen deeply in love, as portrayed in several of Shakespeare's plays. Samuel Stouffer's (1955) classic study of public attitudes toward Communism and civil liberties in the 1950s proceeds from just such an assumption about open questions, as indicated by the title of the first substantive chapter in his book: "Is There a National Anxiety Neurosis?" Throughout the chapter, Stouffer assumes that mention of Communists in response to the initial open questions in his 1954 survey reflects intense concern about Communism. He therefore considers the relative rarity of such responses an indication that extreme concern about Communists was not widespread in the U.S. in the mid-1950s, despite the media attention on Senator Joseph McCarthy and the characterization even today of that period as an "era of hysteria" (Tindall 1988, p. 1272).

However, a different interpretation of the availability of responses to open questions is offered by writers who emphasize the slight basis on which answers are usually produced in survey interviews (e.g., Zaller and Feldman 1988). Unlike people in extreme situations involving physical deprivation or mental anguish, survey respondents are neither under great internal pressure to give a particular response nor forced by the interviewing process to search their minds for deeply significant answers. Thus, their spontaneous responses may reflect what they happen to have heard most recently, perhaps quite accidentally. In any case, survey responses often represent casual thoughts, rather than deep feelings.

With these two theoretical positions in mind, we examine important parts of Stouffer's *Communism, Conformity, and Civil Liberties,* focusing especially on the broad issue he poses at the outset (1955, p. 87): "How much personal anxiety or involvement do Americans feel [in the mid-1950s] with respect to the internal Communist threat or with respect to the loss of civil liberties?" Stouffer found that "very few Americans are worried or even deeply concerned about either issue." As already noted, he draws this conclusion from responses to open-ended questions about people's worries and concerns, since only a small percentage of respondents referred to either threat in their answers to such questions. Having established this conclusion, Stouffer proceeds in the rest of the book to use responses to closed questions to study the association between attitudes toward American Communists and attitudes toward civil liberties, and the association between these attitudes and other variables. Implicitly, Stouffer assumes that open and closed questions tap much the same concerns but that open questions assess "the depth and intensity of opinions, which may later be ascertained systematically by more conventional check-list questions" (1955, p. 20). The exact psychological meaning of answers to the closed questions is left undefined. Instead, Stouffer uses them to create highly reliable multi-item scales (1955, pp. 46–48).

Stouffer never brings together the responses from his open and closed questions, and theoretical issues having to do with their relation to one another are neither discussed nor tested in his book. Nor is there any detailed analysis of responses to the open questions, other than the initial emphasis on their univariate distributions. Our reanalysis attempts to understand better what Stouffer's open questions measure and the association between open-question responses, closed-question responses, and background variables in the 1954 survey. Our interest is not primarily historical—though the Stouffer study has been unusually influential on subsequent research—but rather uses the data to explore measurement issues that are as important today as they were in the mid-1950s.[1] The results of the reanalysis call for both revision and refinement in Stouffer's (and others') assumption about the meaning of responses to open questions about personal concerns.

[1]For example, Stouffer's findings influenced Converse's (1964) widely cited essay on belief systems and also stimulated Sullivan, Piereson, and Marcus's (1982) research on the nature of tolerance. In addition, Stouffer's main set of closed tolerance questions became part of NORC's General Social Survey and are still used in the GSS today.

2. DATA AND METHOD

Stouffer's questionnaire was administered in 1954 to two large samples, a cross-section of the general population (N=4,933) and a sample of community leaders (N=1,500) from mid-sized cities. At the beginning of the questionnaire, respondents were asked, "What kinds of things do you worry about most?" This was followed shortly by the question, "Are there other problems you worry or are concerned about, especially political or world problems?" We focus on answers to this second question, which produced most of the responses that were coded as showing either a concern about Communists or a concern about civil liberties.[2]

The closed measure on Communists that we use is a direct replication of Stouffer's perception-of-the-internal-Communist-danger scale, which was constructed from a series of closed questions (Stouffer 1955, App. C). In addition, all of our findings that are based on the full scale are replicated with one of its components, a single general question on the Communist danger (see Table 1 for wording). We show results for that single question separately. Later in our analysis, we draw also on Stouffer's willingness-to-tolerate-nonconformists scale (1955, App. C), which was intended to measure attitudes toward civil liberties.

[2]Apparently because so few people mentioned either Communists or civil liberties (a total of 27 in the cross-section sample) in response to his first open question about worries, Stouffer coded both types of response the same; therefore, they cannot be distinguished (ICPSR 1986, p.4). Only for the second question, which yielded most of the mentions of both Communists and civil liberties (237 respondents mentioned Communists, 123 mentioned civil liberties) can the two responses be separated. Thus, we present here an analysis based only on the second question. Even if one assumes that the 27 who mentioned Communists and civil liberties in response to the first question mostly mentioned Communists—Stouffer's text simply indicates that the majority referred to Communists—well over 90 percent of all mentions would come from the second question, and thus no serious distortion can result from this way of handling the problem. For the leaders the problem is a little more severe: At least 84 percent of all mentions of Communists come in response to the second question, at most 16 percent in response to the first question. For both the cross-section and the leaders samples, we repeated our analysis by assuming that most of the responses to the first question referred to Communists and then by combining the two questions. The results do not change any of the conclusions reported in this paper. The original questionnaires appear to have been lost, so reanalysis is dependent upon Stouffer's own coding.

3. RESULTS

3.1. *Concern About Communists*

Table 1 draws together results from the univariate analysis of responses to the open and closed questions about concern over Communists, which Stouffer reports in different parts of his book, and it points up a paradoxical finding in the data that he does not

TABLE 1

Distributions of Responses to Open and Closed Questions
(Number of Respondents in Parentheses)

	Cross-Section Sample	Leaders Sample
Responses to open question		
Communism mentioned as a worry or concern	4.8%	12.5%
	(4,933)	(1,500)
Responses to closed questions that form the perception-of-Communist-danger scale		
Relatively great danger	30.3%	26.7%
In between	50.9	44.5
Relatively little danger	18.8	28.9
	100.0	100.0
	(4,933)	(1,500)
Responses to closed question on Communist danger[a]		
Very great danger	21.0%	15.4%
Great danger	25.4	22.0
Some danger	40.7	45.3
Hardly any danger	10.3	15.0
No danger	2.7	2.4
	100.0	100.0
	(4,546)	(1,489)

[a]The question was, "How great a danger do you feel American Communists are to this country at the present time: a very great danger, a great danger, some danger, hardly any danger, or no danger?" The first two alternatives, *a very great danger* and *a great danger,* are scored positive when the question is used as a component of the perception-of-Communist-danger scale. Those who responded *don't know* (387 in the cross-section sample and 11 in the leaders sample) are omitted from this table. Stouffer scored them as negative for scale purposes.

mention. If one regards responses to the open question as a measure of "the depth and intensity" of concern about the Communist threat, then the leaders sample shows much greater concern than the cross-section sample (12.5 percent vs. 4.8 percent; $L^2 = 95.8$, $df = 1$, $p<0.001$). However, if one uses Stouffer's perception-of-the-internal-Communist-danger scale (broken into three categories) or simply focuses on responses to the single most general closed question he used, then the cross-section sample shows more concern than the leaders sample ($p<0.001$ for both comparisons). Thus, there is no straightforward way to determine which sample is more worried by the Communist threat nor which type of question, open or closed, is more useful for assessing personal concern or worry about Communists.

Furthermore, if the responses to the open questions represent anxiety over the Communist threat, the much more frequent mention of Communists on the open question by the leaders sample than in the cross-section sample is even more puzzling, because we later learn that the leaders are more tolerant of Communists *and* that tolerance and perceived danger from Communists are inversely related. However, the difference between the leaders sample and the cross-section sample in their mentions of Communists makes more sense if it reflects the leaders' greater awareness of current political issues and not necessarily their greater anxiety.

This last interpretation gains additional credence when we consider how responses to the open and closed questions relate to standard background variables for the cross-section sample, something not reported by Stouffer for the open question. As Table 2 shows, education, age, and sex are all positively and significantly related to mention of Communists in response to the open question, but education and age are not related to the perception of Communist danger, as measured on the closed-question scale, and sex is related in the opposite direction.[3] This suggests that it may be aware-

[3]Education is coded into five categories (<9, 9–11, 12, 13–15, 16+ years of schooling); age is coded into five categories (21–29, 30–39, 40–49, 50–59, 60 and over); and sex is coded as a dichotomous variable (1=female, 2=male). An earlier reader expressed doubts that the variation for the Communist category on the open question was sufficient to allow much of a correlation with anything, but these highly significant relationships between responses to the open question and background variables suggest otherwise. Below we present even stronger associations for the less frequent mention of civil liberties. With regard to the

TABLE 2
Concern About Communist Danger, by Education, Age, and Sex

	Mention of Communists in Responses to Open Question[a]		Responses to Closed Questions that Form the Perception-of-Communist-Danger Scale[b]	
	Coeff.	Coeff./SE	Coeff.	Coeff./SE
Cross-section sample				
Education	0.35	6.98*	0.00	0.84
Age	0.15	3.02*	−0.01	0.62
Sex	0.37	2.78*	−0.17	4.07*
Leaders sample				
Education	−0.01	0.21	−0.11	3.61*
Age	0.14	1.75	−0.11	2.87*
Sex	−0.20	1.14	−0.70	7.71*

[a]Coefficients are derived from logistic regression analysis including the three predictors.

[b]Coefficients are derived from ordinary least squares regression analysis including the three predictors.

*$p < 0.01$.

ness of national and world issues more than anxiety or intensity that creates the difference between the two types of responses, because if education, age, or sex were related to concern over Communists for more substantive reasons, this would show up in the responses to the several closed questions as well, especially since, as a scale, these are almost certainly more reliable than responses to one open question.

The results of the regression analyses of the two samples (Table 2) may at first appear different, but theoretically they are parallel, except for apparently being affected by compositional differences between the two samples (e.g., the leaders sample is more educated, older, and more male than the cross-section sample). In both samples it is evidently the less educated, the younger, and women whose expressed concern over Communism is greater in responses to the closed questions than in responses to the open question. In the cross-

assumption that men would be more likely to provide a political "mention" to an open question, that is obviously not inevitable but it was true in Stouffer's day and is probably true at present in the general population (e.g., see Schuman and Scott 1989, note 5).

section sample, this increase eliminates the positive associations to education, age, and being male that were found in responses to the open question. In the leaders sample, the nonassociations of responses to the open question with education, age, and sex become significant negative associations on the closed questions.

Additional evidence that responses to the open question may not always reflect simple anxiety appears when we look at the relation between mentioning Communists in response to the open question and mentioning civil liberties in response to the *same* question. (Up to three responses to the open question were coded by Stouffer, so it was possible to be coded into both categories.) Stouffer treats these responses as diametrically opposed, but as Table 3 indicates, in the cross-section sample, the association between mentions of Communists and mentions of civil liberties tends to be *positive,* though the significance level is only borderline. For the leaders, the association is negative, but only slightly so. Thus, far from a coding of Communists on the open question necessarily signifying only anxiety about Communists, it can be combined with an apparent concern for civil liberties.

Next we consider the association between mentions of Communists on the open question and responses to those closed questions

TABLE 3

Association Between Mention of Communists and Mention of Civil Liberties in Responses to the Open Question

	No Mention of Communists	Mention of Communists
Cross-section sample		
No mention of civil liberties	97.6%	95.8%
Mention of civil liberties	2.4	4.2
N	(4,696)	(237)
$L^2 = 2.56$		
$df = 1$		
$p = 0.11$		
Leaders sample		
No mention of civil liberties	96.3%	97.3%
Mention of civil liberties	3.7	2.7
N	(1,313)	(187)
$L^2 = 0.57$		
$df = 1$		

TABLE 4

Association Between Mention of Communists in Responses to Open Question and
Responses to Closed Question on Communist Danger

| Responses to Open Question | Responses to Closed Question on Communist Danger[a] | | | | | Total | N |
	Very Great Danger	Great Danger	Some Danger	Hardly Any Danger	No Danger		
Cross-section sample							
No mention of Communists	20.6%	25.2%	41.0%	10.4%	2.8%	100%	4,310
Mention of Communists	27.5	29.7	33.9	7.6	1.3	100	236
Gamma = 0.18 (SE − 0.05)							
Leaders sample							
No mention of Communists	13.6	21.0	46.9	16.1	2.5	100	1,302
Mention of Communists	28.3	28.9	34.2	7.5	1.1	100	187
Gamma = 0.37 (SE = 0.05)							

[a]See Table 1 for the exact wording of the question. Responses to the question were scored from 1 (*no danger*) to 5 (*very great danger*).

that Stouffer used to measure Perception of the Internal Communist Danger. Table 4 shows the association between responses to the open question and responses to the most general closed question about Communists, because the latter has the advantage of incorporating a simple intensity scale of danger perceived.[4] If mention of Communists in response to the open question reflects great concern about their role in the U.S., such responses should be bunched at the high end of the responses provided for the general closed question (i.e., *very great danger* or *great danger*). In addition, the two measures should be strongly correlated if we use an index of association like gamma, which can reach 1.0 even when the marginals of the two variables have quite different distributions. However, as Table 4

[4]Most of the questions in Stouffer's multi-item scale are about Communists in particular locations (e.g., in defense plants, schools, stores). Therefore, variation in scale scores could be based on variation in both substantive and intensity factors.

shows, the association in the cross-section sample, though significant, is relatively small (gamma=0.18), and only a little more than half of those who mentioned Communists in response to the open question indicated in response to the closed question that Communists are a very great or great danger. The relation is stronger for the leaders (gamma=0.37), but even in that sample, more than 40 percent of those who mentioned Communists to the open question do not consider Communists to be a great danger.[5] When the full closed-question scale of perception of the Communist danger is used, the gamma rises slightly to 0.25 in the cross-section sample, probably because of the increased reliability of the closed scale, but it actually drops slightly to 0.34 in the leaders sample. In sum, many of the people who spontaneously mention Communists as a worry or concern later downplay their concern when asked about it in the closed question.

Finally, we consider the association that was most important to Stouffer's investigation: the association between concern about Communists and willingness to tolerate nonconformists, as measured on Stouffer's scale. In the cross-section sample, the association (gamma) between the perception-of-Communist-danger scale and the tolerance-of-nonconformists scale is -0.15 ($p<0.001$), indicating that those most concerned about Communists are least tolerant of nonconformists—Stouffer's main conclusion. However, when concern about Communists is measured using responses to the open question, the relation to the tolerance scale is slightly *positive* (gamma = +0.07), though nonsignificant (SE = 0.05), suggesting either no relation at all or a trend in the opposite direction. Only among the leaders do the perception-of-Communist-danger scale and the responses to the open question point in the same direction on tolerance. The former association is larger (-0.29, SE = 0.03) than the latter (-0.10, SE = 0.06), perhaps partly because of the greater reliability of the closed-question scale.[6]

[5] The gamma for the leaders sample is significantly higher ($z = 2.68, p > 0.01$) than the gamma for the cross-section sample. See Agresti (1984, p. 190) for the method of calculation.

[6] If the two gammas for the cross-section sample are treated as coming from independent samples, the test statistic for the difference is $z = 4.20, p < 0.001$. The test statistic for the leaders is $z = 2.74, p < 0.01$ (see Agresti 1984, p. 190). (These should be conservative, since the two gammas are actually from the same sample. We have not been able to locate a test for two gammas from the same sample.) The difference in gammas between the cross-section and leaders

Our findings regarding the associations between responses to the open question about Communists and the other variables considered thus far cast considerable doubt on the meaning of the responses. Stouffer's assumption that mentioning Communists indicates "depth and intensity of opinions" about Communists receives very little support. However, before drawing conclusions from this set of findings, we consider more briefly the responses to open and closed questions about civil liberties.

3.2. *Concern About Civil Liberties*

Mentions of civil liberties in response to the open question are much less frequent than mentions of Communists: Only 2.5 percent of the cross-section sample and 3.6 percent of the leaders mentioned civil liberties. Yet there are a number of indications that such responses reflect concern about civil liberties better than mentions of Communists reflect concern about Communists. First, responses to both the open question and the closed questions that form the tolerance scale show that the leaders sample is more tolerant, in Stouffer's terms, than the cross-section sample.[7] Second, the mention of civil liberties in response to the open question and tolerance are much more highly associated than the mention of Communists and the perception-of-Communist-danger scale: gamma=0.46 (SE=0.06) in the cross-section sample; gamma=0.47 (SE=0.10) in the leaders sample.[8] Third, the mention of civil liberties and the tolerance scale are related

samples in the association between the mention of Communists in response to the open question and tolerance scores ($z = 2.18$, $p < 0.05$) suggests that education might be an important interacting variable in the cross-section sample. Among college graduates in the cross-section sample, the association is negative (gamma = -0.24, SE = 0.12), as it is among the leaders. However, three of the four other educational categories show nonsignificant positive associations, the only other negative (and nonsignificant) association being for the least-educated (less than nine years of schooling). We also controlled another potentially interacting variable: whether the respondent mentioned civil liberties as well as Communists in response to the open question. Those who mentioned civil liberties scored higher on the tolerance scale, suggesting that some mentions of Communists reflected concern for civil liberties.

[7] In this paper we need not resolve Sullivan et al.'s (1982) criticism of Stouffer's measure of tolerance.

[8] This might be because the tolerance scale is more reliable than the perception-of-Communist-danger scale, but our estimates of the internal consistencies (coefficient alpha) of the two scales are quite similar: 0.66 and 0.68, respectively, in the cross-section sample, 0.71 and 0.66 in the leaders sample.

to the perception of Communist danger in the same direction and to almost the same degree: gamma=-0.16 and -0.15, respectively, in the cross-section sample; gamma=-0.26 and -0.29 in the leaders sample. Finally, the mention of civil liberties and tolerance are positively and significantly related to education, though the relations are stronger for tolerance, which is also related to age and sex. Younger people and males are more supportive of civil liberties. The mention of civil liberties in response to the open question does not seem to be related to age or sex.[9]

In sum, despite the quite small percentage of people who mention civil liberties in response to the open question, our results suggest that mentioning civil liberties measures concern over civil liberties much better than mentioning Communists measures concern over Communists. Whether responses to the open question truly capture "depth and intensity of opinion" about civil liberties is another matter, and not one that these results can address in any direct way. However, they suggest a hypothesis about the circumstances under which responses to open questions are most likely to reflect personal concern over an issue. The hypothesis is stated at the end of section 4.

4. CONCLUSIONS

Relatively few Americans in 1954 mentioned Communists spontaneously in response to an open question on concerns and worries, and of those, few appear to have done so because of fear of

[9] We used logistic regression to analyze the dichotomous civil liberties variable for the open question. We used OLS regression for the tolerance scale (six ordinal categories). The ratios of coefficients to standard errors are as follows:

	Responses to Open Question	Responses to Closed Questions
Cross-section sample		
Education	5.94	25.24
Age	1.00	-8.49
Sex	-0.81	-8.33
Leaders sample		
Education	2.55	10.79
Age	-0.48	-3.06
Sex	0.33	-6.06

Communists. Mention of Communists seems mostly to reflect higher education and other characteristics commonly found among those aware of national and world issues at that time. Indeed, in the cross-section sample, the mention of Communists and the mention of civil liberties tend to be positively, not negatively, associated, probably because Communists were sometimes mentioned in the context of a concern about civil liberties. In addition, there is only a small relation between the mention of Communists in response to the open question and closed-question responses that characterize Communists as a danger to the U.S. Moreover, although the closed questions about the Communist danger are related to intolerance toward non-conformists, which was Stouffer's main concern, responses to the open question show little or no relation to such intolerance, exactly the opposite of what we expect if we assume that responses to open questions reflect "depth and intensity of opinion."

We conclude that Stouffer's interpretation of the mention of Communists in response to his open question about worries or concerns is incorrect or at least greatly overstated. Yet, paradoxically, our negative results for the open question might actually be seen as bolstering Stouffer's main conclusion in his review of responses to his open questions—namely, that there was little evidence in 1954 of spontaneous worry about an internal Communist threat. If one assumes that responses to an open question about worries or concerns reflect anxiety about Communists, then the anxiety was even less than Stouffer reported. Even those who mentioned Communists often did so either in the context of their concern about civil liberties or as a reflection of their awareness of the then current national issues, not as a sign of intense worry over a Communist threat.

However, there are two serious problems with this conclusion. First, it probably applies to most issues that fill the newspapers and news broadcasts. As Stouffer himself emphasized, most people most of the time are concerned with their own personal lives, not with the national issues that concern politicians and political scientists. The same point was also made, of course, by Converse (1964), who indeed drew in his well-known essay on Stouffer's book. Unless they have direct and personal involvement in war, revolution, or economic disaster, the general population rarely expresses spontaneous worry over any of the issues that dominate the front pages of the newspapers.

A second problem becomes clear when we try to establish the degree to which the American population was caught up in concern over Communists or the threat to civil liberties, both symbolized by Senator McCarthy in the mid-1950s. That there was some genuine concern about Communists is suggested by the finding that more than one fifth of the American population indicated in response to the closed question that Communists were a very great danger to the U.S. However, closed questions have their own problems, and although the response *a very great danger* seems on its face to be straightforward, we must keep in mind that both subtleties of question wording and the demand effects in posing such a question make percentages much less clear-cut in meaning than they seem. It is probably a mistake to believe that the "marginals" or univariate results from any survey question, open *or* closed, can provide an absolute numerical estimate of the proportion of people who are deeply or intensely worried about an issue. Survey questions repeated over time may be able to tell us whether aggregate concerns are increasing or decreasing (Smith 1980, 1985), and appropriately worded questions can (though with more uncertainty) tell us whether one issue is of more concern than others with which it is explicitly compared. But beyond those conclusions, we are in the realm of subjective judgments, where many factors must be considered and integrated.[10] We are not in the realm of straightforward measurement, and it is best to recognize and accept this fact.

As for the broader issue of interpreting responses to open questions about concerns or worries, to the extent that respondents give mainly personal answers about their health, marriage, and jobs, we suspect that these answers do reflect, as Stouffer assumes, what seems to them most important in their lives, even though such content may not seem important to social scientists. However, to the extent that they give answers about national issues that are in the

[10]Stouffer did ask his respondents to state how important Communists in the U.S. were compared with nine other issues (e.g., atom or hydrogen bombs, high taxes), but unfortunately his coding indicates only whether respondents rated Communists as most or second-most important (12 percent of the cross-section sample and 14 percent of the leaders sample rated Communists as first in importance) and does not give equivalent percentages for the other issues. In any case, Schuman and Scott (1987) show that the importance of an issue can vary dramatically, depending on the selection of other issues with which it is compared.

news, it seems likely on the basis of the evidence we have examined that such answers reflect mainly *awareness* of current issues, rather than personal concern over them. The answers can provide both an aggregate measure of the salience of issues within the communication environment and an individual measure of cognitive exposure to news about issues, but not usually a direct and unambiguous measure of emotional intensity, anxiety, or personal involvement. (See Iyengar and Kinder [1987] for a recent study of such agenda setting.)

There may be one noteworthy type of exception to this conclusion. Our finding that the less common responses about civil liberties seem to be more valid than the more common responses about Communists suggests that the exceptions occur for mention of issues that are *not* in the news. Rare responses, such as mentions of vivisection or the gold standard or any number of other issues likely to be categorized under *other,* probably do reflect personal involvement, since their salience cannot be based on the evening news or the morning newspaper. This seemingly upside-down hypothesis is worth testing in the future: The *smaller* the number of people who give a response to a question about their concerns, the more likely such a response reflects genuine personal concern rather than simple awareness of what is in the news.[11]

REFERENCES

Agresti, Alan. 1984. *Analysis of Ordinal Categorical Data.* New York: Wiley.
Converse, Philip E. 1964. "The Nature of Belief Systems in Mass Publics." *Ideology and Discontent,* edited by D. E. Apter. New York: Free Press.
ICPSR. 1968. *Codebook for the Stouffer Study.* Ann Arbor: Inter-University Consortium for Political and Social Research.
Iyengar, Shanto, and Donald R. Kinder. 1987. *News That Matters.* Chicago: University of Chicago Press.

[11]Another approach would be to control for media exposure when using open questions, although our attempt to do so using Stouffer's broad questions on media contact did not appear promising. Media references to Communists were probably so common in 1954 that it would have been difficult to control adequately for exposure. Stouffer also made considerable use of a question about respondent interest in news about Communists, and this does show a strong relation to mention of Communists in response to the open question, especially in the cross-section sample (8.1 percent of the more interested but only 1.7 percent of the less interested mention Communists). But the two questions are so close in meaning that we doubt the appropriateness of using the one as a control for the other.

Levi, Primo. 1959. *Survival in Auschwitz*. New York: Collier.

Schuman, Howard, Jacob Ludwig, and Jon A. Krosnick. 1986. "The Perceived Threat of Nuclear War, Salience, and Open Questions." *Public Opinion Quarterly* 50:519–36.

Schuman, Howard, and Jacqueline Scott. 1987. "Problems in the Use of Survey Questions to Measure Public Opinion." *Science* 236:957–59.

––––––. 1989. "Generations and Collective Memories." *American Sociological Review* 54:359–81.

Scott, W. A. 1968. "Attitude Measurement." *The Handbook of Social Psychology*, 2d ed., vol. 2, edited by G. Lindzey and E. Aronson. Reading, MA: Addison-Wesley.

Smith, Tom W. 1980. "America's Most Important Problem—A Trend Analysis, 1946–1976." *Public Opinion Quarterly* 44: 164–80.

––––––. 1985. "The Polls: America's Most Important Problems. Part I: National and International." *Public Opinion Quarterly* 49:264–74.

Stouffer, Samuel A. 1955. *Communism, Conformity, and Civil Liberties*. New York: Doubleday.

Sullivan, John L., James Piereson, and George E. Marcus. 1982. *Political Tolerance and American Democracy*. Chicago: University of Chicago Press.

Tindall, George Brown. 1988. *America: A Narrative History*. New York: Norton.

Tversky, A., and D. Kahneman. 1982. "Judgment Under Certainty: Heuristics and Biases." Pp. 3–20 in *Judgment Under Uncertainty: Heuristics and Biases*, edited by D. Kahneman, P. Slovic, and A. Tversky. Cambridge: Cambridge University Press.

Zeller, J., and S. Feldman. 1988. "Answering Questions vs. Revealing Preferences: A Simple Theory of the Survey Response." Paper presented at the Annual Meeting of the Political Methodology Society, University of California, Los Angeles.

4

RELIABILITY OF ATTITUDE SCORES BASED ON A LATENT TRAIT MODEL

David J. Bartholomew*
Karl F. Schuessler[†]

In this paper we present a coefficient for measuring the reliability of scores based on a fitting of a logit model with normal prior to k *dichotomous items, and we consider methods of estimating the constituent terms on which that coefficient rests. We organize numerical examples around five topics: (1) the reliability of individual items, (2) reliability and goodness of fit, (3) scale differences in reliability within and between samples, (4) the influence of item slopes on reliability, and (5) variation in sample estimates of the reliability coefficient. We discuss why reliabilities differ within and between samples and present the argument for a random effects model in social research.*

1. MEASUREMENT THEORY

1.1. *Background*

Sociologists have long tried to measure attitudes and the like, relying largely on techniques invented by specialists in psychology

We wish to acknowledge the contributions of Edward Bassin to the method of section 2.4 and to the calculations based thereon. In revising this paper, we were greatly aided by, and took full advantage of, the many useful suggestions of the editor and referees.
*The London School of Economics and Political Science
†Indiana University, Bloomington

(Thurstone and Chave 1929) and statistics (Lord and Novick 1968). Behind this work is the conviction that subjective traits such as happiness and satisfaction, alienation and anomie, can be measured like physical traits are measured.

The usefulness of an instrument for measuring a given construct is in practice judged by its validity and reliability. An instrument is valid if it measures what it purports to measure and not something else. An instrument is reliable if repeated trials yield similar measures. Thus, a good instrument yields similar values if applied to the same individual on different occasions or to different individuals located at the same point on the attitude scale on the same occasion. We use the term in this sense.

The primary concern of this paper is the reliability of scores based on a fitting of the logit/probit latent trait model (defined below) to the replies of N persons to k dichotomous items (*agree/disagree, yes/no*) on a given topic. A secondary concern is the relation of reliability to unidimensionality and goodness of fit.

We derive from first principles the correlation between replicate scores, then go on to specialize that result to the correlation between replicate scores based on the parameters of the logit/probit model. Our account of the statistical theory on which our reliability measure rests is self-contained. That is, nothing else is needed to validate the argument; it was framed for sociological readers generally unversed in psychometric theory. It is of practical importance that an estimate of our model-based coefficient may be obtained from a single administration of the questionnaire; replicated measures are not required. The possibility that reliability is spuriously high because of memory effects is thereby averted. We illustrate the method with calculations based on both actual and simulated sample survey data (see section 2).

1.2 *Reliability as Correlation Between Replicate Scores*

Let X denote any measure that we propose to use. It need not be the sum of the item scores, hereafter called the total score. It could be any function of the responses. For example, it could be the reciprocal of the total score or the sum of the weighted item scores. If we could replicate observations on the same individual, we could obtain two values of X—say, X_1 and X_2. A commonly used definition of reliability is the correlation between X_1 and X_2, here denoted by ρ.

If we have a perfectly reliable measure, we can then precisely predict X_2 given X_1. At the other extreme, where X_1 has no predictive value, the correlation is zero. An equivalent measure is ρ^2, which represents the amount of variation in X_2 that can be statistically explained by X_1, and vice versa. Because the mathematics is a little simpler, we shall use ρ.

Since X_1 and X_2 must be identically distributed, they will have the same variance. Therefore, we can write

$$\rho(X_1, X_2) = \text{cov}(X_1, X_2)/\text{var}(X_1). \tag{1}$$

Now,

$$\begin{aligned}
\text{var}(X_1) &= E(X_1^2) - E^2(X_1) \\
&= EE(X_1^2|y) - \{EE(X_1|y)\}^2 \\
&= E\text{var}(X_1|y) + \text{var}\{E(X_1|y)\},
\end{aligned} \tag{2}$$

where y is the latent "true" score. When two expectation operators occur together, as in $EE(u|v)$, the right-hand one is taken first. The expression is thus equivalent to $E\{E(u|v)\}$. Similarly,

$$\text{cov}(X_1, X_2) = EE(X_1 X_2|y) - \{EE(X_1|y)EE(X_2|y)\}.$$

If y is the only common element of X_1 and X_2, they will be independent conditional on y. Therefore, $E(X_1 X_2|y) = E(X_1|y)E(X_2|y)$. Since $E(X_1|y) = E(X_2|y)$, it follows that

$$\text{cov}(X_1, X_2) = \text{var}\{E(X_1|y)\} \tag{3}$$

and hence that

$$\rho = 1 - \{E\text{var}(X_1|y)/\text{var}(X_1)\}. \tag{4}$$

Perfect reliability thus arises when X_1 is a perfect indicator of y, meaning that the conditional variance of X_1 is zero. If the variance of X_1 is unaffected by conditioning on y, then it is useless as an indicator and ρ is zero.

The practical difficulty in estimating ρ defined in this way lies with the term $E\text{var}(X_1|y)$. There is no problem with $\text{var}(X_1)$, which can be estimated directly from the sample values of X_1.

There are three ways to deal with the difficulty. One, which we shall not pursue here, is by considering subsets of the items, for example, halves or thirds. Another is to establish bounds on ρ, as in the next paragraph (e.g., see Guttman 1945). The third is to express ρ as a function of the parameters of the model that is assumed to underlie the item responses. We shall explore this last approach here, but first we derive a well-known bound for later use. This concerns the special case in which X is the total score.

Suppose there are k items yielding responses $x_1, x_2, \ldots, x_k$. Then,

$$X = \sum_{i=1}^{k} x_i \quad \text{and} \quad \text{Evar} (X|y) = \sum_{i=1}^{k} \text{Evar} (x_i|y). \tag{5}$$

There are no covariance terms because the item responses will be independent, conditional on y, if the x's are uncontaminated indicators of y. If we specialize the result of (2) to a single x, we have

$$\text{var}(x_i) = \text{Evar}(x_i|y) + \text{var} \{E(x_i|y)\}.$$

Since both terms on the right-hand side must be nonnegative, it follows that

$$\text{Evar}(x_i|y) \leq \text{var}(x_i).$$

Referring back to (4), we deduce that, say,

$$\rho \leq 1 - \{\sum_{i=1}^{k} \text{var}(x_i)/\text{var}(\Sigma x_i)\} = \alpha^*. \tag{6}$$

Although we cannot estimate ρ, we can readily estimate α^* because it depends only on the item variances and the variance of the total score, which can be directly estimated from the sample. The bound α^* is closely related to coefficient-α (Lord and Novick 1968, p. 87), which specializes to Kuder and Richardson's formula 20, hereafter KR20 (Lord and Novick 1968, p. 91) when all k items are scored 0 or 1. The connection is

$$\text{coefficient-}\alpha = (k/(k - 1))\alpha^*. \tag{7}$$

The purpose of the multiplier $k/(k - 1)$ is to ensure that coefficient-α attains the value 1 for a perfectly reliable measure. For moderately large values of k, the difference between α and α^* is negligible.

The justification for introducing the coefficient α^* is as follows: If the x's are perfect indicators, they are perfectly correlated. Therefore, $\text{cov}(x_i, x_j) = \text{var}(x_i)$. Hence,

$$\text{var}(\Sigma x_i) = \Sigma \text{var}(x_i) + \sum_{ij} \Sigma \text{var}(x_i)$$
$$= k \Sigma \text{var}(x_i)$$

and

$$\alpha^* = 1 - 1/k, \quad \text{then } \alpha = 1.$$

In section 2, we calculate KR20 and our model-based reliability measure for several data sets to illustrate how they may differ in magnitude.

1.3. The Logit/Probit Model

As noted, our method is to express the correlation between replicate scores, as given by (4), in terms of the parameters of the logit/probit latent trait model. Latent trait models of various kinds have been used for some time in educational testing (Goldstein and Wood 1989) but have been used in sociology only recently (Duncan 1985a, 1985b; Schaeffer 1988; Thissen and Mooney 1990). Of concern here are those models that pertain to dichotomous items of the form *yes/no* or *agree/disagree*. These models, among others, have been considered within the general framework of latent variable models by Bartholomew (1987), who shows that the logit/probit model has attractive statistical properties. It is defined by

$$\text{logit } \pi_i(y) = \alpha_{i0} + \alpha_{i1}y \qquad (i = 1, 2, \ldots, k), \tag{8}$$

where y is the latent true score of an individual and

$$\begin{aligned}
\pi_i(y) &= \{1 + \exp(-\alpha_{i0} - \alpha_{i1}y)\}^{-1} \\
&= \Pr\{x_i = 1|y\} \qquad (x_i = 0, 1).
\end{aligned} \tag{9}$$

For obvious reasons, α_{i0} in (8) will be referred to as the intercept and α_{i1} as the slope. The slope of the response function $\pi_i(y)$ is illustrated for three sets of parameters in Figure 1. The *probit* part of the name refers to the assumption that y is a standard normal random variable. The response probability $\pi_i(y)$ shows how the probability of giving a positive response (e.g., *agree*) to item i depends on the individual's latent true score. Equation (9) shows that it is a monotonically increasing function having the form of a cumulative logistic distribution—hence the name. For such a model we can express both $\text{Evar}(X_1|y)$ and $\text{var}(X_1)$ in terms of the model parameters and hence determine ρ. Examples are given by Bartholomew (1987) and Krebs and Schuessler (1987), who show that when this model fits item-response data, which it often does, we have a method of estimating ρ.[1]

---

[1] A program for fitting the logit/probit model by maximum likelihood, written by Dr. Brian Shea of the London School of Economics, is publicly available in the Numerical Algorithms Group (NAG) Library (1987).

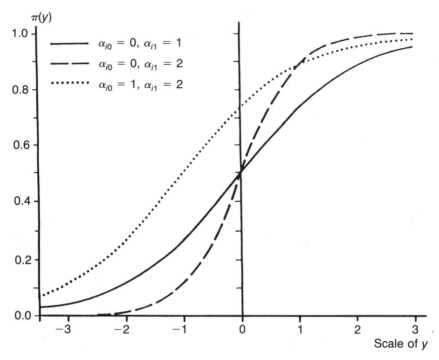

FIGURE 1. Shape of response function $\pi_i(y)$ for three sets of item parameters.

Remark on notation. In some writing (e.g., Bock and Lieberman 1970), a denotes the intercept, b denotes the slope, and θ denotes the latent trait. A different notation appears in Muthén (1978). This is not the place to debate the merits of these notations. We point out, however, that (8) generalizes readily to the case of q latent variables:

$$\text{logit } \pi_i(y) = \alpha_{i0} + \sum_{j=1}^{q} \alpha_{ij} y_j,$$

including the case of $q = 0$:

$$\text{logit } \pi_i(y) = \alpha_{i0},$$

which is sometimes used as a baseline model for judging the predictive efficiency of the chosen latent trait model.

Using (4), we can determine the reliability of any function of the x's, including, of course, the total score. A further advantage of using (4) is that it enables us to judge which function to use as a measure of the latent variable y. It turns out that for the logit/probit model, there is one linear combination of the weighted item scores that is "sufficient," i.e., that contains all the information in the x's about y (Birnbaum 1968, p. 429). It is a special case of the generalized weighted score, given by

$$X = \sum_{i=1}^{k} w_i x_i. \tag{10}$$

By putting $w_i = 1$ for all i, we can obtain results for the total score, $X = \Sigma x_i$. If we put $w_i = \alpha_{i1}$ ($i = 1,2, \ldots ,k$), we have the sufficient statistic for the logit/probit model:

$$X = \sum_{i=1}^{k} \alpha_{i1} x_i. \tag{11}$$

The reliability of this composite score is under investigation here.[2]

To express ρ as given by (4) in terms of the parameters of the logit/probit model (8), we need

$$\mathrm{var}(X) = \sum_{i=1}^{k} \alpha_{i1}^2 \, \mathrm{var}(x_i) + \sum_{i \neq j}\sum \alpha_{i1}\alpha_{j1}\mathrm{cov}(x_i, x_j)$$

and

$$\mathrm{var}(X|y) = \sum_{i=1}^{k} \alpha_{i1}^2 \, \mathrm{var}(x_i|y) + \sum_{i \neq j}\sum \alpha_{i1}\alpha_{j1}\mathrm{cov}(x_i x_j|y).$$

Now, var $(x_i|y) = \pi_i(y)\{1 - \pi_i(y)\}$ and $\mathrm{cov}(x_i, x_j|y) = 0$. Therefore,

$$\mathrm{Evar}(X|y) = \sum_{i=1}^{k} \alpha_{i1}^2 \, \mathrm{E}\pi_i(y) \{1 - \pi_i(y)\}.$$

For the denominator of (4), we first require var(x_i) and cov(x_i, x_j). Since $x_i^2 = x_i$,

$$\mathrm{var}(x_i) = \mathrm{EE}(x_i^2|y) - \{\mathrm{EE}(x_i|y)\}^2$$
$$= \mathrm{EE}(x_i \,|y) - \{\mathrm{E}\pi_i(y)\}^2 = \mathrm{E}\pi_i(y) \{1 - \mathrm{E}\pi_i(y)\},$$
$$\mathrm{cov}(x_i, x_j) = \mathrm{EE}(x_i x_j|y) - \mathrm{E}\{\mathrm{E}(x_i|y)\}\mathrm{E}\{\mathrm{E}(x_j|y)\}$$
$$= \mathrm{EE}(x_i|y)\mathrm{E}(x_j|y) - \mathrm{E}\{\mathrm{E}(x_i|y)\}\mathrm{E}\{\mathrm{E}(x_j|y)\}$$
$$= \mathrm{E}\pi_i(y)\pi_j(y) - \mathrm{E}\pi_i(y)\mathrm{E}\pi_j(y)$$
$$= \mathrm{cov}(\pi_i(y), \pi_j(y)), \, (i \neq j).$$

---

[2]Another possibility would be to choose the w_i's so that X has the maximum reliability in the class of linear functions. Of course we are not limited to linear functions for purposes of scoring people; we might use instead, for example, the mean of the posterior distribution for all respondents with the same score pattern. The relation of (11) to the mean of the posterior is given in Bartholomew (1984a). Also see Bock and Aitkin (1981).

The final expression for the correlation coefficient is then

$$\rho = 1 - \frac{\sum\limits_{i=1}^{k} \alpha_{i1}^2 E\{\pi_i(y) - \pi_i^2(y)\}}{\sum\limits_{i=1}^{k} \alpha_{i1}^2 E\pi_i(y)\{1 - E\pi_i(y)\} + \sum\sum\limits_{i\neq j} \alpha_{i1}\alpha_{j1} \mathrm{cov}(\pi_i(y), \pi_j(y))} \cdot \quad (12)$$

This expression can be written in a variety of forms. To simplify the notation and to clarify the estimation problem, we shall introduce the further notation,

$$p_i = E\pi_i(y), \qquad p_{ii} = E\pi_i^2(y), \qquad p_{ij} = E\pi_i(y)\pi_j(y).$$

We may then express ρ as, say,

$$\rho = \frac{\sum\limits_{i=1}^{k} \alpha_{i1}^2 (p_{ii} - p_i^2) + \sum\sum\limits_{i\neq j} \alpha_{i1}\alpha_{j1}(p_{ij} - p_i p_j)}{\sum\limits_{i=1}^{k} \alpha_{i1}^2 p_i(1 - p_i) + \sum\sum\limits_{i\neq j} \alpha_{i1}\alpha_{j1}(p_{ij} - p_i p_j)} = \frac{A + C}{B + C}. \quad (13)$$

The quantities p_{ii}, p_{ij}, and p_i may be interpreted as unconditional probabilities, where p_i is the probability of a positive response to item i, p_{ij} is the probability of a positive response to both items i and j, and p_{ii} is the probability of a positive response to item i on any two trials. If the x's are perfectly correlated, $p_{ii} = p_i$. If the x's are perfectly uncorrelated, $p_{ii} = p_i^2$. In the former case, $\rho = 1$. In the latter, $\rho = 0$.

If we define a, b, and c as the average values of A, B, and C,

$$a = A/k, \qquad b = B/k, \qquad c = C/k(k-1),$$

then

$$\rho = \frac{a + (k-1)c}{b + (k-1)c}, \quad (14)$$

$$\rho = \frac{a' + (k-1)c'}{1 + (k-1)c'}, \quad (15)$$

where $a' = a/b$ and $c' = c/b$. These latter forms will be useful when we discuss the examples, because they let us standardize the coefficient to a common value of k. Thus, if we have values of a, b, and c for different k, we can use (14) or (15) to estimate what ρ would be for any specified value of k. In the unusual event that $a' = c'$, $\rho = kc'/(1 + (k-1)c')$. In the usual case that $a' > c'$, $\rho > kc'/(1 + (k-1))$. Thus, the greater the value of a' (intraitem association) relative to c' (interitem association), the larger the value of ρ, all else the same. (In appearances, (15) resembles the Spearman-Brown Prophecy Formula. However, unlike (15), that formula assumes parallel items.)

1.4. Estimation of Rho

There are two ways to approach the estimation of ρ. From (12) or (13) it is apparent that we need to estimate the three groups of quantities $\{E\pi_i(y)\}$, $\{E\pi_i(y)\pi_j(y)\}$ $(i \neq j)$, and $\{E\pi_i^2(y)\}$. Starting with (8) we can first estimate $\{\alpha_{i0}\}$ and $\{\alpha_{i1}\}$, then use the estimated versions of $\{\pi_i(y)\}$ to compute the required expectations.[3] If y is assumed to be standard normal, we cannot evaluate the integrals involved in closed form, but we can obtain them by numerical integration. Thus, to obtain, say, p_1, we would calculate the value of the definite integral $p_1 = \int_{-\infty}^{\infty} f(y)h(y)dy$, where $f(y)$ is the response function given by (9), and $h(y)$ is a standard normal random variable.

The second approach depends on the fact that all of the expectations, except $\{E\pi_i^2(y)\}$, can be estimated directly from the frequencies of the score patterns without using the model. This follows from the fact that

$$E\pi_i(y) = E(x_i) = \Pr\{x_i = 1\} = p_i \qquad (i = 1, 2, \ldots, k) \quad (16)$$

and

$$E\pi_i(y)\pi_j(y) = E(x_i x_j) = \Pr\{x_i = 1 \text{ and } x_j = 1\} = p_{ij} \quad (17)$$
$$(i,j = 1, 2, \ldots, k; i \neq j)$$

If N_i is the number of times $x_i = 1$ in the sample and N_{ij} is the number of times x_i and x_j are both 1, then (16) may be estimated by N_i/N and (17) by N_{ij}/N, where N is the total sample size. If the model is a satisfactory fit, both approaches should give similar answers. The remaining expectations, $\{E\pi_i^2(y)\}$, must still be estimated by numerical integration using the model. The final form of this estimate is therefore

---

[3]There are many ways to estimate these parameters. The maximum likelihood method is available as G11SAF and G11SBF in the NAG library, as noted elsewhere. Approximate methods based on the factor analysis of various pseudo-correlation coefficients are described in Bartholomew (1987, sect. 6.2). The other approximate methods, which take as their starting point the cross-product ratios and require minimal computing resources, are described in Bartholomew (1987, sect. 6.3).

$$\hat{\rho} = \frac{\sum_{i=1}^{k} \alpha_{i1}^2 \{p_{ii} - (N_i/N)^2\} + \sum_{i \neq j} \sum \alpha_{i1}\alpha_{j1}(N_{ij} - N_iN_j/N)/N}{\sum_{i=1}^{k} \alpha_{i1}^2 (N_i(1 - N_i/N))/N + \sum_{i \neq j} \sum \alpha_{i1}\alpha_{j1}(N_{ij} - N_iN_j/N)/N} . \tag{18}$$

Apart from the α_{i1} terms, equation (18) depends on the model only through the terms (p_{ii}), which, as noted, must be obtained by numerical integration. In the examples that follow, ρ is based on (13), except for a set of nine social life feeling scales (section 2.3), where it is based on (18) as well as (13), and also on (13) after dropping weights.

2. NUMERICAL APPLICATIONS

In applied work, there are a variety of questions about the interpretation of reliability. Some of these could be answered, in principle at least, by mathematical analysis, which has yet to be carried out. Here we shall try to throw light on such matters by applying the formula to several different data sets, both observed and simulated, with a view to seeing how ρ behaves under different conditions. These analyses have been loosely grouped into five sections according to the issues they raise and seek to clarify.

2.1. Scale and Item Reliability

The question here is how individual items contribute to the overall reliability. We illustrate how this may be investigated using data on four items concerning sources of knowledge about cancer (Bartholomew 1987). Our approach is to compute the reliability coefficient for the items taken one, two, three, and four at a time. The comparison of the resulting values then shows how much each contributes in the presence or absence of the others. The basic data and the X scores based on (11) are given in Table 1.

Maximum likelihood estimates of item parameters come from a fitting of the logit/probit model to the score pattern frequencies of Table 1. These are shown in Table 2. Although the logit/probit model fits fairly well ($G^2 = 11.73$, $df = 6$, $p = 0.068$), scale reliability at 0.646 is not very high.[4] (We return to the relation between goodness of fit and reliability below.) The values of the estimated reliabilities

---

[4]Collapsing two cells with small expected frequencies resulted in a loss of 1 df. Therefore, total $df = 16 - 9 - 1 = 6$.

TABLE 1
Distribution of 1,729 Respondents by $2^k = 16$ Score Patterns

Score Pattern	Observed Frequency	X Score
0000	477	.000
1000	63	.721
0001	12	.768
0010	150	1.344
1001	7	1.489
1010	32	2.065
0011	11	2.112
1011	4	2.833
0100	231	3.359
1100	94	4.081
0101	13	4.127
0110	378	4.703
1101	12	4 848
1110	169	5.425
0111	45	5.471
1111	31	6.192

Note. X score calculated by equation (11).

TABLE 2
Maximum Likelihood Estimates of Item Intercepts ($\hat{\alpha}_{i0}$'s) and Item Slopes
($\hat{\alpha}_{i1}$'s) and their Estimated Standard Errors

Item	Intercept	SE	Slope	SE
1	−1.288	.068	.721	.093
2	.597	.208	3.359	1.069
3	−.140	.064	1.344	.171
4	−2.707	.120	.768	.146

for all possible subsets of the four items come from the application of
(13) to the entries in Table 2. All 15 of these are shown in Table 3.

Examining these entries we see that some items, like item 4,
evidently contribute very little. Dropping item 4 from the complete
set, for example, only reduces the reliability of the scale from 0.646
to 0.641. Item 2 on the other hand is a major contributor. Dropping
this item halves the reliability, and it is remarkable that the reliability
of all four items is not much higher than the reliability of item 2 alone

TABLE 3

Values of $\hat{\rho}$ for Items Four, Three, Two, and One at a Time, Given Item
Parameters of Table 2

1 2 3 4	.646	1 2	.590	1	.083
1 2 3	.641	1 3	.302	2	.582
1 2 4	.601	1 4	.121	3	.256
1 3 4	.322	2 3	.632	4	.046
2 3 4	.636	2 4	.587		
		3 4	.278		

TABLE 4

Values of ρ for Items One at a Time, Given Intercept Constant and Slope
Variable and the Reverse

α_{i0}	α_{i1}	ρ	α_{i0}	α_{i1}	ρ
.597	.721	.100	−1.288	3.359	.577
.597	3.359	.582	.597	3.359	.582
.597	1.344	.252	−.140	3.359	.583
.597	.768	.111	−2.707	3.359	.556

(0.646 compared with 0.582). From all such comparisons it is possible to demonstrate the differing contributions of individual items to the overall reliability.

We digress to illustrate the sensitivity of estimates of reliability to differences in slopes and differences in intercepts. Thus, we ask how the reliabilities of individual items would change if, for example, we changed α_{i0} to .597 leaving α_{i1} unchanged and if we changed α_{i1} to 3.359 leaving α_{i0} unchanged. The results (Table 4) show that the differences between item reliabilities tend to maintain themselves with intercept constant but virtually disappear with slope constant. This result is in line with our general finding that the influence of the intercept on ρ relative to slope is negligible. (The relation of the distribution of item intercepts to the test information function is analyzed in Lord and Novick [1968, pp. 465–68].)

2.2. Reliability and Goodness of Fit

It is not unusual to find that the logit/probit model provides a good fit to the data but that the level of reliability is low. This is

TABLE 5
Maximum Likelihood Estimates of Intercepts and Slopes, $k = 5$, $N = 1,242$

Item	Intercept	SE	Slope	SE
1	.307	.061	.566	.150
2	−.167	.059	.566	.150
3	.610	.067	.593	.156
4	−.341	.063	.553	.149
5	.535	.067	.583	.154

illustrated by our second example based on the replies of 1,245 respondents to five *agree/disagree* items on trust. The actual score-pattern frequencies were purposely altered to yield approximately equal slopes but different intercepts. Table 5 gives the estimated item parameters and their standard errors; and from these coefficients one obtains in due course $a' = 0.069$, $b' = 1.000$, and $c' = 0.068$. Substituting these quantities into equation (15) gives

$$\hat{\rho} = \frac{0.069 + 0.272}{1.000 + 0.272} = 0.268.$$

Given the quite small values of a' and c', corresponding to association within and between items, a low value of ρ might have been foreseen. Inspection of equation (13) shows that for ρ to attain even 0.50, given $k = 5$, a' and c' would have to be close to 0.17. From a different viewpoint, all five slopes would have to be in the neighborhood of 1.00 for ρ to attain a value of 0.50 or so.

This low reliability is coupled with an almost too-good fit of the logit/probit model ($G^2 = 0.781$, $df = 21$, $p = 0.999$). Therefore, there is strong evidence that we are dealing with a unidimensional scale but that the items we are using are poor indicators of it. The remedy would be to increase the number of items if this were possible without losing the good fit. Goodness of fit has more to do with validity than with reliability. If fit is poor, the data are not adequately described by a single latent variable. An index that then purports to scale one dimension will, in fact, be partly influenced by other dimensions and will not be a valid measure of any single dimension. It is possible, of course, to have a poor fit and a high reliability. In such cases, however, the validity of the scale must be suspect; therefore, its reliability is not an issue.

It is worth remarking that when the slopes are equal, the weighting of the item variances (the $p_i(1 - p_i)$), the interitem covariances (the $(p_{ij} - p_i p_j)$), and the intraitem covariances (the $(p_{ii} - p_i^2)$) is unnecessary, since weights constitute a common factor of the numerator and denominator and therefore cancel out. In this example, where the slopes are almost equal, the values of weighted and unweighted reliabilities were almost the same: 0.269 and 0.268. It is also worth mentioning that with equal slopes, there are only $k + 1$ different values that the X score can take. In the general case the number is 2^k, which permits a finer discrimination between individuals.

2.3. Comparing Reliabilities

Our third illustration is based on a recent study of the responses of 2,003 Germans and 1,522 Americans to questions about nine social life feelings, measured by as many scales consisting of *agree/disagree* items (Krebs and Schuessler 1987). In the course of that study, the following questions came up:

1. How can we measure the reliability of logit/probit X scores?
2. Given such a measure, how does it compare with KR20?
3. How can we account for differences in reliabilities both within and between samples?

Equation (13) answers the first question. Table 6 addresses the second question and shows how (18) compares with (13) and how the reliability coefficient is affected by dropping weights. Table 6 sheds little light on why Germans and Americans differ in their reliabilities and why scales differ in reliability within samples. However, in the latter case, it shows that differences in reliabilities are altered by taking into account scale length.

As background and before discussing results, we briefly describe each of the nine social life feeling scales. Details of their construction are in Krebs and Schuessler (1987).

1. *Self-determination.* This ten-item scale measures the feeling that the doctrine of individualism, with its emphasis on effort and initiative, is at odds with one's personal and social experience. It is conceptually akin to internal-external control and personal efficacy.

2. *Trustworthiness of others.* Scores on this six-item scale

measure feelings about the trustworthiness and dependability of other people. It might have been called people cynicism, since its statements portray people as opportunistic, unreliable, uncaring, and callous.

3. *Feeling down.* The nine items in this scale pertain to negative feelings: boredom, loneliness, uselessness, uneasiness. We call it feeling down to avoid the clinical connotations of such terms as *anxiety* and *depression.*

4. *Job satisfaction.* This scale ranks respondents according to how satisfied they are with their job. Its eight items refer to both the tangible and intangible aspects of work. The presence of this scale in the set of nine is an accident caused by the manner in which the content domain of over 900 items was put together.

5. *Faith in democracy.* The seven items in this scale pertain to the responsiveness of public officials to citizen concerns and the impact of citizen participation on government policy and practice. It might have been called faith in the democratic creed.

6. *Feeling up.* This scale measures the degree to which one feels good about one's self and one's situation, in contrast with scale 3, which measures the degree to which one feels bad about one's self.

7. *Political disillusionment.* This scale measures political cynicism or the belief that politicians fail to practice what they preach.

8. *Future outlook.* The ten items in this scale measure feelings about current and anticipated trends in the quality of life, both personal and situational. Scores reflect respondents' degree of pessimism (optimism).

9. *Economic self-determination.* The five items in this scale measure feelings about poverty. A high score indicates that the respondent blames the economic system for poverty. A low score indicates that the respondent blames the individual and his or her work habits. Because it portrays individual effort to overcome poverty as largely futile, it is conceptually similar to scale 1.

Table 6 (column 6) shows that scales differ in their reliabilities within samples partly because of their varying lengths. Other things being equal, the more items the higher the reliability. We can make them comparable by a process of standardization using equation (15). Thus, we use the calculated values of a', b', and c' but use the same standard value for k—in this case, 10. After this adjustment, reliabilities ranged from 0.701 to 0.844 in the American sample and

TABLE 6

Social Life Feeling Scale Reliabilities and Component Terms, a' and c'

(1)	(2)	(3)	(4)	(5)	(6)	(7)	(8)	(9)	(10)
Scale Number	Scale Length (k)	Sample	a'	c'	$\hat{\rho}(k)^a$	KR20[b]	$\hat{\rho}(10)^c$	$\hat{\rho}_u(k)^d$	$\hat{\rho}'(k)^e$
1	10	American	.263	.242	.768	.763	.768	.764	.770
		German	.211	.191	.707	.699	.707	.699	.708
2	6	American	.396	.320	.765	.742	.844	.751	.766
		German	.338	.253	.707	.682	.810	.693	.708
3	9	American	.322	.293	.797	.735	.814	.791	.798
		German	.303	.278	.784	.772	.801	.780	.781
4	8	American	.291	.248	.741	.721	.781	.727	.741
		German	.326	.225	.738	.698	.777	.713	.737
5	7	American	.354	.203	.707	.643	.771	.649	.704
		German	.326	.167	.663	.544	.731	.559	.662
6	8	American	.330	.176	.698	.632	.741	.648	.698
		German	.294	.190	.696	.613	.739	.628	.696
8	8	American	.248	.174	.660	.611	.701	.623	.659
		German	.240	.170	.651	.612	.700	.624	.651
9	10	American	.294	.238	.774	.763	.774	.766	.774
		German	.356	.226	.787	.749	.787	.761	.783
10	5	American	.371	.173	.628	.528	.748	.597	.631
		German	.381	.198	.642	.566	.777	.553	.642

[a]$\hat{\rho}(k)$ = reliability by equation (13), given k (column 2), and a' and c' (columns 4 and 5).
[b]KR20 = coefficient-α for binary responses (column 7).
[c]$\hat{\rho}(10)$ = reliability by equation (13), given $k = 10$, and a' and c' (columns 4 and 5).
[d]$\hat{\rho}_u(k)$ = scale reliability by equation (13) after dropping weights on item variances and covariances.
[e]$\hat{\rho}'(k)$ = reliability by equation (18), given k (column 2).

from 0.700 to 0.801 in the German sample. These are typical values for scales of this length.

Table 6 also shows that though the differences between Germans and Americans are small, the reliability was lower for the Germans seven times out of nine. We surmise that these differences are related to differences in cultural background and to flaws in the translation of the items from English to German. German respondents were perhaps less certain about what was meant. (We return to this kind of question in section 3.)

The values of KR20 (column 7) confirm what we showed in section 1, namely, that KR20 is a conservative estimate of ρ and that the bound is quite close in most cases. It is pertinent that the ratio of ρ to KR20 runs parallel to the ratio of a' to c', implying that if we were to substitute c' for a' in equation (15), we would get values of ρ much closer to KR20.

Reliabilities by (18) appear in column 9. The reliabilities of unweighted scores appear in column 10. Reliabilities by (13) and (18) hardly differ at all, but the reliabilities of unweighted scores are generally lower than the reliabilities of weighted scores. Thus, we lose reliability if we drop weights but neither gain nor lose if we replace p_i with N_i/N and p_{ij} with N_{ij}/N.

For the social researcher, the contents of Table 6 are primarily a reminder that when short scales of dichotomous items are used to measure social life feelings and the like, the standardized reliability ($k = 10$) is seldom likely to be much greater than 0.80 and that scales on different topics (trust, alienation, self-determination) may differ in some degree. Likewise, reliabilities for the same scale may differ from one population to another. In short, the reliability of what might be called sociological scales is specific to both topic and population.

2.4. *Relation of Reliability to Slope Size and Slope Heterogeneity*

The dependence of ρ on the size of the slope coefficients has already been anticipated in sections 2.1 and 2.3. In this section, we show in greater detail by means of computer-generated data how the size and variability of the item slope coefficients contribute to the value of ρ. For this purpose we define the following summary measures:

$$V_0 = \rho \qquad \text{(the reliability coefficient)}$$
$$V_1 = \sum_{i=1}^{k} \alpha_{i1}^2 \qquad \text{(sum of slopes)}$$
$$V_2 = \tfrac{1}{k^2} \Sigma_i \Sigma_j |\alpha_{i1} - \alpha_{j1}| \quad \text{(Gini's mean difference coefficient)}$$
$$V_3 = kV_2/V_1 \qquad \text{(Gini coefficient divided by mean slope)}$$
$$V_4 = V_1 \times V_3 \qquad \text{(an interaction term)}$$

V_1 measures the size of the slopes, and V_3 measures their variability independent of size. Thus, V_3 is a kind of coefficient of variation.

Our method takes $k = 5$ and ten fixed values of V_1, namely, 1, 2, . . . ,10. These span the common range of slope sums found in practice. For each value of V_1, we generated 300 or more sets of slopes as a random partition of V_1 into five parts, for a grand total of

3,650 sets. Values of the forenamed variables were calculated for each of these sets, and the relations among variables were then analyzed to gauge the degree of dependence of ρ on slope size (V_1) and slope heterogeneity (V_3).

The results may be displayed in various ways, each putting the interrelations among the variables in a somewhat different light. Figure 2 shows how the mean value of ρ depends on V_1 and V_3. For any value of V_3, there is a strong curvilinear relationship between ρ and V_1 such that ρ increases as V_1 increases, which reflects the fact

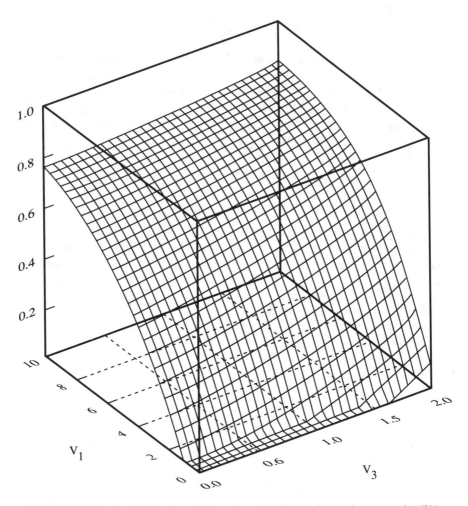

FIGURE 2. Plot of reliability ($\rho = V_0$) on slope size (V_1) and slope heterogeneity (V_3).

TABLE 7
Mean Value of ρ and Number of Cases (in parentheses) by Slope Size (V_1) and Slope Variation (V_3)

V_3	$V_1 = 2$		$V_1 = 10$	
	Mean ρ	N	Mean ρ	N
0.1	0.16	(1)	0.77	(2)
0.3	0.17	(26)	0.77	(28)
0.5	0.19	(104)	0.77	(107)
0.7	0.20	(140)	0.78	(120)
0.9	0.23	(47)	0.79	(33)
1.1	0.26	(25)	0.80	(16)
1.3	0.30	(2)	0.82	(2)
All cases	0.21	(345)	0.78	(308)

that as the response uncertainty of the items decreases, the reliability increases. The effect of V_3 on reliability is much less marked, though we can see that for a given V_1, the reliability increases as the variability of V_3 increases.

A different view of the dependence of ρ on V_1 and V_3 is provided by Table 7, which shows that the mean value of ρ, given V_1, is fairly constant as V_3 changes from 0.1 to 1.3, whereas the mean value of ρ, given V_3, changes markedly as V_1 shifts from 2 to 10. These tendencies hold for the complete ANOVA table (not shown) from which Table 7 was extracted.

Another way to view these tendencies is to square the correlations between ρ and all possible subsets of the four predictor variables for all 3,650 cases. The largest squared correlations for the independent variables one, two, three, and four at a time, respectively, are as follows: $r^2_{01} = 0.92$, $r^2_{0.13} = 0.93$, $r^2_{0.134} = 0.97$, and $r^2_{0.1234} = 0.98$. The dominance of V_1 in determining the value of V_0 is clearly evident from these figures, as is the fact that V_1 and V_3 together, after providing for their interaction, account for most of the variation in V_0.

2.5. Sampling Variation in $\hat{\rho}$

The standard error of $\hat{\rho}$ has yet to be worked out. In the meantime, we give a rough idea of how large its sampling variation might be, using the nine social life feeling scales. At one extreme we deflate each $\hat{\alpha}_{i1}$ by two times its standard error, and at the other we inflate them all by the same amount. Calculating reliability coefficients from these deflated and inflated slopes, and taking the difference between them, gives what we shall call a pseudo-confidence interval. We know that the asymptotic correlations between the individual $\hat{\alpha}_{i1}$'s are small, so the chance that all of the $\hat{\alpha}_{i1}$'s would show such extreme deviations simultaneously, in the same direction, must be very small indeed. We therefore guess that the confidence coefficient for such an interval is very close to one.

These calculations have been carried out for each of the social life feeling scales (Table 6) in each sample, and the results are given in Table 8. They show that within the samples, the width of the interval for $\hat{\rho}$ is inversely related to the magnitude of $\hat{\rho}$, except in scale 4. Loosely speaking the larger the reliability coefficient, the greater its reliability.

Because intervals for scale 4 break the trend and are based on much smaller samples, they draw attention to the relation between interval width and sample size. To illustrate this relationship, we constructed pseudo-confidence intervals for the trustworthiness scale (scale 2) in subsamples of 1,000, 500, and 250 cases randomly drawn

TABLE 8
Pseudo-Confidence Intervals for SLFS $\hat{\rho}$'s

	American ($N = 1,522$)			German ($N = 2,003$)		
SLFS	Lower Limit	Upper Limit	Interval	Lower Limit	Upper Limit	Interval
1	.71	.81	.10	.64	.76	.12
2	.71	.80	.09	.64	.76	.12
3	.74	.83	.09	.73	.82	.09
4[a]	.61	.81	.20	.62	.81	.19
5	.62	.76	.14	.53	.75	.22
6	.58	.77	.19	.59	.77	.18
8	.57	.72	.15	.57	.71	.14
9	.72	.81	.09	.74	.82	.08
10	.47	.72	.25	.54	.71	.17

Note: See text for method of construction.
[a]American (723), German (917).

TABLE 9
Pseudo-Confidence Interval for Reliability ($\hat{\rho}$) of SLFS2 by Sample Size

N	Lower Limit	Upper Limit	Interval Width	$\sqrt{N} \times$ Width
250	.51	.84	.33	5.2
500	.56	.80	.24	5.4
1,000	.62	.78	.16	5.1
2,003	.64	.76	.12	5.4

from the total of all 2,003 German cases. The results are shown in Table 9.

As expected, the width decreases with sample size. We expect the true standard error to be of order $1/\sqrt{N}$ and hence the length of the true confidence interval to be proportional to $1/\sqrt{N}$. We therefore expect our intervals to behave in the same way. But if this were so, the last column of Table 9 would be constant. That there is no systematic variation with N suggests that conclusions drawn from the relative sizes of the intervals under various conditions may be valid.

From our demonstration of sampling variability in $\hat{\rho}$, we can conclude that at least for $\hat{\rho}$ in the range 0.6 to 0.8, the higher values are more reliable than the lower and that the reliability of $\hat{\rho}$ increases as sample size increases, whatever the value of $\hat{\rho}$. If we had a formula for the standard error of $\hat{\rho}$, we would not need such rough methods, but our results do call attention to the inevitable sample variation in $\hat{\rho}$, or the unreliability of a reliability measure.

3. CONCLUDING REMARKS

It is clear from an inspection of the formulas for ρ (equations (12)–(15)) that the size of the reliability coefficient for the logit/probit model depends on the number of items (k) and on the magnitude of the slope coefficients (α_{i1}). In this section we discuss why these coefficients may vary, why ρ is subject to sampling errors, and several technical issues recurrent in discussions on reliability and latent trait modeling.

In an educational context, slope coefficients are often referred to as discrimination parameters, because as α_{i1} increases the response function rises more steeply. This implies that in the center of the distribution it is easier to discriminate between two individuals a given distance apart on the ability scale if α_{i1} is large than if it is small. We can also characterize the α_{i1}'s as measures of the uncertainty about how an individual will respond. For example, if α_{i1} is large, the logistic response function (see Figure 1) will be steep; so for most people, the probability of a positive response will be close to zero or one. In other words, there is little uncertainty about how most individuals will respond; statistically speaking the standard error of the response, zero or one, is very small. As α_{i1} becomes smaller the curve becomes flatter and the probabilities for different individuals become more nearly alike. The overall uncertainty will thus increase, reaching its maximum when α_{i1} is zero.

These uncertainties are reflected in the value of ρ. Items with low uncertainty yield a high reliability, and vice versa. Accounting for the level of X-score reliability (for fixed k) thus involves accounting for the uncertainty in the responses that make up those X scores. Our survey findings suggest several factors that may induce variation in the degree of uncertainty and, hence, in the value of ρ.

1. Items that have meaning in one cultural group may have little or no meaning in another. The size of the corresponding slope coefficient might therefore reflect the degree of meaning that the item has in the cultural group to which it is being applied. For example, the meaning of some items might have become distorted in the translation from English to German, and this might explain why the α_{i1}'s, and hence the reliabilities, are slightly lower in our German samples. Wendt-Hildebrandt (1988) focused on three obstacles to an exact translation of the life feeling scales: ambiguities in the English text, the presence of slang and idiom, and the presence of concepts with little or no meaning for Germans. The difference between Germans and Americans may be traceable to these nearly insoluble problems of getting semantically equivalent questionnaires.

2. Differences in uncertainty may also arise from the differences between the topics. There is some evidence (Krebs and Schuessler 1987, p. 23) that items about one's own feelings (like rejection) are subject to less uncertainty than items about society and its institutions (like the feeling that society is going downhill). The somewhat abstract and impersonal nature of the items composing scales 5 (faith in democracy) and 8 (disillusionment with govern-

ment) might account for their slightly lower reliabilities (adjusted for scale length).

3. For whatever reasons, both Germans and Americans respond with greater certainty to negatively worded items (for example, about the bleakness of the future) than to positively worded items (about the brightness of the future).[5] Thus, scores based on positively worded items tend to have lower reliabilities than scores based on negatively worded items. The differences in the reliabilities between scale 3 (all negative) and scale 6 (all positive) could therefore be due to this direction-of-wording factor and might disappear when that factor is controlled.

4. There is some evidence that certainty in answering is inflated in some measure by respondents' tendency to present themselves in a good light and to endorse what are regarded as socially desirable feelings or attitudes. Whatever the reason, there are respondents who admit to no personal shortcomings, and there are respondents who always express, at least publicly, the socially popular point of view. In this case, certainty of responding is due not to the strength of true feelings but rather to the strength of habits of responding to attitude/feeling questions. But whether due to response sets or to mind sets, perfect consistency in responding tends to raise the level of association between and within items and thereby the level of ρ.

5. It should be clear that the relative instability of the X scores we have calculated (Table 6), as measured by ρ, lies not in measurement error (i.e., not in inaccurate recording) but in the probabilistic nature of responding to questions about social self and social situation, which are often perceived as vague and ambiguous. With the kind of uncertainties of our items, it is clear that highly stable X scores ($\rho > 0.9$, say) are practically unattainable with tests based on 10 or so items. To attain a reliability of .90, say, with no change in scale length, we would have to replace items whose α_{i1}'s are small with items whose α_{i1}'s are sufficiently large. That effort would tend to yield a set of items with slopes alike in their magnitudes, as in a "random effects" Rasch model.

[5]A sociological interpretation of direction-of-wording effects in the American sample is offered in Reiser, Wallace, and Schuessler (1986).

We have noted earlier here and there that the value of $\hat{\rho}$ is determined not only by the size of the test and the uncertainties in the item responses but also by sampling error, because the slope parameters have to be estimated from a sample and therefore cannot be determined precisely. In fact, the standard errors of the estimated slopes may be large, especially if the sample size is small (a few hundreds, say) or if one of the α_{i1}'s is large. For this reason it may be that some of the small differences to which we have ascribed substantive meaning are merely chance variation. Until we have a formula for the standard error of $\hat{\rho}$, we have to rely on available empirical evidence, some of which was given in section 2.

Our final points are statistical rather than substantive and concern (a) errors in predicting one set of replicates from another, (b) the effect of the prior trait distribution $h(y)$ on ρ, (c) the effect of the item marginals (first-order) on ρ, and (d) the place of reliability in latent trait modeling.

We may wish to predict the value of a replicated score, X_2, say, of an individual who has already produced a score X_1. This can be found from the bivariate distribution of X_1 and X_2. For given values of the α_{i1}'s, this will be approximately bivariate normal, because as $k \to \infty$, the central limit theorem assures the approximate normality of X_1 and X_2. Since their correlation is ρ, by definition, we can use the standard result from linear regression that the standard error of prediction is

$$\sigma_{x_2|x_1} = \sigma_{x_1(1-\rho^2)^{1/2}}. \tag{19}$$

In calculating ρ by (13), we took the prior trait distribution to be a standard normal random variable: $h(y) = N(0,1)$. That procedure raises several interrelated questions. First, why use a standard normal variable? Second, would we get the same result if we used a normal distribution with mean $\neq 0$ and variance $\neq 1$? Third, would we get the same value of ρ if we used a quite different prior distribution? Fourth, could we get along without a prior?

Setting y to be $N(0,1)$ is essentially a matter of convention. We simply decide on grounds of convenience to scale the latent trait in such a manner as to render it normal with zero mean and unit standard deviation. If we supposed that y was normal with mean μ and standard deviation σ, we could easily find the effect on α_{i0} and α_{i1}. The new values α_{i0}^* and α_{i1}^* would be

$$\alpha_{i0}^* = \alpha_{i0} - \alpha_{i1}\mu/\sigma,$$
$$\alpha_{i1}^* = \alpha_{i1}/\sigma.$$

This would leave the reliability virtually unchanged, since the replacement of α_{i1} with α_{i1}^* would merely introduce a constant in the numerator and denominator of (13) or (18), which would cancel. We have already noted that ρ is almost independent of the values of the α_{i0}'s.

A change in the form of the prior distribution also has little effect unless the departure from normality is very extreme (see Bartholomew 1988). If the part played by the prior in determining the values of the α's is small enough, we might be able to get along without it. The prior first comes into play in the likelihood function before maximum likelihood estimation. The various approximate methods referred to in footnote 3 do not require the use of the prior distribution at all. If we go on to use (18) to estimate ρ, the only other point at which the prior is required is in estimating the probabilities p_{ii}. Here there appears to be no way of avoiding the use of a prior, though $p_i \geq p_{ii} \geq p_i^2$, whatever the prior, places bounds on the indeterminacy. It may be observed that the value of a' (which is the only term involving p_{ii}) in the example in section 2.2 is small and has only a minor effect on the value of ρ.

In questionnaire studies, different marginals (first-order) are to be expected both within and between samples. We expect different scales to have different marginals when administered to the same group of respondents. We expect the same questionnaire to have different marginals when administered to different groups of respondents. In any given instance, marginals may congregate around .50; in another, around .90; in still another, they may divide themselves into clusters around .25 and .75. Therefore, we should ask, Is the magnitude of ρ affected by the location and distribution of the item marginals? The general answer is "no," because first-order marginals stand in a close relation to the item intercepts and item intercepts have little or no effect on the covariances, both within and between items, and therefore little or no effect on ρ. A mathematical demonstration of this point has yet to be worked out. However, a substantial body of computer-generated results supports our answer.

In the context of ability testing, Samejima (1977) has argued that the notion of the reliability of a test has no place in latent trait theory. Because it is a correlation, it depends not only on the test itself but on the specific group of examinees being tested. Clearly, a measure that cannot be generalized beyond the sample at hand is of little value. Instead, Samejima proposes the standard deviation of the posterior distribution of ability, which appears to be roughly constant over all levels of ability. In making this claim Samejima follows the widespread but rarely justified practice of treating the ability of an individual as a parameter to be estimated. There are theoretical and statistical objections to this, but our main objection is a practical one. Usually we are not interested in the sample as such but in the population from which it has been drawn. The sample survey is a case in point. We therefore treat an attitude (as we would an ability) as a random variable. Many are reluctant to do this because it seems to require the introduction of an otherwise unnecessary assumption about the form of the distribution of the variable about which we can have no direct empirical evidence. The distinction is, however, more apparent than real, since the way ability is parameterized involves arbitrary conventions. In the case of the random-effects model the distribution of ability is *essentially* arbitrary, as shown in Bartholomew (1984*b*). As we said above, in choosing it to be normal, for example, we are saying nothing about the real world. We are merely constructing a scale of measurement that will render the latent variable normally distributed.

It certainly follows from this that our measure of reliability depends upon the population distribution. But this is no handicap, since we see no reason why a test instrument should have the same reliability across populations. We made this point in a practical context at the end of section 2.3.

REFERENCES

Bartholomew, David J. 1984*a*. "Scaling Binary Data Using a Factor Model." *The Journal of the Royal Statistical Society,* ser. B, 46:120–23.
———. 1984*b*. "The Foundations of Factor Analysis." *Biometrika* 71:221–32.
———. 1987. *Latent Variable Models and Factor Analysis.* London: Charles Griffin.
———. 1988. "The Sensitivity of Latent Trait Analysis to Choice of Prior Distribution." *British Journal of Mathematical and Statistical Psychology* 41: 101–107.
Birnbaum, Allan. 1968. "Some Latent Trait Models and Their Use in Inferring an Examinee's Ability." Pp. 395–479 in *Statistical Theories of Mental Test Scores,* edited by Frederic M. Lord and Melvin R. Novick. Reading, MA: Addison-Wesley.

Bock, R. D., and M. Aitkin. 1981. "Marginal Maximum Likelihood Estimation of Item Parameters: An Application of the EM Algorithm." *Psychometrika* 46: 443–59.

Bock, R. D., and M. Lieberman. 1970. "Fitting a Response Model for *n* Dichotomously Scored Items." *Psychometrika* 35: 179–97.

Duncan, Otis Dudley. 1985a. "Rasch Measurement in Survey Research." Pp. 179–229 in *Survey Measurement of Subjective Phenomena,* vol. 1, edited by C. F. Turner and E. Martin. New York: Basic Books.

————. 1985b. "Rasch Measurement: Further Examples and Discussion." Pp. 367–403 in *Survey Measurement of Subjective Phenomena,* vol. 2, edited by C. F. Turner and E. Martin. New York: Basic Books.

Goldstein, Harvey, and Robert Wood. 1989. "Five Decades of Item Response Modelling." *British Journal of Mathematical and Statistical Psychology* 42: 139–67.

Guttman, Louis. 1945. "A Basis for Analyzing Test-Retest Reliability." *Psychometrika* 10:255–82.

Krebs, Dagmar, and Karl F. Schuessler. 1987. *Soziale Empfindungen: Ein Interkultureller Skalenvergleich bei Deutschen und Amerikanern* (Measuring the Social Life Feelings of Germans and Americans: A Cross-Cultural Study). Frankfurt: Campus Verlag.

Lord, Frederic M., and Melvin R. Novick, eds. 1968. *Statistical Theories of Mental Test Scores.* Reading, MA: Addison-Wesley.

Muthén, B. 1978. "Contributions to Factor Analysis of Dichotomous Variables." *Psychometrika* 43:551–60.

Numerical Algorithms Group. 1987. *Library Manual, MK.* Oxford: Numerical Algorithms Group.

Reiser, Mark, Michael Wallace, and Karl F. Schuessler. 1986. "Direction-of-Wording Effects in Dichotomous Social Life Feelings Items," Pp. 1–25 in *Sociological Methodology 1986,* edited by Nancy B. Tuma. San Francisco: Jossey-Bass.

Samejima, F. 1977. "The Use of the Information Function in Tailored Testing." *Applied Psychological Measurement* 1:233–47.

Schaeffer, Nora C. 1988. "An Application of Item Response Theory to the Measurement of Depression." Pp. 271–307 in *Sociological Methodology 1988,* edited by Clifford C. Clogg. Washington, DC: American Sociological Association.

Thissen, David, and Jo Ann Mooney. 1990. "Loglinear Item Response Models with Applications to Data from Social Surveys." Pp. 299–330 in *Sociological Methodology 1990,* edited by Clifford C. Clogg. Oxford: Basil Blackwell.

Thurstone, L. L., and E. J. Chave. 1929. *The Measurement of Attitude.* Chicago: University of Chicago Press.

Wendt-Hildebrandt, Susan. 1988. "On the Problematics of Translating Cross-Cultural Survey Instruments: Theory and Practice." Unpublished manuscript.

❧5❧

CORRECTING MEASURES OF RELATIONSHIP BETWEEN AGGREGATE-LEVEL VARIABLES

*Robert M. O'Brien**

Social scientists often use aggregate-level variables. These variables use the weighted sum of the characteristics of single elements to measure the characteristics of cases. For example, a measure of the formalization of different business organizations (cases) may be based on the mean of the responses of a sample of employees (elements) from each business to a question on the extent to which their work is rule governed. Or a measure of the seriousness of armed robbery, shoplifting, and other crimes (cases) may be based on the mean of the responses of raters (elements). This paper derives estimates of the reliability of aggregate-level variables, describes how to estimate "spurious" covariance components that occur when the same respondents rate an aggregate on more than one variable, and demonstrates how coefficients of relationship can be corrected for both of these sources of error. The methodology is widely applicable and should substantially improve the analysis of aggregate-level variables in social science.

The data used in this study were made available by the Interuniversity Consortium for Political and Social Research. The data for the 1980 High School and Beyond study were originally collected by the National Opinion Research Center (NORC) for the National Center for Education Statistics, U.S. Department of Education. Neither the collector of the original data nor the Consortium bear any responsibility for the analyses or interpretations presented here. I thank Peter Marsden and three anonymous reviewers for very helpful comments and suggestions.
*University of Oregon

125

1. INTRODUCTION

This paper explores some applications and extensions of generalizability theory to analyses involving relationships between aggregate-level variables. An aggregate-level variable uses the weighted sum of the characteristics of single elements to measure a characteristic of cases. These variables are similar to the "analytical properties of collectives" described by Lazarsfeld and Menzel (1969). "These are properties of collectives which are obtained by performing some mathematical operation upon some property of each single member" (1969, p. 503). The definition of aggregate-level variables used here is much broader: The cases need not be collectives nor the elements members.[1] This paper addresses a particular weighted sum of single elements: the mean (which, of course, includes proportions, percentages, and rates). Even this restricted focus is very broad and includes variables such as the mean need-achievement score for nations (based on samples of stories from each nation), the percentage of black students in different high schools, or the average seriousness ratings of different crimes. Here, the cases are nations, schools, and crimes, and the elements are the need-achievement scores for stories, the percentage of students who are black, and respondent ratings of crime seriousness. Sometimes each element contributes to the scores of several cases: e.g., each respondent rates each crime in terms of seriousness. At other times, each element contributes to the score of only a single case: e.g., each high school score is based on the race of only the students *within* it.

Examples of such operationalizations abound in the social sciences: the levels of formalization and centralization in organizations, measured by the mean of responses of individuals within each organization (Aiken and Hage 1968); the need-achievement levels of countries, measured by the proportion of students telling stories with need-achievement imagery (McClelland 1961); the social distance of ethnic groups (Bogardus 1959); the perceived benefits to society of selected occupations (Siegel 1971); the levels of anomie in particular cohorts (Kahn and Mason 1987); the perceived seriousness and harmfulness of different crimes (Warr 1989); and the level of white student's hostil-

---

[1]It does not include Lazarsfeld and Menzel's structural measures, which are "obtained by performing some operation on data about the relations of each member to some or all of the others" (1969, p. 504).

ity towards blacks (Longshore 1982). All of these operationalizations are designed to measure characteristics of cases (organizations, countries, ethnic groups, occupations, cohorts, crimes, schools), and all of them are based on the weighted sums of the characteristics of single elements.

The techniques developed in this paper can be used to (1) measure the reliability of aggregate-level variables, (2) separate respondent-induced covariance due to joint sampling from the covariance between aggregates,[2] and (3) estimate relationships between aggregate-level variables that have been corrected for both these sources of error. The approach works not only with data-collection designs in which elements (say, respondents) are nested within aggregates (which means that each respondent [or element] contributes only to the score of the aggregate [case] of which they are a member) but also with a multitude of other designs. For example, the approach works with designs in which each group of respondents rates all of the aggregates (crossed designs), with designs in which each group of respondents uses multiple items to rate each aggregate on a particular variable, and with designs in which each group of items is rated by individuals who are nested within different aggregates (mixed designs).[3] The effects of these design differences on both the reliability of the aggregate-level variables and on the aggregate-level covariance is taken into account. Finally, the generalizability theory orientation used in this paper leads researchers to examine the impact of treating some aspects of measurement as fixed and others as random. For example, researchers can estimate the reliability of the aggregate-level variables and correct measures of relationship, assuming that the same set of questions are used (fixed) rather than a different set of questions (random).

[2]Cronbach et al. (1972, pp. 268–72) discuss joint sampling in the context of the scores of individuals. For example, in joint sampling, the scores on two variables for an individual are measured in the same testing session. In independent sampling, the scores on the two variables are collected in different (randomly assigned) sessions. In the context of aggregate-level variables, joint sampling occurs whenever respondents or raters rate the aggregates on two or more variables and the aggregate-level variables are based on those ratings. In independent sampling, the scores of aggregates on different variables are based on different raters. Joint sampling produces covariance between the aggregate-level variables.

[3]The formulas for the mixed design are not derived in this paper, but they are straightforward extensions of the procedures outlined below.

The approach yields results that are similar to those presented by Kenny and La Voie (1985) for *separating individual-level from group-level effects* in situations in which respondents have been *randomly* assigned to aggregates and are nested within aggregates: $R:A.$[4] (This notation is read "*R* nested within *A*" and means that each respondent's score is relevant only for the aggregate of which they are a member, i.e., in which they are nested.) The nested situation ($R:A$) is the only one examined by Kenny and La Voie (1985). The techniques presented in this paper are *not* designed to separate individual-level from group-level effects and do not depend on the random assignment of respondents to groups. Instead they are designed to assess the relationship between aggregate-level variables corrected for certain sources of correlated and uncorrelated measurement errors.

2. RELIABILITY, JOINT SAMPLING, AND AGGREGATE-LEVEL VARIABLES

Cronbach et al. (1972, p. 293), in their book on generalizability theory, stated that "the concept of correlated error (i.e., of the linkage introduced by joint sampling) is highly pertinent to causal analysis and has been recognized in that research more often than in psychological measurement. . . . It seems likely that benefits will follow from a careful restatement of some of the problems of causal inference using concepts from generalizability theory." The benefits are indeed many, and they involve more than just the problems associated with correlated errors.

2.1. *Reliability*

Reliability of aggregate-level variables concerns the replicability of results over repeated samplings. For example, how similar are the aggregate-level scores from two different samples of elements (say, respondents) from the same cases (aggregates)? Estimates of the

[4]Kenny and La Voie's (1985) approach does not separate individual and group effects, except when subjects have been randomly assigned to groups. It does correct for the effects of joint sampling. This may be what they mean when they state, "When groups are not formed through random assignment, the strategy outlined in this article may still apply in part" (p. 340).

reliability of aggregate-level variables can help determine whether a larger sample of elements (respondents) is needed to increase the reliability to an acceptable level, and they allow researchers to correct measures of relationship between aggregate-level variables.

2.2. *Joint Sampling*

Ideally, each aggregate-level variable is computed from the scores of a different set of elements. In such a sampling scheme the scores for each variable are based on independent samples of elements. Then, the covariances of the aggregate-level variables are not dependent on the joint sampling of scores from the same set of elements.

Typically, however, one sample of elements (for example, respondents) is used to obtain the aggregate-level scores on several variables or dimensions, and thus, the mean values of different variables for each aggregate are not independent of the particular respondents selected. For example, a sample of respondents who were predominantly easy graders would tend to grade easy on a number of dimensions. An organization might be rated by such respondents as not too centralized, and their satisfaction with working conditions might be rated as high. This would bias estimates of the aggregate-level relationship. One solution to this problem is to estimate this covariance at the individual level (covariance due to the joint sampling of the scores for two or more variables from the same respondents) and remove it from the covariance of the aggregate-level variables. This provides an estimate of the results that would have been obtained if the sampling had been done independently.[5]

The approach used to obtain estimates of reliability and estimates of the covariance due to joint sampling is based on generalizability theory (Cronbach et al. 1972). Before proceeding formally with that approach, we establish some parallels to classical

[5]The method of sampling scores on which to base the aggregate-level variables causes joint sampling effects. If, for example, the aggregates are schools and the aggregate-level variables are percentage black and mean SAT scores and these scores are based on a sample of students from each school, this joint sampling of scores from the same students will cause individual-induced covariance components. If the percentage black and the mean SAT scores were each based on different independent samples of students from each of the schools, joint sampling effects would not occur.

test-score theory, which should make the formal approach more intuitive.[6]

3. SPEARMAN'S CORRECTION AND JOINT SAMPLING

Most social scientists are familiar with Spearman's (1910) formula for correcting observed correlation coefficients for attenuation due to unreliable measurement. The corrected coefficients for aggregate-level variables described in this paper are similar to those produced using Spearman's classic formula. However, the covariance components, which are generated by joint sampling, make the correction problem more complex.

3.1. *Classical Test-Score Theory*

Using the notation of classical test-score theory (e.g., Lord and Novick 1968), we define the observed (deviation) score on the ith variable for the rth respondent (X_{ir}) as a function of the respondent's true (deviation) score on that variable (T_{ir}) plus an error term (e_{ir}). The resulting formula (in deviation score form) is

$$X_{ir} = T_{ir} + e_{ir}. \tag{1}$$

Squaring both sides of (1) and taking expectations (over respondents) provides the variance of X_i (variable i) in terms of the true-score variance, the error variance, and the covariance between T_i and e_i:

$$\text{var}(X_i) = \text{var}(T_i) + \text{var}(e_i) + 2\text{cov}(T_i, e_i). \tag{2}$$

In classical test-score theory, the error term is assumed to be uncorrelated with the true score. Thus, the observed-score variance for the ith variable may be written as

$$\text{var}(X_i) = \text{var}(T_i) + \text{var}(e_i), \tag{3}$$

and the reliability of an observed variable is defined as the systematic or true-score variance divided by the observed-score variance:

---

[6]Most of the results obtained in this paper can also be derived from the generic true-score extension of classical test-score theory (Lord and Novick 1968).

$$\rho(X_i,X_i') = \frac{\text{var}(T_i)}{\text{var}(X_i)} = \frac{\text{var}(X_i) - \text{var}(e_i)}{\text{var}(X_i)} = \frac{\text{var}(T_i)}{\text{var}(T_i) + \text{var}(e_i)}, \quad (4)$$

where $\rho(X_i,X_i')$ represents the reliability of the observed variable.

We can obtain the covariance between two observed variables in terms of the covariance between their true scores and error terms by writing equation (1) twice—once for variable i and once for another variable (variable j)—and then multiplying the left-hand sides of the equations for X_{ir} and X_{jr} by each other and the right-hand sides by each other, and taking expectations. This yields the covariance of X_i with X_j in terms of various covariance components between T_i, T_j, e_i, and e_j:

$$\text{cov}(X_i,X_j) = \text{cov}(T_i,T_j) + \text{cov}(T_i,e_j) + \text{cov}(e_i,T_j) + \text{cov}(e_i,e_j). \quad (5)$$

In classical test-score theory, the random error terms for different variables are assumed to be uncorrelated with each other and with the true scores on other variables. Thus, (5) simplifies to

$$\text{cov}(X_i,X_j) = \text{cov}(T_i,T_j). \quad (6)$$

The correlation between true scores, T_i and T_j, is defined as

$$\rho(T_iT_j) = \frac{\text{cov}(T_i,T_j)}{\sqrt{\text{var}(T_i)} \sqrt{\text{var}(T_j)}}. \quad (7)$$

To determine the correlation between the underlying true scores, we can solve equation (3) for $\text{var}(T_i)$ (and $\text{var}(T_j)$) and equation (6) for $\text{cov}(T_i,T_j)$, and substitute these components for the corresponding components in equation (7):

$$\rho(T_i,T_j) = \frac{\text{cov}(X_i,X_j)}{\sqrt{\text{var}(X_i) - \text{var}(e_i)} \sqrt{\text{var}(X_j) - \text{var}(e_j)}}. \quad (8)$$

When both the numerator and denominator of (8) are divided by the square roots of $\text{var}(X_i)$ and $\text{var}(X_j)$, the result is the standard formula for correcting the bivariate correlation coefficient for unreliability (e.g., Lord and Novick 1968, p. 70; Bohrnstedt 1970, p. 84):

$$\rho(T_i,T_j) = \frac{\rho(X_i,X_j)}{\sqrt{\rho(X_i,X_i')} \sqrt{\rho(X_j,X_j')}}. \quad (9)$$

3.2. *Generic True-Score Theory*

Classical test-score theory can be extended (Lord and Novick 1968) by adding, to the right-hand side of equation (1), components other than a true score and a random error term—for example, a condition of measurement (R_i), such as the time of day at which a test is administered or the sex of the interviewer.[7] Differences in these conditions of measurement add variability to the observed test scores. The resulting formula appears below:

$$X_{ir} = T_{ir} + R_{ir} + e_{ir}. \tag{10}$$

Assume, for the moment, that the true scores are uncorrelated with the measurement errors and with the conditions of measurement and that the conditions of measurement are uncorrelated with the measurement errors. When we square both sides of the equation, take expectations, and eliminate covariances that are zero, we find that

$$\text{var}(X_i) = \text{var}(T_i) + \text{var}(R_i) + \text{var}(e_i). \tag{11}$$

In generic true-score theory, $\text{var}(T_i)$ is the generic true-score variance and $[\text{var}(R_i) + \text{var}(e_i)]$ is the generic error variance. Reliability is again defined as the systematic true-score variance divided by the observed score variance:

$$\rho(X_i, X_i') = \frac{\text{var}(T_i)}{\text{var}(X_i)} = \frac{\text{var}(X_i) - \text{var}(R_i) - \text{var}(e_i)}{\text{var}(X_i)}. \tag{12}$$

Again, to examine the covariance between two observed variables, we write out equation (10) once for variable i and once for another variable (j). Assume that the true score on i is uncorrelated with the conditions of measurement or with the measurement error on j, that the conditions of measurement on i are uncorrelated with the conditions of measurement on j or with the measurement error on variable j, and that the error terms in each equation are uncorrelated with each other. Then when we multiply the left-hand sides of

---

[7]In some senses this approach does not depart from classical test-score theory, discussed by Spearman (1910). It is also similar to the approach that Lord and Novick (1968) discuss under the rubric of generic and specific true scores. Classical test-score theory, however, typically only considers an observed score, a true score, and an undifferentiated error component.

the equations for X_{ir} and X_{jr} by each other and the right-hand sides by each other and take expectations, we find that

$$\text{cov}(X_i,X_j) = \text{cov}(T_i,T_j). \tag{13}$$

Solving equation (11) for $\text{var}(T_i)$ (and $\text{var}(T_j)$) and solving equation (13) for $\text{cov}(T_i,T_j)$ and substituting the results into equation (7) yields

$$\rho(T_iT_j) = \frac{\text{cov}(X_i,X_j)}{\sqrt{\text{var}(X_i)-\text{var}(R_i)-\text{var}(e_i)}\sqrt{\text{var}(X_j)-\text{var}(R_j)-\text{var}(e_j)}}. \tag{14}$$

Spearman (1910) noted that the presence of correlated errors due to the conditions of measurement—in our notation, $\text{cov}(R_i,R_j)$ and $\text{cov}(e_i,e_j)$—could affect his correction formula, and he described how such correlations could occur in practice:

> In experimental psychology, for instance, it is not uncommon for each individual to be tested separately, and for each test in x to be accompanied by a test in y. Suppose, now, any individual to be accidentally indisposed: his results for both x and y will be accidentally depressed; the same will occur, more or less, for the other individuals; hence arises a spurious correlation between x and y. (Spearman 1910, p. 277)

This is an instance of joint sampling, since the two test scores are sampled at the same time under the same conditions, rather than independently. Spearman suggested that if measured, this spurious covariance component, due to the use of the same conditions of measurement, could be subtracted from the observed covariance.[8]

Under joint sampling, the expected values of $\text{cov}(R_i,R_j)$ and $\text{cov}(e_i,e_j)$ are *not* zero, and $\text{cov}(X_i,X_j)$ is

$$\text{cov}(X_i,X_j) = \text{cov}(T_i,T_j) + \text{cov}(R_i,R_j) + \text{cov}(e_i,e_j). \tag{15}$$

Therefore, $\text{cov}(R_i,R_j)$ and $\text{cov}(e_i,e_j)$ must be subtracted from $\text{cov}(X_i,X_j)$ to provide an estimate of $\text{cov}(T_i,T_j)$. When this result is

[8]In the traditional format, a covariance component such as $\text{cov}(R_1,R_2)$ is unlikely to be specifically measured as a condition of measurement because it would require taking measurements of the same individuals under varying conditions.

substituted into the numerator of equation (14), it yields equation (16), which corrects for joint sampling, as well as unreliability:

$$\rho(T_iT_j) = \frac{\text{cov}(X_i,X_j) - \text{cov}(R_i,R_j) - \text{cov}(e_i,e_j)}{\sqrt{\text{var}(X_i)-\text{var}(R_i)-\text{var}(e_i)}\ \sqrt{\text{var}(X_j)-\text{var}(R_j)-\text{var}(e_j)}}\ . \tag{16}$$

In the case of aggregate-level measures, correlated "conditions" (R's) and errors (e's) are likely to occur when, for example, the same individuals within an aggregate are used to obtain the aggregate-level scores on two or more variables, or when the same respondents rate several aggregates on two or more variables. Here, *the aggregates are analogous to individuals, and the respondents represent different conditions of measurement.* Such joint sampling creates correlated conditions and errors of measurement. Below, we show how these correlated "error" components can be measured and removed from estimates of aggregate-level relationships.

4. AGGREGATE-LEVEL VARIABLES AND JOINT SAMPLING: THE *R:A* DESIGN

The simplest way to describe the derivation of measures of reliability for aggregate-level variables and how to remove the respondent-induced covariance components due to joint sampling from the relationship between them is to examine a situation in which different respondents rate each aggregate and the means of their responses are used as the aggregate-level scores. For example, we might examine a random sample of workers from different enterprises who rated their organizations on several variables. The means of their responses are the scores of the enterprises on the different variables. Or we could examine school-level scores that are based on the means of the responses of a random sample of school children attending different schools to items designed to rate their schools on several dimensions.

Although we speak of respondents rating aggregates, the same approach and equations hold when the "respondents" do not respond (e.g., when a researcher notes their sex, race, or SAT score) or when "respondents" are not individuals (e.g., when they are the scores on stories that have been coded for need for achievement). Respondents are more concrete, but their responses are merely an example of the more abstract elements that may be averaged to create aggregate-level scores.

4.1. *Deriving the Aggregate-Level Variances*

Since the same steps will be used to derive variance and covariance components in other designs, we number the steps used in the derivations for the $R{:}A$ design. In step 1 we write out the linear equation for the model:

$$X_{iar} = \mu_i + (\mu_{ia} - \mu_i) + (\mu_{iar} - \mu_{ia}) + e_{iar}, \tag{17}$$

where the subscript i is the variable, a is the aggregate, and r is the respondent. X_{iar} is the score of the rth respondent on the ith variable in the ath aggregate; μ_i (the grand mean for variable i) is the expected value of X_{iar} over all aggregates and respondents; μ_{ia} (the aggregate mean on variable i) is the expected value of X_{iar} over all respondents; and μ_{iar} is the expected value of X_{iar}, i.e., the expected score on variable i of the rth respondent in the ath aggregate. In the language of classical test-score theory, μ_{iar} is the expected value of the propensity distribution of the observed variable for a fixed person in the ath aggregate (Lord and Novick 1968, p. 30). The first term on the right-hand side of the equation is the grand mean on the ith variable, the second $(\mu_{ia} - \mu_i)$ is the aggregate effect for the ith variable, the third $(\mu_{iar} - \mu_{ia})$ is the respondent effect on the ith variable, and the last is the random error component on the ith variable.[9]

In step 2 we subtract μ_i from both sides of the equation for X_{iar} (here, equation (17)). In step 3 we square both sides of the equation and take the expectations. In step 4 we eliminate those expectations with values of zero.

All of the terms on the right-hand side of the equation for $(X_{iar} - \mu_i)$ (here, $(\mu_{ia} - \mu_i)$, $(\mu_{iar} - \mu_{ia})$, and e_{iar}) are assumed to be uncorrelated. These assumptions are based on the way in which these terms have been constructed (e.g., as deviations from population means) and on random sampling. For example, given random

---

[9]The linear equations that we write for all of the models in this paper can be simplified to the same two components. For example, equation (17) can be simplified to $X_{iar} = \mu_{iar} + e_{iar}$. In the language of classical test-score theory, a person's score is equal to his or her true score (the expected value of the person's propensity distribution) plus error. We can write the extended formula (equation (17)) because it is possible to estimate the deviation of the aggregate's mean from the grand mean $(\mu_{ia} - \mu_i)$ and the deviation of the respondent's score from the mean of the aggregate $(\mu_{iar} - \mu_{ia})$. Other designs allow other components to be estimated, but they can all be simplified to $X_{iar} = \mu_{iar} + e_{iar}$.

sampling of respondents, the deviation of the randomly sampled respondent's expected score (μ_{iar}) from the aggregate's mean on the ith variable (μ_{ia}) should be uncorrelated with the deviation of the mean of the aggregate on the ith variable (μ_{ia}) from the mean of variable i (μ_i). Both of these components should be uncorrelated with the deviation of the respondent's score from the expected value of the respondent's propensity distribution for the ith variable in the ath aggregate (e_{iar}). Step 4 yields an equation for the observed-score variance of respondents in terms of various variance components:

$$\sigma_i^2(X_{ar}) = \sigma_i^2(a) + \sigma_i^2(r{:}a) + \sigma_i^2(e). \qquad (18)$$

Here, $\sigma_i^2(X_{ar})$ is the expected observed-score variance, $\sigma_i^2(a)$ is the variance due to aggregates, $\sigma_i^2(r{:}a)$ is the variance due to respondents nested within aggregates (i.e., the variance due to the sampling of respondents within aggregates), and $\sigma_i^2(e)$ is the variance due to random measurement error. (Note the parallel between this equation and equation (11).)

In step 5, for notational and conceptual convenience, we combine the $(r{:}a)$ component with the error term (e), with which it is completely confounded, into a single variance component $(r{:}a,e)$.[10] Then, we divide the variance components on the right-hand side of the equation for the observed-score variances (here, the right-hand side of equation (18)) by the number of times they are sampled. This generates the variance components for the observed *aggregate-level means* on variable i ($X_{ia.}$):

$$\sigma_i^2(\overline{X}_{a.}) = \sigma_i^2(a) + \sigma_i^2(r{:}a,e)/n_r, \qquad (19)$$

where n_r is the number of respondents on the ith variable. Here, this number is assumed to be equal for each aggregate; the case in which it is not equal for each aggregate is discussed later.[11]

---

[10]The $(r{:}a)$ and (e) components are confounded in this model, since each respondent answers only a single question about the aggregate. Therefore, the respondent component cannot be separated from the measurement error. Thus, we will use the symbol $(r{:}a,e)$ in our further discussions and similar notation in other designs in which this confounding occurs.

[11]The number of respondents on variable i in each aggregate could be labeled n_{iar}, but for notational simplicity we use n_r. This simplification is especially helpful when we examine the covariance between two variables below. When necessary, we will use more extended notation.

It is not surprising that as n_r increases, the contribution of the error term (variance in the aggregate-level means due to the random sampling of respondents and other sources of random error) to the variance of the aggregate-level means decreases and that this decrease is proportional to n_r, as is usual for the variance of means of randomly sampled observations (see, e.g., Hays 1981, p. 186).[12] These are the variance components of interest to us, since they are the variances associated with aggregate-level means.

In step 6 we solve (in this case, equation (19)) for the variance due to differences between aggregates:

$$\sigma_i^2(a) = \sigma_i^2(\overline{X}_{a.}) - \sigma_i^2(r{:}a,e)/n_r. \tag{20}$$

That is, the variance between the observed aggregate-level means $(\sigma_i^2(\overline{X}_{a.}))$ has been adjusted for variance in the observed means that is due to the variability of the ratings of aggregates by the respondents within aggregates and random measurement error.

The aggregate-level reliability coefficient may be derived by dividing the variance due to differences between aggregates by the expected observed-score variance of the aggregate-level means (see O'Brien 1990b), that is, by dividing the systematic variance between aggregates by the expected observed-score variance between aggregate-level means:[13]

$$E[\rho(\overline{X}_{ia.}\overline{X}'_{ia.})] = \frac{\sigma_i^2(a)}{\sigma_i^2(a) + \sigma_i^2(r{:}a,e)/n_r}, \tag{21}$$

where $E[\rho(\overline{X}_{ia.}\overline{X}'_{ia.})]$ represents the expected correlation between the aggregate-level means. If another random sample of respondents (elements), using the same design, were used to generate a new set of aggregate-level means, this is the expected value of the correlation between the two sets of means (see Cronbach et al. [1972, pp. 100–101] for this interpretation of the "generalizability coefficient" in an

[12]If we were interested in the expected variance of the grand mean (the mean across the n_r respondents and the n_a aggregates), this component would be divided by $(n_a)(n_r)$, and the variance due to aggregates would be divided by n_a.

[13]Note the parallel between equation (21) and equation (4), the classical test-score theory formula for the reliability: i.e., the systematic true-score variance divided by the sum of the true-score variance and the error variance (Lord and Novick 1968, p. 57). Note also that as the number of respondents increases, the reliability of the aggregate-level measure increases.

$R{:}A$ situation).[14] We will return shortly to the problem of finding estimates for these variance components.

4.2. Deriving the Covariance Between Aggregate-Level Variables

The covariance between $\overline{X}_{ia.}$ and $\overline{X}_{ja.}$ is derived in an analogous manner. In step 1 we write out the linear equation for the model (equation (17)), but this time we write it out once for variable X_{iar} and once for another variable, X_{jar}. In step 2 we subtract μ_i and μ_j from each side of the equations for X_{iar} and X_{jar}, respectively. In step 3 we multiply the left-hand sides of these equations by each other and the right-hand sides by each other, then take the expectations. In step 4 we eliminate those components with expectations of zero.

Across equations the covariance between the terms appearing on the right-hand sides of the equations for $(X_{iar} - \mu_i)$ and $(X_{jar} - \mu_j)$ are zero for all "noncorresponding" terms, e.g., between $(\mu_{ia} - \mu_i)$ and $(\mu_{jar} - \mu_{ja})$, $(\mu_{jar} - \mu_{ja})$ and e_{iar}, and $(\mu_{ia} - \mu_i)$ and e_{jar}. But the covariance between "corresponding" terms is not assumed to be zero, i.e., between $(\mu_{ia} - \mu_i)$ and $(\mu_{ja} - \mu_j)$, $(\mu_{iar} - \mu_{ia})$ and $(\mu_{jar} - \mu_{ja})$, and e_{iar} and e_{jar}. Again, random sampling is used to justify the assumption of zero covariances. For example, in the population the deviation of randomly sampled respondents from the mean of the aggregate on variable j $(\mu_{jar} - \mu_{ja})$ should not be related to the deviation of the same aggregate from the grand mean on variable i $(\mu_{ia} - \mu_i)$. There is good reason (under joint sampling), however, to expect that the covariance between corresponding terms is not zero. For example, we expect that (in the population) the covariance between individuals' scores on a test of math and verbal ability (in a school study) or between their responses to questions concerning centralization and management style (in a study of organizations) will not be zero. The covariance between errors of measurement for variables i and j

---

[14]Raters are assumed to be randomly sampled from an infinite population of raters, which is almost never a realistic assumption. Cornfield and Tukey (1956) address this problem. For example, we might ask if we can use a model that assumes random sampling from an infinite population when students are sampled from classrooms. This assumption is implicit in ANOVA procedures: That is, students are viewed as a sample of a larger population of potential members of particular classrooms. It is the reliability of the scores of these potential members of the aggregates that is of interest (Cornfield and Tukey 1956).

may arise from a number of sources. For example, the respondent may be in a particularly good mood or may be particularly perceptive on the day that the questions are asked, creating correlated errors across measures.

We are now ready for step 4, the elimination of the covariance components with expectations of zero. This results in an equation for the observed covariance between X_{iar} and X_{jar} in terms of various covariance components:

$$\sigma_{ij}(X_{ar}) = \sigma_{ij}(a) + \sigma_{ij}(r{:}a) + \sigma_{ij}(e), \qquad (22)$$

where $\sigma_{ij}(X_{ar})$ is the expected observed-score covariance between variables i and j, $\sigma_{ij}(a)$ is the covariance between the observed scores for i and j that is due to the covariance between the (population) means of the aggregates, $\sigma_{ij}(r{:}a)$ is the covariance between the observed scores for i and j that is due to covariance of the scores of randomly sampled respondents within aggregates, and $\sigma_{ij}(e)$ is the covariance between the observed scores for i and j that is due to the covariance of the measurement errors for i and j.

Since we are interested in the observed-score covariance at the aggregate level rather than at the individual level, step 5 divides each of the components on the right-hand side of the equation (here, equation (22)) by the number of times they are sampled. Here, n_{iar} (the number of respondents in an aggregate on variable i) equals n_{jar} (the number of respondents in an aggregate on variable j), since we are dealing with covariances that are computed from pairs of variables. For the present we consider the case in which the number of respondents in each aggregate is the same. Later we will examine the case of unequal numbers of respondents within aggregates. For now, we use n_r to represent the number of respondents ($n_r = n_{iar} = n_{jar}$). Thus, the expected observed-score covariance for the aggregate-level means is

$$\sigma_{ij}(\overline{X}_{a.}) = \sigma_{ij}(a) + \sigma_{ij}(r{:}a,e)/n_r. \qquad (23)$$

This formula indicates that as the number of respondents within aggregates increases, the relative contribution of the covariance within aggregates (which contains the covariance due to joint sampling) to the observed covariance between the aggregate-level scores decreases.

In step 6 we solve (in this case (23)) for the aggregate-level covariance, i.e., the covariance due to systematic differences between aggregates (the observed covariance corrected for covariance due to joint sampling):

$$\sigma_{ij}(a) = \sigma_{ij}(\overline{X}_{a.}) - \sigma_{ij}(r{:}a,e)/n_r. \tag{24}$$

4.3. Correcting Measures of Relationships Between Aggregate-Level Variables

We are now ready to estimate the relationships between aggregate-level means that have been corrected for the effects of random error variance and for joint sampling.

To estimate the correlation between aggregate-level scores once random measurement error and covariance due to joint sampling have been removed, we need to find an estimate for

$$\mathrm{E}[\rho_{ij}(a)] = \frac{\sigma_{ij}(a)}{\sqrt{\sigma_i^2(a)}\,\sqrt{\sigma_j^2(a)}}, \tag{25}$$

where E is the expectation operator and $\rho_{ij}(a)$ is the corrected population correlation between the aggregate-level variables (corrected for unreliability and for joint sampling).

Using the right-hand sides of equations (20) and (24) to provide the corresponding components in (25), we obtain the following equation for the corrected bivariate correlation coefficient:[15]

$$\mathrm{E}[\rho_{ij}(a)] = \frac{\sigma_{ij}(\overline{X}_{a.}) - \sigma_{ij}(r{:}a,e)/n_r}{\sqrt{\sigma_i^2(\overline{X}_{a.}) - \sigma_i^2(r{:}a,e)/n_r}\,\sqrt{\sigma_j^2(\overline{X}_{a.}) - \sigma_j^2(r{:}a,e)/n_r}}. \tag{26}$$

Note the parallel between equations (26) and (16). We can obtain an estimate of $\rho_{ij}(a)$ by substituting estimates for the variance and covariance components on the right-hand side of equation (26):[16]

---

[15]Although the estimates of variance components suggested in this paper are unbiased, the ratio of unbiased estimates is not itself an unbiased estimate, even though it is a consistent estimate of the ratio (Olkin and Pratt 1958; Lord and Novick 1968). Fortunately, the bias is not likely to be severe, especially if the number of elements on which each variance component is based is large. In the $R{:}A$ design, respondents are the only conditions of measurement, and n_r is the number of elements sampled. In other designs discussed in this paper, interviewers and questions are additional conditions of measurement, and each have their own separate variances.

[16]The accuracy of the estimates of the variance components described below depends not only on their own variances but also on the number of

TABLE 1
Expected Mean Squares for Four Designs

Observed Mean Square	Expected Mean Square
R:A design	
A	$\sigma_i^2(e) + n_r\,\sigma_i^2(a) + \sigma_i^2(r{:}a)$
R:A	$\sigma_i^2(e) + \sigma_i^2(r{:}a)$
R:K:A design	
A	$\sigma_i^2(e) + n_r n_k\,\sigma_i^2(a) + n_r\,\sigma_i^2(k{:}a) + \sigma_i^2(r{:}k{:}a)$
K:A	$\sigma_i^2(e) + n_r\,\sigma_i^2(k{:}a) + \sigma_i^2(r{:}k{:}a)$
R:K:A	$\sigma_i^2(e) + \sigma_i^2(r{:}k{:}a)$
A*R design	
A	$\sigma_i^2(e) + n_r\,\sigma_i^2(a) + \sigma_i^2(ar)$
R	$\sigma_i^2(e) + n_a\,\sigma_i^2(r) + \sigma_i^2(ar)$
A*R	$\sigma_i^2(e) + \sigma_i^2(ar)$
A*R*Q design	
A	$\sigma_i^2(e) + n_r n_q\,\sigma_i^2(a) + n_r\,\sigma_i^2(aq) + n_q\,\sigma_i^2(ar) + \sigma_i^2(aqr)$
Q	$\sigma_i^2(e) + n_a n_r\,\sigma_i^2(q) + n_r\,\sigma_i^2(aq) + n_a\,\sigma_i^2(qr) + \sigma_i^2(aqr)$
R	$\sigma_i^2(e) + n_a n_q\,\sigma_i^2(r) + n_q\,\sigma_i^2(ar) + n_a\,\sigma_i^2(qr) + \sigma_i^2(aqr)$
A*Q	$\sigma_i^2(e) + n_r\,\sigma_i^2(aq) + \sigma_i^2(aqr)$
A*R	$\sigma_i^2(e) + n_q\,\sigma_i^2(ar) + \sigma_i^2(aqr)$
Q*R	$\sigma_i^2(e) + n_a\,\sigma_i^2(qr) + \sigma_i^2(aqr)$
A*Q*R	$\sigma_i^2(e) + \sigma_i^2(aqr)$

Note. These formulas apply to the case in which the number of respondents or interviewers, or both, is the same for each aggregate.

$$\hat{\sigma}_i^2(X_{a.}) = \sum_a (X_{ia.} - X_{i..})^2/(n_a - 1),$$

$$\hat{\sigma}_{ij}(\overline{X}_{a.}) = \sum_a (\overline{X}_{ia.} - \overline{X}_{i..})(\overline{X}_{ja.} - \overline{X}_{j..})/(n_a - 1),$$

$$\hat{\sigma}_{ij}(r{:}a,e) = \sum_a \sum_r (X_{iar} - \overline{X}_{ia.})(X_{jar} - \overline{X}_{ja.})/[n_a(n_r - 1)].$$

Again, the situation in which n_r is not equal across aggregates is discussed later.

It is also possible to solve equation (25) in terms of the expected mean squares and the expected mean products that appear in Tables 1 and 2. For example, $\sigma_i^2(a)$ in (25) may be estimated using the

elements on which they are based. In this design the accuracy of the estimate of the $(r{:}a)$ variance component depends upon the number of respondents, and the accuracy of the (a) component depends upon the number of aggregates (Smith 1978, 1982). The same is true for the accuracy of the estimates of the covariance components.

TABLE 2
Expected Mean Products for Four Designs

Observed Mean Product	Expected Mean Product
$R{:}A$ design	
A	$\sigma_{ij}(e) + n_r\sigma_{ij}(a) + \sigma_{ij}(r{:}a)$
$R{:}A$	$\sigma_{ij}(e) + \sigma_{ij}(r{:}a)$
$R{:}K{:}A$ design	
A	$\sigma_{ij}(e) + n_r n_k \sigma_{ij}(a) + n_r \sigma_{ij}(k{:}a) + \sigma_{ij}(r{:}k{:}a)$
$K{:}A$	$\sigma_{ij}(e) + n_r \sigma_{ij}(k{:}a) + \sigma_{ij}(r{:}k{:}a)$
$R{:}K{:}A$	$\sigma_{ij}(e) + \sigma_{ij}(r{:}k{:}a)$
A^*R design	
A	$\sigma_{ij}(e) + n_r \sigma_{ij}(a) + \sigma_{ij}(ar)$
R	$\sigma_{ij}(e) + n_a \sigma_{ij}(r) + \sigma_{ij}(ar)$
A^*R	$\sigma_{ij}(e) + \sigma_{ij}(ar)$
A^*R^*Q design	
A	$\sigma_{ij}(e) + n_r n_q \sigma_{ij}(a) + n_r \sigma_{ij}(aq) + n_q \sigma_{ij}(ar) + \sigma_{ij}(arq)$
Q	$\sigma_{ij}(e) + n_a n_r \sigma_{ij}(q) + n_r \sigma_{ij}(aq) + n_a \sigma_{ij}(qr) + \sigma_{ij}(arq)$
R	$\sigma_{ij}(e) + n_a n_q \sigma_{ij}(r) + n_q \sigma_{ij}(ar) + n_a \sigma_{ij}(qr) + \sigma_{ij}(arq)$
A^*Q	$\sigma_{ij}(e) + n_r \sigma_{ij}(aq) + \sigma_{ij}(aqr)$
A^*R	$\sigma_{ij}(e) + n_q \sigma_{ij}(ar) + \sigma_{ij}(aqr)$
Q^*R	$\sigma_{ij}(e) + n_a \sigma_{ij}(qr) + \sigma_{ij}(aqr)$
A^*Q^*R	$\sigma_{ij}(e) + \sigma_{ij}(aqr)$

Note. These formulas apply to the case in which the number of respondents or interviewers, or both, is the same for each aggregate.

expected mean squares (MS) for the $R{:}A$ design in Table 1. Subtracting $MS_i(R{:}A)$ from $MS_i(A)$ and dividing by n_r yields

$$\hat{\sigma}_i^2(a) = [MS_i(A) - MS_i(R{:}A)]/n_r. \qquad (27)$$

The covariance in (25) may be estimated by using the expected mean products (MP) from the $R{:}A$ design from Table 2. Subtracting $MP_{ij}(R{:}A)$ from $MP_{ij}(A)$ and dividing by n_r yields

$$\hat{\sigma}_{ij}(a) = [MP_{ij}(A) - MP_{ij}(R{:}A)]/n_r. \qquad (28)$$

Substituting these mean squares and mean products into equation (25) and multiplying both the numerator and denominator by n_r provides an estimate of the aggregate-level correlation that has been corrected for both unreliability and for joint sampling:

$$\hat{\rho}_{ij}(a) = \frac{MP_{ij}(A) - MP_{ij}(R{:}A)}{\sqrt{MS_i(A) - MS_i(R{:}A)}\sqrt{MS_j(A) - MS_j(R{:}A)}}. \quad (29)$$

Formulas for computing mean squares appear in any standard analysis-of-variance text (e.g., Keppel 1982; Myers 1966), but formulas for calculating mean products do not. Such formulas are easy to derive by analogy to those for mean squares:

$$MS_i(A) = \sum_a n_r(\overline{X}_{ia.} - \overline{X}_{i..})^2/(n_a - 1),$$

$$MP_{ij}(A) = \sum_a n_r(\overline{X}_{ia.} - \overline{X}_{i..})(\overline{X}_{ja.} - \overline{X}_{j..})/(n_a - 1),$$

$$MS_i(R{:}A) = \sum_a \sum_r (X_{iar} - \overline{X}_{ia.})^2/[n_a(n_r - 1)],$$

$$MP_{ij}(R{:}A) = \sum_a \sum_r (X_{iar} - \overline{X}_{ia.})(X_{jar} - \overline{X}_{ja.})/[n_a(n_r - 1)].$$

Note that $MS_i(A) = n_r\hat{\sigma}_i^2(\overline{X}_a)$, $MP_{ij}(A) = n_r\hat{\sigma}_{ij}(\overline{X}_a)$, $MS_i(R{:}A) = \hat{\sigma}_i^2(r{:}a)$, and $MP_{ij}(R{:}A) = \hat{\sigma}_{ij}(r{:}a)$. We can make similar straightforward translations between mean squares and mean products and variance and covariance components for other designs.

Although equation (25) is written in terms of variances and covariances due to aggregates, it is instructive to reexpress it in terms of the correlation between aggregates (corrected for joint sampling) and the reliability of each of the aggregate-level variables. We can do this for equation (25) by dividing both the numerator and denominator by the square roots of $[\sigma_i^2(a) + \sigma_i^2(r{:}a,e)/n_r]$ and $[\sigma_j^2(a) + \sigma_j^2(r{:}a,e)/n_r]$. This converts the numerator into the correlation between the aggregate-level variables corrected for joint sampling, and it converts the two terms in the denominator to the square roots of the ratios of systematic aggregate-score variance to the expected observed-score variance, i.e., to the square roots of the reliabilities of these two variables (see equation (21)). For equation (29), this is the equivalent of dividing the numerator and denominator by the square roots of $MS_i(A)$ and $MS_j(A)$. The estimates in the denominator are then equivalent to the square roots of the estimates of aggregate-level reliability given by O'Brien (1990b).

This reexpression demonstrates that the corrected aggregate-level correlations derived using our procedure are corrected for unreliability and for joint sampling. Equation (29) is equivalent to the correction suggested by Kenny and La Voie (1985), although they do not seem to be aware that their coefficient corrects measures of relationship for unreliability.

Equations paralleling (25) and (29) can be derived for regression coefficients. For example, for i regressed on j, the corrected aggregate-level regression coefficient is

$$E[\beta_{ij}(a)] = \frac{\sigma_{ij}(a)}{\sigma_j^2(a)},\qquad(30)$$

where β_{ij} is the unstandardized regression coefficient of i regressed on j. Again, we can estimate this expected value by substituting estimates of the variance and covariance components into equation (30) or by using mean squares and mean products:

$$\hat{\beta}_{ij}(a) = \frac{MP_{ij}(A) - MP_{ij}(R{:}A)}{MS_j(A) - MS_j(R{:}A)}.\qquad(31)$$

Finally, we can apply the same procedure of substituting variance and covariance components to equation (21) to derive estimates of the aggregate-level reliability. Or we can estimate the reliability using mean squares:[17]

$$\hat{\rho}(\overline{X}_{ia}\overline{X}'_{ia}) = \frac{MS_i(A) - MS_i(R{:}A)}{MS_i(A)}.\qquad(32)$$

4.4 Unequal Numbers of Respondents Within Aggregates

In most sociological applications, the number of respondents in each of the aggregates will not be the same. In this situation, n_r in the equations above must be replaced with k_o, a constant derived for the expected value of the mean squares in cases in which number of respondents in each group may differ (see Snedecor 1946). The constant k_o equals $[1/(n_a - 1)][\sum_a n_{ra} - (\sum_a n_{ra}^2/\sum_a n_{ra})]$, where n_a is the number of aggregates and n_{ra} is the number of respondents in each aggregate, which can vary from aggregate to aggregate (see Snedecor 1946, p. 241). The summation is over aggregates. Fortunately, when we derive (29), (31), and (32), the k_o's divide out, leaving these estimates the same, whether the aggregate-level means are based on the same or different numbers of respondents.

Although the k_o's cancel each other out in these formulas, they

---

[17]Using Table 1 for the $R{:}A$ design, we can derive the denominator of (21) in terms of mean squares: $[MS_i(A) - MS_i(R{:}A)]/n_r - MS_i(R{:}A)/n_r$. In equation (27) we have already derived the term in the numerator: $[MS_i(A) - MS_i(R{:}A)]/n_r$. Multiplying both the numerator and denominator by n_r yields equation (32).

are needed if researchers want to estimate $\sigma_i^2(a)$, $\sigma_j^2(a)$, or $\sigma_{ij}(a)$. To estimate these components, the error components in (20) and (24) must be divided by k_o rather than by n_r. Further, the ratio n_{ra}/k_o, where n_{ra} is the number of respondents in the ath aggregate, is needed as a weighting factor in the computation of the values to substitute for $\hat{\sigma}_i^2(\overline{X}_{a.})$ and $\hat{\sigma}_{ij}(\overline{X}_{a.})$ in these two equations. Specifically, $[\Sigma(n_{ra}/k_o)(\overline{X}_{ia.} - X_{i..})^2]/(n_a - 1)$ is substituted for $\hat{\sigma}_i^2(\overline{X}_{a.})$, and $[\Sigma(n_{ra}/k_o)(\overline{X}_{ia.} - \overline{X}_{i..})(\overline{X}_{ja.} - \overline{X}_{j..})]/(n_a - 1)$ is substituted for $\hat{\sigma}_{ij}(\overline{X}_{a.})$. Then, when $\hat{\sigma}_i^2(r{:}a,e)/k_o$ and $\hat{\sigma}_{ij}(r{:}a{:}e)/k_o$ are subtracted (respectively) from these values, we get unbiased estimates of $\sigma_i^2(a)$ and $\sigma_{ij}(a)$.

When the number of respondents sampled from each aggregate is not the same, we must choose between pooled and unpooled estimates of $\sigma_i^2(r{:}a,e)$, which equals $MS_i(R{:}A)$. Cronbach et al. (1972, p. 208) note that most analysis-of-variance programs assume that the number of respondents sampled from each aggregate is the same or, if not the same, that the population variances for each aggregate are the same or uncorrelated with group size. Estimates of $\sigma_i^2(r{:}a,e)$ from such programs are called pooled estimates. If the n_{ra} are not all the same and none of these assumptions is tenable, $\sigma_i^2(r{:}a,e)$ should be estimated using the (unweighted) mean of the within-group variances (estimated variances of the respondents nested within aggregates calculated separately for each group). Estimates of $\sigma_i^2(r{:}a,e)$ based on this procedure are called unpooled estimates. Cronbach et al. (1972, p. 208) note that the pooled and unpooled estimates are not likely to differ greatly. The same procedures can be used to calculate an unpooled version of $MP_{ij}(R{:}A)$, i.e., using the unweighted mean of the within-group covariances that have been calculated separately for each group.

5. ANOTHER LEVEL OF NESTING: THE $R{:}K{:}A$ DESIGN

The approach outlined above can be extended to obtain correction equations for any level of nesting. For instance, respondents in each aggregate may be interviewed by interviewers of different sexes. For the example below, assume that a study involves respondents who are interviewed in different cities by interviewers who work only in that city. In such a study, respondents are nested within interviewers and interviewers are nested within cities. The notation for such a design is $R{:}K{:}A$, and the linear model for this design is

$$X_{iakr} = \mu_i + (\mu_{ia} - \mu_i) + (\mu_{iak} - \mu_{ia}) + (\mu_{iakr} - \mu_{iak}) + e_{iakr}. \qquad (33)$$

Most of these components are now recognizable from the discussion of the $R{:}A$ model above. Perhaps we should note that $(\mu_{iak} - \mu_{ia})$ is the interviewer effect, the deviation of the mean score for the kth interviewer from the mean score of the aggregate in which the interviews were conducted, and that $(\mu_{iakr} - \mu_{iak})$ is the respondent effect, the deviation of the rth respondent in the ath aggregate from the mean of the interviewer who conducted the interview with that respondent in the ath aggregate. Assume again that once we have subtracted μ_i from both sides of (33), the terms on the right-hand side of the equation are uncorrelated with other terms on the same side of the equation, i.e., that the component for aggregates $(\mu_{ia} - \mu_i)$ is uncorrelated with the component for interviewers $(\mu_{iak} - \mu_{ia})$, respondents $(\mu_{iakr} - \mu_{iak})$, and e_{iakr}; that the component for interviewers is uncorrelated with that for respondents and e_{iakr}; and that the component for respondents is uncorrelated with e_{iakr}. These assumptions are reasonable given that e_{iakr} is a random error term, that the other components are deviations from the grand mean, the aggregate's mean, and the interviewer's mean within the ath aggregate, and that the sampling of respondents and interviewers is random. Similarly, when we write out equation (33) for two different variables (i and j) and subtract μ_i and μ_j from both sides of the appropriate equations to derive the covariance components, we assume that "noncorresponding" terms are uncorrelated. We proceed as before, using the six steps for deriving both the variance and covariance components. Substituting these results into (25) provides an equation for the bivariate correlation corrected for both unreliability and for joint sampling:

$$E[\rho_{ij}(a)] = \frac{\sigma_{ij}(\overline{X}_{a..}) - \sigma_{ij}(k{:}a)/n_k - \sigma_{ij}(r{:}k{:}a,e)/n_k n_r}{\sqrt{\begin{array}{c}\sigma_i^2(\overline{X}_{a..}) - \sigma_i^2(k{:}a)/n_k \\ - \sigma_i^2(r{:}k{:}a,e)/n_k n_r\end{array}} \sqrt{\begin{array}{c}\sigma_j^2(\overline{X}_{a..}) - \sigma_j^2(k{:}a)/n_k \\ - \sigma_j^2(r{:}k{:}a,e)/n_k n_r\end{array}}} \cdot \quad (34)$$

These components can be estimated in a manner similar to that outlined above for the variance and covariance components in equation (26):

$$\hat{\sigma}_i^2(\overline{X}_{a..}) = \sum_a (\overline{X}_{ia..} - \overline{X}_{i...})^2/(n_a - 1),$$

$$\hat{\sigma}_i^2(k{:}a) = \sum_a \sum_k (\overline{X}_{iak.} - \overline{X}_{ia..})^2/n_a(n_k - 1),$$

$$\hat{\sigma}_{ij}(r{:}k{:}a) = \sum_a \sum_k \sum_r (X_{iakr} - \overline{X}_{iak.})(X_{jakr} - \overline{X}_{jak.})/n_a n_k(n_r - 1).$$

Again, the translation between variances and covariances and mean squares and mean products is straightforward:

$$MS_i(A) = n_k n_r \hat{\sigma}_i^2(\overline{X}_{a..}),$$
$$MS_i(K{:}A) = n_r \hat{\sigma}_i^2(k{:}a),$$
$$MP_{ij}(R{:}K{:}A) = \hat{\sigma}_{ij}(r{:}k{:}a).$$

Not surprisingly, the variance and covariance components in (25) may be solved in terms of the mean squares and mean products for the $R{:}K{:}A$ design in Tables 1 and 2. Then these estimates may be substituted into (25) and simplified by dividing both the numerator and denominator by $n_k n_r$. Equation (35) shows the results of following these steps:

$$\hat{\rho}_{ij}(a) - \frac{MP_{ij}(A) - MP_{ij}(K{:}A)}{\sqrt{MS_i(A) - MS_i(K{:}A)}\sqrt{MS_j(A) - MS_j(K{:}A)}}. \quad (35)$$

Using the same method and equation (30), we get the corrected aggregate-level regression coefficient of i on j:

$$\hat{\beta}_{ij}(a) = \frac{MP_{ij}(A) - MP_{ij}(K{:}A)}{MS_j(A) - MS_j(K{:}A)}. \quad (36)$$

The reliability of $\overline{X}_{ia..}$ is

$$\hat{\rho}(\overline{X}_{ia.}, \overline{X}'_{ia.}) = \frac{MS_i(A) - MS_i(K{\cdot}A)}{MS_i(A)}. \quad (37)$$

Again, if the number of respondents and the number of interviewers within each aggregate are not the same, then the weights given to the variance components for the expected mean squares in Tables 1 and 2 are incorrect. The correct weights are given in Snedecor (1946, p. 240). When we derive the estimates for (35), (36), and (37), however, these weights divide out, yielding the same results whether or not the numbers of interviewers or respondents within each aggregate are the same.

As with the $R{:}A$ design, if one is unwilling to make the assumptions outlined earlier, which justify the pooling of variance estimates, then the pooled estimates of $MS_i(K{:}A)$ and $MP_{ij}(K{:}A)$ cannot be used in (35), (36), or (37). Again, unpooled estimates can be used.

6. CROSSED DESIGNS

6.1. *The R∗A Design*

In the R^*A design each respondent rates each aggregate. That is, respondents (or raters) are crossed with aggregates. For example, an organizational researcher may ask "experts" to rate a series of organizations on their openness to innovation and on their degree of centralization in decision making. Or a set of respondents may rate the seriousness, harmfulness, and wrongfulness of a series of crimes (Warr 1989). Slovic, Fischhoff, and Lichtenstein (1985) used respondents to rate different activities and technologies in terms of variables such as dread, control over risks, and severity of consequences. In the first case, the organizations are the aggregates, in the second, crimes are the aggregates, and in the third, activities or technologies are the aggregates. Again, although we are using the responses of respondents as an example of elements that can be used to develop aggregate-level measures, we could use very different types of elements to develop such measures. For example, we could sample noise levels in work settings (each measure of the noise level would be an element) and calculate the average level of noise pollution in work settings as an aggregate-level measure of one aspect of an environment.

The derivations of the appropriate coefficients for this design parallel those for the nested designs, with two important differences. First, in this design, it is possible to measure the interaction between respondents and aggregates, since each respondent rates each aggregate. Second, since each respondent rates each aggregate, variability between respondents' ratings (main effects due to respondents) does not contribute to variability between the ratings of aggregates, but interactions between respondents and aggregates do add to the aggregate-level variability. The linear model for this design may be written as

$$X_{iar} = \mu_i + (\mu_{ia} - \mu_i) + (\mu_{ir} - \mu_i) + (\mu_{iar} - \mu_{ia} - \mu_{ir} + \mu_i) + e_{iar}, \quad (38)$$

where X_{iar} is the rth respondent's rating on the ith variable of the ath aggregate; μ_i (the grand mean on the ith variable) is the expected value of X_{iar} over all aggregates and raters; μ_{ia} (the aggregate mean on the ith variable) is the expected value of X_{iar} over all respondents; μ_{ir}

(the respondent mean on the ith variable) is the expected value of X_{iar} over all aggregates; and μ_{iar} is the expected value of X_{iar} (the expected value of the rth respondent's propensity distribution for the ath aggregate on the ith variable). The final term, e_{iar}, is a random-error variable with an assumed mean of zero (the deviation of the respondent's score from the expected value of the propensity distribution).

In step 2, we subtract μ_i and μ_j from both sides of equations for X_{iar} and X_{jar} derived from equation (38). Again, it is assumed that the components on the right-hand side of each equation are uncorrelated with other terms on the right-hand side of the equation. It is also assumed that noncorresponding terms are uncorrelated across the equations for two different variables ($X_{iar} - \mu_i$ and $X_{jar} - \mu_j$) constructed from equation (38). These assumptions are again justified on the basis of random sampling of the respondents who rate each of the aggregates.

Then, to decompose the observed-score variance, we square both sides of the equation for ($X_{iar} - \mu_i$), take expectations (step 3), and then eliminate the covariance components that are zero (step 4). We obtain the following decomposition in terms of variance components:

$$\sigma_i^2(X_{ar}) = \sigma_i^2(a) + \sigma_i^2(r) + \sigma_i^2(ar) + \sigma_i^2(e). \qquad (39)$$

To decompose the covariance between X_{iar} and X_{jar}, we multiply the equations resulting from step 2 above, take expectations, and eliminate the covariances that are zero. We obtain the following covariance components:

$$\sigma_{ij}(X_{ar}) = \sigma_{ij}(a) + \sigma_{ij}(r) + \sigma_{ij}(ar) + \sigma_{ij}(e). \qquad (40)$$

Again, we are interested in the variance and covariance components for the aggregate-level scores, so we divide the variance and covariance components by the number of times that they are sampled (step 5).[18] Here, since each aggregate is rated by the same respondents, the variability between raters does not contribute to the variability between aggregate-level means; thus, this component is eliminated from the variance and covariance between the aggregate-level means. *The main effect of any variable that crosses all aggregates*

---

[18]Since the (ar) and (e) components are confounded, we combine them, below, into a single component: (ar,e).

does not contribute to the variance or covariance between aggregates. Solving for the aggregate-level variance and covariance (step 6) yields

$$\sigma_i^2(a) = \sigma_i^2(\overline{X}_{a.}) - \sigma_i^2(ar,e)/n_r, \tag{41}$$

$$\sigma_{ij}(a) = \sigma_{ij}(\overline{X}_{a.}) - \sigma_{ij}(ar,e)/n_r. \tag{42}$$

To estimate the corrected correlation between the aggregate-level variables in the $R*A$ design, we substitute the right-hand sides of equations (41) and (42) for the corresponding variance and covariance components in equation (25). This yields

$$E[\rho_{ij}(a)] = \frac{\sigma_{ij}(\overline{X}_{a.}) - \sigma_{ij}(ar,e)/n_r}{\sqrt{\sigma_i^2(\overline{X}_{a.}) - \sigma_i^2(ar,e)/n_r}\ \sqrt{\sigma_j^2(\overline{X}_{a.}) - \sigma_j^2(ar,e)/n_r}}. \tag{43}$$

Deriving estimates for these variance and covariance components again is straightforward. For example,

$$\hat{\sigma}_{ij}(\overline{X}_{a.}) = \sum_a (\overline{X}_{ia.} - \overline{X}_{i..})(\overline{X}_{ja.} - \overline{X}_{j..})/(n_a - 1),$$

$$\hat{\sigma}_{ij}(ar,e) = \frac{\sum_a \sum_r (X_{iar} - \overline{X}_{ia.} - \overline{X}_{ir.} + \overline{X}_{i..})(X_{jar} - \overline{X}_{ja.} - \overline{X}_{jr.} + \overline{X}_{j..})}{(n_a - 1)(n_r - 1)}.$$

Again, Tables 1 and 2 (now for the $R*A$ design) can be used to solve for the variance and covariance components in equation (25) in terms of mean squares and mean products. When we divide both the numerator and denominator by n_r, we get

$$\hat{\rho}_{ij}(a) = \frac{MP_{ij}(A) - MP_{ij}(AR)}{\sqrt{MS_i(A) - MS_i(AR)}\ \sqrt{MS_j(A) - MS_j(AR)}}. \tag{44}$$

Similarly, the estimate for the corrected aggregate-level regression of i on j in terms of mean squares and mean products is

$$\hat{\beta}_{ij}(a) = \frac{MP_{ij}(A) - MP_{ij}(AR)}{MS_j(A) - MS_j(AR)}. \tag{45}$$

The reliability coefficient for $\overline{X}_{ia.}$ is calculated by dividing the variance due to systematic differences between aggregates by the expected observed-score variance for the aggregate-level means:

$$\hat{\rho}(\overline{X}_{ia.}\overline{X}'_{ia.}) = \frac{\hat{\sigma}_i^2(a)}{\hat{\sigma}_i^2(a) + \hat{\sigma}_i^2(ar,e)/n_r}. \tag{46}$$

This can also be expressed in terms of mean squares and mean products:

$$\hat{\rho}(\overline{X}_{ia}\overline{X}'_{ia}) = \frac{MS_i(A) - MS_i(AR)}{MS_i(A)}. \tag{47}$$

The mean square and mean product components are calculated in a straightforward way for designs in which each respondent rates each aggregate on each variable. Again, the formulas for the mean square components are found in any standard analysis-of-variance text (e.g., Myers 1966; Keppel 1982) and are easily extended to mean product components. For example, for the completely crossed design, R^*A,

$$MS_i(A) = [\textstyle\sum_a n_r(\overline{X}_{ia.} - \overline{X}_{i..})^2]/[n_a - 1)],$$

$$MP_{ij}(A) = [\textstyle\sum_a n_r(\overline{X}_{ia.} - \overline{X}_{i..})(\overline{X}_{ja.} - \overline{X}_{j..})]/[n_a - 1)],$$

$$MS_i(AR) = \textstyle\sum_a \sum_r (X_{iar} - \overline{X}_{ia.} - \overline{X}_{ir.} + \overline{X}_{i..})^2/[(n_a - 1)(n_r - 1)],$$

$$MP_{ij}(AR) = \frac{\sum_a \sum_r (X_{iar} - \overline{X}_{ia.} - \overline{X}_{ir.} + \overline{X}_{i..})(X_{jar} - \overline{X}_{ja.} - \overline{X}_{jr.} + \overline{X}_{j..})}{(n_a - 1)(n_r - 1)}.$$

Estimates of variance and covariance components based on the formulas presented earlier for the R^*A design or based on the mean square and mean product approach assume that each respondent rates each aggregate. Fortunately, in many social science applications, each respondent rates each of the aggregates. For example, each member of a research team may rate each of several organizations on centralization and formalization, and each of a series of respondents may rate the potential harm of a set of environmental hazards and people's control over their occurrence. But there are situations in which crossing is incomplete. For example, experts may rate only those organizations with which they are familiar.

When each respondent rates only some of the organizations, the estimation of variance components is problematic. Although variance components in such designs may be estimated using less-traditional approaches (e.g., the minimum variance quadratic unbiased estimation technique suggested by Hartley, Rao, and LaMotte [1978]), these procedures are not yet fully accepted.[19] Shavelson and

[19]This and several other techniques for estimating variance components in unbalanced designs are available in the VARCOMP procedure of SAS (Statistical Analysis System 1985). They may be applied to crossed and nested designs and to designs that combine both crossed and nested factors.

Webb (1981) compared results based on the Hartley et al. procedure with those based on the elimination of cases. They found that the results were quite similar but suggested that sampling to produce a balanced design "affords greater flexibility in choosing computational procedures" (p. 160). Brennan (1983, p. 111) notes that there is reason to be optimistic "as long as the unbalancing is with respect to nesting." Thus, in crossed designs, having raters who do not rate each aggregate creates problems for which there are no fully agreed-upon solutions. Fortunately, in most sociological applications these designs are more likely to be balanced than nested designs.

In many applications, when using crossed designs it may make sense to use only data that are balanced. For example, a researcher might use only data from these respondents who rated each of a set of environmental hazards on each of the items and discard those cases (in a listwise fashion) that have missing data for some of the hazards on some of the items. Obviously, such a decision depends on the number of cases that are eliminated by this procedure. When the design requires that different respondents rate only a portion of the hazards, *ad hoc* procedures need to be developed.

6.2. *The A*R*Q Design*

Imagine a case in which each rater rates each organization (or country or crime) using two four-item Likert scales (each four-item scale measuring a different variable). This design is called $A*R*Q$, since the questions (items) are crossed with each (appear with each) respondent and aggregate, and the respondents are crossed with each question and aggregate. Here, we discuss such a design to explicate the difference between fixed and random factors. The model for this design is

$$X_{iarq} = \mu_i + (\mu_{ia} - \mu_i) + (\mu_{ir} - \mu_i) + (\mu_{iq} - \mu_i) + (\mu_{iaq} - \mu_{ia} - \mu_{iq} + \mu_i)$$
$$+ (\mu_{iar} - \mu_{ia} - \mu_{ir} + \mu_i) + (\mu_{iqr} - \mu_{iq} - \mu_{ir} + \mu_i) \qquad (48)$$
$$+ (\mu_{iarq} - \mu_{iar} - \mu_{iaq} - \mu_{iqr} + \mu_{ia} + \mu_{ir} + \mu_{iq} - \mu_i) + e_{iarq},$$

where X_{iarq} is the rth respondent's response to the qth question on the ith variable for the ath aggregate. The same procedures that were used above can be applied to this design. First, to compute the covariance we create a second equation for variable X_{jarq}, where j is substituted for i in equation (48). Then we subtract the grand means for X_{iarq} and X_{jarq} from both sides of their respective equations and assume that all of the terms on the right-hand side of an equation are uncorrelated with one another and that the terms on the right-hand side of the equation for $(X_{iarq} - \mu_i)$ have a zero covariance with the noncorresponding terms on the right-hand side of the equation for $(X_{jarq} \times \mu_j)$. Further, we note that in this design, the same questions and the same raters are used to determine the aggregate-level score for each aggregate and, thus, that the variability between respondents, questions, and the interaction of respondents with questions do not contribute to the variability between the aggregate-level scores. Therefore, they are eliminated from the equations for the variance and covariance between aggregates. Interactions between raters and aggregates, questions and aggregates, and the third-order interaction among questions, raters, and aggregates do affect the variability between aggregates because they are different for different aggregates. We derive the variance and covariance as before, and at step 6 we get the following equations:

$$\sigma_i^2(a) = \sigma_i^2(\overline{X}_{a..}) - \sigma_i^2(ar)/n_r - \sigma_i^2(aq)/n_q - \sigma_i^2(arq,e)/n_r n_q, \quad (49)$$

$$\sigma_{ij}(a) = \sigma_{ij}(\overline{X}_{a..}) - \sigma_{ij}(ar)/n_r - \sigma_{ij}(aq)/n_q - \sigma_{ij}(arq,e)/n_r n_q. \quad (50)$$

We can substitute the right-hand sides of equations (49) and (50) for the corresponding terms in (25) and then use straightforward estimates for these variance and covariance components. Alternatively, we can use Tables 1 and 2 to find estimates of $\sigma_i^2(a)$, $\sigma_j^2(a)$, and $\sigma_{ij}(a)$ in terms of mean squares and mean products for the $A*R*Q$ design. Substituting these estimates into (25) and simplifying yields

$$\hat{\rho}_{ij}(a) = \frac{MP_{ij}(A) - MP_{ij}(AQ) - MP_{ij}(AR) + MP_{ij}(ARQ)}{\sqrt{\begin{array}{c}MS_i(A) - MS_i(AQ) \\ - MS_i(AR) + MS_i(ARQ)\end{array}}\sqrt{\begin{array}{c}MS_j(A) - MS_j(AQ) \\ - MS_j(AR) + MS_j(ARQ)\end{array}}}. \quad (51)$$

Similarly, solving equation (30) yields

$$\hat{\beta}_{ij}(A) = \frac{MP_{ij}(A) - MP_{ij}(AQ) - MP_{ij}(AR) + MP_{ij}(ARQ)}{MS_j(A) - MS_j(AQ) - MS_j(AR) + MS_j(ARQ)}. \quad (52)$$

The reliability of $\overline{X}_{ia..}$ is

$$\hat{\rho}(\overline{X}_{ia..}\,\overline{X}'_{ia..}) = \frac{MS_i(A) - MS_i(AQ) - MS_i(AR) + MS_i(ARQ)}{MS_i(A)}. \quad (53)$$

7. FIXED VERSUS RANDOM FACTORS

Although the distinction between fixed and random factors could be applied to some of the designs discussed earlier in this paper, this is the first design in which the distinction is likely to be used. The issue is the universe to which we want to generalize. In other words we might ask, Which corrected coefficient are we concerned with? Is it the coefficient of relationship between these two variables at the aggregate level for the same set of questions and a different set of respondents, or for the same set of respondents and a different set of questions, or for a different set of questions and a different set of respondents?[20]

When a factor, such as respondents or questions, is treated as fixed, the correction is for aggregate-level scores based on the same set of respondents or questions. The interaction variance component between the aggregate and the fixed factor contributes to the systematic (replicable) variance between the aggregate-level scores, and the interaction covariance component between the aggregate and the fixed factor contributes to the systematic (replicable) covariance between the aggregate-level scores. This occurs because these components are then part of the aggregate-level score, as defined—e.g., the aggregate-level correlation between these variables as measured with these items or the aggregate-level correlation between these variables as measured with these respondents.

When both factors, questions and respondents, are considered random, we want to estimate the following corrected correlation:

$$E[\rho_{ij}(a)] = \frac{\sigma_{ij}(a)}{\sqrt{\sigma_i^2(a)}\sqrt{\sigma_j^2(a)}} . \tag{54}$$

When questions are considered a fixed factor, this becomes

$$E[\rho_{ij}(a)] = \frac{\sigma_{ij}(a) + \sigma_{ij}(aq)/n_q}{\sqrt{\sigma_i^2(a)+\sigma_i^2(aq)/n_q}\sqrt{\sigma_j^2(a)+\sigma_j^2(aq)/n_q}} . \tag{55}$$

[20]The different set of questions must be drawn from a universe of similar questions, and the different set of raters must be drawn from a universe of similar raters. Some authors recommend that in general, items are best viewed as random (Cornfield and Tukey 1956; Hopkins 1984). They argue that researchers almost always want to generalize across both items and respondents. They ask, Do researchers ever want to generalize to the level of centralization in organizations as measured by a particular four-item scale, rather than to centralization as measured by these types of items?

Note that this equation includes the interaction of questions with aggregates as a source of systematic (replicable) variance and covariance for the aggregate-level scores. When questions are considered fixed (i.e., unchanging from replication to replication), any additional variance or covariance that they cause among the aggregates is replicable from replication to replication. Thus, these components need to be included in the corrected aggregate-level correlation coefficient. When respondents are treated as a fixed factor, the following formula is appropriate:

$$E[\rho_{ij}(a)] = \frac{\sigma_{ij}(a) + \sigma_{ij}(ar)/n_r}{\sqrt{\sigma_i^2(a) + \sigma_i^2(ar)/n_r}\,\sqrt{\sigma_j^2(a) + \sigma_j^2(ar)/n_r}}. \qquad (56)$$

Again, using the rationale from the preceding paragraph, we find that the aggregate-by-rater interaction components for covariance and variance are part of the systematic covariance and variance of the aggregates.

The variance and covariance components for (aq) or (ar) can be estimated directly and substituted into equations (55) or (56), or we can derive estimates of these corrected coefficients in terms of mean squares and mean products.

Combinations of mean squares and of mean products derived below provide estimates of both of the systematic (replicable) variance components in the denominator and both of the systematic covariance components in the numerator of (55). Table 2 for the A^*R^*Q design can be used to find $\sigma_{ij}(a) + \sigma_{ij}(aq)/n_q$ in equation (55) in terms of mean products, $[MP_{ij}(A) - MP_{ij}(AR)]/n_r n_q$, and Table 1 for the A^*R^*Q design can be used to find $\sigma_i^2(a) + \sigma_i^2(aq)/n_q$ in terms of mean squares, $[MS_i(A) - MS_i(AR)]/n_r n_q$.

Tables 3 and 4 contain these and similar estimates of the variance components in the denominators and the covariance components in the numerators of the corrected coefficients for all of the designs discussed in this paper. Using these tables, we can easily find the appropriate estimates of the systematic covariance components for the numerator (always from Table 4) and the systematic variance components for the denominator (always from Table 3) for the corrected aggregate-level regression and correlation coefficients for any combination of fixed or random effects for the designs discussed in

TABLE 3

Formulas for Calculating the Corrected Systematic (Replicable) Aggregate-
Level Variance Components of Four Common Designs

Factors	Design
Respondents nested within aggregates: $R{:}A$	
(R^r)	$[MS_i(A) - MS_i(R{:}A)]/n_r$
(R^f)	Need replications for raters
Respondents nested within interviewers nested within aggregates: $R{:}K{:}A$	
$(R^r$ and $K^r)$	$[MS_i(A) - MS_i(K{:}A)]/n_r n_k$
$(R^r$ and $K^f)$	$[MS_i(A) - MS_i(R{:}K{:}A)]/n_r n_k$
$(R^f$ and $K^r)$	Need replications for raters
$(R^f$ and $K^f)$	Need replications for raters
Respondents by aggregates: $R{*}A$	
(R^r)	$[MS_i(A) - MS_i(AR)]/n_r$
(R^f)	Need replications for raters
Aggregates by respondents by questions: $A{*}R{*}Q$	
$(R^r$ and $Q^r)$	$[MS_i(A) - MS_i(AQ) - MS_i(AR) + MS_i(ARQ)]/n_r n_q$
$(R^r$ and $Q^f)$	$[MS_i(A) - MS_i(AR)]/n_r n_q$
$(R^f$ and $Q^r)$	$[MS_i(A) - MS_i(AQ)]/n_r n_q$
$(R^f$ and $Q^f)$	Need replications for raters

Note. The superscript r denotes a random effect, and the superscript f denotes a
fixed effect.

this paper. In several cases, however, we cannot estimate the coefficients when raters are considered fixed.[21]

For example, to estimate equation (55), in which questions are
considered fixed and respondents are random, look up the components of the $A{*}R{*}Q$ design for random respondents (R^r) and fixed
questions (Q^f) in Tables 3 and 4, substitute them for the components
in the numerator and denominator of (55), and simplify:

[21]For example, in the $R{*}A$ design with respondents considered fixed
from replication to replication, the equation for the reliability of variable 1
should be $[\sigma_i^2(a) + \sigma_i^2(ar)/n_r]$, which is the systematic or replicable variance
divided by the expected observed-score variance, which is $[\sigma_i^2(a) + \sigma_i^2(ar,e)/n_r]$.
The problem is that the variances for the (ar) and the (e) component are completely confounded, so that the correct component for the numerator cannot be
estimated. When respondents are considered random, the variance due to respondents *and* error should be removed from the numerator, and this component can be estimated. Since the correct components for fixed respondents could
be estimated if multiple measures were available for each respondent, we note
that several designs in Tables 3 and 4 need replications for raters.

$$\hat{\rho}_{ij}(a) = \frac{MP_{ij}(A) - MP_{ij}(AR)}{\sqrt{MS_i(A) - MS_i(AR)} \sqrt{MS_j(A) - MS_j(AR)}}. \quad (57)$$

Since the denominator for the reliability coefficient is always the expected observed aggregate-score variance for the design, i.e., for the $A*R*Q$ design with n_r respondents and n_q questions, the expected observed-score variance for the aggregate-level variable is $\sigma_i^2(a) + \sigma_i^2(aq)/n_q + \sigma_i^2(ar)/n_r + \sigma_i^2(aqr)/n_r n_q$, which is estimated from Table 1 for the $A*R*Q$ design as $MS_i(A)/n_r n_q$. We can estimate the reliability as the systematic variance for the design divided by the expected observed-score variance. Placing the appropriate systematic variance for the $A*R*Q$ design with random respondents and fixed questions into the numerator and the expected observed-score variance into the denominator and simplifying yields

$$\hat{\rho}(\overline{X}_{ia.}, \overline{X}'_{ia.}) = \frac{MS_i(A) - MS_i(AR)}{MS_i(A)}. \quad (58)$$

TABLE 4

Formulas for Calculating the Corrected Systematic (Replicable) Covariance Components Between Aggregate-Level Variables for Four Common Designs

Factors	Design
Respondents nested within aggregates: $R:A$	
(R^r)	$[MP_{ij}(A) - MP_{ij}(R:A)]/n_r$
(R^f)	Need replications for raters
Respondents nested within interviewers nested within aggregates: $R:K:A$	
$(R^r$ and $K^r)$	$[MP_{ij}(A) - MP_{ij}(K:A)]/n_r n_k$
$(R^r$ and $K^f)$	$[MP_{ij}(A) - MP_{ij}(R:K:A)]/n_r n_k$
$(R^f$ and $K^r)$	Need replications for raters
$(R^f$ and $K^f)$	Need replications for raters
Respondents by aggregates: $R*A$	
(R^r)	$[MP_{ij}(A) - MP_{ij}(AR)]/n_r$
(R^f)	Need replications for raters
Aggregates by respondents by questions: $A*R*Q$	
$(R^r$ and $Q^r)$	$[MP_{ij}(A) - MP_{ij}(AQ) - MP_{ij}(AR) + MP_{ij}(ARQ)]/n_r n_q$
$(R^r$ and $Q^f)$	$[MP_{ij}(A) - MP_{ij}(AR)]/n_r n_q$
$(R^f$ and $Q^r)$	$[MP_{ij}(A) - MP_{ij}(AQ)]/n_r n_q$
$(R^f$ and $Q^f)$	Need replications for raters

Note. The superscript r denotes a random effect, and the superscript f denotes a fixed effect.

Using Tables 3 and 4, researchers can derive estimates of the reliability of aggregate-level means and of corrected correlation and regression coefficients for the relationship between aggregate-level variables for any of the designs discussed in this paper.

8. SOME EMPIRICAL EXAMPLES

We apply the $R{:}A$ design to the High School and Beyond (HSB) study (NORC 1980), in which students were interviewed within schools, and examine relationships at the school level. Particularly important is the large number of aggregates (schools) sampled, which means that the reliability estimates and the corrected coefficients of relationship are likely to have little sampling error.

The HSB study used two-stage sampling. In the first stage, schools were selected: 1,122 schools were selected, 735 of which were public schools. In the second stage, students within schools were selected. A random sample of 36 seniors and 36 sophomores were selected from each school. In schools with fewer than 36 seniors or 36 sophomores, all eligible students at these levels were included.

The first analysis uses data from sophomores in the total sample of 1,122 schools. To appear in the analysis, a school needed the responses of ten or more sophomores to the specific question on which the aggregate-level variable was based. Table 5 presents the reliability estimates for 16 different aggregate-level variables (see O'Brien and Jones 1986).[22]

The school-level variables in Table 5 fall into five broad categories. Variables 1–3 measure the average SES of the families of the students, 4–8 measure average achievement levels of the students, 9 and 10 measure (respectively) the percentage of students with mothers in the home and the percentage of students with fathers in the home, 11 and 12 measure the perceived quality of the school's libraries and the school's instruction, and 13–16 measure the extent of specific behavioral problems at the schools.[23] The first column of Table 5

---

[22]O'Brien and Jones (1986) also correct aggregate-level correlation coefficients for unreliability. They fail, however, to correct these coefficients for respondent-induced covariance components due to joint sampling.

[23]Details of the coding of these variables can be found in O'Brien and Jones (1986).

TABLE 5
Aggregate-Level Reliability Estimates for 16 School-Level Variables

	Reliability		N of
	Unpooled	Pooled	Schools
1. Mother's education	.803	.806	951
2. Father's education	.842	.844	901
3. Family income	.806	.808	959
4. Vocabulary	.882	.882	940
5. Reading	.823	.821	939
6. Math 1	.869	.868	941
7. Math 2	.813	.813	935
8. Writing	.838	.838	924
9. Percentage of mothers present	.268	.281	979
10. Percentage of fathers present	.668	.672	979
11. Percentage rating library good	.800	.801	974
12. Percentage rating instruction good	.739	.743	959
13. Percentage citing attendance problem	.795	.796	978
14. Percentage citing cutting problem	.894	.893	979
15. Percentage citing obeying problem	.632	.634	977
16. Percentage citing fighting problem	.735	.737	978

Source. NORC 1980.

contains the names of the variables, the second contains estimates of the aggregate-level reliability based on the unpooled estimates of $MS_i(R{:}A)$, the third contains estimates of the reliability based on the pooled estimate of $MS_i(R{:}A)$, and the final column lists the numbers of schools (aggregates) on which these estimates are based. The reliability estimates are based on equation (32). As noted by Cronbach et al. (1972, p. 208), the reliability coefficients based on pooled and unpooled estimates are "unlikely to differ appreciably."

As expected, the pooled and unpooled estimates of the reliability do not differ greatly (never by more than .004). The reliability of these aggregate-level variables is also generally quite high. The reliabilities of the three measures of family SES are in excess of .80, as are the reliabilities of all of the achievement variables. Only in the case of the percentage of students with mothers in the home is the aggregate-level reliability (.268 or .281) clearly deficient. The reliability of these variables depends upon the variability of the means (or percentages) between aggregates (the greater the variability, the greater the reliability), the homogeneity of variance within aggregates (the greater the homogeneity, the greater the reliability), and the number of students sampled within each school (the larger the number sampled, the greater the reliability). O'Brien and Jones (1986, p. 24) speculate that the low aggregate-level reliability coefficient for the percentage of mothers in the home is due to a ceiling effect. Since 92 percent of the mothers are present in the home for the total sample of students, there is less opportunity for this variable to differ between schools than, for example, the father-present variable (75 percent of the fathers are present in the home).

In the second analysis, the HSB data are revisited. This time data from the 735 schools in the public school sample are used to generate detailed results for four variables selected from the HSB study. One of these indicates whether the student's mother is in the home, another indicates whether the student's father is in the home, a third indicates respondents' ratings of the extent to which students in their school obey instructions from teachers, and a fourth indicates students' ratings of how their school friends feel about students who get good grades (a high score indicating that they feel positive toward such students). In this analysis, ten or more sophomores from a school must have answered all four questions for the school to be included in the analysis (720 of 735 schools met this criterion).

Table 6 presents results from the analysis of these four variables. The pooled and unpooled reliability estimates in Table 6 are very similar; they never differ by more than .01. The reliabilities of the school-level obedience scores (.61 for the pooled version) and of the estimate of the percentage of students from homes in which the father is present (.63) are reasonably high, but the reliabilities of the estimate of the percentage of students from homes in which the mother is present (.28) and the estimate of the popularity of students who get good grades (.33) are quite low.

It is clear that the corrections suggested in this paper make a substantial difference in the correlations among the four variables.[24]

[24]The correlations in Table 6 are based on pooled estimates of $MS_i(R:A)$ and on pooled estimates of $MP_i(R:A)$. Basing the corrected correlations on unpooled estimates of these quantities does not change any of the corrected correlations in Table 6 by more than plus or minus .01.

TABLE 6

Reliability Estimates and Corrected and Observed Correlations for Four Aggregate-Level Variables

	Father Present	Mother Present	Obey Instructions	Popularity of Good Students	Reliabilities	
					Pooled	Unpooled
Father present	1.00	.72	.31	.29	.63	.62
Mother present	.55	1.00	.10	.26	.28	.27
Obey instructions	.20	.05	1.00	.35	.61	.61
Popularity of good students	.12	.07	.18	1.00	.33	.33

Source. NORC 1980.

Note. The entries below the main diagonal are the observed correlations between the aggregate-level variables. The entries above the main diagonal are the corrected correlations between the aggregate-level variables.

For example, at the school level, the observed correlation (below the main diagonal) between the measures of the extent to which students obey teachers and the popularity of students who get good grades is .18, and the corrected correlation (above the diagonal) is .35. Most of this increase is due to the low reliability of the measure of the popularity of students who get good grades (.33 for the pooled estimate). Correcting the correlation for the relationship between the proportion of students whose father is in the home and the extent to which students obey teachers is less dramatic, though substantial: The observed correlation is .20, and the corrected correlation is .31.[25]

I am currently working with data that are appropriate for the R^*A design. They were collected from 42 respondents who rated a series of 97 activities, substances, and technologies, e.g., home gas furnaces, surgery, caffeine, steroids, nuclear power, and water flouridation. These 97 activities, substances, and technologies are the aggregates, since their scores are based on the weighted average of the respondents' scores. These aggregates are rated on variables such as voluntariness of risk, immediacy of effect, extent to which the risks are known to science, and dread.[26]

The reliabilities of the aggregate-level measures of the 18 variables range from .77, for the extent to which the risks are known to science, to .98, for the extent to which the risk is dreaded. All of the variables are reasonably reliable at the aggregate level, so the observed and corrected correlations do not differ dramatically. For example, one of the largest differences is in the correlation between the extent to which the risks are known to science and the extent to which the process is observable if something goes wrong: The observed correlation is $-.55$, and the corrected correlation is $-.63$.

[25]Most of the difference between the observed and corrected correlations for these four aggregate-level variables is due to corrections for unreliability. For example, correcting only for joint sampling—i.e., using $[MP_{ij}(A) - MP_{ij}(R:A)]/[\sqrt{MS_i(A)} \sqrt{MS_j(A)}]$ rather than equation (29)—results in corrected correlations of .30 between mother present and father present, .19 between father present and obeying teachers, .13 between father present and popularity of students who get good grades, .04 between mother present and obeying teachers, .08 between mother present and popularity of students who get good grades, and .16 between obeying teachers and popularity of students who get good grades.

[26]These data were made available by Paul Slovic, Department of Psychology, University of Oregon.

9. CONCLUSIONS

This paper has focused on aggregate-level variables, i.e., on variables that are designed to measure a characteristic of cases and that are based on a weighted sum of the characteristics of single elements. The weighted sum that we have examined are means (which, of course, include rates, proportions, and percentages).

The methodology we have described addresses two major challenges faced by those analyzing aggregate-level variables: (1) estimating the reliability of aggregate-level measures and (2) estimating the covariance components that arise from joint sampling, i.e., from the covariance between aggregates when the same raters or respondents rate aggregates on a series of variables. We have demonstrated how measures of relationship between aggregate-level variables can be corrected for both joint sampling and for unreliability. Finally, we have discussed how to conceptualize certain factors as fixed or random and how these conceptualizations affect both estimates of reliability and the corrected coefficients of relationship.

There are problems with the approach that need to be mentioned. For example, although it is possible to build confidence intervals around the aggregate-level reliability coefficients discussed in this paper (O'Brien 1990a), there is no easy way to build confidence intervals around the corrected correlation and regression coefficients. Some work using the delta method in similar circumstances is relevant (Hakstian, Schroeder, and Rogers 1988), but it needs to be extended to the coefficients derived in this paper. Since the variance and covariance components are estimates, they can "go out of range." For example, we can estimate a negative variance component for $\sigma_i^2(a)$ from equation (20) or a correlation greater than one (or less than minus one) from equation (26). These results are less likely when the samples are large: e.g., large samples of respondents in each organization and large numbers of organizations in a study. Finally, software for conducting these analyses is not widely available. The author has written some Fortran programs (which are available upon request). They were used to analyze the data reported in the previous section.

Despite these problems the corrections outlined in this paper are important and *should* be used by those who analyze aggregate-level variables of the type described here. They do not require additional data collection, and they can make a substantial difference in the conclusions that are drawn from a study. There is no excuse for using coefficients that, because of joint sampling and unreliability, provide poor estimates of the aggregate-level relationships.

REFERENCES

Aiken, Michael, and Jerald Hage. 1968. "Organizational Interdependence and Intra-Organizational Structure." *American Sociological Review* 33:912–30.

Bogardus, Emory S. 1959. *Social Distance.* Yellow Springs, OH: Antioch University Press.

Bohrnstedt, George W. 1970. "Reliability and Validity in Attitude Measurement." Pp. 80–99 in *Attitude Measurement,* edited by G. F. Summers. Chicago: Rand McNally.

Brennan, Robert L. 1983. *Elements of Generalizability Theory.* Iowa City: American Testing Program.

Cornfield, Jerome, and John W. Tukey. 1956. "Average Values of Mean Squares in Factorials." *Annals of Mathematical Statistics* 27:907–49.

Cronbach, Lee J., Goldine C. Gleser, Harinder Nanda, and Nageswari Rajaratnam. 1972. *The Dependability of Behavioral Measurement: Theory of Generalizability for Score Profiles.* New York: Wiley.

Hakstian, Ralph A., Marsha L. Schroeder, and W. Todd Rogers. 1988. "Inferential Procedures for Correlation Coefficients Corrected for Attenuation." *Psychometrika* 53:27–43.

Hartley, H. O., J. N. K. Rao, and Lynn LaMotte. 1978. "A Simple Synthesis-Based Method of Variance Component Estimation." *Biometrics* 34:233–42.

Hays, William L. 1981. *Statistics.* 3d ed. New York: Holt, Rinehart and Winston.

Hopkins, Kenneth D. 1984. "Generalizability Theory and Experimental Design: Incongruity Between Analysis and Inference." *American Educational Research Journal* 21:703–12.

Kahn, Joan R., and William M. Mason. 1987. "Political Alienation, Cohort Size, and the Easterlin Hypothesis." *American Sociological Review* 52:155–69.

Kenny, David A., and Lawrence La Voie. 1985. "Separating Individual and Group Effects." *Journal of Personality and Social Psychology* 48:339–48.

Keppel, Geoffrey. 1982. *Design and Analysis: A Researcher's Handbook.* 2d ed. Englewood Cliffs, NJ: Prentice-Hall.

Lazarsfeld, Paul F., and Herbert Menzel. 1969. "On the Relationship Between Individual and Collective Properties." Pp. 499–510 in *A Sociological Reader on Complex Organizations,* edited by Amitai Etzioni. New York: Holt, Rinehart and Winston.

Longshore, Douglas. 1982. "Race Composition and White Hostility: A Research Note on the Problem of Control in Desegregated Schools." *Social Forces* 61:73–78.

Lord, Frederick M., and Melvin R. Novick. 1968. *Statistical Theories of Mental Test Scores.* Reading, MA: Addison-Wesley.

McClelland, David C. 1961. *The Achieving Society.* New York: Free Press.

Myers, Jerome L. 1966. *Fundamentals of Experimental Design.* Boston: Allyn and Bacon.

NORC. 1980. *High School and Beyond Information For Users Base Year (1980) Data: Version 1.* Chicago: NORC.

O'Brien, Robert M. 1990*a*. "Confidence Intervals for Generalizability Coefficients." Unpublished Manuscript.

――――. 1990*b*. "Estimating the Reliability of Aggregate-Level Variables Based on Individual-Level Characteristics." *Sociological Methods and Research* 18:473–504.

O'Brien, Robert M., and Barnie Jones. 1986. "The Reliability of School-Level Aggregate Variables: An Application of Generalizability Theory." *Journal of Research and Development in Education* 20:21–27.

Olkin, I., and V. W. Pratt. 1958. "Unbiased Estimation of Certain Correlation Coefficients." *Annals of Mathematical Statistics* 29:201–11.

Shavelson, Richard J., and Noreen M. Webb. 1981. "Generalizability Theory: 1973–80." *British Journal of Mathematical and Statistical Psychology* 34. 133–66.

Siegel, Paul M. 1971. "Prestige in the American Occupational Structure." Ph.D. diss., University of Chicago.

Slovic, Paul, Baruch Fischhoff, and Sarah Lichtenstein. 1985. Pp. 91–125 in *Perilous Progress: Managing the Hazards of Technology,* edited by R. Kates, C. Hohenemser, and J. Kasperson. Boulder: Westview Press.

Smith, Phillip L. 1978. "Sampling Errors of Variance Components in Small Sample Generalizability Studies." *Journal of Educational Statistics* 3:319–46.

――――. 1982. "A Confidence Interval Approach for Variance Component Estimates in the Context of Generalizability Theory." *Educational and Psychological Measurement* 42:459–66.

Snedecor, George W. 1946. *Statistical Methods: Applied to Experiments in Agriculture and Biology.* Ames, IA: Iowa State College Press.

Spearman, C. 1910. "Correlation Calculated from Faulty Data." *British Journal of Psychology* 3:271–95.

Statistical Analysis System. 1985. *SAS User's Guide: Statistics, Version 5 Edition.* Cary, NC: SAS Institute.

Warr, Mark. 1989. "What Is the Perceived Seriousness of Crimes?" *Criminology* 27:795–821.

6

STATISTICAL POWER IN NONRECURSIVE LINEAR MODELS

*William T. Bielby**
Ross L. Matsueda[†]

In nonrecursive models, estimates of simultaneous relationships are often subject to high sampling variability. In this paper, we apply classical procedures for computing statistical power to the issue of sampling variability in estimates of reciprocal causal effects. Using a model of married women's attitudes regarding work and family size as an example, we show how the power to detect nonrecursive relationships depends on the model's parametric structure. Specifically, we show how the power of statistical tests depends on the strength of instrumental variables, the number of overidentifying restrictions, and the covariation among disturbances. We conclude by discussing the implications of our results for applications of nonrecursive models in the social sciences.

1. INTRODUCTION

Social scientists are often interested in estimating reciprocal causal relationships among variables measured contemporaneously.

An earlier version of this paper was presented at the 1987 Annual Meetings of the American Sociological Association, Chicago. This research was supported in part by the Academic Senate of the University of California, Santa Barbara, and the Graduate School of the University of Wisconsin—Madison.
*University of California, Santa Barbara
[†]University of Wisconsin, Madison

167

For example, economists attempt to estimate simultaneous relationships among sets of supply-and-demand equations (Liu 1963), sociologists seek to disentangle the reciprocal influence of one peer on
another (Duncan, Haller, and Portes 1968), and demographers try to
determine whether childbearing determines labor force participation, or vice versa (Waite and Stolzenberg 1976; Smith-Lovin and
Tickamyer 1978; Cramer 1980). In principle, such reciprocal effects
can be routinely estimated using nonrecursive estimators such as
two-stage least squares (2SLS), three-stage least squares (3SLS), and
maximum likelihood (ML). In practice, however, researchers often
find that nonrecursive models provide estimates of simultaneous relationships that are subject to high sampling variability, making it difficult to rule out chance in drawing inferences. Thus, researchers are
unable to draw definitive conclusions about crucial relationships.

In single-equation linear models and in recursive multiple-
equation models, the problem of high sampling variability typically
arises because of multicollinearity or small sample size. However,
sampling variability can be a more serious problem in nonrecursive
models. Even with relatively large samples and exogenous variables
that are only modestly correlated, estimates of relationships among
endogenous variables can be quite unstable; i.e., they can have
large amounts of sampling variability. The problem, sometimes
called weak empirical identification or poor instrumental variables,
is usually handled informally, using rules of thumb and *ad hoc*
indexes. In this paper, we argue that the problem can be viewed as
one of statistical power and can be addressed by classical methods
for protecting against type II error, the error of failing to reject a
false null hypothesis.

We proceed in four steps. First, we review estimation and
testing within nonrecursive models and provide an intuitive explanation of the problem of high sampling variability in estimates of reciprocal effects. We focus on full-information estimation, using 3SLS to
present analytical results. Second, we show how statistical power can
be calculated using a power function for a test of general linear
constraints. Third, we present calculations that show how the power
to detect nonrecursive relationships depends on the parametric structure of the model. As an example, we use a model of married
women's attitudes regarding work and family size. We conclude by

discussing the implications of our results for applications of nonrecursive models in the social sciences.

2. NONRECURSIVE MODELS: ESTIMATION

To set up the analyses presented below, we first briefly review estimation of nonrecursive models by the method of 3SLS. We focus on 3SLS for three reasons. First, power is a function of the estimator's asymptotic covariance matrix, and for the 3SLS estimator, that matrix can be expressed in terms of moments among exogenous and endogenous variables. Since moments can be expressed in terms of parameters of the model, 3SLS estimation allows us to explore how parametric structure influences power. Second, the asymptotic covariance matrix for the 3SLS estimator is identical to that for the full-information maximum likelihood (FIML) estimator (Theil 1971, p. 526); therefore, all of our results apply to nonrecursive models estimated by FIML methods.[1] Third, conceptualizing estimation as a three-stage process provides insights into the sources of sampling variability that are not as apparent when estimation is approached from the principle of maximum likelihood.

Consider the following system of simultaneous equations:

$$\mathbf{y}_i = \mathbf{B}\mathbf{y}_i + \mathbf{\Gamma}\mathbf{x}_i + \mathbf{\epsilon}_i, \tag{1}$$

where $\mathbf{y}_i$ is a vector consisting of the ith observation on p jointly determined endogenous variables, $\mathbf{x}_i$ is the ith observation on g exogenous variables, $\mathbf{\epsilon}_i$ is a vector of disturbances for the p equations, and $\mathbf{B}$ and $\mathbf{\Gamma}$ are coefficient matrices of order $p \times p$ and $p \times g$, respectively. The model assumes that $E(\mathbf{\epsilon}_i) = \mathbf{0}$, $E(\mathbf{x}_i\mathbf{\epsilon}_i') = \mathbf{0}$, and $E(\mathbf{\epsilon}_i\mathbf{\epsilon}_i') = \mathbf{\Sigma}$. We assume that formal conditions for identification hold in all models discussed below (Theil 1971, pp. 489–95). In addition, we assume that the structural disturbances are multinormally distributed.

---

[1]The equivalence of FIML and 3SLS holds only for simultaneous equation models in observable variables and not for the more general covariance structure model with latent variables. In general, the FIML asymptotic covariance matrix cannot be expressed directly in terms of observable moments. Thus, the relationship between power and parametric structure in such models cannot be explored with closed expressions relating asymptotic covariances to observable moments and parametric structure (see Matsueda and Bielby 1986 for details).

For the jth equation in the set of p equations, all n observations can be represented as

$$\mathbf{y}_j = \mathbf{Y}_j\boldsymbol{\beta}_j + \mathbf{X}_j\boldsymbol{\gamma}_j + \boldsymbol{\epsilon}_j \tag{2}$$

or as

$$\mathbf{y}_j = \mathbf{Z}_j\boldsymbol{\delta}_j + \boldsymbol{\epsilon}_j, \tag{3}$$

where $\mathbf{Z}_j = [\mathbf{Y}_j\,\mathbf{X}_j]$ and $\boldsymbol{\delta}_j' = [\boldsymbol{\beta}_j'\,\boldsymbol{\gamma}_j']$. In these expressions, $\mathbf{y}_j$ is an $n \times 1$ vector of observations of the jth dependent variable; $\mathbf{Y}_j$ is an $n \times p_j$ matrix of observations of the p_j endogenous variables in equation j; $\mathbf{X}_j$ is an $n \times g_j$ matrix of observations of the g_j exogenous variables in the equation; and $\boldsymbol{\beta}_j$ and $\boldsymbol{\gamma}_j$ are coefficient vectors of order $p_j \times 1$ and $g_j \times 1$, respectively. Given the disturbance specification for the system, it follows that $E(\boldsymbol{\epsilon}_j) = \mathbf{0}$, $E(\mathbf{X}'\boldsymbol{\epsilon}_j) = \mathbf{0}$, and $E(\boldsymbol{\epsilon}_j\boldsymbol{\epsilon}_j') = \sigma_{jj}\mathbf{I}$.

Given expression (3), the p structural equations for all n observations combined can be expressed as

$$\mathbf{y} = \mathbf{Z}\boldsymbol{\delta} + \boldsymbol{\epsilon}, \tag{4}$$

where

$$\mathbf{y} = \begin{bmatrix} \mathbf{y}_1 \\ \mathbf{y}_2 \\ \vdots \\ \mathbf{y}_p \end{bmatrix} \quad \mathbf{Z} = \begin{bmatrix} \mathbf{Z}_1 & 0 & \cdots & 0 \\ 0 & \mathbf{Z}_2 & \cdots & 0 \\ \vdots & \vdots & & \vdots \\ 0 & 0 & \cdots & \mathbf{Z}_p \end{bmatrix} \quad \boldsymbol{\delta} = \begin{bmatrix} \boldsymbol{\delta}_1 \\ \boldsymbol{\delta}_2 \\ \vdots \\ \boldsymbol{\delta}_p \end{bmatrix} \quad \boldsymbol{\epsilon} = \begin{bmatrix} \boldsymbol{\epsilon}_1 \\ \boldsymbol{\epsilon}_2 \\ \vdots \\ \boldsymbol{\epsilon}_p \end{bmatrix}$$

In the above expressions, $\mathbf{y}$ and $\boldsymbol{\epsilon}$ are each $np \times 1$ matrices, $\mathbf{Z}$ is $np \times q$, and $\boldsymbol{\delta}$ is $q \times 1$, where q is the total number of coefficients in the system ($[p_j + g_j]$, summed over all p equations).

2.1. The 2SLS Estimator

The coefficient vector for the jth equation, $\boldsymbol{\delta}_j$, can be estimated consistently with the 2SLS estimator:

$$\mathbf{d}_j = (\mathbf{A}_j'\mathbf{A}_j)^{-1}\mathbf{A}_j'\mathbf{y}_j, \tag{5}$$

where $\mathbf{A}_j = \mathbf{X}(\mathbf{X}'\mathbf{X})^{-1}\mathbf{X}'\mathbf{Z}_j$ (Theil 1971, p. 451). Matrix $\mathbf{A}_j$ can also be expressed as $[\hat{\mathbf{Y}}_j\,\mathbf{X}_j]$, where $\hat{\mathbf{Y}}_j$ is $\mathbf{X}(\mathbf{X}'\mathbf{X})^{-1}\mathbf{X}'\mathbf{Y}_j$ or the predicted value of right-hand-side endogenous variables obtained from the reduced-form regression.[2] Thus, equation (5) is equivalent to OLS estimation for the second-stage regression of y_j on $\hat{Y}_j$ and X_j. The asymptotic covariance matrix of the 2SLS estimator is

$$V(d_j) = \sigma_{jj}(A_j'A_j)^{-1}, \tag{6}$$

which is simply the OLS computation for the covariance matrix of the second-stage estimates.

2.2. The 3SLS Estimator

The 3SLS estimator for δ (with known Σ) is

$$\hat{\delta} = (Z'[\Sigma^{-1} \otimes X(X'X)^{-1}X'Z)^{-1}Z'[\Sigma^{-1} \otimes X(X'X)^{-1}X']y, \tag{7}$$

were $\otimes$ is the Kronecker product operator. The asymptotic covariance matrix for the 3SLS estimator (Theil 1971, pp. 510–12)[3] is

$$V(\hat{\delta}) = (Z'[\Sigma^{-1} \otimes X(X'X)^{-1}X']Z)^{-1}. \tag{8}$$

For any two-equation system (i.e., when $p = 2$), the asymptotic covariance matrix can be expressed as follows (Theil 1971, p. 515):

$$V(\hat{\delta}) = \begin{bmatrix} \sigma^{11}A_1'A_1 & \sigma^{12}A_1'A_2 \\ \sigma^{21}A_2'A_1 & \sigma^{22}A_2'A_2 \end{bmatrix}^{-1}, \tag{9}$$

where σ^{jk} is the (j,k) element of Σ^{-1}. Computationally, 3SLS is equivalent to joint GLS estimation of the p second-stage equations

---

[2] Since $Z_j = [Y_j \ X_j]$, A_j can be expressed as

$$A_j = [X(X'X)^{-1}X'Y_j \ X(X'X)^{-1}X'X_j].$$

However, the first term in A_j, $X(X'X)^{-1}X'Y_j$, is equivalent to XP_j, where P_j is the OLS estimate of the reduced-form coefficient vector for the right-hand-side endogenous variables. Thus, $XP_j = \hat{Y}_j$ or the predicted values for Y_j from the first-stage regression. The second term in A_j, $X(X'X)^{-1}X'X_j$, is equal to X_j, since X_j is perfectly predicted from the full set of exogenous variables in X. Therefore, $A_j = [\hat{Y}_j \ X_j]$.

[3] When Σ is unknown, estimators of δ and $V(\hat{\delta})$ are obtained by replacing Σ with S, the sample disturbance covariances computed from 2SLS residuals. In this paper we are interested in calculations of statistical power given specific parameter values under the null hypothesis. In calculating power, the investigator assumes specific values for all parameters, including Σ. Consequently, our results are based on expressions for known Σ.

as a seemingly unrelated regression system (Zellner 1962; Theil 1971, p. 510).

In a two-equation system, the asymptotic covariance matrix for $\hat{\boldsymbol{\delta}}_1$, the estimator of the coefficients of the first equation, is

$$V(\hat{\boldsymbol{\delta}}_1) = \sigma_{11}[A_1'A_1 + \{\rho^2/(1 - \rho^2)\}A^*]^{-1}, \tag{10}$$

where $A^* = A_1' (I - A_2(A_2' A_2)^{-1}A_2')A_1$ and ρ is $\sigma_{12}/(\sigma_{11}\sigma_{22})^{1/2}$, the correlation between ϵ_1 and ϵ_2 (Theil 1971, p. 515). The second term in brackets in equation (10) vanishes if either $\rho = 0$ or the model is just-identified (Theil 1971, p. 511). In either case, the 3SLS and 2SLS estimators are identical, with covariance matrix $\sigma_{11}(A_1' A_1)^{-1}$.

Insight into sources of sampling variability in the two-equation case can be gained by viewing A_1 and A_2 as the right-hand-side variables of second-stage estimation equations. If the model is just-identified or if $\rho = 0$, then $V(\hat{\boldsymbol{\delta}}_1) = \sigma_{11}([\hat{Y}_1 X_1]'[\hat{Y}_1 X_1])^{-1}$ is simply the OLS variance-covariance matrix computed from the second-stage regression. In this situation, all the results obtained by Bielby and Kluegel (1977) for the general linear model apply to the second-stage regression. In particular, the sampling variability of $\hat{\beta}_1$ will increase as $\hat{Y}_1$ becomes increasingly collinear with X_1. Below, we explore how that collinearity varies as a function of the model's parameters.

When ρ differs from zero and the model is over-identified, the sampling variability of $\hat{\beta}_1$ decreases as both ρ^2 and the generalized variance of A^* increase. But A^* is equivalent to the sum-of-squares and cross-products matrix of the second-stage right-hand-side variables in the first equation after they have been residualized on the second-stage right-hand-side variables of the second equation. In other words, for an over-identified model with correlated disturbances, sampling variability in estimates of the coefficients of equation (1) will increase with (a) collinearity between the exogenous variables unique to the y_1 equation and the remaining exogenous variables in the model and (b) collinearity between $\hat{Y}_1$ and the y_2 equation second-stage right-hand-side variables, $\hat{Y}_2$ and X_2.[4] Below,

---

[4] In a two-equation seemingly unrelated regression model, the relative efficiency of GLS over equation-by-equation OLS is a decreasing function of the canonical correlations between the exogenous variables in the two equations (Theil 1971, pp. 322–23). Thus, the relative efficiency of 3SLS over 2SLS can be expressed as a decreasing function of the canonical correlations between A_1 and A_2.

we explore how these conditions vary as a function of the model's parameters.

3. NONRECURSIVE MODELS: THE GENERAL LINEAR HYPOTHESIS AND THE POWER OF STATISTICAL TESTS

Any linear hypothesis within a nonrecursive system of equations can be expressed as H_o: $\mathbf{R\delta} = \mathbf{c}$, where $\mathbf{R}$ is a $t \times q$ matrix (of rank t) composed of coefficients for t constraints among the q parameters, and $\mathbf{c}$ is a $t \times 1$ matrix of constants. The test statistic is

$$\nu = (\mathbf{c} - \mathbf{R\hat{\delta}})'[\mathbf{RVR'}]^{-1}(\mathbf{c} - \mathbf{R\hat{\delta}}), \tag{11}$$

where $\mathbf{V}$ is short for $\mathbf{V(\hat{\delta})}$. Under the null hypothesis, the test statistic, ν, is asymptotically distributed as a chi-square variate with t degrees of freedom (Judge et al. 1985, p. 614). Following Gallant and Jorgenson (1979), it can be shown that under the alternative hypothesis H_A: $\mathbf{R\delta} \neq \mathbf{c}$, ν is asymptotically distributed noncentral chi square with noncentrality parameter[5]

$$\tau = (\mathbf{c} - \mathbf{R\delta})'[\mathbf{RVR'}]^{-1}(\mathbf{c} - \mathbf{R\delta}). \tag{12}$$

Using equations (8) and (12), we can compute the statistical power of the test of t constraints by specifying the model under the alternative hypothesis and calculating values for $\mathbf{V}$ and τ. Given τ, we can obtain power from tables for the noncentral chi-square distribution (Hayman, Govindarajulu, and Leone 1970). Those tables were used to construct Figure 1, which shows the relationship between statistical power and the noncentrality parameter τ for both one- and two-degrees-of-freedom tests, given type I error rates of .05 and .001. The figure indicates how large the noncentrality parameter must be to achieve a certain level of protection against type I and type II errors. For example, for a one-degree-of-freedom test, to achieve a type II error of .90, the noncentrality parameter must be

[5]For a derivation of the noncentrality parameter of the likelihood-ratio test statistic for nonlinear simultaneous equation systems estimated by maximum likelihood, see Gallant and Holly (1980). More generally, this result was independently applied to linear covariance structure models by Satorra and Saris (1985) and Matsueda and Bielby (1986). As noted above, the results for 3SLS presented here are asymptotically equivalent to maximum likelihood results (Theil 1971, pp. 525–26).

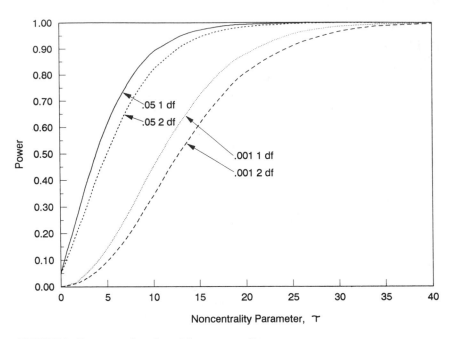

FIGURE 1. Power as a function of the noncentrality parameter, τ.

just over 10 at $\alpha = .05$ and just over 20 at $\alpha = .001$. For a two-degrees-of-freedom test, the corresponding noncentrality parameters must be 13 and 24. Furthermore, to achieve type I and type II error rates of .05 ($\alpha = .05$ and power $= .95$), the noncentrality parameter must be at least 13 for the one-degree-of-freedom test and 16 for the two-degrees-of-freedom test.

For a given nonrecursive model, once sample size, null and alternative hypotheses, and level of protection against type I error have been specified, the noncentrality parameter—and therefore the power of the test—is a function of the variance-covariance matrix **V**, which in turn is a function of the model's parameters. Accordingly, power of tests within nonrecursive models can be computed in four steps:

1. Given the values of a model's parameters under the alternative hypothesis, the implied moments among endogenous and exogenous variables are computed.

2. Those moments are used to compute **V**, according to equation (8) or (for a two-equation model) equation (9).
3. The noncentrality parameter τ is computed using equation (12).[6]
4. Given τ, power is obtained from tables of the noncentral chi-square distribution. Equivalently, power can be obtained from computerized representations of those tables, such as LIS-POWER under LISREL VII (Jöreskog and Sörbom 1989).

In the analyses below, we examine the impact of parametric structure on power and vary a parameter of the model across a range of values. Steps 1–4 are repeated for each specific value of the parameter of interest.

4. PARAMETRIC STRUCTURE AND STATISTICAL POWER

The power to detect parameters of a simultaneous equation model is influenced by the overall parametric structure of the model. In the single-equation linear model, $\mathbf{y} = \mathbf{X}\boldsymbol{\beta} + \boldsymbol{\epsilon}$, the noncentrality parameter for the general linear hypothesis $\mathbf{R}\boldsymbol{\beta} = \mathbf{c}$ is

$$\tau = (\mathbf{c} - \mathbf{R}\boldsymbol{\beta})'[\mathbf{R}\mathbf{V}\mathbf{R}']^{-1}(\mathbf{c} - \mathbf{R}\boldsymbol{\beta}), \qquad (13)$$

where $\mathbf{V} = \sigma_{\epsilon\epsilon}(\mathbf{X}'\mathbf{X})^{-1}$. Thus, for the classical linear model, power is a function of the disturbance variance, $\sigma_{\epsilon\epsilon}$, the degree to which parameters depart from the hypothesized linear relationship, $\mathbf{c} - \mathbf{R}\boldsymbol{\beta}$, and

---

[6]In analyses below, computations for the first three steps were obtained from matrix expressions using GAUSS statistical software (Edlefsen and Jones 1986) described in the appendices. Alternatively, the noncentrality parameter can be computed in LISREL using the procedure described by Matsueda and Bielby (1986, pp. 132–33): The *alternative* model is fit to the implied moments; the asymptotic covariance matrix **V** is computed from the correlation of estimates and standard errors produced by LISREL; and the noncentrality parameter is computed from equation (12). Our procedure for computing the noncentrality parameter differs from the approximation suggested by Satorra and Saris (1985) and Jöreskog and Sörbom (1989), which is biased asymptotically. Their approximation to the noncentrality parameter is the chi-square statistic obtained by fitting the model under the *null* hypothesis to the moments implied by the alternative model. For models that can be represented by equation (1), our procedure is tractable and asymptotically unbiased. Our approach can be intractable for more complex covariance structure models with latent variables, but the biased approximation is always tractable. On this point, see Satorra and Saris (1985, pp. 85–89) and Matsueda and Bielby (1986, pp. 148–52).

the moments among the exogenous variables, $\mathbf{X'X}$ (Bielby and Kluegel 1977).

Despite the similarity of equations (12) and (13), the impact of parametric structure on power is considerably more complicated in a nonrecursive model than in a single-equation model, because in the former case, the variance-covariance matrix, $\mathbf{V}$, is a function of moments involving endogenous right-hand-side variables (see equations (8)–(10)). These moments are not exogenous to the model and are therefore functions of the model's parameters. Thus, the power of a test regarding the parameters of one equation is typically a function of parameters of other equations in the model.

In this section we present results from simulations that show how the power of selected tests varies as a function of several features of the parametric structure of the model. First is the strength of instrumental variables. Specifically we examine power as a function of the strength of the effect in the second equation of exogenous variables excluded from the first equation. Second, we examine statistical power as a function of the number of instrumental variables (or over-identifying restrictions). Specifically, we compare power calculations for a just-identified model (with one exogenous variable excluded from each of two equations) with calculations for an over-identified model (with two exclusions in each equation). Finally, we compute statistical power as a function of the strength of the reciprocal relationship between two endogenous variables and the degree of covariation between the structural disturbances.

4.1. *The Hypothetical Model*

Our example is a hypothetical nonrecursive model of married women's attitudes regarding (a) the desirability of working outside the home while one's children are young and (b) the desirability of having a large family. Below, we refer to these as *work attitude* and *family attitude,* respectively. We assume that they are measured on the same metric and that they are negatively related to one another. The model, diagrammed in Figure 2, has two endogenous variables (work attitude and family attitude) and five exogenous variables (woman's years of schooling, woman's work experience, husband's occupational status, husband's educational status, and number of siblings). Hypothetical baseline values for a just-identified model are

$$\mathbf{B} = \begin{bmatrix} 0 & -.20 \\ -.40 & 0 \end{bmatrix},$$

$$\mathbf{\Gamma} = \begin{bmatrix} .20 & .15 & -.40 & .10 & 0 \\ -.30 & 0 & -.15 & -.20 & .20 \end{bmatrix},$$

$$\mathbf{\Sigma}_{\epsilon\epsilon} = \begin{bmatrix} .60 & -.10 \\ -.10 & .50 \end{bmatrix}, \text{ and}$$

$$\mathbf{\Sigma}_{xx} = \begin{bmatrix} 1 & -.10 & .34 & .55 & -.25 \\ -.10 & 1 & -.02 & -.08 & -.30 \\ .34 & -.02 & 1 & .62 & -.03 \\ .55 & -.08 & .62 & 1 & -.04 \\ -.25 & -.30 & -.03 & -.04 & 1 \end{bmatrix}.$$

To simplify the selection of baseline parameter values, we have re-scaled the exogenous variables to standard-deviation units (variances of one). However, results presented below do not depend on scaling of the measured variables.[7]

The model is just-identified and assumes that γ_{15} and γ_{22} are zero, i.e., that number of siblings has no effect on work attitude and that work experience has no effect on family attitude.[8] Values for a baseline over-identified model are identical to those above except that γ_{14} and γ_{23} are assumed to equal zero.

Given these baseline parameter values, the just-identified model is "weakly" identified, in the sense that estimates of β_{12} and β_{21} are subject to substantial sampling variability. This is reflected in the low statistical power of tests of each of these parameters. For example, for a sample size of 1,000, a type I error rate (α) of .05, and a just-identified model, the power to detect $\beta_{12} = -0.20$ with a one-degree-of-freedom (nondirectional) t test is only .39. For a type I error rate of $\alpha = .001$, the power to detect $\beta_{12} = -0.20$ is just .05.[9]

[7]The coefficients of the models reported below are not fully standardized, since the variance of each endogenous variable is a function of the parameters of the model and cannot be fixed at one.

[8]The model is just-identified if parameters to be estimated include all elements of $\mathbf{\Sigma}$ (the covariance matrix among disturbances), all elements of $\mathbf{\Sigma}_{xx}$ (the covariance matrix among exogenous variables), the off-diagonal elements of $\mathbf{B}$, and the nonzero elements of $\mathbf{\Gamma}$.

[9]We obtained these figures as follows. First, we generated implied moments from the baseline parameter values and sample size. Second, we used these moments to compute $\mathbf{V}$ from equation (9). Third, given $\mathbf{V}$, we used equation (12) to compute the noncentrality parameter τ of 2.581. Fourth, we referred to power tables for one degree of freedom and $\tau = 2.581$ to obtain power at $\alpha = .05$ and at $\alpha = .001$.

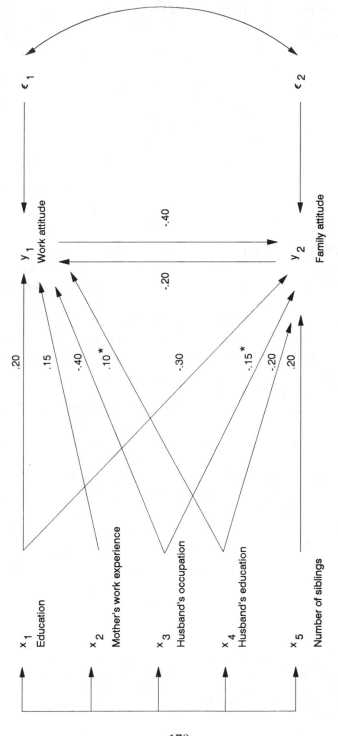

FIGURE 2. Hypothetical nonrecursive model. An asterisk indicates that the coefficient is set to zero for the over-identified model.

178

The corresponding power to detect $\beta_{21} = -0.40$ is 0.82 when $\alpha = .05$ and 0.34 when $\alpha = .001$.

We examine three tests of the reciprocal causal relationship between y_1 and y_2. Each represents a test typically conducted in the evaluation of nonrecursive models. First, we examine the one-degree-of-freedom test of a single coefficient relating the two endogenous variables ($\beta_{12} = 0$). This test determines whether one endogenous variable has any effect on the other. Second, we examine the two-degrees-of-freedom test that the reciprocal effects between the two variables are jointly zero ($\beta_{12} = \beta_{21} = 0$). This evaluates whether there is any relationship in either direction between the endogenous variables. Third, we examine the one-degree-of-freedom test that the difference between the coefficients is zero ($\beta_{12} - \beta_{21} = 0$). This test of whether the causal effect is larger in one direction or the other is of considerable interest in research on fertility and labor force participation (Lehrer and Nerlove 1986).

4.2. Power and the Strength of Instrumental Variables

We noted above that in a just-identified model, the sampling variability of estimates of reciprocal effects increases with the collinearity between predicted endogenous and exogenous variables on the right-hand side of the second-stage regression. Thus, in our example of a just-identified model, the sampling variability of the estimate of β_{12} increases as $\hat{y}_2$ becomes collinear with x_1 through x_4. Since $\hat{y}_2$ is a linear function of all five exogenous variables, the reduced-form effect of x_5 on y_2 is the only source of nonredundant variation in $\hat{y}_2$. For given values of β_{12} and β_{21}, the degree to which $\hat{y}_2$ varies independently of x_1 through x_4 is determined by the structural coefficient γ_{25}. As γ_{25} approaches zero, $\hat{y}_2$ approaches perfect collinearity with x_1 through x_4. Conversely, as the magnitude of γ_{25} increases, the sampling variability of the estimate of β_{12} decreases. Thus, in our hypothetical example, we interpret γ_{25} as an index of the strength of x_5 as an instrumental variable for the first equation.

To index the degree of collinearity in the second-stage regression, we can use either the proportion of variance explained in $\hat{y}_2$ by x_1 through x_4 (Cramer 1980) or the corresponding variance-inflation factor, $1/(1 - R^2)$ (Chaterjee and Price 1977). However, these are merely descriptive indices. Neither takes into account how sample size influences sampling variability, nor are these R^2 measures sensitive to all of the parameters that influence sampling variability (Maddala 1988, pp. 228–29). Thus, these measures are of limited use in addressing the problem of sampling variability within the context of formal statistical inference. By defining the issue as protection against type I and type II error, we can systematically analyze how sample size, parametric structure, and type I error rates affect inference in nonrecursive models.

Figure 3 shows the power of a one-degree-of-freedom chi-square test of β_{12} as a function of the strength of the instrumental variable x_5. The null hypothesis, $\beta_{12} = 0$, is contrasted with the alternative hypothesis, $\beta_{12} = -0.20$. For the just-identified model, the solid line shows that the noncentrality parameter, τ, increases curvilinearly with γ_{25}, the structural effect of x_5 on y_2.[10] (See Appendix A for a description of the GAUSS program that produced the computations upon which Figure 3 is based.) According to Figure 3, γ_{25} has to approach 0.4 before the noncentrality parameter exceeds 10, roughly the value at which power reaches .90 for $\alpha = .05$. Given the parameter values in the hypothetical just-identified model, when $\alpha = .001$, γ_{25} must approach 0.6 before τ exceeds 24, roughly the value at which power reaches .99. Thus, for a sample size of 1,000, the effect of x_5, the instrumental variable, on y_2, the right-hand-side endogenous variable, must be considerable if we are to have a reasonable probability of detecting a value of $\beta_{12} = -0.20$. At the baseline value of $\gamma_{25} = .20$,

---

[10] For the special case of the one-degree-of-freedom test of β_{12} in the just-identified model, the relationship between γ_{25} and τ can be expressed analytically. The sampling variance of the estimate of β_{12} computed from the second-stage regression is

$$\text{Var}(\hat{\beta}_{12}) = \sigma_{11}(\hat{y}_2'M_1\hat{y}_2)^{-1},$$

where $M_1 = (I - X_1(X_1' X_1)^{-1}X_1')$, so the noncentrality parameter is

$$\tau = (\beta_{12}^2/\sigma_{11})(\hat{y}_2'M_1\hat{y}_2).$$

Further, $\hat{y}_2' M_1\hat{y}_2 = \pi_2X'M_1X\pi_2' + u_2' X(X'X)^{-1}X'M_1X(X'X)^{-1}X'u_2 + 2\pi_2X'u_2$, where π_2 is the second row of the matrix of reduced-form coefficients, $(I - B)^{-1}\Gamma$. The term $2\pi_2X'u_2$ is linear in γ_{25}, while the term $\pi_2X'M_1X\pi_2'$ is quadratic in γ_{25}.

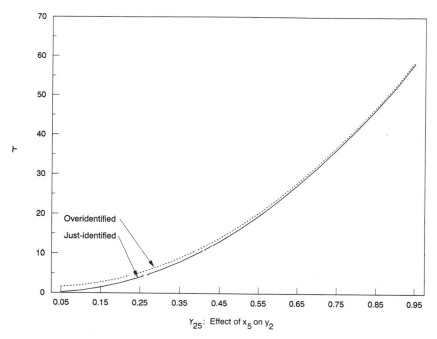

FIGURE 3. Noncentrality parameter τ as a function of γ_{25}: One-df test, $\beta_{12} = 0$.

a sample size of 3,874 would yield a noncentrality parameter of 10 for a power of approximately .9 at $\alpha = .05$.[11]

Figure 3 shows that the one-degree-of-freedom test is slightly more powerful for the over-identified model than for the just-identified model. The gain in power is relatively small because x_4 is also a relatively weak instrumental variable ($\gamma_{24} = -0.2$). Thus, we can conclude that for the hypothetical model posed in Figure 2, the probability of detecting an effect of family attitude on work attitude is weak even when two exogenous variables can be excluded from each structural equation.

Figure 4 shows the noncentrality parameter as a function of the strength of the instrumental variable x_5 for the two-degrees-of-freedom test that β_{12} and β_{21} are jointly zero (i.e., $\beta_{12} = 0 \ and \ \beta_{21} = 0$). The noncentrality parameter is evaluated at baseline values of the reciprocal effects of -0.20 for β_{12} and -0.40 for β_{21}.

[11]The noncentrality parameter, τ, is proportional to sample size n. For $n = 1,000$, $\tau = 2.581$ at $\gamma_{25} = 0.20$. Therefore, τ is 10 when $n = (10/2.581) \times 1,000 = 3,874$.

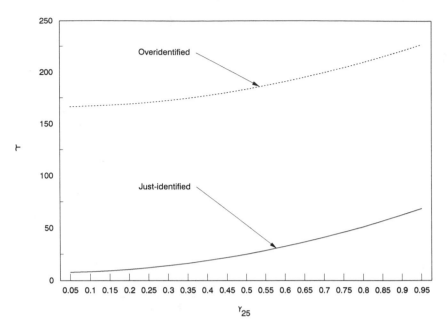

FIGURE 4. Noncentrality parameter τ as a function of γ_{25}: Two-df test, $\beta_{12} = \beta_{21} = 0$.

According to Figure 4, the power to reject the hypothesis of no reciprocal causation depends decisively on whether the model is over- or just-identified. For a two-degrees-of-freedom test at $\alpha = .05$, power reaches .90 when the noncentrality parameter is approximately 12.5. At $\alpha = .001$, power does not reach .90 until the noncentrality parameter is 24. For the just-identified model, the noncentrality parameter approaches 12.5 at $\gamma_{25} = 0.44$ and 24 at $\gamma_{25} = 0.61$. Therefore, for the just-identified model, reciprocal causation will not be detected at a reasonable level of type II error unless x_5 is a strong instrument for the first equation. This is because x_2, the instrumental variable for the second equation, is a weak instrument ($\gamma_{12} = 0.15$). Thus, estimates of *both* β_{12} and β_{21} are subject to substantial sampling variability when γ_{25} is small.

In contrast, for the over-identified model at $\alpha = .001$, the power to reject the null hypothesis of no reciprocal causation exceeds .999 regardless of the strength of x_5 as an instrumental variable.[12] We

[12]The power of a two-degrees-of-freedom test at $\alpha = .001$ exceeds .999 when the noncentrality parameter reaches 46.

have already noted in the over-identified model, both x_4 and x_5 are weak instruments for the first equation. However, x_3 is a strong instrument for the second equation ($\gamma_{13} = -0.4$). The standard error of the estimate of β_{21} is reduced by nearly 80 percent when x_3 is added as an instrument for the y_2 equation. Thus, the strong protection against type II error in the over-identified model is due to the precision with which we can estimate β_{21}, even when β_{12} cannot be estimated precisely.

We conclude from these results that statistical power varies in complicated ways with the hypothesis being tested, with the strength of the instrumental variables, and with the identification of the model. In the hypothetical model posed here, the likelihood of detecting the causal impact of y_2 on y_1 is low, regardless of whether the model is just- or over-identified, unless the instrument for the y_1 equation is quite strong (indeed, implausibly strong for the substantive example considered here). In contrast, the likelihood of rejecting the hypothesis of no reciprocal causation between y_1 and y_2 is high for the over-identified model, regardless of the strength of the instrument for the y_1 equation.

This conclusion is reinforced when we examine the probability of detecting whether the causal relationship among the endogenous variables is stronger in one direction than the other. The null hypothesis is $\beta_{12} - \beta_{21} = 0$, and the alternative is $\beta_{12} = -0.2$ and $\beta_{21} = -0.4$. Figure 5 shows that for the just-identified model, the noncentrality parameter is less than 2.0, regardless of the strength of the instrument (x_5) for the y_1 equation. In other words, with a just-identified model, we must have a sample of over 5,000 to have a reasonable likelihood of detecting a difference between β_{12} and β_{21} (when the actual population values are -0.2 and -0.4, respectively).

In contrast, in the over-identified model, the probability of detecting the difference between β_{12} and β_{21} rises sharply with γ_{25}, the strength of x_5 as an instrument for the first equation. Nevertheless, even in the over-identified model, a noncentrality parameter of 10 is not reached until γ_{25} exceeds 0.45. Thus, given a sample size of 1,000, two over-identifying restrictions, the parameter values in our baseline model, and weak to modest instruments for the y_1 equation, we have little chance of detecting whether causal effects are stronger in one direction than in the other.

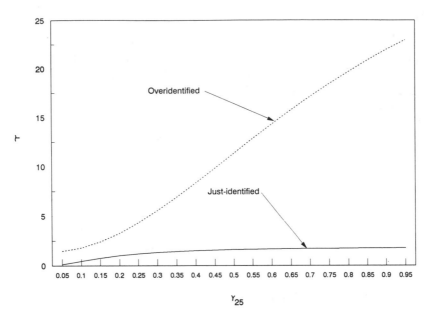

FIGURE 5. Noncentrality parameter τ as a function of γ_{25}: One-df test, $\beta_{12} - \beta_{21} = 0$.

4.3. *Power and the Size of Reciprocal Effects*

To examine how the size of reciprocal effects influences the power of various tests, we assume an alternative hypothesis, $\beta_{12} = 0.5\beta_{21}$, and compute the noncentrality parameter as a function of β_{12}. All other parameters (except β_{21}) are set to their baseline values for the just- and over-identified models. Figure 6 shows the influence of reciprocal effects on power for the one-degree-of-freedom test of the null hypothesis that $\beta_{12} = 0$ and for the hypothesis that $\beta_{21} = 0$.

Again, because of the differential strength of the instruments for the two equations, over-identification is much more consequential for the test of β_{21} than for the test of β_{12}. For a type I error rate of .05, the power to reject $\beta_{21} = 0$ exceeds .90 (i.e., the noncentrality parameter exceeds 10) when β_{12} and β_{21} are as small as -0.05 and -0.10, respectively, for the over-identified model. For the just-identified model, the same level of power is not reached until β_{12} and β_{21} are -0.23 and -0.46, respectively.

In contrast, the probability of detecting departures from the null hypothesis, $\beta_{12} = 0$, is weak regardless of whether the model is

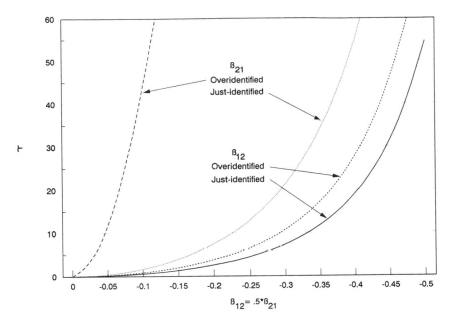

FIGURE 6. Noncentrality parameter τ as a function of $\beta_{12} = 0.5*\beta_{21}$: One-$df$ tests, $\beta_{12} = 0$ and $\beta_{21} = 0$.

over-identified. For the over-identified model and a type I error rate of .05, the power to reject $\beta_{12} = 0$ does not exceed .90 until β_{12} and β_{21} are -0.30 and -0.60, respectively. Thus, for the hypothetical model posed here, we would have a difficult time detecting an effect of family attitude on work attitude even when there is a sizeable effect in the population. In contrast, there is a high probability that we would detect even a small effect in the other direction (work attitude on family attitude) in the over-identified model.

Figure 7 reveals that the chances of detecting whether the reciprocal effect is larger in one direction than in the other are low unless the difference between the effects is quite large. The null hypothesis is the one-degree-of-freedom test $\beta_{12} - \beta_{21} = 0$, and again the alternative is $\beta_{12} = 0.5\beta_{21}$, with the noncentrality parameter computed across a range of values for β_{12}. For the just-identified model, the noncentrality parameter does not exceed 10 until $\beta_{12} = -0.43$ and $\beta_{21} = -0.86$. Even in the over-identified model, the noncentrality parameter does not exceed 10 until the reciprocal effects are -0.31 and -0.62, despite the precision with which β_{21} is estimated.

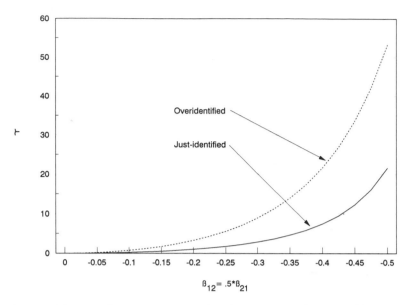

FIGURE 7. Noncentrality parameter τ as a function of $\beta_{12} = 0.5^*\beta_{21}$: One-$df$ test, $\beta_{12} - b_{21} = 0$.

In sum, given the baseline values of our hypothetical model and a sample size of 1,000, our ability to detect reciprocal causal effects between work attitude and family attitude is limited. The only effect that we are likely to detect with a minimally acceptable level of certainty is the effect from attitude about working mothers (y_1) to attitude about large families (y_2), and then only if the model is over-identified. Detecting whether the causal effect is greater in one direction than in the other is especially problematic unless the effects are quite large. This is because of weak instruments for the y_1 equation.

4.4. *Power and the Size of the Disturbance Correlation*

Equation (10) above shows that for an over-identified model, the sampling variability of 3SLS coefficient estimates decreases as the absolute value of ρ, the correlation among structural distur-bances, increases. Thus, the power of a one-degree-of-freedom test of a hypothesis about a single coefficient increases as ρ departs from zero. This is illustrated by the solid line in Figure 8 for the test of the

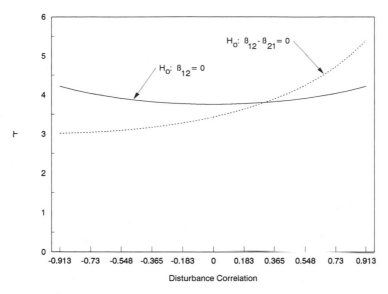

FIGURE 8. Noncentrality parameter τ as a function of correlation between disturbances: One-*df* tests, $\beta_{12} = 0$ and $\beta_{12} - \beta_{21} = 0$.

null hypothesis $\beta_{12} = 0$. The noncentrality parameter for the over-identified baseline model was computed as a function of the disturbance covariance over the range -0.5 to $+0.5$, which corresponds to a range of -0.913 to $+0.913$ for the correlation between the structural disturbances.

Given the particular baseline parameters we chose, the disturbance covariation has little effect on the power to detect β_{12} under the alternative hypothesis $\beta_{12} = -0.20$. The noncentrality parameter computed at $\rho = 0$ ($\tau = 3.75$) is 89 percent as large as that computed at $|\rho| = 0.916$ ($\tau = 4.212$). According to Figure 1, at a type I error rate of .05, the power of the test is close to .50, regardless of the size of the disturbance correlation.

The disturbance correlation is more consequential for the one-degree-of-freedom test of the difference between the coefficients, which corresponds to the null hypothesis $\beta_{12} - \beta_{21} = 0$. For that test (under the over-identified baseline model), the noncentrality parameter increases with ρ at an increasing rate. At $\rho = -0.913$ the noncentrality parameter ($\tau = 3.01$) is only 56 percent as large as it is at $\rho = +0.913$ ($\tau = 5.39$). At a type I error rate of .05, the corresponding probabilities of rejecting the null hypothesis are .42 and .64, respectively.

The power of a test on a single coefficient will always be lowest when $\rho = 0$, given any specific values of the other parameters in an over-identified model. However, the power to detect departures from $\beta_{12} - \beta_{21} = 0$ need not necessarily increase with ρ. The sampling variability of $\hat{\beta}_{12} - \hat{\beta}_{21}$ is

$$\text{Var}(\hat{\beta}_{12}) + \text{Var}(\hat{\beta}_{21}) - 2\text{Cov}(\hat{\beta}_{12}, \hat{\beta}_{21}).$$

In our particular example, the sampling covariance increases with ρ, thereby decreasing the sampling variability of the difference between the coefficient estimates (and increasing the power of the test). Moreover, in our example, the sampling covariance dominates the sampling variances in the above expression. That is, the rate at which the sampling covariance increases as ρ ranges from -0.916 to 0 (which reduces the sampling variability of the difference) more than offsets the increases in the sampling variability of $\hat{\beta}_{12}$ and $\hat{\beta}_{21}$ over the same range.

Finally, equation (10) implies that the impact of the disturbance correlation on sampling variability (and therefore power) is contingent upon $\mathbf{A}^*$, which in turn depends on the strength of instrumental variables. Consequently, the sensitivity of τ to chnages in ρ should be greater for the test of β_{21} than for the test of β_{12}, since the y_2 equation has stronger instruments than the y_1 equation. This is apparent when we compare Figure 9 with Figure 8. The proportionate change in the noncentrality parameter is indeed greater for the test of $\beta_{21} = 0$ (against the alternative $\beta_{21} = -0.40$). For that test, the noncentrality parameter evaluated at $\rho = 0$ ($\tau = 158.51$) is 84 percent as large as that computed at $|\rho| = 0.916$ ($\tau = 189.05$).

In sum, in an over-identified model, the sampling variability of 3SLS estimates of individual coefficients decreases with the magnitude of the covariance between structural disturbances, thereby increasing the power of tests on individual coefficients.[13] However, for a test of coefficients from more than one equation, the impact of the error covariance on statistical power is contingent upon the overall parametric structure of the model.

---

[13]The relative efficiency of 3SLS compared with 2SLS also increases with the magnitude of the covariance between structural disturbances.

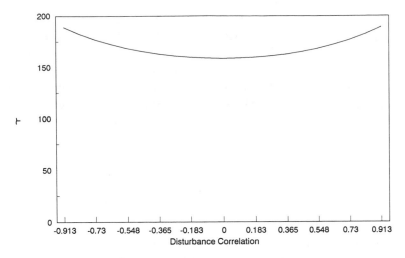

FIGURE 9. Noncentrality parameter τ as a function of correlation between disturbances: One-df test, $\beta_{21} = 0$.

5. SUMMARY AND CONCLUSIONS

In nonrecursive models, sampling variability and the probability of detecting causal effects among endogenous variables can depend on the parametric structure of the model in ways quite different from what sociologists encounter in classical regression and recursive structural equation models. Depending on the hypothesis tested, the power of the test can vary in complicated ways with the strength of the instrumental variables, with the number of over-identifying restrictions, and with the covariation among disturbances. Consequently, rules of thumb regarding appropriate sample sizes, magnitudes of coefficients that are substantively significant, and so on, can be grossly misleading. The likelihood of detecting asymmetric causal relationships, a central issue in research on fertility behavior (Smith-Lovin and Tickamyer 1978; Rindfuss, Bumpass, and St. John 1980) and on work and family interaction (Berk and Berk 1978; Bielby and Bielby 1989), can be especially problematic.

Our results suggest several ways in which sociological applications of nonrecursive models can be improved. For example, sociologists should be more sensitive to the issue of type II error when interpreting results from nonrecursive models. As our example illustrates, having a viable substantive rationale for restrictions that identify a model's parameters does not guarantee that valid inferences will be drawn from *estimates* of those parameters. An effect of an endogenous variable that is formally identified can often be difficult to detect, even when the sample size is large by sociological standards. Without explicitly assessing the type II error rate, sociologists are likely to conclude incorrectly that effects are absent (or symmetric) more often than they realize.

Sociological applications of nonrecursive models should systematically address the issue of type II error in tests of hypotheses concerning the effects of endogenous variables. For example, a researcher conducting such an analysis with our hypothetical model would be confronted with several issues. First, she or he would probably conclude that a sample of 1,000 is too small to assess (a) the effect of family attitude on work attitude and (b) asymmetry in the reciprocal relationship between the endogenous variables. Second, the researcher would note that the probability of detecting a causal effect of work attitude on family attitude depends decisively on whether the additional restriction that renders the y_2 equation over-identified ($\gamma_{23} = 0$) can be justified substantively. Indeed, depending on the researcher's loss function regarding the trade-off between bias and efficiency, she or he might conclude that the substantial gain in power obtained by imposing the over-identifying restriction more than offsets the bias introduced by small departures from the restriction in the population. As Figures 5–7 illustrate, depending upon the hypothesis, the potential gain in power due to the addition of a strong instrument can be comparable to that of a very substantial increase in sample size.

Of course, the specific findings presented in Figures 3–9 depend upon the values of the baseline parameters we have chosen. Had we chosen lower correlations among exogenous variables, smaller disturbance variances, or more over-identifying restrictions, the power of the statistical tests we examined would have been greater. The analysis of statistical power is always problem-dependent. To specify null and alternative hypotheses completely requires the specification of plausible values of the model's parameters under both sets of circumstances. If, for example, an analyst were to choose values for exogenous moments based on consistent sample estimates of those moments, then power calculations would be contingent upon those sample values. In a substantive area different from the one we have chosen, sample sizes, collinearity among exogenous variables, and the magnitudes of effects could be quite different, yielding very different calculations of statistical power.

Nevertheless, the *procedures* we have presented are widely applicable. Indeed, they apply to any model that can be specified in terms of the classical textbook econometric model described in equation (1). These include nonrecursive models with more than one equation, fully recursive models, and seemingly unrelated regression models, among others. The same four steps that we have used here to compute power can be applied to any of these models, and the GAUSS program described in the appendices can be modified to accommodate any of these specific instances of the classical simultaneous equation model. Moreover, equations (8) and (12) allow the researcher to express the mathematical relationship between a model's parameters and the noncentrality parameter for a statistical test.

Our analyses open several areas for future research. One is to explore more formally the trade-offs between bias and efficiency according to different loss functions when an exogenous variable is known to have a very strong effect on one endogenous variable and (at most) a small effect on another endogenous variable. Another is to examine the impact of multiple indicators on the probability of detecting effects in nonrecursive models. We have shown elsewhere that for recursive models, additional indicators can have an impact on power that is comparable to a substantial increase in sample size (Matsueda and Bielby 1986). The extension of these results to nonrecursive models would allow researchers to evaluate the relative costs and benefits of increased sample size versus additional indicators during the design stage of a research project.

APPENDIX A
A GAUSS PROGRAM FOR COMPUTING
NONCENTRALITY PARAMETERS

For any test of parameters in a linear structural equation model, the associated noncentrality parameter can be expressed as a function of the asymptotic covariance matrix, V, of the estimator for the model's coefficients, as in equation (12) above. In this paper we exploit the fact that for a 3SLS estimator of a simultaneous equation model, V can be expressed in terms of moments among the observable variables, which in turn can be expressed in terms of the model's parameters. The GAUSS program in Appendix B shows how we have computed the relationship between a model's parameters and the noncentrality parameters associated with various statistical tests.

The program applies to the just-identified model in Figure 2 and the analysis of power as a function of the strength of the instrumental variables. It computes the noncentrality parameters associated with the three tests, $\beta_{12} = 0$, $\beta_{12} = \beta_{21} = 0$, and $\beta_{12} - \beta_{21} = 0$, as a function of parameter γ_{25}. Specifically, all parameters of the model other than γ_{25} are set to values that correspond to the alternative hypothesis, while γ_{25} is varied from 0.05 to 0.95 in increments of 0.05. For each value of γ_{25} (i.e., for each iteration of the loop), the program computes the implied moments, the 3SLS asymptotic covariance matrix, and the three noncentrality parameters of interest. The four columns of numbers in Appendix C are the output of the program. They are plotted as the solid lines in Figures 3, 4, and 5. We computed the over-identified model by changing the *gamm=* expression to let $\gamma_{14} = \gamma_{23} = 0$ and by changing the *let rowsx1* and *let rowsx2* expressions to reflect the two additional exclusions of exogenous variables.

We computed power as a function of the size of reciprocal effects by modifying the program to iterate on β_{21} and setting β_{12} equal to $0.5\beta_{21}$. Finally, we computed power as a function of the size of the disturbance correlation by modifying the program to iterate on σ_{12}.

Although the program has been set up for a system with five exogenous variables, it can easily be modified to accommodate any two-equation system by changing the dimensions of the appropriate matrices. Moreover, the program can be generalized to more than two equations by using the more general expression in equation (8) instead of equation (9) to compute the asymptotic covariance matrix. Further, the effects of other parameters on power can be assessed by modifying the program to iterate on the parameter of interest. Finally, the effect on power of different baseline parameter values can be assessed by changing the entries in step 1, part 1.

APPENDIX B
GAUSS PROGRAM FOR COMPUTING NONCENTRALITY PARAMETERS AS A FUNCTION OF γ_{25}, JUST-IDENTIFIED MODEL

```
/* program to compute noncentrality parameter for test of */
/* general linear hypothesis in a simultaneous equations */
/**context. William T. Bielby and Ross L. Matsueda, 7/90 */
/* this version computes tau as a function of gamma25 */
/* for the just-identified model—see Figure 3, 4, 5 */
format 6,3;
output file = c:\power\generic.out reset;
outwidth 250;
n=1000;

/* Step 1, part 1: SPECIFY PARAMETER VALUES */
/* this is set up to iterate on gamma25 */
let sdx[5,1]=1 1 1 1 1;
dx=diagrv(eye(5),sdx);
/* above is s.d. of x's */
let rx[5,5]=
   1     -.10     .34     .55    -.25
 -.10      1     -.02    -.08    -.30
   .34    -.02     1      .62    -.03
   .55     .08     .62     1     -.04
 -.25     -.30    -.03    -.04     1   ;
/* above is correlation of x's */
sigxx=dx*rx*dx;
gamm25=.05;
b21 = .400;
b12 = .200;
do while gamm25 <1.0;
/* above iterates on parameter of interest */
gamm=( .200~ .150~ -.400~ .100~ .000) |
     (-.300~ .000~ -.150~ -.200~ gamm25);
/* above is initial gamma matrix, we'll iterate on gamma25 */
beta = (1~b12) | (b21 ~1);
let see[2,2]=.600 -.100 -.100 .500;
```

```
/* above are beta and psi matrices (LISREL IV notation) */
seinv=invpd(see);
seinv11=seinv[1,1];
seinv22=seinv[2,2];
seinv12=seinv[1,2];

/* Step 1, part 2: COMPUTE ENDOGENOUS MOMENTS */
sigyx=inv(beta)*gamm*sigxx;
sigyy=inv(beta)*gamm*sigxx*gamm'*(inv(beta))' +
inv(beta)*see*(inv(beta))';
sigxy=sigyx';
vary=diag(sigyy);
dy=eye(2).*sqrt(vary);
ryx=inv(invpd(dy)*beta*dy)*invpd(dy)*gamm*dx*rx;
ryy=invpd(dy)*sigyy*inv(dy);
let rowsx1= 1 2 3 4 ; /* x variables included in eq 1 */
let rowsy1=2; /* y vars included in equation 1 */
sxy1=submat(sigxy,0,rowsy1); /* cov matrix of eq 1 x vars w */
/* eq 1 y vars */
sy1x=sxy1';
sx1x=submat(sigxx,rowsx1,0); /* cov matrix of eq 1 x vars w */
/* all x vars */
xxinv=invpd(sigxx);
/* similar computations for equation 2 follow */
let rowsx2 = 1 3 4 5;
let rowsy2=1;
sxy2=submat(sigxy,0,rowsy2);
sy2x=sxy2';
sx2x=submat(sigxx,rowsx2,0);

r=(ryy~ryx) | (ryx'~rx);
std=(diag(dy) | diag(dx))';
/* above are correlations and standard deviations */
/* can be output to LISREL

/* Step 2: COMPUTE VARIANCE-COVARIANCE */
/* MATRIX OF 3SLS ESTIMATOR */
/* what follows is 3sls asymptotic covariances following Theil */
```

```
/* z1 includes eq 1 rght hnd vars, z2 includes eq 2 rght hnd vars */
sz1x=sy1x | sx1x; /* var-cov matrix of z1 vars with all x vars */
sz2x=sy2x | sx2x; /* var-cov matrix of z2 vars with all x vars */
a11=n*sz1x*xxinv*sz1x';
a12=n*sz1x*xxinv*sz2x';
a22=n*sz2x*xxinv*sz2x';
covest=invpd((seinv11*a11~seinv12*a12)
| (seinv12*a12'~seinv22*a22)); /* see Theil, p. 515, top */
stderr=sqrt(diag(covest));
varb12=covest[1,1];
varb21=covest[6,6];
b12=beta[1,2];
b21=beta[2,1];


/* Step 3: COMPUTE NONCENTRALITY PARAMETERS */
/* FOR VARIOUS TESTS */
tau1=b12*b12/varb12;
tau2=b21*b21/varb21;


/* create submatrix for tests on b21 and b12 */
rowscv=1~6;
vr=submat(covest,rowscv,rowscv);


/* compute 2 df tau for b12 = b21 = 0 */
tau2df=(b12~b21)*invpd(vr)*(b12 | b21);
h=(1~-1);


/* compute 1df tau for b12 - b21 = 0 */
taudiff=(h*(b12 | b21))'*invpd(h*vr*h')*(h*(b12 | b21));


/* OUTPUT */
/* create output vector of all parameters to plot */
outpar=gamm25~tau1~tau2df~taudiff;
;
print /m0 /rd /m1 outpar;
gamm25=gamm25+.05;
endo;
```

APPENDIX C
OUTPUT OF GAUSS PROGRAM

	Noncentrality Parameter, τ		
γ_{25}	(1) $\beta_{12}=0$	(2) $\beta_{12}=\beta_{21}=0$	(3) $\beta_{12}-\beta_{21}=0$
0.050	0.161	7.777	0.144
0.100	0.645	8.398	0.455
0.150	1.452	9.343	0.769
0.200	2.581	10.612	1.020
0.250	4.033	12.204	1.206
0.300	5.808	14.121	1.340
0.350	7.906	16.361	1.438
0.400	10.326	18.926	1.511
0.450	13.068	21.814	1.567
0.500	16.134	25.026	1.610
0.550	19.522	28.562	1.644
0.600	23.233	32.422	1.671
0.650	27.266	36.606	1.693
0.700	31.622	41.114	1.711
0.750	36.301	45.946	1.726
0.800	41.303	51.101	1.739
0.850	46.627	56.581	1.750
0.900	52.274	62.384	1.759
0.950	58.243	68.511	1.768

REFERENCES

Berk, Richard A., and Sarah F. Berk. 1978. "A Simultaneous Equation Model for the Division of Household Labor." *Sociological Methods and Research* 6:431–68.

Bielby, William T., and Denise D. Bielby. 1989. "Family Ties: Balancing Commitments to Work and Family in Dual Earner Households." *American Sociological Review* 54:776–89.

Bielby, William T., and James R. Kluegel. 1977. "Simultaneous Statistical Inference and Statistical Power in Survey Research Applications of the General Linear Model." Pp. 283–312 in *Sociological Methodology 1977*, edited by D. R. Heise. San Francisco: Jossey-Bass.

Chaterjee, S., and B. Price. 1977. *Regression Analysis by Example*. New York: Wiley.

Cramer, James C. 1980. "Fertility and Female Employment: Problems of Causal Direction." *American Sociological Review* 45:167–90.

Duncan, O. D., A. O. Haller, and A. Portes. 1968. "Peer Influences on Aspirations: A Reinterpretation." *American Sociological Review* 74:119–37.

Edlefsen, Lee E., and Samuel D. Jones. 1986. *GAUSS Programming Language Manual*. Kent, WA: Aptec Systems.

Gallant, A. Ronald, and A. Holly. 1980. "Statistical Inference in an Implicit, Nonlinear, Simultaneous Equation Model in the Context of Maximum Likelihood Estimation." *Econometrica* 48:697–720.

Gallant, A. Ronald, and Dale W. Jorgenson. 1979. "Statistical Inference for a System of Simultaneous, Non-Linear, Implicit Equations in the Context of Instrumental Variable Estimation." *Journal of Econometrics* 11:275–302.

Hayman, G. E., A. Govindarajulu, and F. C. Leone. 1970. "Tables of the Cumulative Non-Central Chi Square Distribution." Pp. 1–78 in *Selected Tables in Mathematical Statistics*, vol. 1, edited by H. L. Harter and D. B. Owen. Providence: American Mathematical Society.

Jöreskog, Karl G., and Dag Sörbom. 1989. *LISREL VII: A Guide to the Program and Applications*. Chicago: SPSS Inc.

Judge, George D., William E. Griffiths, R. Carter Hill, and Tsoung-Chao Lee. 1985. *The Theory and Practice of Econometrics*. 2d ed. New York: Wiley.

Lehrer, Evelyn, and Marc Nerlove. 1986. "Female Labor Force Behavior and Fertility in the United States." Pp. 181–276 in *Annual Review of Sociology*, vol. 12, edited by Ralph Turner and James J. Short. Palo Alto: Annual Reviews.

Liu, T. C. 1963. "An Exploratory Quarterly Model of Effective Demand in the Post-war U.S. Economy." *Econometrica* 31:301–48.

Maddala, G. S. 1988. *Introduction to Econometrics*. New York: Macmillan.

Matsueda, Ross L., and William T. Bielby. 1986. "Statistical Power in Covariance Structure Models." Pp. 120–58 in *Sociological Methodology 1986*, edited by Nancy Tuma. Washington, DC: American Sociological Association.

Rindfuss, R. R., L. Bumpass, and C. St. John. 1980. "Education and Fertility: Implications for the Roles Women Occupy." *American Sociological Review* 45:431–47.

Satorra, Albert, and William E. Saris. 1985. "Power of the Likelihood Ratio Test in Covariance Structure Analysis." *Psychometrica* 50:83–90.

Smith-Lovin, Lynn, and Ann R. Tickamyer. 1978. "Labor Force Participation, Fertility Behavior, and Sex Role Attitudes." *American Sociological Review* 43:541–56.

Theil, Henri. 1971. *Principles of Econometrics*. New York: Wiley.

Waite, Linda J., and Ross M. Stolzenberg. 1976. "Intended Childbearing and Labor Force Participation of Young Women: Insights from Nonrecursive Models." *American Sociological Review* 41:235–52.

Zellner, Arnold. 1962. "An Efficient Method of Estimating Seemingly Unrelated Regressions and Tests for Aggregation Bias." *Journal of the American Statistical Association* 57:348–68.

7

LOGLINEAR MODELS FOR RECIPROCAL AND OTHER SIMULTANEOUS EFFECTS

*Robert D. Mare**
Christopher Winship[†]

This paper presents new models for simultaneous relationships among endogenous categorical variables. Previous investigators have argued that the loglinear/logit framework is insufficiently rich for the development of simultaneous equation models and that only models that postulate latent continuous variables (e.g. multivariate probit models) can represent simultaneous relationships among categorical variables. This paper shows that by using latent class methods, we can develop loglinear models for simultaneous effects that are analogous to linear models in simultaneous equation theory. These models, which are extensions of conventional loglinear and logit models for cross-classified data, are suitable when an independent variable is jointly determined with the dependent variable in a single-equation logit model or when there are reciprocal effects between two endogenous categorical variables. The models proposed here are extensions of recently developed

This research was supported by grants from the National Institute of Child Health and Human Development (HD-25748-01 and HD-25749-01), the National Science Foundation, and the Graduate School of the University of Wisconsin—Madison. Computations were performed using the facilities of the Center for Demography and Ecology of the University of Wisconsin—Madison, which are supported by the Center for Population Research of the NICHD (HD-5876). The authors are grateful to Charles Halaby, Yu Xie, Peter Marsden, and anonymous reviewers for helpful comments on an earlier draft of this paper.

*University of Wisconsin, Madison
[†]Northwestern University

loglinear models for missing and other partially observed data. They have several advantages over the multivariate probit approach, including avoidance of the assumption of latent multivariate normally distributed variables, a closer link between units of measurement and structural parameters, and relative ease of computation.

1. INTRODUCTION

1.1. *The Problem of Simultaneity*

A standard tool for the analysis of complex social phenomena is the structural equation model, which specifies the relationships between dependent variables and independent variables. This model is particularly valuable when several outcomes are jointly (simultaneously) determined, that is, when each endogenous variable depends on the other endogenous variables under investigation. For example, in the interaction between spouses, the behavior of one spouse may affect the behavior of the other spouse, and vice versa (e.g., Duncan 1974; Duncan and Duncan 1978). The behavior of each spouse is both an independent variable and a dependent variable in a model of reciprocal effects. In other instances the joint determination of endogenous variables is more subtle. For example, one may wish to examine the effects of participation in a job-training program on the probability of employment at a subsequent date. Ideally, program participation is an exogenous variable that affects a single endogenous variable; but in the absence of random assignment of persons to the program, the structural relationship between participation and employment may be obscured by systematic selection of individuals into (or out of) the program. Although employment status is the endogenous variable of primary interest, program participation is also endogenous and is jointly determined with employment (e.g., Heckman and Hotz 1989).

For continuous endogenous variables, simultaneous equation models are well-established extensions of the general linear model (e.g., Goldberger and Duncan 1973; Amemiya 1985; Duncan 1975). When one or more endogenous variables are discrete, however, more complex methods are used. Typically, simultaneous equation models for discrete endogenous variables are multivariate probit models (e.g., Mallar 1977; Heckman 1978; Muthén 1984). These simultaneous models rely critically on the assumption that discrete endogenous variables are realizations of latent *continuous* variables. That is, structural relations are specified in terms of continuous variables, thereby allowing interpretations that are similar to those from conventional structural equation models for observed continuous variables. In these models, the link between the latent continuous variables and the observed discrete variables is specified in auxiliary measurement equations, and estimation usually requires the assumption that conditional on the exogenous variables, the latent continuous variables follow a multivariate normal distribution.

1.2. *Simultaneous Equations: A Loglinear Approach*

An alternative strategy for analysis of simultaneous relations among discrete variables is to extend standard loglinear and logit models for categorical data (e.g., Bishop, Fienberg, and Holland 1975; Goodman 1978; Haberman 1978–79; Fienberg 1980). On the surface, this strategy seems attractive: (a) It expresses structural relations among variables in a way more closely tied to the way that variables are measured; (b) it avoids the analytic fiction that discrete endogenous variables always arise from latent continuous variables; (c) it avoids the assumption of (conditional) multivariate normality of endogenous variables; and (d) it avoids the computational burden that arises in probit models for polytomous outcomes or for more than two or three dichotomous outcomes (e.g. Daganzo 1979).

This strategy for simultaneous equation modeling for discrete endogenous variables, however, has *not* been followed. Indeed, many analysts have concluded that loglinear models cannot be used to analyze simultaneous relationships among endogenous variables.

Goodman (1973) presents methods for analysis of recursive causal systems using loglinear models but represents relationships between jointly determined variables by only their partial association. By this formulation, the reciprocal effects between pairs of endogenous variables are not identified, and the structural relations between variables are not distinguished from their partial associations.

Brier (1978) shows that elementary loglinear models for two endogenous variables imply two logit equations in which the reciprocal effects of the endogenous variables are equal. He concludes that "generally, reciprocal effects can never be separated in systems of logistic models. . . . The only techniques that allow simultaneous estimation of reciprocal effects involve the concept of latent continuous variables" (1978, pp. 124, 126).

In a widely used text, Fienberg states: "Can we set up non-recursive systems of logit models for categorical variables, with properties resembling those of the nonrecursive systems of linear structural equations? The answer to this question is no" (1980, p. 134).

Heckman (1978, p. 950) asserts that "the loglinear model is not sufficiently rich in parameters to distinguish structural association among discrete random variables from purely statistical association among discrete random variables. The distinction between structural and statistical association is at the heart of simultaneous equation theory." Heckman argues that the error structure of the logit model is too restrictive to allow the model to represent simultaneous relationships. Specifically, because the logit model does not allow for correlated errors across equations, it is inappropriate for estimating simultaneous effects.

This paper shows that models for simultaneous effects among endogenous variables can in fact be specified and estimated by extending loglinear models for cross-classified data. In particular, we develop models that expand the standard loglinear model by incorporating partially observed variables. These variables are observed for some cases but are unobserved for others. The use of partially observed variables allows for a sufficiently rich parametric structure to model simultaneity within the framework of loglinear models. These simultaneity models do not rely on the assumption of latent continuous variables; nor do they make distributional assumptions beyond the usual multinomial sampling assumptions of the loglinear model. The models are analogous to standard simultaneous equation models for continuous variables in that they permit the separation of structural relations of variables from their statistical associations and, in models of simultaneity between two endogenous variables, the isolation of distinct reciprocal effects. At the same time, this approach to simultaneous equation modeling retains the conceptual and practical advantages of loglinear and logit approaches.

The models presented in this paper build on recently developed models for cross-classified data in which some variables are missing for some observations. Fay (1986), Little and Rubin (1987),

Baker and Laird (1988), and Winship and Mare (1989) present loglinear models for tables with missing data, including data that are not missing at random. Haberman (1988) presents a general computational algorithm for estimating loglinear models on indirectly or partially observed contingency tables.

Section 2 of this paper describes data that we will use to illustrate our models and discusses alternative structural relationships that may be investigated with the data. Section 3 presents a model for a single structural relationship that is potentially confounded by simultaneity between the dependent variable and one of the regressors. This model is analogous to the dummy-endogenous-variable model that is based on extensions of multivariate probit analysis (Heckman 1978; Maddala 1983). Section 4 presents a model for reciprocal effects between two endogenous variables. This model is analogous to the simultaneous equation model that has been commonly applied in sociology (e.g., Duncan, Haller, and Portes 1968; Stolzenberg and Waite 1977; Marini 1984). We show how each of these two models can be formulated and estimated on a partially observed contingency table and present illustrative empirical results. Section 5 discusses the identifiability of the simultaneous equation models presented here. Section 6 discusses some limitations of the proposed models and problems for further research.

2. AN EXAMPLE

2.1. *Simultaneous Equation Models for Reciprocal Effects*

Table 1 cross classifies two-wave panel data on whether or not high school boys perceive themselves to be members of their school's leading crowd and whether their attitude toward the leading crowd is favorable or unfavorable. These data are from a study by Coleman (1961), in which high school students were interviewed in October 1957 and in May 1958. Membership is measured by a response to the question, "Are you a member of the leading crowd?" Attitude is measured by the respondent's agreement or disagreement with the statement, "If a fellow wants to be part of the leading crowd around here, he sometimes has to go against his principles" (Coleman 1964, p. 168). These data have been analyzed by Coleman (1964), Good-

TABLE 1

Cross-Classification of Panel Data on Membership In and Attitude Toward the Leading Crowd in High School

			Wave 2			
		Member		Nonmember		
Membership (C) Attitude (D)		Favorable	Unfavorable	Favorable	Unfavorable	
Membership (A)	Attitude (B)					
Member	Favorable	458	110	140	49
Member	Unfavorable	171	56	182	87
Nonmember	Favorable	184	531	75	281
Nonmember	Unfavorable	85	338	97	554

Source. Coleman 1964.

204

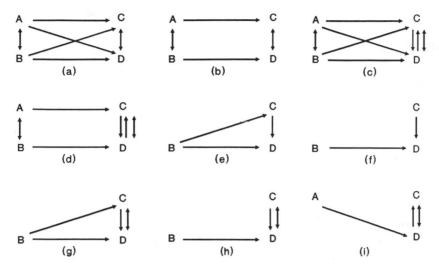

FIGURE 1. Models for two endogenous variables.

man (1973, 1974), Fienberg (1980), Duncan (1985), and Haberman (1988).

Although many models can be applied to these data, we emphasize those that represent simultaneous relationships between membership in and attitude toward the leading crowd. Figure 1 represents alternative models for the leading-crowd data, where A, B, C, and D denote membership in the leading crowd at wave 1, attitude toward the leading crowd at wave 1, membership at wave 2, and attitude at wave 2, respectively. In model a, both membership and attitude at wave 1 affect both membership and attitude at wave 2. Within each wave, membership and attitude are associated, but the direction of the effect is unspecified. Thus, although model a allows for mutual causation of membership and attitude *over time,* it does not represent their simultaneous effects on each other. This model can be estimated as a loglinear model with the terms AB, AC, AD, BC, BD, and CD. Model b is similar to model a, except that it omits the cross-lagged associations between membership and attitude. It can be estimated as a simple loglinear model with terms AB, AC, BD, and CD.

Unlike models a and b, models c and d include the reciprocal effects of membership and attitude on each other at wave 2. These effects are represented by the single-headed arrows that connect C and D. In addition, models c and d include residual association between C and D that remains once the dependence of C and D on each other and on A and B are taken into account. This residual association is represented by the double-headed arrows connecting C and D in models c and d. Whereas model c also allows for cross-lagged effects, model d omits these effects. These models could be specified as pairs of simple logit models. For example, model c could be represented as a loglinear model or as two logit models for the probability that a boy is in the leading crowd (given A, B, and D) and that he has a favorable attitude toward the leading crowd (given A, C, and D). By this formulation, however, the partial effects of D on C and of C on D are necessarily equal and thus are no more informative than the CD partial association in model a (Brier 1978). The same result holds for model d. The logit models, moreover, cannot distinguish the reciprocal effects between C and D from the association that remains once their dependence on A, B, and each other is taken into account. In contrast, if C and D were continuous variables, a conventional simultaneous equation model (or the analogous multivariate probit model [Heckman 1978]) for model d would yield distinct estimates of the effects of C on D and D on C. In this approach, variables B and A are instrumental variables for C and D, respectively. Moreover, by this approach it is possible to identify both the reciprocal effects of C and D and also the residual correlation between C and D net of their dependence on A, B, and each other. Model c, however, is not identified in a conventional simultaneous equation approach.

Although conventional loglinear and logit models cannot isolate the reciprocal effects of C and D in model d, extensions of the loglinear model can. These extensions, which we shall term *structural loglinear models*, also enable one to distinguish the two reciprocal effects of C and D from their remaining partial association once causal relationships are taken into account. Whereas extensions of loglinear models can contain all of the parameters for model d, they cannot do so for model c. These new models, which are presented in section 4, enable one to isolate all of the effects that can be obtained in conventional simultaneous equation models. Before we present these models, however, we consider simpler simultaneous equation models.

2.2. *Simultaneous Equation Models for One Equation with Endogenous Regressor*

A simpler model is required when one has a single dependent variable but one or more independent variables can be jointly determined with the dependent variable. This problem arises in the study of job-program effects on employment mentioned above, but it can also be illustrated with the leading-crowd data in Table 1. Suppose that variable A is not observed, that instead of Table 1 we have a 2^3 table of attitude at wave 1 (B) by membership at wave 2 (C) by attitude at wave 2 (D), and that we are mainly interested in the effects of membership on attitude. Models e–i in Figure 1 apply to 2^3 tables. Models e and f are simple models for the effects of B and C on D and can be specified and estimated as elementary loglinear models. Models g, h, and i, in contrast, represent joint determination of C and D. The single headed arrow between C and D denotes the effect of C on D. The double-headed arrow represents additional association between the variables not due to the effect of C on D. This association may occur because D affects C as in models c and d; because other variables, not included in the table, affect both C and D; or because C and D have measurement errors that are correlated.

As in the four-variable model with reciprocal effects, the parameters of models g, h, and i cannot be retrieved from conventional loglinear models. In contrast, if C and D were continuous variables, conventional simultaneous equation methods could be used to estimate model i, in which A serves as an instrumental variable for D. In the conventional simultaneous equation approach, models g and h are not identified. The structural loglinear models proposed in this paper, however, can isolate the parameters of models h and i, but not model g. Models h and i are analogous to the dummy-endogenous-variable model proposed by Heckman (1978) within the multivariate probit framework. We discuss this model in the next section.

3. STRUCTURAL LOGLINEAR AND LOGIT MODELS FOR A SINGLE EQUATION WITH SIMULTANEITY

In this section we describe single-equation models for categorical variables in which one independent variable is jointly determined with the dependent variable. We begin by outlining a general approach to distinguishing between structural and spurious association in categorical variables. Then we apply this approach to the simultaneous equation model.

3.1. *Structural Effects and Partial Observability*

In nonexperimental data, observations on the joint distributions of dependent and independent variables almost always confound the structural relationships between variables with spurious association. Spurious associations arise because unmeasured variables may affect both the independent and the dependent variables; because respondents may be selected (or select themselves) into categories of the independent variable on the basis of their expected outcomes on the dependent variable, creating "feedback" between the dependent and independent variables; or because of correlated errors of measurement in the dependent and independent variables. Spurious association between observed variables arises because observations are not randomly assigned to levels of the independent variable.[1]

Another way of viewing spuriousness is that it results from *incomplete observation* on the dependent variable. For each respondent, we observe the dependent variable for a single level of an independent variable but do not observe what the dependent variable would have been had the respondent been assigned to other levels of that independent variable (Rubin 1978). In most nonexperimental studies, one must infer effects from differences in the dependent variable across levels of an independent variable that are observed for different respondents; that is, one must infer from comparisons *between persons* who are not necessarily identical on unmeasured variables. If, on the other hand, one could observe *distinct* dependent variables for each individual for each value of an independent variable, then one could make much stronger causal inferences from comparisons *within persons* who are, by definition, identical on unmeasured variables across levels of the independent variables. In the absence of repeated observations on the same respondent across levels of an independent variable, one can nonetheless *model* the par-

---

[1]For concreteness our discussion refers to "respondents," "persons," and "individuals" throughout. Obviously, our models apply to other units of analysis as well.

tially observed data. Although one cannot estimate effects for each person, one can estimate the average effect of a variable across persons. Rubin (1978) provides a general model for causal inference in which outcomes on the dependent variable on unobserved levels of the independent variables are regarded as "missing data." Winship and Mare (1989) show how loglinear models for missing data enable one to make inferences about respondents' behavior when it is not observed. Before extending these models to simultaneous equations, we describe their formulation for the more elementary case of a single endogenous variable. In practice, if the dependent variable is the only endogenous variable (that is, if all independent variables are exogenous), then elementary loglinear and logit models and the models for partially observed data presented here provide identical estimates of effects. We begin with this case, however, to illustrate the approach in its simplest form, before going on to the more complex case of jointly determined variables.

Suppose that we have a single endogenous variable D and a single exogenous variable B, each of which takes the values 1 or -1. For example, B and D may denote attitude toward the leading crowd at waves 1 and 2, respectively, and thus be observed in a collapsed version of Table 1. The observed data, therefore, are a 2×2 frequency table. To assess the effect of B on D, we can use an elementary logit model,

$$\text{logit}[p(D = 1 \mid B)] = \beta + \beta_j^B, \tag{1}$$

where the subscript j indexes levels of B and $\sum_j \beta_j^B = 0$.

An alternative formulation recognizes that for each respondent, we observe D for only one level of B and we do not observe D for the level of B that the respondent did not experience. Define two additional variables, D_1 and D_0, that denote respondents' values on D when B equals 1 and -1, respectively. For respondents for whom $B = 1$, $D_1 = D$ and D_0 is unobserved; for respondents for whom $B = -1$, $D_0 = D$ and D_1 is unobserved. Here, B is an indicator for whether D_1 or D_0 is observed. In the language of experiments it indicates the treatment to which an individual is assigned. Since B is exogenous, it is independent of D_1 and D_0. Whether $B = 1$ or -1 is not related to the outcome on D_1 and D_0. Assignment to levels of B is at "random."

We can represent the relationship between our three variables in a partially observed 2^3 table with dimensions B, D_1, and D_0. This

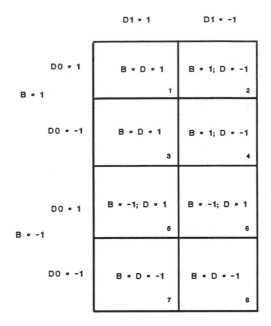

FIGURE 2. Expanded form of table with one exogenous and one endogenous variable.

table is illustrated in Figure 2, which shows the mapping between the observed data on B and D and the partially observed relations among B, D_1, and D_0. This table can be modeled as a latent class/ loglinear model using methods described by Winship and Mare (1989) and below. The loglinear model that is equivalent to the logit model (1) is the model of one-way effects (independence): BD_1D_0. This equivalence is explained below. The assumption that B is independent of D_1 and D_0 (that is, the assumption that B is exogenous) is essential to the identification of the model. The D_1D_0 interaction is not identified. For convenience it is set to zero.

To understand the relationship between the above loglinear model and the logit model (1), consider two logit equations that the above loglinear model implies:

$$\text{logit}[p(D_1 = 1)] = \beta^{D1}, \tag{2}$$

$$\text{logit}[p(D_0 = 1)] = \beta^{D0}. \tag{3}$$

The effect of B on D is the difference in levels between D_1 and D_0, that is, $\beta^{D1} - \beta^{D0}$. The average level of D in the population is $(\beta^{D1} + \beta^{D0})/2$. Equations (2) and (3) cannot be estimated using standard methods, since D_1 and D_0 are not fully observed. That B is independent of D_1 and D_0, however, implies that

$$\text{logit}[p(D_1 = 1) \mid B = 1] = \beta^{D1}, \tag{4}$$

$$\text{logit}[p(D_0 = 1) \mid B = 0] = \beta^{D0}. \tag{5}$$

These two equations can be estimated using standard methods, since D_1 and D_0 are fully observed for the specified value of B in each question. The estimation of (4) and (5) is equivalent to the estimation of (1). Combining the dependent variables in equations (4) and (5) gives the dependent variable in equation (1). The relationships between the parameters in the three equations are as follows: $\beta = (\beta^{D1} + \beta^{D0})/2$, $\beta_1^B = (\beta^{D1} - \beta^{D0})/2$, and $\beta_0^B = (\beta^{D0} - \beta^{D1})/2$.

If B is exogenous, estimation of equation (1) and estimation of a loglinear model with only the one-way effects in Figure 2 yield identical results. Nothing more about the relationship between B and D is learned by using the latent class approach. One can always postulate a separate dependent variable for each combination of levels of the independent variables, but this is unnecessary whenever one assumes that all of the independent variables are exogenous. In this case, by assumption, the effects that derive from the between-respondent comparisons on the dependent variable across levels of the independent variable are satisfactory.

As discussed in detail below, when an independent variable is jointly determined with the dependent variable, it becomes fruitful to distinguish between respondents' observed outcomes on endogenous variables and those that they would have obtained if their values on the independent variables were different from those observed. It is possible to model these relationships by using latent class loglinear models that are more complicated than the one-way effects model above. This is the key to our approach.

3.2. General Form of the Single-Equation Model with Simultaneity

Our approach is applicable to models h and i in Figure 1, although our initial discussion will be confined to model h. Model i, which can be estimated by a similar approach, is discussed in section 5.2.

To separate the structural effect of C on D from the statistical association between these variables, we use a model in which each respondent has two outcomes on variable C and two outcomes on variable D. That is, we distinguish between respondents' actual responses on D and their hypothetical responses if they had a value of C different from the one that we observe; and we distinguish between respondents' actual responses on C and their hypothetical responses if they had a value of D different from the one that we observe. Let B, C, and D take on values of 1 or -1. Now define four new variables: D_1 and D_0, which denote respondents' outcomes for alternative values of C, and C_1 and C_0, which denote respondents' outcomes for alternative values of D.

D_1, D_0, C_1, and C_0 are partially observed variables inasmuch as whether we observe them depends on the particular value of C and D that we observe. The logical relations among C, D, C_1, C_0, D_1, and D_0 are as follows: (a) if $C = D = 1$, then $C_1 = 1$, $D_1 = 1$, and C_0 and D_0 are unobserved; (b) if $C = 1$ and $D = -1$, then $C_0 = 1$, $D_1 = -1$, and C_1 and D_0 are unobserved; (c) if $C = -1$ and $D = 1$, then $C_1 = -1$, $D_0 = 1$, and C_0 and D_1 are unobserved; (d) if $C = D = -1$, then $C_0 = -1$, $D_0 = -1$, and C_1 and D_1 are unobserved. This implies that $C = [(D + 1)C_1 + (1 - D)C_0]/2$ and that $D = [(C + 1)D_1 + (1 - C)D_0]/2$.

Despite the partial observability of C_1, C_0, D_1, and D_0, a general model for the dependence of D on C is

$$p(D_1 = 1 \mid B, C_1, C_0) = F_1(B, C_1, C_0), \tag{6}$$

$$p(D_0 = 1 \mid B, C_1, C_0) = F_0(B, C_1, C_0), \tag{7}$$

where F_1 and F_0 denote functions that will be specified more fully below. Equations (6) and (7) are a structural model for D inasmuch as they represent the effects of B and C on D apart from the actual sample values of B, C, and D. As we will show more explicitly below, the model separates the structural effect of C on D from the sample association between C and D. In these respects, this model is analogous to the endogenous switching regression model (Maddala 1983; Mare and Winship 1988), which separates the structural effects of a categorical variable from systematic, sample-specific selection of observations into levels of the categorical variable that are potentially correlated with the dependent variable.

		$D1 = 1$		$D1 = -1$	
		$DO = 1$	$DO = -1$	$DO = 1$	$DO = -1$
$C1 = 1$	$CO = 1$	$C = D = 1$ 1	$C = D = 1$ 2	$C = 1; D = -1$ 3	$C = 1; D = -1$ 4
	$CO = -1$	$C = D = 1$ 5	$C = D = 1$ $C = D = -1$ 6	 7	$C = D = -1$ 8
$C1 = -1$	$CO = 1$	$C = -1; D = 1$ 9	 10	$C = 1; D = -1$ $C = -1; D = 1$ 11	$C = 1; D = -1$ 12
	$CO = -1$	$C = -1; D = 1$ 13	$C = D = -1$ 14	$C = -1; D = 1$ 15	$C = D = -1$ 16

FIGURE 3. Expanded form of table with two endogenous variables (conditional on exogenous variables).

3.3. Structural Loglinear Model for the Expanded Table

We specify and estimate structural loglinear models for an expanded, partially observed contingency table with dimensions B, C_1, C_0, D_1, and D_0.[2] Figure 3 illustrates the expanded table for the jth category of B. We observe none of the individual cells of the expanded table. Instead, each observed combination of C and D for a given level of B can fall into four cells in the expanded table. For example, if $C = -1$ and $D = 1$ for an observation, then it is potentially a member of cell 9, 11, 13, or 15 of the expanded table. Two

[2]An alternative approach to the single-equation model with an endogenous independent variable is to specify a model for an expanded table with dimensions B, C, D_1, and D_0, that is, to consider alternative outcomes on D for different values of C but to assume that $C_1 = C_0 = C$. This approach yields a model that is similar but not identical to the one presented here. The relationship between these two models is a subject for further research. The model presented here generalizes more easily to the simultaneous equation model presented in section 4.

cells of the expanded table are logically impossible (7 and 10), and for two other cells of the expanded table (6 and 11), two distinct cells of the observed table provide information.

Since B has two categories, a general loglinear model for the expanded table would have 28 parameters ($32 - 4 = 28$, because of the four logically impossible cells), which would not be estimable because the observed table has only eight cells. Thus, we use a more restricted model. In keeping with model h in Figure 1, we assume that B does not directly affect C. This is analogous to the assumption in standard simultaneous equation theory that B is an instrument for C. Thus, all interactions that include the BC_1 and BC_0 terms are set to zero. In addition, we assume that all interactions that include the D_1D_0 and C_1C_0 terms are zero. This implies that conditional on B, D_1 and D_0 are independent and C_1 and C_0 are independent.[3] Assuming that observations are obtained under multinomial sampling, a restricted loglinear model is

$$\log p_{jklmn} = \lambda + \lambda_j^B + \lambda_k^{C1} + \lambda_l^{C0} + \lambda_m^{D1} + \lambda_n^{D0}$$
$$+\lambda_{jm}^{BD1} + \lambda_{jn}^{BD0} + \lambda_{km}^{C1D0} + \lambda_{kn}^{C1D0} + \lambda_{lm}^{C0D1} + \lambda_{ln}^{C0D0}, \qquad (8)$$

where p_{jklmn} denotes the probability that an individual falls into the jth category of B ($j = -1,1$), the kth category of C_1 ($k = -1,1$), the lth category of C_0 ($l = -1,1$), the mth category of D_1 ($m = -1,1$), and the nth category of D_0; the intercept λ is determined by the constraint that $\Sigma_{jklmn}P_{jklmn} = 1$; the remaining λ's are parameters; and $\Sigma_j\lambda_j^B = \Sigma_k\lambda_k^{C1} = \Sigma_l\lambda_l^{C0} = \Sigma_m\lambda_m^{D1} = \Sigma_n\lambda_n^{D0} = \Sigma_j\lambda_{jm}^{BD1} = \Sigma_m\lambda_{jm}^{BD1} = \Sigma_j\lambda_{jn}^{BD0} = \Sigma_n\lambda_{jn}^{BD0} = \Sigma_k\lambda_{km}^{C1D1} = S_m\lambda_{km}^{C1D1} = \Sigma_k\lambda_{kn}^{C1D0} = \Sigma_n\lambda_{kn}^{C1D0} = \Sigma_l\lambda_{lm}^{C0D1} = \Sigma_m\lambda_{lm}^{C0D1} = \Sigma_l\lambda_{ln}^{C0D0} = \Sigma_n\lambda_{ln}^{C0D0} = 0$.

Model (8) is not identified inasmuch as it contains 12 parameters, four more than the number of observed cells. However, a more restrictive version of (8), which is identified, captures the essential features of model h in Figure 1. In particular, we assume that D does not affect C, i.e., that $\lambda_k^{C1} = \lambda_l^{C0}$. We also assume that $\lambda_{km}^{C1D1} = \lambda_{kn}^{C1D0}$

[3] Unlike the interactions in the endogenous switching model based on linear and probit equations (Maddala 1983; Mare and Winship 1988), these interactions are identified in structural loglinear models under certain conditions. The assumption that they are zero is usually not realistic. In the examples presented in this paper, however, the models fit well when these interactions are omitted. Footnotes 4 and 6 report results for models in which these interactions are included. For the most part, the estimates do not change, although standard errors are larger.

$= \lambda_{lm}^{C0D1} = \lambda_{ln}^{C0D0}$, a restriction explained below. Equation (8) includes distinct effects of B on D_1 and D_0. This amounts to a three-way interaction between B, C, and D. Model h in Figure 1, however, assumes a single effect of B on D (irrespective of the value of C). Thus, we assume that $\lambda_{jm}^{BD1} = \lambda_{jn}^{BD0}$, i.e., that B does not interact with C in affecting D.

We impose the above constraints by using two new variables, C^* and D^*. These variables help to simplify the equations below and to provide a direct connection to the structure of the design matrices discussed below. C^* is indexed by s and has three levels, 1, 0, -1. The index s of C^* is the sum of the indexes of C_1 and C_0, k and l respectively; that is, $s = (k + l)/2$. The parameters for C^*, for example λ^{C^*}, are the sums of the parameters for C_1 and C_0, for example $\lambda_s^{C^*} = \lambda_k^{C1} + \lambda_l^{C0} = 2\lambda_k^{C1}$. D^* is defined analogously for the variables D_1 and D_0. D^* has index t, where $t = (n + m)/2$, and $\lambda_t^{D^*} = \lambda_m^{D1} + \lambda_n^{D0} = 2\lambda_m^{D1}$. When C^* and D^* are used in higher-way effects, the above relations generalize. Thus, including the term $\lambda_{jt}^{BD^*}$ implies that $\lambda_{jm}^{BD1} = \lambda_{jn}^{BD0}$, with $\lambda_{jt}^{BD^*} = \lambda_{jm}^{BD1} + \lambda_{jn}^{BD0} = 2\lambda_{jm}^{BD1}$. Using C^* and D^* implies that the terms involving C_1, C_0, D_1, and D_0 are implicitly included in an expression and that they have been constrained to be equal in the way noted above: $\lambda_{st}^{C^*D^*} = \lambda_{km}^{C1D1} + \lambda_{kn}^{C1D0} + \lambda_{lm}^{C0D1} + \lambda_{ln}^{C0D0} = 4\lambda_{km}^{C1D1}$. This term represents the residual association of C and D net of the structural relationship(s) between the two variables. Inclusion of this term implies that all terms to which it sums are included and constrained to be equal. As we show below, the definitions of C^* and D^* are consistent with the way design effects are defined when equality constraints are imposed.

Under these assumptions and notation, the model becomes

$$\log p_{jklmn} = \lambda + \lambda_j^B + \lambda_{kl}^{C^*} + \lambda_m^{D1} + \lambda_n^{D0} + \lambda_{jmn}^{BD^*} + \lambda_{st}^{C^*D^*}. \quad (9)$$

Model (9) is a structural loglinear model for the effects of C on D, taking account of the residual association between these two variables. The *structural* coefficient for the effect of C on D is $2(\lambda_m^{D1} - \lambda_n^{D0})$. To see this, note that λ_m^{D1} denotes the average level of D when $C = 1$, whereas λ_n^{D0} denotes the average level of D when $C = -1$. Thus, the effect of C is proportional to the difference between these two parameters. The *partial association* between C and D is $2\lambda_{st}^{C^*D^*}$. The latter parameter corresponds to the double-headed arrow in model h of Figure 1 and measures the tendency of respondents for whom $C_1 =$

1 and $C_0 = 1$ to be more (or less) likely to have $D_1 = 1$ and $D_0 = 1$. If the model contained separate parameters $\lambda_{st}^{C^*D1}$ and $\lambda_{st}^{C^*D0}$ (instead of $\lambda_{st}^{C^*D^*}$), then these two parameters would correspond to the effects of nonrandom selection from the levels of D_1 and D_0 into categories of C and would be analogous to correlated disturbances in endogenous switching regression models (e.g., Maddala 1983; Mare and Winship 1988). In this model, however, we estimate only a single parameter for nonrandom selection, yielding a model that is analogous to the dummy endogenous variable model (Heckman 1978, p. 938).

3.4. Logit Form of the Model

To show the link between the structural loglinear model and the general model presented in section 3.2, we write (9) as two logit models, one for D_1 and one for D_0. That is,

$$\text{logit}[p(D_1 = 1 \mid B,C_1,C_0)] = \beta^{D1} + \beta_j^{BD^*} + \beta^{C^*D^*}, \qquad (10)$$

$$\text{logit}[p(D_0 = 1 \mid B,C_1,C_0)] = \beta^{D0} + \beta_j^{BD^*} + \beta^{C^*D^*}, \qquad (11)$$

where $\beta^{D1} = 2\lambda_m^{D1}, \beta^{D0} = 2\lambda_n^{D0}, \beta_j^{BD^*} = 2\lambda_{jt}^{BD^*}$, and $\beta^{C^*D^*} = 2\lambda_{st}^{C^*D^*}$. Equations (10) and (11) correspond to the general model of (6) and (7), but we can also write the model as a single equation:

$$\text{logit}[p(D_q = 1 \mid B,C_1,C_0)] = \beta^D + \beta_q^{DC} + \beta_j^{BD^*} + \beta^{C^*D^*}, \qquad (12)$$

where D_q is a variable taking the value 1 or -1 for the qth category of C ($q = 0,1$); β^D is the grand mean of the logit of the probability that $D_q = 1$ [$\beta^D = (\beta^{D1} + \beta^{D0})/2$]; β_q^{DC} is the structural effect of C on D (that is, $\beta_1^{DC} = \beta^{D1} - \beta^{D0}$, and $\beta_0^{DC} = \beta^{D0} - \beta^{D1}$); and the remaining notation is as defined above. Model (12), therefore, contains parameters for the structural effects of B and C on D, as well as for the association between C and D that remains once the dependence of D on C and B is taken into account.

3.5. Estimation with an Empirical Illustration

We can obtain the parameters of (12) from the corresponding loglinear model (9), which we estimate by treating the unobserved cells in Figure 3 as "missing" data (Winship and Mare 1989). We get maximum likelihood estimates of expected cell frequencies and parameters of (9) using Haberman's (1988) DNEWTON program for loglinear models estimated from indirectly observed contingency tables. Haberman (1988) describes the computational algorithm, and Winship and Mare (1989) provide an example of its application to simple contingency tables with missing data. The estimation procedure requires that one specify (a) a design matrix for the relationship between the parameters to be estimated and the expected frequencies of the expanded table and (b) a mapping between the observed cell frequencies and the cells of the expanded table.

For model (9) applied to the three-variable BCD version of the leading-crowd data in Table 1, we present the design matrix and cell mapping in Table 2. The rows of Table 2 refer to cells in the expanded table. The columns of the design matrix labeled *Model Terms* correspond to parameters in equation (9). The columns for B, C^*, D_0, and D_1 are contrast-coded indicator variables. These variables are d^B, d^{C^*}, d^{D0}, and d^{D1}, respectively. (The variable d^{C^*} is the average of the separate indicator variables for C_1 and C_0, say d^{C1} and d^{C0}.) Then the columns for BD^* and C^*D^* are $d^B(d^{D0} + d^{D1})/2$ and $d^{C^*}(d^{D0} + d^{D1})/2$, respectively. This coding imposes the restrictions $\lambda_{jm}^{BD1} = \lambda_{jn}^{BD0}$, $\lambda_k^{C1} = \lambda_l^{C0}$, and $\lambda_{km}^{C1D1} = \lambda_{kn}^{C1D0} = \lambda_{lm}^{C0D1} = \lambda_{ln}^{C0D0}$ on (8) above.

The first column shows how the observed frequencies are mapped into 28 of the cells in the expanded table. The four cells corresponding to the two levels of cells 7 and 10 in Figure 3 are not included in this list because they are logically impossible. Thus, their frequencies are constrained to be zero.

As noted above there are potentially 28 parameters associated with the model for the expanded table in Figure 3. But Table 2 includes 32 rows because cells 6 and 7 in Figure 3 receive observations under two outcomes for each of the two levels of B. We have listed the contribution of each outcome separately. If we had combined the contributions, which would lead to the same results, Table 2 would have 28 rows. The last column of the table contains expected frequencies for a model to be discussed below.

The top panel of Table 3 presents likelihood-ratio chi-square (G^2) statistics for model (9) plus several simpler models fit to the BCD version of Table 1. Model I includes the structural effect of C on D (as implied by the terms D_0 and D_1), but no partial association between these variables. Model II includes the partial association (as implied by the term C^*D^*), but no structural effect. Model III includes both the structural effect and the partial association. Models I

TABLE 2

Design Matrix, Cell Mapping, and Expected Frequencies for Single-Equation
Model with Endogenous Regressor for Collapsed Version of
Leading-Crowd Data

Observed Frequency	C	D	B	C^*	D_1	D_0	BD^*	C^*D^*	Expected Frequencies (Expanded Table) Model III
642	1	1	1	1	1	1	1	2	338.248
642	1	1	1	1	1	−1	0	0	34.175
642	1	1	1	0	1	1	1	0	209.986
642	1	1	1	0	1	−1	0	0	57.722
256	1	1	−1	1	1	1	−1	2	105.465
256	1	1	−1	1	1	−1	0	0	32.310
256	1	1	−1	0	1	1	−1	0	65.473
256	1	1	−1	0	1	−1	0	0	54.572
215	1	−1	1	1	−1	1	0	0	66.609
215	1	−1	1	1	−1	−1	−1	−2	6.730
215	1	−1	1	0	−1	1	0	0	112.503
215	1	−1	1	0	−1	−1	−1	0	30.925
279	1	−1	−1	1	−1	1	0	0	62.974
279	1	−1	−1	1	−1	−1	1	−2	19.293
279	1	−1	−1	0	−1	1	0	0	106.363
279	1	−1	−1	0	−1	−1	1	0	88.654
641	−1	1	1	0	1	1	1	0	209.986
641	−1	1	1	0	−1	1	0	0	112.503
641	−1	1	1	−1	1	1	1	−2	130.360
641	−1	1	1	−1	−1	1	0	0	190.018
394	−1	1	−1	0	1	1	−1	0	65.473
394	−1	1	−1	0	−1	1	0	0	106.363
394	−1	1	−1	−1	1	1	−1	−2	40.646
394	−1	1	−1	−1	−1	1	0	0	179.648
330	−1	−1	1	0	1	−1	0	0	57.722
330	−1	−1	1	0	−1	−1	−1	0	30.925
330	−1	−1	1	−1	1	−1	0	0	97.493
330	−1	−1	1	−1	−1	−1	−1	2	142.110
641	−1	−1	−1	0	1	−1	0	0	54.572
641	−1	−1	−1	0	−1	−1	1	0	88.654
641	−1	−1	−1	−1	1	−1	0	0	92.172
641	−1	−1	−1	−1	−1	−1	1	2	407.386

TABLE 3

Likelihood-Ratio Chi-Square Statistics for Three-Variable Models for
Leading-Crowd Data

Model	G^2	df
Structural loglinear models		
I. B, C^*, D_1, D_0, BD	57.64	2
II. $B, C^*, D^*, BD^*, C^*D^*$	14.02	2
III. $B, C^*, D_1, D_0, BD^*, C^*D^*$	0.07	1
Elementary loglinear models		
IV. BD, CD	32.44	2
V. BC, CD	263.46	2
VI. BC, BD	31.18	2
VII BC, BD, CD	0.04	1

TABLE 4

Parameter Estimates in Logit Form of Structural Loglinear Models for the
Three-Way Table

Variable[a]	Model I		Model II		Model III	
	$\hat{\beta}$	$SE(\hat{\beta})$	$\hat{\beta}$	$SE(\hat{\beta})$	$\hat{\beta}$	$SE(\hat{\beta})$
Intercept	.297	.037	.364	.040	.403	.090
$D_1 - D_0$	.416	.075			-.667	.218
B	1.162	.072	1.192	.070	1.110	.076
C^*D^*			1.080	.124	2.000	.324

[a]B is attitude toward the leading crowd in wave 1; C is membership in the leading crowd in wave 2, and D is attitude toward the leading crowd in wave 2.

and II are both nested within III, and as the G^2 statistics indicate, both the structural and the partial associations are statistically significant and are needed to provide an adequate model for these data.

Table 4 presents logit parameter estimates for these models. As indicated by the parameter estimates for B in all three models, the odds of a favorable attitude toward the leading crowd in wave 2 are higher for persons having a favorable attitude in wave 1 than for persons having an unfavorable attitude. The estimated effect of membership in the leading crowd in wave 2 (C), however, depends on which model is estimated. Models I and II imply that members of the leading crowd in wave 2 have more favorable attitudes toward the leading crowd in wave 2, whereas model III reveals a more complex relationship. Membership in the leading crowd *reduces* the probability of a favorable attitude in wave 2, but the partial association of membership and attitude is positive. This suggests that although belonging to the leading crowd makes one less likely to view the leading crowd favorably, unmeasured common causes of membership and attitude induce a positive association between these two variables. Although this example is simple, it illustrates that one can distinguish structural from residual associations using our methods.[4]

The lower panel of Table 3 reports G^2 statistics for several elementary loglinear models. The fit of the model of no three-way interaction, model VII, is close but not identical to that of model III. Whereas model VII includes all two-way interactions, model III uses the two-way interaction of B and C to identify the two parameters governing the relationship between C and D. Although models III and VII fit the *observed* data similarly, they yield different expected frequencies for the *expanded* table. Unlike the expected frequencies for model VII, the expected frequencies for model III vary across cells of the expanded table that correspond to the same cells of the observed table. The choice between models III and VII should be determined in part by the assumption that is made about the structural relationship between the variables, that is, whether B directly affects C. This choice is analogous to the problem of making assumptions about instrumental variables in standard simultaneous equation models.

4. STRUCTURAL LOGLINEAR AND LOGIT MODELS FOR RECIPROCAL EFFECTS

4.1. *General Form of the Model*

We now extend the approach described in section 3 to the model for reciprocal effects. This corresponds to model d in Figure 1 and will be illustrated with the four-way table for the leading-crowd data. Our model again views each respondent as having *two pairs* of outcomes, a pair for each of variables C and D. Defining all notation as above, let A be an additional exogenous variable, taking values of

---

[4]We also estimated model III allowing for a $D_1 D_0$ association. Under this model, $G^2 = 0$ (0 *df*). The estimated association parameter is -0.376 (SE = 1.212), other parameter estimates for the model change somewhat, and their standard errors are larger than when the $D_1 D_0$ association is omitted. The parameter for $D_1 - D_0$ becomes -0.422 (SE = 0.338).

1 or -1, that affects C but not D. A general model for the mutual dependence of C and D is

$$p(C_1 = 1 \mid A,B,D = 1) = G_1(A,D_0,D_1), \tag{13}$$

$$p(C_0 = 1 \mid A,B,D = -1) = G_2(A,D_0,D_1), \tag{14}$$

$$p(D_1 = 1 \mid A,B,C = 1) = G_3(B,C_0,C_1), \tag{15}$$

$$p(D_0 = 1 \mid A,B,C = -1) = G_4(B,C_0,C_1), \tag{16}$$

where the G_i denote functions that will be specified more fully below. Equations (13)–(16) are a structural model for C and D and include not only the effects of A and D on C and of B and C on D, but also the residual association between C and D. These effects are described below.

4.2. Structural Loglinear Model for the Expanded Table

We specify and estimate a loglinear model for an expanded, partially observable table with dimensions A, B, C_1, C_0, D_1, and D_0. The full expanded table has $2^6 = 64$ cells. Figure 3 now shows the cross-classification of C_1, C_0, D_1, and D_0 given a combination of values of A and B ($A = i$, $B = j$). The relationships between the observed values of C and D and the cells of the expanded table are the same as for the single-equation model.

A general loglinear model for the expanded table has 56 parameters (since there are eight structural zeros due to cells 7 and 10 in Figure 3), whereas the observed table has only 16 cells. Thus, we impose a number of restrictions. In keeping with model d of Figure 1, we assume that partial associations between A and D_0, A and D_1, B and C_0, B and C_1, and higher-way interactions involving these pairs of terms are zero. These are analogous to instrumental-variable assumptions. As before, we assume that all interactions that include the $C_1 C_0$ or $D_1 D_0$ terms are zero. Additional discussion of these two assumptions is given in section 6 below. Assuming that observations are obtained under multinomial sampling, a restricted loglinear model is

$$\begin{aligned} \log P_{ijklmn} = {} & \lambda + \lambda_i^A + \lambda_j^B + \lambda_k^{C1} + \lambda_l^{C0} + \lambda_m^{D1} + \lambda_n^{D0} + \lambda_{ij}^{AB} \\ & + \lambda_{ik}^{AC1} + \lambda_{il}^{AC0} + \lambda_{jm}^{BD1} + \lambda_{jn}^{BD0} + \lambda_{km}^{C1D1} + \lambda_{kn}^{C1D0} + \lambda_{lm}^{C0D1} \\ & + \lambda_{ln}^{C0D0}, \end{aligned} \tag{17}$$

where P_{ijklmn} denotes the probability that an individual falls into the ith category of A ($i = -1,1$), the jth category of B ($j = -1,1$), the kth category of C_1 ($k = -1,1$), the lth category of C_0 ($l = -1,1$), the mth category of D_1 ($m = -1,1$), and the nth category of D_0; the intercept λ is determined by the constraint that $\Sigma_{ijklmn}P_{ijklmn} = 1$; the remaining λ's are parameters; and $\Sigma_i\lambda_i^A = \Sigma_j\lambda_j^B = \Sigma_k\lambda_k^{C1} = \Sigma_l\lambda_l^{C0} = \Sigma_m\lambda_m^{D1} = \Sigma_n\lambda_n^{D0} = \Sigma_i\lambda_{ij}^{AB} = \Sigma_j\lambda_{ij}^{AB} = \Sigma_i\lambda_{ik}^{AC1} = \Sigma_k\lambda_{ik}^{AC1} = \Sigma_i\lambda_{il}^{AC0} = \Sigma_l\lambda_{il}^{AC0} = \Sigma_j\lambda_{jm}^{BD1} = \Sigma_m\lambda_{jm}^{BD1} = \Sigma_j\lambda_{jn}^{BD0} = \Sigma_n\lambda_{jn}^{BD0} = \Sigma_k\lambda_{km}^{C1D1} = \Sigma_m\lambda_{km}^{C1D1} = \Sigma_k\lambda_{kn}^{C1D0} = \Sigma_n\lambda_{kn}^{C1D0} = \Sigma_l\lambda_{lm}^{C0D1} = \Sigma_m\lambda_{lm}^{C0D1} = \Sigma_l\lambda_{ln}^{C0D0} = \Sigma_n\lambda_{ln}^{C0D0} = 0.$

Equation (17) contains more parameters than are required by the reciprocal-effects model. Thus, we impose some further restrictions. Equation (17) includes distinct effects of A on C_1 and C_0 (that is, the effect of A on C interacts with D) and effects of B on D_1 and D_0 (that is, the effect of B on D interacts with D). In contrast, model d in Figure 1 assumes a single effect of A on C and B on D. Thus, we also assume that $\lambda_{ik}^{AC1} = \lambda_{il}^{AC0}$ and that $\lambda_{jm}^{BD1} = \lambda_{jn}^{BD0}$. These restrictions imply that

$$\log p_{ijklmn} = \lambda + \lambda_i^A + \lambda_j^B + \lambda_k^{C1} + \lambda_l^{C0} + \lambda_m^{D1} + \lambda_n^{D0} + \lambda_{ij}^{AB} + \lambda_{jt}^{BD^*} + \lambda_{is}^{AC^*} + \lambda_{st}^{C^*D^*}, \tag{18}$$

where C^* and D^* are as defined above.

Equation (18) is a structural loglinear model for the reciprocal effects of C and D. The effect of C on D is $2(\lambda_m^{D1} - \lambda_n^{D0})$, and the effect of D on C is $2(\lambda_k^{C1} - \lambda_l^{C0})$. Note that λ_m^{D1} denotes the average level of D when $C = 1$ and that λ_n^{D0} denotes the average level of D when $C = -1$. Thus, the effect of C on D is proportional to the difference between these two parameters. Similarly, λ_k^{C1} and λ_l^{C0} denote the average levels of C when $D = 1$ and $D = -1$, respectively, and the effect of D on C is proportional to the difference between these two parameters. The partial association between C and D is $\lambda_{st}^{C^*D^*}$. It measures the association between C and D that remains once their reciprocal effects and the effects of A and B are taken into account. Whereas model (17) includes four parameters for associations among C_1, C_0, D_1, and D_0, model (18) includes only a single parameter, which is analogous to the residual correlation in the structural form of a conventional simultaneous equation model.

4.3. Logit Form of the Model

To show the link between the structural loglinear model and the general model presented in section 4.1, we write (18) as four logit equations, one each for C_1, C_0, D_1, and D_0. That is,

$$\text{logit}[p(C_1 = 1 \mid A, D_1, D_0)] = \beta^{C1} + \beta_i^{AC^*} + \beta^{C^*D^*}, \quad (19)$$

$$\text{logit}[p(C_0 = 1 \mid A, D_1, D_0)] = \beta^{C0} + \beta_i^{AC^*} + \beta^{C^*D^*}, \quad (20)$$

$$\text{logit}[p(D_1 = 1 \mid B, C_1, C_0)] = \beta^{D1} + \beta_j^{BD^*} + \beta^{C^*D^*}, \quad (21)$$

$$\text{logit}[p(D_0 = 1 \mid B, C_1, C_0)] = \beta^{D0} + \beta_j^{BD^*} + \beta^{C^*D^*}, \quad (22)$$

where $\beta^{C1} = 2\lambda_k^{C1}, \beta^{C0} = 2\lambda_l^{C0}, \beta^{D1} = 2\lambda_m^{D1}, \beta^{D0} = 2\lambda_n^{D0}, \beta_i^{AC^*} = 2\lambda_{is}^{AC}, \beta_j^{BD^*} = 2\lambda_{jt}^{BD^*}$, and $\beta^{C^*D^*} = 2\lambda_{st}^{C^*D^*}$. Equations (19–22) correspond to the general model given by (13)–(16), but we can also write the model as two logit equations, one for C and one for D:

$$\text{logit}[p(C_r = 1 \mid A, D_1, D_0)] = \beta^C + \beta_r^{CD} + \beta_i^{AC^*} + \beta^{C^*D^*}, \quad (23)$$

$$\text{logit}[p(D_q = 1 \mid B, C_1, C_0)] = \beta^D + \beta_q^{DC} + \beta_j^{BD^*} + \beta^{C^*D^*}, \quad (24)$$

where C_r is a variable taking the value 1 or -1 for the rth category of D ($r = 0,1$); D_q is a variable taking the value 1 or -1 for the qth category of C ($q = 0,1$); β^C is the grand mean of the logit of the probability that $C_r = 1$ [$\beta^C = (\beta^{C1} + \beta^{C0})/2$]; β^D is the grand mean of the logit of the probability that $D_q = 1$ [$\beta^D = (\beta^{D1} + \beta^{D0})/2$]; β_r^{CD} is the structural effect of D on C (that is, $\beta_1^{CD} = \beta^{C1} - \beta^{C0}$, and $\beta_0^{CD} = \beta^{C0} - \beta^{C1}$); β_q^{DC} is the structural effect of C on D (that is, $\beta_1^{DC} = \beta^{D1} - \beta^{D0}$, and $\beta_0^{DC} = \beta^{D0} - \beta^{D1}$); and the remaining notation is as defined above.

Equations (23) and (24), therefore, contain structural parameters for the effects of B and D on C and the effects of A and C on D, as well as the association between C and D that remains once their dependence on each other and on A and B is taken into account. Note that the structural parameters are unrestricted and that in general, $\beta_r^{CD} \neq \beta_q^{DC}$. That $\beta^{C^*D^*}$ enters both (23) and (24) implies that the two logit models should be estimated jointly. This contrasts with Brier's (1978) formulation in which the logit model for each dependent variable is estimated separately and yields identical parameters for the reciprocal relationship between C and D.

4.4. Empirical Illustration

As in the case of the single-equation logit model, we obtain the parameters for the two-equation logit model (23)–(24) from its corresponding structural loglinear model for the expanded table (18). Table 5 presents the design matrix and cell mapping for (18). As in Table 2, the rows in Table 5 refer to cells in the expanded table.

TABLE 5

Design Matrix, Cell Mapping, and Expected Frequencies for Reciprocal-Effects Model for Four-Variable Leading-Crowd Data

Observed Frequency	C	D	C_1	C_0	D_1	D_0	A	B	AB	AC^*	BD^*	C^*D^*	Expected Frequencies (Expanded Table) Model III
458	1	1	1	1	1	1	1	1	1	1	1	2	308.1
458	1	1	1	1	1	-1	1	1	1	1	0	0	47.9
458	1	1	1	-1	1	1	1	1	1	0	1	0	74.8
458	1	1	1	-1	1	-1	1	1	1	0	0	0	22.0
140	1	-1	1	1	-1	1	1	1	1	1	0	0	92.5
140	1	-1	1	1	-1	-1	1	1	1	1	-1	-2	14.4
140	1	-1	1	-1	-1	1	1	1	1	0	0	0	30.0
140	1	-1	1	-1	-1	-1	1	1	1	0	-1	0	8.8
110	-1	1	-1	1	1	1	1	1	1	0	1	0	52.8
110	-1	1	-1	1	1	-1	1	1	1	0	0	0	30.0
110	-1	1	-1	-1	1	1	1	1	1	-1	1	-2	12.8
110	-1	1	-1	-1	1	-1	1	1	1	-1	0	0	13.8
49	-1	-1	-1	1	-1	1	1	1	1	0	0	0	22.0
49	-1	-1	-1	1	-1	-1	1	1	1	0	-1	0	12.5
49	-1	-1	-1	-1	-1	1	1	1	1	-1	0	0	7.1
49	-1	-1	-1	-1	-1	-1	1	1	1	-1	-1	2	7.7
171	1	1	1	1	1	1	1	-1	-1	1	-1	2	88.9
171	1	1	1	1	1	-1	1	-1	-1	1	0	0	43.6
171	1	1	1	-1	1	1	1	-1	-1	0	-1	0	21.6
171	1	1	1	-1	1	-1	1	-1	-1	0	0	0	20.0
182	1	-1	1	1	-1	1	1	-1	-1	1	0	0	84.3
182	1	-1	1	1	-1	-1	1	-1	-1	1	1	-2	41.4
182	1	-1	1	-1	-1	1	1	-1	-1	0	0	0	27.3
182	1	-1	1	-1	-1	-1	1	-1	-1	0	1	0	25.4
56	-1	1	-1	1	1	1	1	-1	-1	0	-1	0	15.2
56	-1	1	-1	1	1	-1	1	-1	-1	0	0	0	27.3
56	-1	1	-1	-1	1	1	1	-1	-1	-1	-1	-2	3.7
56	-1	1	-1	-1	1	-1	1	-1	-1	-1	0	0	12.6

ID												R
87	-1	-1	-1	-1	-1	-1	-1	-1	0	0	0	20.0
87	-1	-1	-1	-1	-1	-1	1	-1	0	1	0	35.9
87	-1	-1	-1	-1	1	-1	-1	-1	-1	0	0	6.5
87	1	-1	1	-1	-1	1	-1	-1	-1	1	2	22.1
184	1	1	1	1	1	-1	1	1	-1	1	2	41.6
184	1	1	1	1	1	1	1	1	-1	0	0	6.5
184	1	1	1	1	-1	1	1	1	0	1	0	108.2
184	1	1	1	1	1	1	1	1	0	0	0	31.8
75	-1	-1	-1	-1	-1	1	-1	1	1	0	0	12.5
75	-1	-1	-1	-1	-1	1	-1	1	1	-1	-2	1.9
75	-1	-1	-1	-1	-1	-1	-1	-1	0	0	0	43.4
75	-1	-1	-1	-1	-1	-1	-1	-1	0	1	0	12.8
531	-1	-1	-1	1	-1	-1	-1	-1	0	-1	0	76.5
531	-1	-1	-1	-1	-1	-1	-1	-1	0	0	-2	43.4
531	-1	-1	-1	-1	1	1	1	1	1	1	0	199.1
531	-1	-1	-1	1	1	1	1	1	1	0	0	213.8
281	-1	-1	-1	-1	-1	-1	-1	-1	0	0	0	31.8
281	-1	-1	-1	-1	-1	-1	-1	-1	0	-1	0	18.1
281	-1	-1	-1	-1	1	1	1	1	1	0	0	110.7
281	-1	-1	-1	1	1	1	1	1	1	1	2	118.9
85	-1	-1	-1	-1	1	1	-1	1	1	-1	2	12.8
85	-1	-1	-1	-1	1	1	-1	1	1	0	0	6.3
85	-1	1	-1	-1	-1	-1	-1	-1	0	1	0	33.2
85	-1	-1	-1	-1	-1	-1	-1	-1	0	0	0	30.8
97	-1	1	-1	-1	-1	1	-1	1	1	0	0	12.1
97	-1	1	-1	-1	-1	1	-1	1	1	-1	-2	5.9
97	-1	-1	-1	-1	-1	-1	-1	-1	0	0	0	42.1
97	-1	-1	-1	-1	-1	-1	-1	-1	0	1	0	39.1
338	-1	-1	-1	-1	-1	-1	-1	-1	0	-1	0	23.5
338	-1	-1	-1	-1	-1	-1	-1	-1	0	0	-2	42.1
338	-1	-1	-1	-1	1	1	1	1	1	1	0	61.1
338	-1	1	1	1	1	1	1	1	1	0	0	207.3
554	-1	-1	-1	-1	-1	-1	-1	-1	0	0	0	30.8
554	-1	-1	-1	-1	-1	-1	-1	-1	0	-1	0	55.3
554	-1	1	-1	-1	1	1	1	1	1	0	0	107.3
554	-1	1	1	1	1	1	1	1	1	1	2	364.2

TABLE 6
Likelihood-Ratio Chi-Square Statistics for Four-Variable Models for
Leading-Crowd Data

Model	G^2	df
Structural loglinear models		
I. AB, AC^*, BD^*, C^*D^*	9.78	7
II. $AB, C_1, C_0, D_1, D_0, AC^*, BD^*$	30.28	6
III. $AB, C_1, C_0, D_1, D_0, AC^*, BD^*,$ C^*D^*	1.17	5
Elementary loglinear models		
IV. AB, AC, BD, CD	17.91	7
V. AB, AC, AD, BC, BD	15.72	6
VI. AB, AC, AD, BC, BD, CD	1.21	5

Except for the C and D columns, each column of the design matrix corresponds to a parameter in (18). The columns for C_1, C_0, D_1, and D_0 are contrast-coded indicator variables that denote positions in Figure 3. If we denote these variables as d^A, d^B, d^{C1}, d^{C0}, d^{D1}, and d^{D0}, respectively, then the columns for higher-way interaction are formed as follows: $d^{AB} = d^A d^B$; $d^{AC^*} = d^A(d^{C1} + d^{C0})/2$; $d^{BD^*} = d^B(d^{D1} + d^{D0})/2$; and $d^{C^*D^*} = (d^{C1} + d^{C0})(d^{D1} + d^{D0})/4$. This coding reflects the equality restrictions that we impose on (17). The first column shows the observed frequency that is mapped into each cell of the expanded table. The final column reports the expected frequencies for one of the models that is discussed below.[5]

The top panel of Table 6 presents G^2 statistics for (18) plus several simpler models fit to Table 1. Model I includes the partial association between C and D but no structural relationships between these two variables. This model fits the data well. Model II includes the structural effects of C on D and D on C but not the partial association between the two variables. This model fits the data

[5]The structure of Table 5 is analogous to that of Table 2. Table 5 has 64 rows, 16 for each of the four combinations of A and B. As shown in Figure 3, for each combination of A and B, only 14 of the 16 combinations of C_1, C_0, D_1, and D_0 are logically possible. Within levels of A and B, Table 5 contains a row for each of the 14 combinations, for a total of 56 rows. Figure 3 contains eight additional rows for cells 6 and 11 because these cells receive observations from more than one source. This leads to a total of 64 rows in Table 5. See the discussion of Table 3 for further details.

TABLE 7
Parameter Estimates in Logit Form of Structural Loglinear Models for the
Four-Way Table

Variable[a]	Model I		Model II		Model III	
	$\hat{\beta}$	SE($\hat{\beta}$)	$\hat{\beta}$	SE($\hat{\beta}$)	$\hat{\beta}$	SE($\hat{\beta}$)
Effects on C						
Intercept	−.168	.044	−.115	.044	−.234	.051
$C_1 - C_0$			.142	.146	.347	.160
A	2.444	.086	2.498	.086	2.372	.094
Effects on D						
Intercept	.329	.039	.287	.039	.320	.041
$D_1 - D_0$			.314	.064	−.658	.247
B	1.176	.072	1.174	.074	1.150	.074
C^*D^*	.344	.104			1.276	.264

[a]A is membership in the leading crowd in wave 1; B is attitude toward the leading crowd in wave 1; C is membership in the leading crowd in wave 2; and D is attitude toward the leading crowd in wave 2.

poorly. Model III includes both the structural effect and the partial association between C and D. This model fits the data extremely well, both absolutely and relative to models I and II. The expected frequencies of the expanded table under model III are reported in the final column of Table 5.

Table 7 presents estimates of the logit parameters for these models. In all three models, membership in the leading crowd in wave 1 substantially increases the odds of membership in wave 2. Likewise, holding a favorable attitude toward the leading crowd in wave 1 substantially increases the odds of a favorable attitude in wave 2. The three models, however, yield different results about the relationships between membership in wave 2 and attitude in wave 2. Model I indicates a net positive association between membership and favorable attitude. Model II indicates that the reciprocal effects of membership and attitude are both positive, but only the effect of membership on attitude is statistically significant. The estimate for the latter effect, moreover, is more than twice the estimate for the effect of attitude on membership. Model III, in contrast, indicates that a favorable attitude toward the leading crowd in wave 2 signifi-cantly raises the odds of joining the leading crowd in wave 2. But membership in the leading crowd reduces the chances of holding a favorable attitude. Model III also shows a positive partial association between membership and attitude. These results are consistent with those reported in Table 4 for the three-variable table. The simultaneous equation model in the latter table also indicated a negative effect of membership on attitude once the joint determination of the two variables was taken into account. These calculations illustrate that the structural loglinear model enables us to isolate the separate reciprocal effects of a pair of endogenous variables and to distinguish these effects from their residual association.[6]

The lower panel of Table 6 reports G^2 statistics for several elementary loglinear models. The fit of the model of no three-way (all two-way) interactions, model VI, to the observed data is very close to the fit for model III, but it is not identical. The structural and elementary loglinear models are distinct, and the parameters of one model cannot be derived from those of the other. The choice between models VI and III should be determined by one's analytic goals and the plausibility of the assumption that A does not directly affect D and that B does not directly affect C.

5. IDENTIFICATION

General rules for the identification of structural loglinear models have not yet been developed, but some guidance is available from results on the identifiability of models for missing data in loglinear models. In this section we show the link between the identifiability of our models and that of certain models for missing data. This enables us to show that the models presented in sections 3 and 4 are in fact identified and to suggest some general guidelines for identification of structural loglinear models. The identification conditions presented in this section are sufficient but not necessary conditions.

5.1. Identification of Models for Missing Categorical Data

The structural loglinear models presented in this paper are extensions of models for categorical data in which some variables are

---

[6]We also estimated model III allowing for C_1C_0 and D_1D_0 associations. For this model, $G^2 = 0.806$ (3 df). The estimated parameters for these terms are, respectively, -0.931 (SE = 4.60) and 0.756 (SE = 0.938). Under this specification the estimate for $D_1 - D_0$ is -0.390 (SE = 0.2115) and for $C_1 - C_0$ is 0.332 (SE = 0.1743). In general, standard errors are larger under this model.

not fully observed (Little and Rubin 1987; Winship and Mare 1989). In (9) and (18), C_1, C_0, D_1, and D_0 are each partially observed, and for each of them, a fully observed variable denotes whether or not they have "missing data." Variable C_1 is observed when $D = 1$ and missing when $D = -1$, whereas C_0 is observed and missing under the opposite conditions. Likewise, D_1 is observed when $C = 1$ and missing when $C = -1$, whereas D_0 is observed and missing under the opposite conditions. Each of these partially observed variables, moreover, is potentially subject to *nonignorable nonresponse* (NINR); that is, whether or not the variables are missing is associated with the level of the variable itself (e.g., Winship and Mare 1989). For example, D_1 in (8) and (17) is associated with C_1 and C_0 and thereby with C, which determines whether or not D_1 is observed. This implies that the identifiability of model terms involving C_1, C_0, D_1, and D_0 should be governed by rules similar to those that apply to other, simpler contingency tables in which a variable is subject to NINR.

These rules can be summarized as follows. Consider a two-way $(J \times K)$ table with dimensions X and Y. Let all observations be present for X, but let some observations be missing for Y. A third variable, M, denotes whether data are missing on Y. A potentially identifiable NINR model is $(XY)(YM)$, that is, a model in which the fully observed variable X is associated with the partially observed variable Y but is conditionally independent of whether data are missing on Y. This model is identified if $J \geq K$, that is, if the number of categories of the fully observed variable is at least as large as the number of categories of the partially observed variable (Little and Rubin 1987, pp. 238–39). More generally, NINR models are identified if (a) for every partially observed variable, there exists a fully observed variable that is conditionally independent of whether data are missing on the partially observed variable and (b) the number of categories of the partially observed variable does not exceed the number of categories of the fully observed variable (Winship and Mare 1989).

5.2. Identification of Structural Loglinear Models

To establish the identifiability of structural loglinear models (9) and (18), we rely on the results for models with missing data stated above plus the fact that some parameters for models of the expanded table can be identified without any overidentifying restrictions on the structural model. Consider a simplified version of (18),

$$\log p_{klmn} = \lambda + \lambda_s^{C*} + \lambda_t^{D*} + \lambda_{st}^{C*D*}, \tag{25}$$

which implies the inclusion of the terms $\lambda_k^{C1} = \lambda_l^{C0}$, $\lambda_m^{D1} = \lambda_n^{D0}$, and $\lambda_{km}^{C1D1} = \lambda_{kn}^{C1D0} = \lambda_{lm}^{C0D1} = \lambda_{ln}^{C0D0}$ and where p_{klmn} denotes the probability that an individual falls into the kth category of C_1 ($k = -1,1$), the lth category of C_0 ($l = -1,1$), the mth category of D_1 ($m = -1,1$), and the nth category of D_0; the intercept λ is determined by the constraint that $\Sigma_{klmn} p_{klmn} = 1$; and all other notation is as defined above. Model (25) represents the two-way association between the average values of C_1 and C_0 and of D_1 and D_0. This model can be identified directly from the observed 2×2 CD table without other identifying restrictions. The four parameters of the model are nonlinear functions of the four frequencies in the observed CD table.[7] Because λ_s^{C*}, λ_t^{D*}, and λ_{st}^{C*D*} are always identified from the CD table alone, to establish the identifiability of (9) and (18) it suffices to show that parameters for C_1, C_0, D_1, and D_0 and for the relationships between these variables and the exogenous variables are identified.

In the structural loglinear model for a single equation with an endogenous independent variable, model (9), we can identify λ_s^{C*} and λ_{st}^{C*D*} from the observed CD table, as noted above. We identify λ_j^B and λ_{jt}^{BD*} directly from observed data on the joint distribution of B, C, and D. (The associations between B and D_1 and between B and D_0 are directly observed when $C = 1$ and $C = -1$, respectively. Model (9) constrains these two associations to be equal.) We identify λ_m^{D1} and λ_n^{D0} using the rules for identification of missing-data models discussed above. Under the model, B is conditionally independent of C_1 and C_0, given D_1 and D_0, and is thus conditionally independent of C, which determines whether D_1 and D_0 are missing (since C is determined by C_1, C_0, D_1, and D_0). Thus, B is fully observed and conditionally independent of whether data are missing on D_1 and D_0. Since the number of categories of B equals the number of categories in D_1 and D_0, the inclusion of B in the model identifies λ_m^{D1} and λ_n^{D0}. Thus, model (9) and its corresponding logit form, model (12), are identified.

---

[7] To see this, write the expected frequencies of the *expanded* table in terms of the parameters of (24) and collapse the expanded table to the observed table. If x_{uv} denotes the observed frequency in the 2×2 table for the uth level of C and the vth level of D ($u = 1,2$; $v = 1,2$), then

$$x_{uv} = \sum_{klmn \, \epsilon \, uv} [\exp (\lambda + \lambda_{kl}^{C*} + \lambda_{mn}^{D*} + \lambda_{st}^{C*D*})].$$

In the structural loglinear model for reciprocal effects, model (18), we can identify $\lambda_{st}^{C^*D^*}$ from the observed CD table, as noted above. We identify $\lambda_i^A, \lambda_j^B, \lambda_{ij}^{AB}, \lambda_{jt}^{BD^*}$, and $\lambda_{is}^{AC^*}$ directly from the observed data on the joint distributions of A, B, C, and D. We identify λ_m^{D1} and λ_n^{D0} from the rules for identification of missing-data models. The inclusion of B, which is associated with D_1 and D_0 but conditionally independent of C, identifies these two parameters. Likewise, we identify λ_k^{C1} and λ_l^{C0} by the inclusion of A, which is associated with C_1 and C_0 but conditionally independent of D. Thus, model (18) and its corresponding logit form, equations (23)–(24), are identified.

Our analysis of the identifiability of models (9) and (18) suggests that parameters of structural loglinear models can be identified by restrictions on the parameters for the effects of the exogenous variables. In particular, a sufficient condition for the identification of the effect of one endogenous variable on another is that the model include an exogenous variable that affects the dependent endogenous variable but not the independent endogenous variable and that the exogenous variable have at least as many categories as the dependent endogenous variable. This principle is illustrated by the use of B to identify λ_m^{D1} and λ_n^{D0} in (9) and λ_m^{D1} and λ_n^{D0} and by the use of A to identify λ_k^{C1} and λ_l^{C0} in (18).

These identification conditions resemble those that govern the use of instrumental variables to identify conventional simultaneous equation models, but they differ in one key respect. In conventional simultaneous equation models, instrumental variables are *excluded* from the structural equation of interest but affect the endogenous independent variable in the equation. In the models described above, however, the exogenous variables are *included* in the structural equation of interest but are conditionally independent of the endogenous independent variable. This distinction is operationally significant only for the single-equation model. For the two-equation model, the same pattern of restrictions on the relationships among the four variables applies in the conventional simultaneous equation and the structural loglinear models. A single-equation model that follows the more usual conventions of simultaneous equation model estimation is model i in Figure 1. In this model the exogenous variable A affects the endogenous independent variable D but not the dependent endogenous variable C. It is possible to show that the structural loglinear model for i is also identified, using modified versions of the arguments presented above. For the sake of brevity, we do not present these arguments here.

6. CONCLUSION

We have proposed models for jointly determined categorical variables that are extensions of loglinear and logit models for cross-classified data. We have shown that it is possible to develop loglinear models that are analogous to standard linear simultaneous equation models. The models proposed here can be estimated using the same algorithms and software that are available for loglinear models of partially or indirectly observed contingency tables.

An issue for further research on these models concerns the robustness of their results to alternative identifying restrictions. In estimating structural loglinear models, we have made a number of assumptions. The two most important are (a) that the $C_1 C_0$ and $D_1 D_0$ interactions are zero (that is, $\lambda_{lk}^{C1C0} = \lambda_{mn}^{D1D0} = 0$) and (b) that all the nonstructural associations between C and D are equal (that is, $\lambda_{km}^{C1D1} = \lambda_{kn}^{C1D0} = \lambda_{lm}^{C0D1} = \lambda_{ln}^{C0D0}$). Some of these restrictions can be relaxed, but the model would be underidentified if all were relaxed simultaneously. Thus, it is not possible to test individual restrictions when all other parameters are unrestricted. As noted in footnotes 4 and 6, our empirical results change slightly when $C_1 C_0$ and $D_1 D_0$ are not restricted to zero in the examples presented. Analyses of hypothetical data not reported here, however, suggest that different specifications may produce different estimates of $\beta^{C1} - \beta^{C0}$ and $\beta^{D1} - \beta^{D0}$. Thus, our models may not always be robust to the specification of the error structure. This issue awaits further investigation.

Our discussion has been confined to models with two dichotomous endogenous variables, but these methods generalize to models with polytomous variables and more than two outcomes. Models with more complex dependent variables may require much larger expanded tables than the simple case presented here. For example, a table that contains one dichotomous and one four-category dependent variable has $2 \times 4 = 8$ cells for each unique combination of the exogenous variables and $2^4 \times 4^2 = 256$ cells in the corresponding expanded table. Larger models obviously require more computation than the elementary models presented here.

The models presented in this paper apply when one is concerned only with simultaneous relationships between discrete variables. If a discrete variable exerts its effect not only discretely but also as an indicator of an underlying continuous variable, then models other than those presented here are more suitable (Heckman 1978; Maddala 1983; Winship and Mare 1983).

REFERENCES

Amemiya, Takeshi. 1985. *Advanced Econometrics*. Cambridge, MA.: Harvard University Press.

Baker, Stuart G., and Nan M. Laird. 1988. "Regression Analysis for Categorical Variables with Outcome Subject to Nonignorable Response." *Journal of the American Statistical Association* 83:62–69.

Bishop, Yvonne M., Stephen E. Fienberg, and Paul W. Holland. 1975. *Discrete Multivariate Analysis*. Cambridge, MA: MIT Press.

Brier, Stephen S. 1978. "The Utility of Systems of Simultaneous Logistic Response Equations." Pp. 119–29 in *Sociological Methodology 1979*, edited by K. F. Schuessler. San Francisco: Jossey-Bass.

Coleman, James S. 1961. *The Adolescent Society: The Social Life of the Teenager and its Impact on Education*. Glencoe, IL: Free Press.

————. 1964. *Introduction to Mathematical Sociology*. New York: Free Press.

Daganzo, Carlos. 1979. *Multinomial Probit: The Theory and its Application to Demand Forecasting*. New York: Academic Press.

Duncan, Beverly, and Otis Dudley Duncan. 1978. *Sex Typing and Social Roles*. New York: Academic Press.

Duncan, Otis Dudley. 1974. "A Model of Interaction Between Spouses." Unpublished manuscript. University of Arizona, Department of Sociology.

————. 1975. *Introduction to Structural Equation Models*. New York: Academic Press.

————. 1985. "New Light on the 16-fold Table." *American Journal of Sociology* 91:88–128.

Duncan, Otis Dudley, Archibald O. Haller, and Alejandro Portes. 1968. "Peer Influences on Aspirations: A Reinterpretation." *American Journal of Sociology* 74:119–37.

Fay, Robert E. 1986. "Causal Models for Patterns of Nonresponse." *Journal of the American Statistical Association* 81:354–65.

Fienberg, Stephen E. 1980. *The Analysis of Cross-Classified Categorical Data*. Cambridge, MA: MIT Press.

Goldberger, Arthur S., and Otis Dudley Duncan. 1973. *Structural Equation Models in the Social Sciences*. New York: Seminar Press.

Goodman, Leo A. 1973. "Causal Analysis of Data from Panel Studies and Other Kinds of Surveys. *American Journal of Sociology* 78:1135–91.

————. 1974. "The Analysis of Systems of Qualitative Variables When Some of the Variables are Unobservable. I. A Modified Latent Structure Approach." *American Journal of Sociology* 79:1179–1259.

———. 1978. *Analyzing Qualitative/Categorical Data.* Cambridge, MA: Abt Books.

Haberman, Shelby J. 1978–79. *Analysis of Qualitative Data.* 2 vols. New York: Academic Press.

———. 1988. "A Stabilized Newton-Raphson Algorithm for Log-Linear Models for Frequency Tables Derived by Indirect Observation." Pp. 193–211 in *Sociological Methodology 1988,* edited by C. C. Clogg. Washington, DC: American Sociological Association.

Heckman, James J. 1978. "Dummy Endogenous Variables in a Simultaneous Equation System." *Econometrica* 46:931–59.

———. 1978. "Sample Selection Bias as a Specification Error." *Econometrica* 47:153–61.

Heckman, James J., and V. Joseph Hotz. 1989. "Choosing Among Alternative Nonexperimental Methods for Estimating the Impact of Social Programs: The Case of Manpower Training." *Journal of the American Statistical Association* 84:862–74.

Little, Roderick J. A., and Donald B. Rubin. 1987. *Statistical Analysis with Missing Data.* New York: Wiley.

Maddala, G. S. 1983. *Limited-Dependent and Qualitative Variables in Econometrics.* Cambridge: Cambridge University Press.

Mallar, Charles D. 1977. "The Estimation of Simultaneous Probability Models." *Econometrica* 45:1717–22.

Mare, Robert D., and Christopher Winship. 1988. "Endogenous Switching Regression Models for the Causes and Effects of Discrete Variables." Pp. 132–60 in *Common Problems/Proper Solutions: Avoiding Error in Quantitative Research,* edited by J. S. Long. Beverly Hills: Sage University Press.

Marini, Margaret M. 1984. "Women's Educational Attainment and the Timing of Entry into Parenthood." *American Sociological Review* 49:491–511.

Muthén, Bengt. 1984. "A General Structural Equation Model with Dichotomous, Ordered Categorical, and Continuous Latent Variable Indicators." *Psychometrika* 49:115–32.

Rubin, Donald B. 1978. "Bayesian Inference for Causal Effects: The Role of Randomization." *Annals of Statistics* 6:34–58.

Stolzenberg, Ross M., and Linda J. Waite. 1977. "Age, Fertility Expectations, and Plans for Employment." *American Sociological Review* 42:769–82.

Winship, Christopher, and Robert D. Mare. 1983. "Structural Equations and Path Analysis for Discrete Data." *American Journal of Sociology* 89: 54–110.

———. 1989. "Loglinear Models for Missing Data: A Latent Class Approach." Pp. 331–67 in *Sociological Methodology 1989,* edited by C. C. Clogg. Oxford: Basil Blackwell.

8

OBSERVATIONAL RESIDUALS IN FACTOR ANALYSIS AND STRUCTURAL EQUATION MODELS

Kenneth A. Bollen*
Gerhard Arminger†

In the last decade there has been a surge of interest in the role of outliers and residuals in statistical analyses. However, there is a surprising neglect of these topics in factor analysis and in other structural equation models with latent variables. In this paper we propose ways to calculate unstandardized residuals, derive standardized residuals, suggest tests of statistical significance for residuals, and illustrate the procedures with empirical and simulated data. Our significance tests for the residuals are based on asymptotic theory, but our examples indicate that the tests are helpful even with N's of 60 to 100.

The last decade has seen a surge of interest in the role of outliers and influential cases in statistical analyses. The scores of techniques designed to detect such observations fall into two categories: *model-free*

We thank Walt Davis for computing assistance and the referees and Peter Marsden for their comments. The first author gratefully acknowledges the support of the Institute for Research in the Social Sciences and the University Research Council at the University of North Carolina, and the National Science Foundation (SES-8908361). An earlier version of this paper was presented at the Annual Meetings of the American Sociological Association, August 1990, Washington, DC.

*University of North Carolina, Chapel Hill
†University of Wuppertal

methods and *model-based* methods. As the name suggests, model-free methods apply regardless of the statistical model that is formulated. Simple examples include univariate stem-and-leaf plots, histograms, and bivariate scattergrams. Barnett and Lewis (1984, pp. 243–80) review many multivariate model-free outlier-detection procedures.

Model-based diagnostics take into account the structure of a model, so the value of a diagnostic statistic can vary with the model structure. The "hat" matrix and studentized residuals in regression analysis are examples (e.g., Belsley, Kuh, and Welsch 1980; Cook and Weisberg 1982). The values of these statistics usually vary with the set of explanatory variables.

There is a surprising neglect of outliers and influential cases in factor analysis and other structural equation models with latent variables. Some researchers have recommended model-free diagnostics for detecting outliers in general structural equation models (e.g., Bentler 1985, p.54–55; Bollen 1987, 1989, pp.28–31). But it is also useful to have model-based diagnostics, such as residuals from latent variable models.

There are at least two reasons for the neglect of such residuals. First, the latent nature of factors makes calculation of residuals less straightforward than in, say, regression analysis. Second, factor analysts and structural equation modelers concentrate on the covariance or correlation matrices rather than on the individual cases. Once these matrices are in hand, analysts tend to forget about the specific observations that generated them. The term *residuals* is most often associated with the differences between observed and predicted covariances (correlations) rather than with the residuals for individuals.

Why should we compute individual residuals? The answer to this question for factor analysis and general structural equation models is the same as that for other areas in statistics. First, large residuals may highlight cases that are highly influential on one or more parameter estimates. For example, a large residual may identify a case that distorts our assessment of the relationship between factors or between factors and observed variables. A factor (or a latent variable) may even be "created" by an outlier. Furthermore, careful examination of outliers may identify cases that require closer scrutiny, revealing coding errors or suggesting possible variables that have been omitted from the analysis. Finally, outliers can create Heywood cases or improper solutions (Bollen 1987).

The purposes of this paper are (a) to suggest ways to calculate unstandardized residuals in factor analysis and structural equation models, (b) to derive standardized residuals, (c) to suggest tests of statistical significance for residuals, and (d) to illustrate the procedures with empirical and simulated data. We begin with the factor analysis model and notation. Then we present sections on unstandardized and standardized residuals in factor analysis. Empirical and simulation examples illustrate these results. Next we explain the calculation of residuals in general structural equation models. The conclusions follow.

1. FACTOR ANALYSIS MODEL

The factor analysis model is

$$\mathbf{y}_i = \mathbf{\Lambda}\mathbf{\eta}_i + \mathbf{\epsilon}_i \qquad (i = 1, 2, \ldots, N), \tag{1}$$

where $\mathbf{y}_i$ is a $p \times 1$ vector of observed random variables, $\mathbf{\eta}_i$ is an $m \times 1$ vector of i.i.d. random latent variables (i.e. "factors"), $\mathbf{\epsilon}_i$ is a $p \times 1$ vector of i.i.d. random error variables, and $\mathbf{\Lambda}$ is the $p \times m$ matrix of "factor loadings" that contains the parameters linking the factors, $\mathbf{\eta}_i$, to the indicators, $\mathbf{y}_i$. Furthermore, we assume that

$$E(\mathbf{\eta}_i) = \mathbf{0}, \tag{2}$$

$$E(\mathbf{\epsilon}_i) = \mathbf{0}, \tag{3}$$

$$E(\mathbf{\eta}_i\mathbf{\epsilon}_i') = \mathbf{0}, \tag{4}$$

$$E(\mathbf{\epsilon}_i\mathbf{\epsilon}_i') = \mathbf{\Theta}, \tag{5}$$

for all i, where (2) is a simplifying assumption and (5) shows that $\mathbf{\Theta}$ is the covariance matrix for $\mathbf{\epsilon}_i$. At this point we make no assumptions about the form of the specific distributions for $\mathbf{\epsilon}_i$, $\mathbf{\eta}_i$, or $\mathbf{y}_i$. We do assume that the factor analysis model is identified.

2. UNSTANDARDIZED RESIDUALS

From (1) it is clear that the error for the ith observation is

$$\mathbf{\epsilon}_i = \mathbf{y}_i - \mathbf{\Lambda}\mathbf{\eta}_i. \tag{6}$$

Equation (6) is analogous to the equation for the error in a regression model. The major difference is that in regression analysis, we observe values of the dependent and explanatory variables, whereas in factor analysis, only y_i, the dependent variables, are directly observed. Thus, it is necessary to find values for η_i to estimate ϵ_i. By necessity the estimated factor scores are a weighted function of the observed variables, y_i. Using $\hat{\eta}_i$ to denote the estimates of the factors of the ith observation, we have

$$\hat{\eta}_i = \mathbf{W}y_i, \tag{7}$$

where $\mathbf{W}$ is the $m \times p$ matrix of weights used to transform y_i into the $\hat{\eta}_i$. The $\hat{\eta}_i$ is often called the estimate of the factor score (see, e.g., Mulaik 1972; Williams 1978; Steiger 1979; Bartholomew 1981).

Substituting (7) into (6) we obtain

$$\begin{aligned} e_i &= y_i - \mathbf{\Lambda}\hat{\eta}_i \\ &= (\mathbf{I} - \mathbf{\Lambda W})y_i, \end{aligned} \tag{8}$$

where e_i is the *unstandardized residual,* which is an estimate of ϵ_i.[1] Obviously our selection of $\mathbf{W}$ in (7) plays a key role in forming $\hat{\eta}_i$ and e_i. Several choices for $\mathbf{W}$ exist (see McDonald and Burr 1967; Saris, de Pijper, and Mulder 1978). The most popular procedure is based on least squares estimation principles. It chooses $\mathbf{W}$ so that

$$\Sigma_{i=1}^{N} (\eta_i - \hat{\eta}_i)'(\eta_i - \hat{\eta}_i) \tag{9}$$

is minimized. This leads to the regression method weight matrix, say, $\mathbf{W}_r$, of

$$\mathbf{W}_r = \mathbf{\Sigma}_{\eta\eta}\mathbf{\Lambda}' \, \mathbf{\Sigma}_{yy}^{-1} \quad , \tag{10}$$

where $\mathbf{\Sigma}_{yy}^{-1}$ is the inverse of the population covariance matrix of y_i and $\mathbf{\Sigma}_{\eta\eta}$ is the population covariance matrix of η_i. Using equations (8) and (10), we get the unstandardized residuals based on the regression method:

$$e_i^{(r)} = (\mathbf{I} - \mathbf{\Lambda}\mathbf{\Sigma}_{\eta\eta}\mathbf{\Lambda}'\mathbf{\Sigma}_{yy}^{-1})y_i, \tag{11}$$

where the superscript (r) indicates that these are the residuals based on the regression method.

A second well-known choice for $\mathbf{W}$ is Bartlett's method:

$$\mathbf{W}_b = (\mathbf{\Lambda}'\mathbf{\Theta}^{-1}\mathbf{\Lambda})^{-1} \mathbf{\Lambda}'\mathbf{\Theta}^{-1}. \tag{12}$$

[1]If outliers are present, they can affect the estimated factor score and in turn the residuals that are calculated with the factor score estimate. We explore these consequences in the second simulation example.

This weight is derived by choosing $\mathbf{W}_b$ so as to minimize the sum of the squared errors divided by their standard deviations (Lawley and Maxwell 1971, p. 109). In this sense, its rationale is based on weighted least squares minimization.

The Bartlett-based residuals are

$$\mathbf{e}_i^{(b)} = (\mathbf{I} - \Lambda(\Lambda'\Theta^{-1}\Lambda)^{-1}\Lambda'\Theta^{-1}) \, \mathbf{y}_i, \tag{13}$$

where the superscript (b) signifies that these are based on Bartlett's method.[2]

We can describe the relationship between the residuals $\mathbf{e}_i$ and the errors $\boldsymbol{\epsilon}_i$ in several ways. One is to manipulate equation (8) to obtain

$$\mathbf{e}_i = \Lambda(\boldsymbol{\eta}_i - \hat{\boldsymbol{\eta}}_i) + \boldsymbol{\epsilon}_i. \tag{14}$$

This shows that $\mathbf{e}_i$ reflects not only the desired random variables $\boldsymbol{\epsilon}_i$ but also the discrepancy of the estimated factor scores $\hat{\boldsymbol{\eta}}_i$ from the latent factors $\boldsymbol{\eta}_i$. When equations (1), (2), and (3) hold, $E(\mathbf{e}_i)$ equals $E(\boldsymbol{\epsilon}_i)$ and both equal zero.

The correlations of $\mathbf{e}_i$ with $\boldsymbol{\epsilon}_i$ provide another means to examine the closeness of the two errors. By definition the population correlation (CORR) is

$$\text{CORR}(\mathbf{e}_i,\boldsymbol{\epsilon}_i') = \mathbf{D}_e^{-1}\text{COV}(\mathbf{e}_i,\boldsymbol{\epsilon}_i')\mathbf{D}_\epsilon^{-1}, \tag{15}$$

where $\mathbf{D}_e^{-1}$ and $\mathbf{D}_\epsilon^{-1}$ are diagonal matrices with the reciprocals of the population standard deviations of $\mathbf{e}_i$ and $\boldsymbol{\epsilon}_i$, respectively, down their main diagonals, and $\text{COV}(\mathbf{e}_i,\boldsymbol{\epsilon}_i')$ is the population covariance matrix of $\mathbf{e}_i$ with $\boldsymbol{\epsilon}_i$.

[2]Maximum likelihood (ML) is a third estimation strategy for the residuals that we also considered. However, we see several difficulties. One is that if all the factor scores, disturbances, and factor-model parameters are unknown and treated simultaneously, the ML estimators do not exist (Anderson and Rubin 1956). We could approximate the ML estimator by taking Λ, $\Sigma_{\eta\eta}$, and Θ as known and substituting the corresponding sample estimates for them (see Bartholomew 1981, p. 98). A more serious problem is that using ML estimators for the errors requires that the error for each individual and for every variable be a constant *parameter*. We can imagine some contexts in which we would be willing to consider the values of the latent substantive factors for each individual as parameters, but we find it hard not to consider errors as random variables that would change from trial to trial even for the same individual. Thus, treating the errors as parameters, as is required for an ML estimator, seems inappropriate. Of course, this does not rule out the application of the ML estimator for the unknown parameters in Λ, $\Sigma_{\eta\eta}$, and Θ.

The covariance matrix between $\boldsymbol{\epsilon}_i$ and the residuals $\mathbf{e}_i$ is

$$\begin{align}
\text{COV}(\mathbf{e}_i, \boldsymbol{\epsilon}_i') &= \text{COV}[(\mathbf{I} - \boldsymbol{\Lambda}\mathbf{W})\mathbf{y}_i, \boldsymbol{\epsilon}_i'] \\
&= (\mathbf{I} - \boldsymbol{\Lambda}\mathbf{W})\boldsymbol{\Theta}. \tag{16}
\end{align}$$

When we use the regression-based residuals, $\mathbf{e}_i^{(r)}$ and $\mathbf{W} = \mathbf{W}_r$, equation (16) becomes

$$\begin{align}
\text{COV}(\mathbf{e}_i^{(r)}, \boldsymbol{\epsilon}_i') &= (\mathbf{I} - \boldsymbol{\Lambda}\mathbf{W}_r)\boldsymbol{\Theta} \\
&= \boldsymbol{\Theta}\boldsymbol{\Sigma}_{yy}^{-1}\boldsymbol{\Theta}, \tag{17}
\end{align}$$

and when we use $\mathbf{e}_i^{(b)}$ and $\mathbf{W} = \mathbf{W}_b$, we get

$$\begin{align}
\text{COV}(\mathbf{e}_i^{(b)}, \boldsymbol{\epsilon}_i') &= (\mathbf{I} - \boldsymbol{\Lambda}\mathbf{W}_b)\boldsymbol{\Theta} \\
&= \boldsymbol{\Theta} - \boldsymbol{\Lambda}(\boldsymbol{\Lambda}'\boldsymbol{\Theta}^{-1}\boldsymbol{\Lambda})^{-1}\boldsymbol{\Lambda}'. \tag{18}
\end{align}$$

From the variances of $\mathbf{e}_i$ we can determine $\mathbf{D}_e^{-1}$. Using (8) and the definition of variance, we get the variance of $\mathbf{e}_i$:

$$\text{VAR}(\mathbf{e}_i) = (\mathbf{I} - \boldsymbol{\Lambda}\mathbf{W})\boldsymbol{\Sigma}_{yy}(\mathbf{I} - \boldsymbol{\Lambda}\mathbf{W})', \tag{19}$$

where VAR stands for the population variance. For the regression-based residuals this is

$$\text{VAR}(\mathbf{e}_i^{(r)}) = \boldsymbol{\Theta}\boldsymbol{\Sigma}_{yy}^{-1}\boldsymbol{\Theta}, \tag{20}$$

and for the Bartlett-based residuals it is

$$\text{VAR}(\mathbf{e}_i^{(b)}) = \boldsymbol{\Theta} - \boldsymbol{\Lambda}(\boldsymbol{\Lambda}'\boldsymbol{\Theta}^{-1}\boldsymbol{\Lambda})^{-1}\boldsymbol{\Lambda}'. \tag{21}$$

Comparing equations (20) to (17) and (21) to (18) we see that the variances of $\mathbf{e}_i^{(r)}$ and $\mathbf{e}_i^{(b)}$ equal the corresponding covariances of $\mathbf{e}_i^{(r)}$ with $\boldsymbol{\epsilon}_i$ and $\mathbf{e}_i^{(b)}$ with $\boldsymbol{\epsilon}_i$. Setting $\mathbf{D}_e^{-1}$ equal to the reciprocal of the square root of the main diagonal of either (20) or (21) and setting $\mathbf{D}_\epsilon^{-1}$ equal to the reciprocal of the square root of the main diagonal of $\boldsymbol{\Theta}$, we can obtain the correlations of $\mathbf{e}_i$ with $\boldsymbol{\epsilon}_i$ from equation (15).

The variances of $\mathbf{e}_i$ given in equations (19) to (21) have importance beyond their role in calculating the correlations of $\mathbf{e}_i$ with $\boldsymbol{\epsilon}_i$. We also use these variances to calculate the standardized residuals that are presented in the next section.

In practice we do not have the population parameters for $\boldsymbol{\Lambda}$, $\boldsymbol{\Sigma}_{\eta\eta}$, $\boldsymbol{\Theta}$, or $\boldsymbol{\Sigma}_{yy}$ that are required to form $\mathbf{e}_i$, $\text{VAR}(\mathbf{e}_i)$, $\text{CORR}(\mathbf{e}_i, \boldsymbol{\epsilon}_i)$, and the other quantities described in this section. Instead we must rely on the sample values $\hat{\boldsymbol{\Lambda}}$, $\hat{\boldsymbol{\Sigma}}_{\eta\eta}$, $\hat{\boldsymbol{\Theta}}$, and $\hat{\boldsymbol{\Sigma}}_{yy}$ to compute the sample residuals

$\hat{\mathbf{e}}_i$. Our simulations explore the consequences of relying on the sample values rather than the parameters.

3. STANDARDIZED RESIDUALS

In an analysis of the unstandardized residuals, we can plot the sample values of $\hat{\mathbf{e}}_i$ for all cases in histograms, stem-and-leaf plots, or index plots. These can help us identify those residuals that are substantially larger than the others for the same variable. One difficulty, however, is that the magnitude of the residuals is partially a function of the units of measurement. It would be useful to standardize the residuals so that they are less affected by the sometimes arbitrary scaling of variables. The derivations here are given, as before, for the residuals $\mathbf{e}_i$ rather than the sample residuals $\hat{\mathbf{e}}_i$.

One possible standardization is

$$e_{ji}/\sqrt{[\Theta]_{jj}}, \tag{22}$$

where e_{ji} is the unstandardized residual for the jth variable and the ith observation, and $[\Theta]_{jj}$ is the error variance for the jth variable. We refer to this as naive standardization. Since e_{ji} generally takes different values from case to case, so will the standardized residual. We can apply equation (22) to all variables and all cases to provide a naive standardized residual that takes account of the standard deviation of the residuals.

A major difficulty with this standardization is that the standardizing factor, $1/\sqrt{[\Theta]_{jj}}$, contains the standard deviation of ϵ_{ji}, the true measurement error. The standard deviation of e_{ji} differs from this. Specifically, equation (19) gives the general formula for the VAR($\mathbf{e}_i$), and equations (20) and (21) show their forms for the regression-based and Bartlett-based residuals. In nearly all cases these lead to different standard deviations for e_{ji} and ϵ_{ji}.

This suggests an alternative standardization of

$$e_{ji}/\sqrt{[\text{VAR}(\mathbf{e}_i)]_{jj}}, \tag{23}$$

where $[\text{VAR}(\mathbf{e}_i)]_{jj}$ is the jth diagonal element of VAR($\mathbf{e}_i$) (see equation (19)). Similarly we compute the standardized regression-based residual as

$$e_{ji}^{(r)}/\sqrt{[\text{VAR}(\mathbf{e}_i^{(r)})]_{jj}} \tag{24}$$

and the Bartlett-based standardized residual as

$$e_{ji}^{(b)}/\sqrt{[\text{VAR}(e_i^{(b)})]_{jj}}. \qquad (25)$$

When we apply equations (23), (24), or (25), we get a random variable with a mean of zero and a standard deviation of one.

If we assume that $\boldsymbol{\epsilon}_i$ and $\boldsymbol{\eta}_i$ are normally distributed, then $\mathbf{y}_i$ is normally distributed. This implies that $\mathbf{e}_i$ is normally distributed (see equation (8)). Thus, with these additional assumptions, the standardized residuals in (23) to (25) are standardized normal variables, and we can test the statistical significance of their departures from zero or any other constant.

Obviously, $\text{VAR}(\mathbf{e}_i)$, $\text{VAR}(\mathbf{e}_i^{(r)})$, and $\text{VAR}(\mathbf{e}_i^{(b)})$ are population quantities and must be estimated with sample variances (e.g., $\text{var}(\mathbf{e}_i)$) that use sample estimates of the corresponding population values. This suggests that the normal distribution for the standardized residuals is an approximation that is best in large samples. We will briefly examine this issue with our simulations.

Furthermore we can form a simultaneous test of statistical significance for two or more sample residuals for an observation. We compute the quadratic form, which is analogous to the naive standardization in equation (22):

$$q_i = \mathbf{e}_i'\boldsymbol{\Theta}^{-1}\mathbf{e}_i, \qquad (26)$$

which looks like a chi-square variate with p degrees of freedom. The problem is that $\boldsymbol{\Theta}$ gives the variance of $\boldsymbol{\epsilon}_i$, not of $\mathbf{e}_i$, so that q_i need not be chi-square distributed.

Alternatively, using the correct variance of $\mathbf{e}_i$ we form

$$h_i = \mathbf{e}_i'[\text{VAR}(\mathbf{e}_i)]^{-1}\,\mathbf{e}_i, \qquad (27)$$

which follows a chi-square distribution with p degrees of freedom. With the regression-based residuals $\mathbf{e}_i^{(r)}$, $\text{VAR}(\mathbf{e}_i^{(r)})$ from (20) replaces $\text{VAR}(\mathbf{e}_i)$ in (27), whereas with the Bartlett-based residuals $\mathbf{e}_i^{(b)}$, $\text{VAR}(\mathbf{e}_i^{(b)})$ from (21) is used. As before, we must use sample estimates of the variances and the other parameters.

In the typical case in which the specific observations are not specified in advance and the standardized residuals or the preceding chi-square tests are applied to all cases, a multiple-testing problem emerges. Specifically, testing each case at a type I error level of .05 leads to a type I probability considerably greater than .05 for the family of hypotheses. A Bonferroni correction is the simplest way to adjust for this. For instance, if we wish an overall alpha level of no more than .05 and we perform tests on 100 standardized residuals, each test should use a critical z value that corresponds to an alpha of .05/100, or .0005 (or for a two-tailed test, .00025). More generally, to maintain a type I probability of no more than alpha when performing k tests, set the alpha level for each test to α/k for one-tailed tests and $\alpha/2k$ for the more typical two-tailed tests. If we have hundreds of standardized residuals to test, we may wish to select an overall type I probability of .10 or even .20, rather than the common .05 level, since applying the usual Bonferroni correction with a .05 level could lead to excessively conservative critical values. In addition to the formal tests of statistical significance described in this section, we advise readers to pay attention to graphical plots of the standardized residuals to identify cases that are distant from the others.

4. SIMULATIONS

In this section we use simulated data that are generated from a known structure and from known distributions. We explore several questions about the standardized residuals:

1. How well does the simpler naive standardization method work?
2. What is the impact of using sample estimates $\hat{\Sigma}_{yy}$, $\hat{\Lambda}$, $\hat{\Sigma}_{\eta\eta}$, and $\hat{\Theta}$ in place of the population parameters when using the other types of standardized residuals?
3. Do the expected numbers of significant standardized residuals appear for "well-behaved" data?
4. Can we identify known problem cases with the standardized residuals?

Our simulations are not an exhaustive analysis of the properties of these residuals. Rather, they are meant to determine whether the standardized residuals hold promise.

4.1. *Simulation 1*

The first simulation addresses questions (1) to (3). The known model is fitted, the variables are generated from normal distributions, and no problem cases are purposely introduced. We begin with an example with less than optimal conditions. Specifically, we allow only two indicators per factor and use a modest-size sample. The population factor analysis model has the following parameter values:

$$
\begin{bmatrix} y_1 \\ y_2 \\ y_3 \\ y_4 \end{bmatrix} = \begin{bmatrix} 1 & 0 \\ .8 & 0 \\ 0 & 1 \\ 0 & .8 \end{bmatrix} \begin{bmatrix} \eta_1 \\ \eta_2 \end{bmatrix} + \begin{bmatrix} \epsilon_1 \\ \epsilon_2 \\ \epsilon_3 \\ \epsilon_4 \end{bmatrix}, \tag{28}
$$

$$
\Sigma_{\eta\eta} = \begin{bmatrix} 1 & \\ .5 & 1 \end{bmatrix}, \quad \Theta = \begin{bmatrix} 1 & & & \\ 0 & 1 & & \\ 0 & 0 & 1 & \\ 0 & 0 & 0 & \end{bmatrix}. \tag{29}
$$

The random variables η_1 and ϵ_1 to ϵ_4 are generated as i.i.d., $N(0,1)$ using the CALL RANNORM function in SAS (SAS Institute 1988). The 0.5 correlation between η_2 and η_1 is created by forming η_2 as a function of η_1 and a random disturbance. Variables y_1 to y_4 are generated using equation (28). The sample size is 100. The ML estimator from SAS's structural equation procedure, PROC CALIS (Hartmann 1989), is applied to each sample. Samples that result in nonconvergent solutions (i.e., that did not converge in 50 iterations) or that result in negative error variances are removed. New samples are drawn and the model is estimated until 100 samples with converged and proper solutions are obtained.

For each of the four variables, we expect to find about five statistically significant standardized residuals when the type I error level is .05. Table 1 lists the mean number of statistically significant ($\alpha = .05$) standardized residuals and the standard deviation of the count using the naive standardization of $e_{ji}/\sqrt{[\Theta]_{jj}}$ and $\hat{e}_{ji}/\sqrt{[\hat{\Theta}]_{jj}}$. The first uses the known population values of Θ, Λ, and W, and the second uses the sample estimates $\hat{\Theta}$, $\hat{\Lambda}$, and $\hat{W}$.

Perhaps the most striking result in Table 1 is that the mean count is far too low; all averages are considerably below the expected number of five. Although the regression-based residuals tend to be larger than the Bartlett-based ones, both types of naive standardized residuals tend to take values that are underestimates. It is also noteworthy that using sample estimates in place of the population parameters makes little difference. These findings suggest that the naive standardized residuals should not be used.

TABLE 1

Mean Counts and Standard Deviations (in parentheses) for 100 Samples of
Statistically Significant ($\alpha = .05$) Residuals Standardized by Population
Parameter of $\sqrt{[\Theta]}_{jj}$ or by Sample Estimate of $\sqrt{[\hat{\Theta}]}_{jj}$

Residual Calculation	Residuals Standardized by Population Parameters				Residuals Standardized by Sample Estimates			
	1	2	3	4	1	2	3	4
Regression-based	1.4	2.5	1.4	2.4	1.6	2.3	1.8	2.3
	(1.0)	(1.3)	(1.2)	(1.6)	(1.4)	(1.6)	(1.6)	(1.6)
Bartlett-based	0.2	1.3	0.1	1.2	0.7	1.5	0.8	1.4
	(0.4)	(0.9)	(0.4)	(1.1)	(1.1)	(1.7)	(1.3)	(1.7)

TABLE 2

Mean Counts and Standard Deviations (in parentheses) for 100 Samples of
Statistically Significant ($\alpha = .05$) Residuals Standardized by the Population
Parameter of $\sqrt{[\text{VAR}(e_i)]}_{jj}$ or by the Sample Estimate of $\sqrt{[\text{var}(e_i)]}_{jj}$

Residual Calculation	Mean Count							
	Residuals Standardized by Population Parameters				Residuals Standardized by Sample Estimates			
	1	2	3	4	1	2	3	4
Regression-based	4.9	4.9	4.9	4.9	4.7	4.6	4.7	5.0
	(2.3)	(1.9)	(2.0)	(2.4)	(1.6)	(1.5)	(1.6)	(1.5)
Bartlett-based	5.1	5.1	5.1	5.1	4.5	4.5	4.9	4.9
	(2.2)	(2.2)	(2.0)	(2.0)	(1.4)	(1.4)	(1.4)	(1.4)

A more favorable picture emerges from the results in Table 2.
It presents the mean count of statistically significant standardized
residuals when the standard deviations of the sample residuals are
used. The standardized residuals in the left half of Table 2 use the
population parameters to create e_{ji} and the population standard deviation of it (see equations (23) to (25)). The ones in the right half
substitute the sample counterparts to these quantities. Both methods
of standardization lead to values close to the expected number of
significant residuals. This is even true when the sample estimates
replace the population parameters in the formulas, though the
sample-based mean counts are slightly further from the expected
numbers than the population-based counts. Furthermore, the stan-

dard deviation of the counts is lower for the sample-based estimates than for the population counts.

4.2. *Simulation 2*

The previous example suggests that the standardized residuals formed using the variance of e_{ji} work fairly well in moderate-size samples ($N = 100$) and with only two indicators per factor. To further study the standardized residuals, we created another data set but introduced some problem observations. Specifically, the population factor analysis model has the following parameters:

$$
\begin{array}{c}
y_1 \\
y_2 \\
y_3 \\
y_4 \\
y_5 \\
y_6
\end{array}
=
\begin{array}{cc}
1 & 0 \\
.8 & 0 \\
.8 & .8 \\
.8 & 1 \\
0 & .8 \\
0 & .8
\end{array}
\begin{bmatrix} \eta_1 \\ \eta_2 \end{bmatrix}
+
\begin{array}{c}
\epsilon_1 \\
\epsilon_2 \\
\epsilon_3 \\
\epsilon_4 \\
\epsilon_5 \\
\epsilon_6
\end{array}
, \tag{30}
$$

$$
\Sigma_{\eta\eta} =
\begin{bmatrix} 1 & \\ .5 & 1 \end{bmatrix},
\quad
\Theta =
\begin{bmatrix}
1 & & & & & \\
0 & 1 & & & & \\
0 & 0 & 1 & & & \\
0 & 0 & 0 & 1 & & \\
0 & 0 & 0 & 0 & 1 & \\
0 & 0 & 0 & 0 & 0 & 1
\end{bmatrix}. \tag{31}
$$

This model is more complicated than the previous one because some of the variables are influenced by two latent variables rather than one. We generated the random variables in the same way as in the first simulation except that we used equation (30) to generate the y variables. The sample size is 100. Since the naive standardization performed so poorly in the last simulation, we do not consider it further. To introduce outliers, we let $E(\epsilon_6) = 5$ for the last ten cases in the sample by adding 5 to y_6 for $i = 91$ to 100 before calculating the covariance matrix and estimating the model. We then standardized the sample residuals by dividing them by $\sqrt{[\mathrm{var}(e_i)]_{jj}}$. We repeated this for 100 samples that had convergent solutions and nonnegative error variances using the procedures described for the first simulation example.

Tables 3 and 4 list means of the last 15 standardized residuals

TABLE 3

Means of Last 15 Standardized Residuals for 100 Samples, Standardized by $\sqrt{[\mathrm{var}(\mathbf{e}_i)]}_{jj}$ with Regression-Based Method

| Case | \multicolumn{6}{c}{Standardized Residual} |
	1	2	3	4	5	6
86	−0.11	0.07	0.10	0.07	−0.01	−0.35
87	0.02	−0.16	−0.04	0.13	0.12	−0.34
88	0.05	−0.15	−0.02	0.05	0.10	−0.28
89	0.03	−0.09	0.09	0.04	−0.04	−0.34
90	0.11	−0.04	0.00	0.09	0.03	−0.31
91	0.01	−0.03	−0.22	−0.12	−0.18	2.45
92	0.09	0.20	−0.08	−0.29	−0.27	2.39
93	0.09	0.04	−0.27	−0.15	−0.26	2.37
94	0.08	0.01	−0.14	−0.33	−0.18	2.46
95	−0.05	0.13	−0.02	−0.32	−0.11	2.33
96	0.04	0.05	−0.29	−0.19	−0.31	2.54
97	0.02	0.11	0.11	−0.28	−0.49	2.46
98	0.14	0.18	−0.17	−0.42	−0.30	2.43
99	−0.00	0.13	−0.16	0.30	−0.42	2.36
100	0.27	0.21	−0.24	−0.47	−0.16	2.35

TABLE 4

Means of Last 15 Standardized Residuals for 100 Samples, Standardized by $\sqrt{[\mathrm{var}(\mathbf{e}_i)]}_{jj}$ with Bartlett-Based Method

| Case | \multicolumn{6}{c}{Standardized Residual} |
	1	2	3	4	5	6
86	−0.19	0.05	0.10	0.08	0.03	−0.34
87	0.09	−0.17	−0.04	0.12	0.13	−0.36
88	0.08	−0.15	−0.00	0.05	0.14	−0.28
89	0.01	−0.11	0.07	0.07	0.01	−0.35
90	0.05	−0.08	−0.01	0.06	0.07	−0.29
91	0.27	0.21	−0.33	−0.38	−0.60	2.33
92	0.24	0.32	−0.17	−0.53	−0.60	2.32
93	0.38	0.22	−0.40	−0.38	−0.59	2.29
94	0.36	0.18	−0.22	−0.57	−0.57	2.35
95	0.33	0.13	−0.13	−0.53	−0.54	2.22
96	0.32	0.23	−0.41	−0.37	−0.66	2.45
97	0.12	0.22	−0.03	−0.49	−0.82	2.38
98	0.30	0.28	−0.26	−0.55	−0.58	2.38
99	0.23	0.28	−0.24	−0.40	−0.76	2.28
100	0.39	0.29	−0.27	−0.63	−0.44	2.30

for all six variables using the regression-based method and the Bartlett-based method, respectively. In both cases we have substituted sample estimates for the population parameters needed to calculate the standardized residuals.

In Table 3 we see that when outliers were not introduced (cases 86 to 90), the means are near zero. Though not shown here, their standard deviations are near one. There is a tendency for the residuals for y_6 to be negative (about -0.3). For the outlying observations (cases 91 to 100), the means for the y_1 to y_5 residuals are near zero and their standard deviations are near one. The means of the last ten standardized residuals for y_6 are positive, as expected, and typically about 2.4 in magnitude. The standard deviations of the y_6 standardized residuals are roughly 0.5 to 0.6, which is lower than the variability of the other standardized residuals. Thus, for the most part we could detect the ten problem cases with the sample standardized residuals.

One other feature is worth nothing. The residuals for y_3 to y_5 tend to be negative but small for cases 91 to 100. This is partially due to y_6, which contains the positive outliers and which enters the construction of the factor score. This makes the factor score estimate somewhat larger than it would be without the outliers for the last ten observations.

Table 4 shows that the Bartlett-based sample standardized residuals are also positive and relatively large for the last ten cases on y_6. However, the tendency for the outliers in y_6 to create negative residuals for the other variables that load on the same factor is stronger.

We repeated the introduction of outliers for the last ten cases but created outliers for y_3 rather than y_6. We chose y_3 because this variable loads on both factors, while y_6 loads only on the second. To conserve space we do not display these results, but the patterns of the standardized residuals were similar to those described for the y_6 residuals. Generally, the cases with the constant added to them were detectable, and there was some tendency for the standardized residuals for other variables that load on the same factor to be negative. This latter trend was most evident for the Bartlett-based residuals.

An implication of these results is that the standardized residuals help to reveal outlying observations on a *specific variable,* but the outlier may create small to moderate opposite-signed residuals for the same cases for the variables that load on the same factor. There are at least two ways to determine whether these secondary outliers are artifactual. One is to form bivariate scattergrams of all pairs of variables that load on the same factor. By examining the plots you can tell which variable has deviant cases. However, if the factor complexity of the variables is greater than one, this may not be ideal. An alternative is to screen the residuals to see which variable has the largest ones, then reconstruct the factor scores and residuals omitting the suspected variable. For instance, suppose that we have four indicators for a factor. We find that the fourth variable has the biggest residuals. Use the first three indicators to construct the factor score and then use this factor score to form the standardized residuals for all variables. This allows us to check the magnitude of residuals unobstructed by outliers on a specific variable. The process is followed for the other variables as needed.

5. EMPIRICAL EXAMPLE

In this section we illustrate the proposed statistics with an empirical example. The data are three judges' estimates of the percentage of the sky that contains clouds in each of 60 photographic slides. We choose this example because in a previous analysis using a model-free procedure, outliers were detected in these data, and it would be troublesome if the residuals do not also highlight these cases. This example also provides an opportunity to discuss the treatment of negative error variances in calculating residuals.

A table containing the raw data is in Bollen (1989, pp. 30–31). The lower half of the sample covariance matrix is

$$S = \begin{bmatrix} 1{,}301 & & \\ 1{,}020 & 1{,}463 & \\ 1{,}237 & 1{,}200 & 1{,}404 \end{bmatrix}. \tag{32}$$

The estimates of the factor analysis parameters are

$$\hat{\Lambda} = \begin{bmatrix} 1.00 \\ 0.97 \\ 1.18 \end{bmatrix}, \qquad \text{var}(\eta_1) = [1{,}052], \tag{33}$$

$$\hat{\Theta} = \begin{bmatrix} 249 & & \\ 0 & 474 & \\ 0 & 0 & -51 \end{bmatrix}. \tag{34}$$

Examination of $[\hat{\Theta}]_{33}$ reveals a negative error variance (or Heywood case). This creates an additional problem for the naive standardized residual (i.e., $e_{ji}/\sqrt{[\hat{\Theta}]_{jj}}$) because the method assumes that $[\hat{\Theta}]_{jj} > 0$. The Heywood case also undermines our ability to calculate the correlation between $\mathbf{e}_i$ and ϵ_i because this necessitates using the square root of the diagonal of $\boldsymbol{\Theta}$, which requires positive variances.

Outliers are one potential cause of Heywood cases, so it is important that we have the ability to compute the residuals to help identify unusual observations. We found that setting the negative variance to a small positive value $(+10)$ and using $\hat{\boldsymbol{\Sigma}}_{yy} = \hat{\boldsymbol{\Lambda}}\hat{\boldsymbol{\Sigma}}_{\eta\eta}\hat{\boldsymbol{\Lambda}}' + \hat{\boldsymbol{\Theta}}$ (instead of $\mathbf{S}$) as an estimator of $\boldsymbol{\Sigma}_{yy}$ gave us useful regression-based standardized residuals.[3] The results using the Bartlett-based residuals are not shown, but they were quite similar.

Figure 1 is an index plot of the three sets of standardized residuals by the observation number. Outliers are evident for the first and second residuals but not for the third. The two largest standardized residuals in absolute values are -3.74, for the second variable and the 52nd observation, and $+3.68$ for the first variable and the 40th observation. The three judges' estimates of the percentage of cloud cover for these two cases are as follows:

Case Number	y_1	y_2	y_3
52	100	5	95
40	95	0	40

These are two of the three cases identified as outliers in Bollen (1989, pp. 29–31). The third is case 51, whose standardized residual has the third highest absolute value. In Bollen (1989) the main diagonal of the projection matrix, $\mathbf{A} = \mathbf{Z}(\mathbf{Z}'\mathbf{Z})^{-1}\mathbf{Z}'$, where $\mathbf{Z}$ is the matrix of observed variables (deviated from their means) for all N cases, was used to highlight the extreme cases. The standardized residuals not only highlight the cases with outliers, but in this example they also indicate the variables with noticeable residuals.

An investigation of the three cases with the largest absolute

---

[3]Though much more experience is needed for firm advice, a general strategy for calculating standardized residuals in the presence of Heywood cases is to set the offending estimate to roughly 1 percent of the variance of the corresponding observed variable.

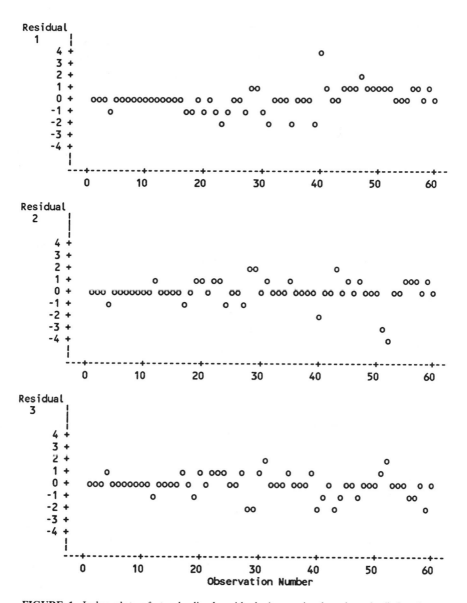

FIGURE 1. Index plots of standardized residuals (regression-based method) for three estimates of cloud cover ($N = 60$).

values of the standardized residuals revealed that these pictures had a great deal of haze. The haziness resulted in divergent estimates. The outliers point to the inappropriateness of this method under hazy conditions. Furthermore, removing these observations and re-analyzing the data leads to

$$\hat{\Lambda} = \begin{bmatrix} 1.00 \\ 1.14 \\ 1.12 \end{bmatrix}, \qquad \mathrm{var}(\eta_1) = [1{,}052], \tag{35}$$

$$\hat{\Theta} = \begin{bmatrix} 106 & & \\ 0 & 157 & \\ 0 & 0 & 58 \end{bmatrix}. \tag{36}$$

Thus, the outliers appear to be the cause of the negative error variance in the analysis of the original sample.

Finally, the pattern of + and − signs of the residuals suggests that the measurement errors might suffer from autocorrelation across observations. This is possible because the observations are in the order in which the judges saw them. An ARIMA analysis of the residuals indicates a possible AR(1) process for the measurement errors for the second and third judges and weaker evidence for the first.

6. EXTENSION TO GENERAL STRUCTURAL EQUATION MODELS

The preceding results apply to general structural equation models as well. The key to demonstrating this is to write the relation between the observed and latent variables in the form of a factor analysis model and then to apply the earlier formulas. For instance, using Jöreskog and Sörbom's (1989) LISREL notation, we have

$$\eta_i = B\eta_i + \Gamma\xi_i + \zeta_i, \tag{37}$$

$$y_i = \Lambda_y\eta_i + \epsilon_i, \tag{38}$$

$$x_i = \Lambda_x\xi_i + \delta_i. \tag{39}$$

Equation (37) is the latent variable model, where η_i is the vector of latent endogenous variables, ξ_i is the vector of latent exogenous variables, ζ_i is the vector of latent disturbances, and B and Γ are the coefficient matrices for the variables that follow them. Equations (38) and (39) provide the measurement model, where y_i and x_i are the observed variables, Λ_y and Λ_x are coefficient matrices (factor loadings), and ϵ_i and δ_i are the measurement error vectors.

Unstandardized and standardized residuals are easy to obtain. Define $z_i' = [y_i' \ x_i']'$, $L_i' = [\eta_i' \ \xi_i']'$, $v_i' = [\epsilon_i' \ \delta_i']'$, and

$$\Lambda = \begin{bmatrix} \Lambda_y & O \\ O & \Lambda_x \end{bmatrix}.$$

Then, equations (38) and (39) become

$$z_i = \Lambda L_i + v_i, \tag{40}$$

which is in the same form as equation (1). Substituting the covariance matrices Σ_{zz}, Σ_{LL}, and Σ_{vv} for Σ_{yy}, $\Sigma_{\eta\eta}$, and Θ in the previous derivations allows us to calculate the unstandardized and standardized residuals for LISREL models.

To illustrate this, let $\hat{L}_i = Wz_i$. Then,

$$v_i = (I - \Lambda W)z_i, \tag{41}$$

where v_i is the vector of residuals when $\hat{L}_i$ substitutes for L_i. The variance of v_i is

$$\text{VAR}(v_i) = (I - \Lambda W)\Sigma_{zz}(I - \Lambda W)'. \tag{42}$$

The unstandardized residuals in the regression method are

$$v_i = (I - \Lambda \Sigma_{LL}\Lambda' \Sigma_{zz}^{-1})z_i. \tag{43}$$

Their variance-covariance matrix is

$$\text{VAR}(v_i) = \Sigma_{vv}\Sigma_{zz}^{-1}\Sigma_{vv}, \tag{44}$$

and the standardized residuals are

$$v_{ji}/\sqrt{[\text{VAR}(v_i)]_{jj}}. \tag{45}$$

Substituting the sample estimates for the unknown parameters creates $\hat{v}_i$ and the standardized $\hat{v}_i$ for the measurement error residuals in the general structural equation model.

We can also estimate the error in the equation, ζ_i. To do so we treat ζ_i as a latent variable and use the regression method of estimating factor scores. Specifically, the unstandardized residuals are

$$\hat{\zeta}_i = W_\zeta z_i, \tag{46}$$

with

$$W_\zeta = \Sigma_{\zeta z} \Sigma_{zz}^{-1}, \tag{47}$$

where $\Sigma_{\zeta z} = [\text{VAR}(\zeta)\,(I - B)^{-1\prime}\Lambda_y'\quad 0]$. The standardization factors are the inverses of the square roots of the diagonal elements in

$$\text{VAR}(\hat{\zeta}_i) = W_\zeta \Sigma_{zz} W_\zeta'. \tag{48}$$

Of course, as before, we need to replace parameters by their sample counterparts.

To illustrate the extension of the residual techniques to general structural equation models, we use the model in Figure 2. The panel model has two latent endogenous variables, political democracy in 1960 (η_1) and 1965 (η_2), and one latent exogenous variable, industrialization in 1960 (ξ_1). Data are available for 75 developing countries. Industrialization is measured with three indicators, and political democracy for 1960 and 1965 is measured with the same four indicators. The measurement errors for the same indicator at two points in time are allowed to correlate, as are errors for measures that come from the same data source. (A detailed description of the variables, the model, and the ML estimates is in Bollen [1989].)

Here we present the standardized residuals for the measurement errors calculated according to the preceding results. Figure 3 provides stem-and-leaf plots and box plots for the 11 sets of standardized residuals for the 11 observed variables in the order of y_1 to y_8 followed by x_1 to x_3.[4] Strict application of the Bonferroni adjustment in testing the statistical significance of the standardized residuals would not identify any of these cases as outliers. However, from a substantive point of view it might prove useful to investigate some of the countries with the largest standardized residuals to see if they provide any insight into the adequacy of the model and the quality of the data. For instance, residual 5 in Figure 3 corresponds to a 1965 rating of freedom of the press by Nixon (1965). The two largest absolute values are for Sri Lanka (-2.8) and Ghana (-2.7). The

---

[4]In the box plots the "+" signifies the sample mean and the center horizontal line is the median. The bottom and top horizontal lines of the box are the 25th and 75th percentiles. Sample skewness and kurtosis for each variable were not excessively large (all less than 1 in absolute value).

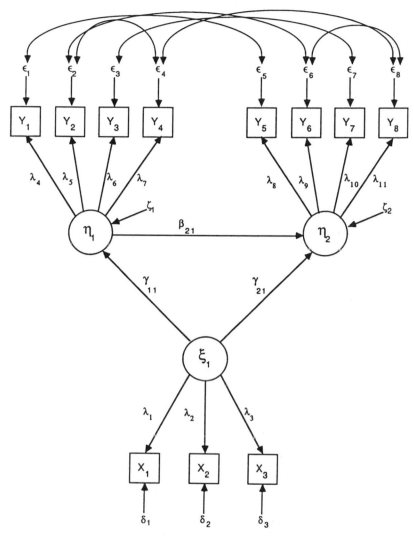

FIGURE 2. Industrialization (ξ_1) and political democracy (η_1 and η_2) panel model for developing countries, 1960 to 1965 (N = 75).

large negative values mean that these ratings were lower than would be predicted from the degree of political democracy in these countries. Indeed Nixon (1965, p. 9) specifically mentions Sri Lanka and Ghana as having much lower ratings in his 1965 survey than in his 1960 survey. Lowenstein provides an independent rating of freedom

Residual 1

Stem	Leaf	#	Box Plot
2		0	
1	577777778	6	
1	0111	4	
0	566677788999	12	+−−−−−+
0	001111222334	12	|　　+　　|
−0	43333221111100	14	*−−−−−−*
−0	9888877665	10	+−−−−−+
−1	321110	6	
−1	9775555	7	
−2	1	1	

−−−−+−−−−+−−−−+−−−−+

Residual 2

Stem	Leaf	#	Box Plot
2	8	1	
2	044	3	
1	5	1	
1	0112223	7	
0	6788899999	10	+−−−−−+
0	0011112222233334	16	*−−−−−−*
−0	443322221	9	|　　+　　|
−0	987777776666	12	+−−−−−+
−1	43322211111110	14	
−1	5	1	
−2	0	1	

−−−−+−−−−+−−−−+−−−−+

Residual 3

Stem	Leaf	#	Box Plot
2	5	1	
2			
1	89	2	
1	01122333	8	
0	555666667778899	15	+−−−−−+
0	0000112223344444	16	*−−+−−*
−0	4433321110	10	|　　　|
−0	9998887665	10	+−−−−−+
−1	33221100	8	
−1	55	2	
−2	3	1	
−2	76	2	

−−−−+−−−−+−−−−+−−−−+

FIGURE 3. Stem-and-leaf plots and box plots of standardized residuals (regression-based method) for 11 observed variables in industrialization and political democracy model ($N = 75$).

Residual 4

Stem	Leaf	#	Box Plot
2	1	1	0
1	889	3	|
1	0344444	7	|
0	555666799	9	+-----+
0	01111111111222223333444	23	*-----*
-0	4332222211110	13	| + |
-0	98766655	8	+-----+
-1	310	3	|
-1	665	3	|
-2	4331	4	0
-2	5	1	0

```
----+----+----+----+
```

Residual 5

Stem	Leaf	#	Box Plot
2	5	1	0
2	1	1	|
1	59	2	|
1	011233334	9	|
0	55556789	8	+-----+
0	1222222233334444	16	| |
-0	3332222111111100	16	*--+--*
-0	98888877665	11	+-----+
-1	210000	6	|
-1	5	1	|
-2	10	2	|
-2	87	2	0

```
----+----+----+----+
```

Residual 6

Stem	Leaf	#	Box Plot
2	5	1	|
2	34	2	|
1	7789	4	|
1	01233	5	|
0	666677778999	12	+-----+
0	1222234	7	| + |
-0	444443332211100	15	*-----*
-0	999987776666666555	18	+-----+
-1	33221000	8	|
-1	987	3	|

```
----+----+----+----+
```

FIGURE 3 Continued

Residual 7

Stem	Leaf	#	Box Plot
2	4	1	
1	5678	4	
1	001123333	9	
0	5555566778888	13	+-----+
0	011222224444	12	*--+--*
−0	443332220	9	
−0	9988877766666655	16	+-----+
−1	443200	6	
−1	98	2	
−2	00	2	
−2	6	1	

```
----+----+----+----+
```

Residual 8

Stem	Leaf	#	Box Plot
2	114	3	
1	66	2	
1	01124	5	
0	5555666677788999	16	+-----+
0	0001222222333444	16	*--+--*
−0	333221000	9	
−0	99988777655	11	+-----+
−1	3321110	7	
−1	9887	4	
−2	0	1	
−2	8	1	

```
----+----+----+----+
```

Residual 9

Stem	Leaf	#	Box Plot
2	2	1	
1	55577	5	
1	112234	6	
0	555666667888899	15	+--!--+
0	0001122233344	13	*--+--*
−0	4333211100	10	
−0	9998887777755	13	+-----+
−1	321110	6	
−1	95	2	
−2	3110	4	

```
----+----+----+----+
```

FIGURE 3 Continued

Residual 10

Stem	Leaf	#	Box Plot
2	02	2	
1	8	1	
1	1112222334	10	
0	5555555677778899	16	+ − − − − − +
0	00122223334	11	* − − − − − *
−0	44433210	8	| + |
−0	998877766665555	15	+ − − − − − +
−1	432110	6	
−1	9977	4	
−2	32	2	

```
    − − − − + − − − − + − − − − + − − − − +
```

Residual 11

Stem	Leaf	#	Box Plot
2	6	1	0
2	1	1	
1	6778	4	
1	00022334	8	
0	555555555789	12	+ − − − − − +
0	0112333333	10	| + |
−0	44433222111000	14	* − − − − − *
−0	99977776555	11	+ − − − − − +
−1	44433333110	11	
−1	8	1	
−2	20	2	

```
    − − − − + − − − − + − − − − + − − − − +
```

FIGURE 3 Continued

of the press for roughly the same time period (1966) and ranks both Sri Lanka and Ghana relatively higher than Nixon did (Taylor and Hudson 1972, p. 52). This suggests that the 1965 Nixon ratings for these two countries were downwardly biased.

We also computed the standardized residuals for the latent variable disturbance terms, ζ_1 and ζ_2. The stem-and-leaf plots and the box plots for these are in Figure 4. No extreme residuals appear, though a couple are fairly large. In the first equation, Spain has the largest negative standardized residual (-2.6), and the Philippines has the largest positive residual (2.6). The negative residual for Spain reflects the dictatorship of Franco, which kept democracy below what would be predicted from its level of industrialization. In con-

Standardized Residuals for $\hat{\zeta}_1$

Stem	Leaf	#	Box Plot
2	6	1	
2	4	1	
1	55	2	
1	0144444	7	
0	55566677778999	14	+--⊥--+
0	00001112222344	14	*--+--*
-0	4432222221100	13			
-0	987777655	9	+--T--+
-1	43211100	8	
-1	8655	4	
-2	3	1	
-2	6	1	

----+----+----+----+

Standardized Residuals for $\hat{\zeta}_2$

Stem	Leaf	#	Box Plot
2	023	3	
1	55	2	
1	1234	4	
0	56666777788889999	17	+--⊥--+
0	0122333344444	13	*-----*
-0	4433221000	10		+	
-0	998877666555	12	+--T--+
-1	44332200	8	
-1	76665	5	
-2			
-2	7	1	

----+----+----+----+

FIGURE 4. Stem-and-leaf plots and box plots of standardized residuals (regression-based method) for $\hat{\zeta}_1$ and $\hat{\zeta}_2$ in industrialization and political democracy model ($N = 75$).

trast, in 1960 the Philippines had a surprisingly democratic system given its modest industrialization. In the second equation, Ghana has the biggest absolute value for a residual (-2.7). This is due to the collapse of a relatively democratic system and a turn toward a single-party dictatorship after 1960.

7. CONCLUSIONS

In this paper we proposed a general approach to calculating unstandardized and standardized residuals in factor analysis models and extended it to general structural equation models. We also provided tests of statistical significance for residuals and a simultaneous chi-square test for more than one residual. The significance tests assume that large samples are used. However, our simulations and empirical illustrations indicate that the tests are helpful even with N's of 60 to 100. We believe that these tests are a useful diagnostic tool for latent variable models. But at the same time we recognize that much more experience with them must be gained before we can fully assess their properties.

We opened the paper with the suggestion that residuals from latent variable models are useful for outlier and influential case diagnostics. We close by elaborating this point. Residuals from latent variable models are *one* means to identify outlying cases. These observations are outliers because they are not well-predicted by the model. A subset of these outliers might be influential in that their omission from the model leads to substantial changes in the coefficient estimates, standard errors, likelihood-ratio test statistic, R^2s, or other estimates. The simplest way to assess influence is to omit various combinations of the cases with large residuals and to examine the changes in the results. Once influential cases are found, the task is to explain why they are outliers. The potential causes are many: coding errors, incorrect functional form, omitted variables, structural shifts, etc. The corrections depend on the cause and can range from the simplest case of rectifying coding errors or variable transformation to the more extreme situation of respecifying a model. Omission of cases aids the assessment of influence, but it is hardly ever a solution to outliers.

Finally, we emphasize that examining only residuals will not reveal all outliers and influential cases. Drawing upon the findings of regression diagnostics, we see that it is possible for a case to have a small standardized residual but a large influence (Bollen and Jackman 1990, pp. 264–65). This points to the need to develop other statistics similar to DFBETAS, Cook's D, and DFITS used in regression analysis. Such diagnostics in structural equation models are complicated by the numerical minimization required in estimation. It may be possible to use approximations that do not require fully iterative solutions, as Pregibon (1981) has done in logistic regression. Until then, it would be prudent to use model-free outlier diagnostics in conjunction with the residuals proposed here.

REFERENCES

Anderson, T. W., and H. Rubin. 1956. "Statistical Inference in Factor Analysis." *Third Berkeley Symposium on Mathematical Statistics and Probability* 5:111–50.

Barnett, Vic, and Toby Lewis. 1984. *Outliers in Statistical Data.* New York: Wiley.

Bartholomew, D. J. 1981. "Posterior Analysis of the Factor Model." *British Journal of Mathematical and Statistical Psychology* 34:93–99.

Belsley, D. A., E. Kuh, and R. E. Welsch. 1980. *Regression Diagnostics: Identifying Influential Data and Sources of Collinearity.* New York: Wiley.

Bentler, P. M. 1985. *Theory and Implementation of EQS: A Structural Equations Program.* Los Angeles:BMDP Statistical Software.

Bollen, K. A. 1987. "Outliers and Improper Solutions: A Confirmatory Factor Analysis Example." *Sociological Methods and Research* 15:375–84.

———. 1989. *Structural Equations with Latent Variables.* New York: Wiley.

Bollen, K. A., and R. W. Jackman. 1990. "Regression Diagnostics: An Expository Treatment of Outliers and Influential Cases." Pp. 257–91 in *Modern Methods of Data Analysis,* edited by J. Fox and J. S. Long. Newbury Park, CA:Sage.

Cook, R. D., and S. Weisberg. 1982. "Criticism and Influence Analysis in Regression." Pp. 313–62 in *Sociological Methodology 1982,* edited by S. Leinhardt. San Francisco:Jossey-Bass.

Hartmann, W. 1989. *The CALIS Procedure: Extended User's Guide.* Cary, NC: SAS Institute.

Jöreskog, K. G., and D. Sörbom. 1989. *LISREL 7: A Guide to the Program and Applications.* Chicago:SPSS Inc.

Lawley, D. N., and A. E. Maxwell. 1971. *Factor Analysis as a Statistical Method.* London:Butterworth.

McDonald, R. P., and E. J. A. Burr. 1967. "A Comparison of Four Methods of Constructing Factor Scores." *Psychometrika* 32:381–401.

Mulaik, S. 1972. *The Foundations of Factor Analysis.* New York:McGraw-Hill.

Nixon, R. 1965. "Freedom in the World's Press: A Fresh Appraisal with New Data." *Journalism Quarterly* 42:3–15, 118–19.

Pregibon, D. 1981. "Logistic Regression Diagnostics." *Annals of Statistics* 9:705–24.

SAS Institute. 1988. *SAS Language Guide for Personal Computers.* Cary, NC: SAS Institute.

Saris, W. E., W. M. de Pijper, and J. Mulder. 1978. "Optimal Procedures for Estimation of Factor Scores." *Sociological Methods and Research* 7:85–106.

Steiger, J. H. 1979. "Factor Indeterminacy in the 1930s and the 1970s: Some Interesting Parallels." *Psychometrika* 44:157–68.

Taylor, C., and M. Hudson. 1972. *World Handbook of Political and Social Indicators.* 2d ed. New Haven: Yale University Press.

Williams, J. S. 1978. "A Definition for the Common-Factor Analysis Model and the Elimination of Problems of Factor Score Indeterminacy." *Psychometrika* 43:293–306.

9

TIME-AGGREGATION BIAS IN CONTINUOUS-TIME HAZARD-RATE MODELS

Trond Petersen*

In analyses of event-history data, the estimators for the parameters of the process (i.e., of the hazard rate) typically assume that the available measures of time are continuous. The assumption that time is exactly or continuously measured is rarely met. Instead, researchers typically know that the amount of time spent in a state lies between, say, j − 1 and j months, but not the exact time within that window. Researchers then customarily set the duration in the state equal to j and treat this as the exact duration. Or, if censoring occurred between j − 1 and j, they set the censoring time equal to j. These practices give rise to some bias in the estimates, called time-aggregation bias. In this paper I address two issues in connection with time-aggregation bias. First, I discuss the size of the bias when an estimator based on exact measurements of durations is applied to grouped measurements of durations. Second, I discuss how one can minimize the time-aggregation bias when using an estimator that assumes exact measurements of durations. This amounts to asking the following question: If an event occurred between duration j − 1 and j, what is the optimal choice for the assigned duration t? Or, if censoring occurred between j − 1

For comments on a previous version of the paper, I thank Clifford Clogg, Peter Marsden, Gary Chamberlain, Burton Singer, Lawrence Wu, and five anonymous reviewers. For research assistance I thank Kenneth Koput and James Wade. An earlier version of the paper circulated as Petersen (1983). This research was supported by the National Institute on Aging (AG04367) and by the Institute of Industrial Relations at the University of California, Berkeley. The opinions expressed in the paper are those of the author.
*University of California, Berkeley

263

and j, *what is a good assignment for the censoring time within that interval? Choosing* j − .5 *as the assigned duration seems to produce good results.*

1. INTRODUCTION

Sociologists often use continuous-time hazard-rate models to analyze the amount of time a person, organization, or some other unit spends in a social state. In these analyses it is assumed that the unit can enter and leave the state at any point in time. That is, the process is continuous in time. The estimators used to estimate the parameters of the process (i.e., the hazard rate) typically assume that the available measures of time are continuous, that is, that the exact amount of time spent in the state is measured.

The assumption that time is exactly measured is rarely met. We usually only know that a state was entered in a given time interval—say, a month—and that it was left or censored during a later time interval—say, a month. From those two pieces of information we cannot compute the exact duration in a state, only that it lies between, say, $j − 1$ (or even worse $j − 2$) and j months.[1] Researchers then customarily set the duration in the state—either censored or noncensored—equal to j and treat this as the exact duration. This practice generates some bias in the estimates, called *time-aggregation bias.*

The most natural solution to the problem of time aggregation is to develop estimators that take account of the grouped nature of the data on the durations.[2] These estimators assume that the process evolves continuously in time, but they adjust for the fact that measurements of time are not continuous (see, e.g., Harris, Meier, and Tukey 1950; Holford 1976, 1980; Thompson 1977; Prentice and Gloeckler 1978; Allison 1982; Cox and Oakes 1984, pp. 53–59; Heijtan 1989, pp. 172–74). Specifically, for an observation that experienced a transition between duration $j − 1$ and j, the likelihood contribution becomes the *probability* of experiencing a transition

---

[1]One may also consider the more general window $j − κ$ to j, where $κ$ is some positive constant that may be greater than one or two. The qualitative conclusions of this paper would be unaffected by this change.

[2]In sociological research, the most popular solution has been to use discrete-time methods. These are discussed briefly in section 6.

between $j - 1$ and j. Each term in this probability can be derived from the hazard rate. The likelihood based on this probability yields *consistent* estimates of the parameters of the hazard rate. If, in contrast, the researcher assumes that the exact duration is j, the likelihood contribution of the observation becomes the *probability density* of experiencing a transition at duration j. The likelihood based on this probability density yields *inconsistent* estimates of the parameters of the hazard rate.

It is always preferable to use the estimator that adjusts for the grouping of time measurements. But researchers almost never choose to do so, partly because of convention, and partly for four other reasons. First, it is often impractical to develop the relevant estimator. In many cases this requires writing special-purpose estimation routines. Second, when there is more than one state that can be entered when a transition occurs, using the estimator that adjusts for the grouping of the data requires that the parameters of all the relevant rates be estimated simultaneously. This may be computationally burdensome.[3] Using the estimator that assumes exact measurements of durations allows one to estimate first the rate to state 1, then the rate to state 2, and so on. Computationally this is much easier. Third, the estimator that adjusts for the grouping of time measurements requires the researcher to specify a model for the censoring process and to estimate its parameters along with the parameters of the failure-time process.[4] Unfortunately, little is usually known about the censoring process, and the researcher rarely has an intrinsic interest in it. Fourth, even though the problem of time-aggregation bias is known, the researcher may believe that it is negligible, that the inconsistent estimates may not be very different from the consistent estimates.

For these four reasons, the estimator that assumes that durations are exactly measured is often used and seems, from a practical point of view, to be preferable, despite its bias. In this paper I address two issues in connection with time-aggregation bias of this

[3]The complexity of this problem may be even greater in continuous-state-space models. For the latter, see Petersen (1988, 1990a). The same problem arises in multistate models in which each destination-specific rate depends on a common unobservable and in the discrete-time formulation of multistate processes (see, e.g., Arminger 1984, p. 476).

[4]This is also the case for the discrete-time formulation. But researchers rarely deal with it, assuming instead that censoring occurred at the end of the interval in question.

estimator. First, I discuss the size of the bias when the estimator is applied to grouped measurements of durations. This discussion shows when the problem is likely or unlikely to affect severely the conclusions reached. Second, I discuss how one can minimize the time-aggregation bias when using the estimator. This amounts to asking the following question: If an event occurred between duration $j - 1$ and j, what is the optimal choice for the assigned duration t? That is, which choice of t minimizes the time-aggregation bias? Is it $t = j - 1$, or $t = j$, or some other value of t between $j - 1$ and j? The same question can be asked for censored cases.

Minimizing the time-aggregation bias for noncensored cases is relatively straightforward, as shown in section 3 below. Dealing with censored cases is more complicated, because one must specify the mechanism that censors cases within a time interval. A simple, but less general, conclusion addressing censored cases is derived in section 5.

The remainder of the paper is organized as follows. In section 2, I formally derive the inconsistency of the estimator that assumes exact measurements of durations when the assumption is not met. This is done for an exponential model under the assumption of no censoring. For that model, analytic results can be obtained. For more general models, analytic results cannot be obtained; one must resort to the less satisfactory solution of simulations. In section 3 I derive an explicit formula for the optimal choice of assigned duration t, again for the exponential model. In section 4 I comment on how to generalize the formula to models with covariates, duration dependence, and multiple states.[5] In section 5 I discuss assignment of durations for censored cases. I use the result derived there in the empirical example in section 3, where censoring is present. In section 6 I discuss discrete-time models. In section 7 I summarize the results.

[5]Throughout, the focus will be on fully parametric models. In semiparametric estimation routines, such as the partial likelihood principle of Cox (1975), time aggregation usually gives rise to ties. The expressions for dealing with these easily become unwieldy (for a discussion, see Heijtan 1989, pp. 172–74). Therefore, researchers often use a standard approximation (Breslow 1974). It works well when the number of events relative to the number of individuals at risk in an interval is small (see, e.g., Kalbfleisch and Prentice 1980, pp. 74–75). With no ties and the ranking of durations unaffected by the time aggregation, the partial likelihood gives rise to consistent estimates because only the rank of the duration, not its specific value, is used in the estimation.

2. THE ESTIMATORS AND THEIR PROPERTIES: CONSISTENCY AND BIAS

In this section I first derive three estimators: (a) the regular estimator of the rate when durations are exactly measured, (b) the estimator of the rate when durations are grouped but are assumed to be exactly measured, and (c) the estimator of the rate when durations are grouped and the estimator takes account of the grouping of durations. Then I show that estimator (b) is inconsistent and that (c) is consistent. Finally, I study the size of the bias in estimator (b).

2.1. *The Three Estimators*

Consider the rate

$$\lambda(t) = \alpha \qquad \text{where } \alpha > 0. \tag{1}$$

Let T_i be the random variable denoting the duration in a state on individual i and let t_i be its realization, where t_i may be censored or not censored. The density function for t_i, in the case of a noncensored observation, is

$$f(t_i) = \alpha \times \exp(-\alpha t_i). \tag{2}$$

The second term on the right-hand side of (2) is the survivor function:

$$G(t_i) \equiv P(T_i \geq t_i). \tag{3}$$

I consider the case with no censored observations and a sample of size N. Censored observations are not considered at this stage, because that necessitates specifying the process whereby censoring occurs. The treatment of censored cases must therefore proceed along less general lines, as outlined in section 5.

The ML estimator of α in the case of no censored observations is

$$\alpha_e = N / \sum_{i=1}^{N} t_i, \tag{4}$$

where the subscript e denotes that the durations are exactly measured.

When durations are grouped, we observe only that a transition took place between, say, month $j_i - 1$ and month j_i. Suppose we treat j_i as the exact duration. The ML estimator of α, based on the grouped data but assuming exact measurements of durations, then becomes

$$\alpha_u = N/\sum_{i=1}^{N} j_i, \tag{5}$$

where the subscript u denotes that the estimator does not adjust for the grouping of duration measurements.

Finally, I consider the ML estimator that adjusts for the grouping of duration measurements. For a case that experienced a transition between $j_i - 1$ and j_i, the likelihood contribution becomes

$$\begin{aligned}
P(j_i - 1 < T_i \le j_i) &= G(j_i - 1) \times [1 - G(j_i \,|\, j_i - 1)] \\
&= \exp[-\alpha(j_i - 1)] \times [1 - \exp(-\alpha)], \tag{6}
\end{aligned}$$

where $G(j_i \,|\, j_i - 1)$ is the conditional survivor function (see, e.g., Harris et al. 1950, p. 263; Lawless 1982, p. 260). It gives the probability of surviving beyond j_i, given survival at $j_i - 1$.

The ML estimator α_g resulting from (6) is

$$\alpha_g = \ln[\sum_{i=1}^{N} j_i/(\sum_{i=1}^{N} j_i - N)], \tag{7}$$

or

$$\exp(\alpha_g) = \sum_{i=1}^{N} j_i/(\sum_{i=1}^{N} j_i - N), \tag{8}$$

where the subscript g denotes that the estimator adjusts for the grouping of duration measurements. I refer to the likelihood in (6) as the *grouped likelihood*. Equation (8) will be used in section 2.2.

I mentioned in section 1 that many researchers choose not to implement the estimator that adjusts for the grouping of duration measurements because it is too cumbersome in multistate models. To illustrate, consider the simplest of cases, the case in which there are two states to which transitions can be made and the rates are constant, α_1 and α_2. Let Z be the random variable denoting the state entered upon a transition, and let z denote its realization. The probability that a transition occurs between $j_i - 1$ and j_i and that it is to state z then becomes

$$P(j_i - 1 < T_i \leq j_i, Z = z) = \exp[-(\alpha_1 + \alpha_2)(j_i - 1)]$$

$$\times \{1 - \exp[-(\alpha_1 + \alpha_2)]\} \times \frac{\alpha_z}{\alpha_1 + \alpha_2}$$

(9)

(for the general formula, see, e.g., Elandt-Johnson and Johnson 1980, p. 274, eq. 9.15).

The second and third terms on the right-hand side of (9) will, after logarithms are taken, not factor into separate components for each of the destination-specific rates. Therefore, joint maximization of the rates is required. For example, suppose that there are 5 rates and that there are 20 variables in each rate. In the estimator that adjusts for the grouping of measurements, we must invert a matrix of dimension 100×100 in each iteration. This is computationally burdensome. In the estimator that assumes exact measurements of durations, we must run five separate estimations. In estimating each rate, we must invert a matrix of dimension 20×20 in each iteration.

2.2. Consistency of the Estimators

To study the consistency of the estimators in (5) and (7), we need one preliminary result. Let J_i be the random variable whose realization is j_i. We must evaluate the expectation of J_i. This is straightforward but technically onerous. I state the result here but defer the proof to the appendix:

$$E(J_i) = 1/[1 - \exp(-\alpha)].$$

(10)

Proof of (10): See the appendix.

We can now study the consistency of (5) and (7). By the Strong Law of Large Numbers (henceforth SLLN, see Rao 1973, p. 115) we get

$$(1/N) \sum_{i=1}^{N} j_i \xrightarrow{\text{a.s.}} E(J_i) = 1/[1 - \exp(-\alpha)],$$

(11)

where a.s. (almost surely) means almost sure convergence (see, e.g., White 1984, sect. II.2). Hence, using (11) in (5) we get (by White 1984, prop. 2.11, p. 17)

$$\alpha_u = N/\sum_{i=1}^{N} j_i \xrightarrow{\text{a.s.}} 1 - \exp(-\alpha).$$

(12)

The convergence result in equation (12) establishes that the estimator α_u in (5) is inconsistent. It generates time-aggregation bias.[6] The size of this bias is explored in section 2.3.

The consistency of the estimator in (7) is easily established. By the SLLN and (11) we see that for $\exp(\alpha_g)$ in (8),

$$\exp(\alpha_g) = \sum_{i=1}^{N} j_j / (\sum_{i=1}^{N} j_i - N) \xrightarrow{\text{a.s.}} \exp(\alpha). \tag{13}$$

It then follows from (13) that (by White 1984, prop. 2.11, p. 17)

$$\alpha_g = \ln[\sum_{i=1}^{N} j_i / (\sum_{i=1}^{N} j_i - N)] \xrightarrow{\text{a.s.}} \alpha. \tag{14}$$

Thus, the estimator α_g that adjusts for the grouping of the duration measurements is consistent.

2.3. Magnitude of the Bias

The inconsistency of the estimator α_u is obviously not a desirable property. Nevertheless, the following valuable property of the estimator can be established: The magnitude of the bias will under some circumstances be negligible. The bias will then have little impact on the substantive conclusions reached. The objective of this section is to establish the circumstances under which this is the case. One of the circumstances identified relates to the nature of the process studied, that is, to how fast changes occur. The other relates to the crudeness with which durations are measured, that is, to the width of the window Δt within which the true durations are known to lie.

In (12) we established that

$$\alpha_u \xrightarrow{\text{a.s.}} 1 - \exp(-\alpha).$$

To assess the size of the bias, note first that for a small α,

$$\alpha \approx 1 - \exp(-\alpha). \tag{15}$$

[6]In addition to the asymptotic bias, there will be bias in small samples, a problem pertaining to both asymptotically biased and unbiased estimators. It is not discussed further here.

For $\alpha = 0$, the approximation is exact. But $\alpha = 0$ is not permissible (see (1)). Thus, when α is small, the estimator α_u converges to a value that is close to the true α. This will be explored further below. Note also that

$$\alpha > 1 - \exp(-\alpha) \qquad \text{for all } \alpha > 0. \tag{16}$$

Hence, the estimator α_u always asymptotically underestimates the true α. This confirms our intuitions. The assigned durations j_i are always bigger than the true durations t_i. Therefore, the process is portrayed as moving slower than it really does. Conversely, had we assigned the durations $j_i - 1$ instead of j_i we would have asymptotically overestimated the true α: The process would be portrayed as moving faster than it really does.[7]

The size of the bias in α_u will be investigated as follows. The quantity to be studied is the relative bias, now to be defined. First, from the true coefficient α subtract the estimator α_u. Then divide the difference between the two by the true coefficient, assuming that it is different from zero. The ensuing expression is $b_u = (\alpha - \alpha_u)/\alpha$. When multiplied by 100 it gives, for a fixed value of α, the percentage by which the estimator α_u misses the parameter α. The relative bias, then, is defined as the value towards which b_u converges almost surely, that is, the asymptotic value of b_u. Call this B_u. It is given by

$$B_u = \{\alpha - [1 - \exp(-\alpha)]\}/\alpha. \tag{17}$$

To assess how this bias varies with α, take the derivative of B_u with respect to α. This yields

$$\partial B_u/\partial \alpha = [1 - \exp(-\alpha) - \alpha \times \exp(-\alpha)]/\alpha > 0. \tag{18}$$

Equation (18) shows that the relative bias increases with α. The relative bias is small when α is close to zero but gets larger as α grows.

The next result follows directly from the one just stated. Fix the pace at which changes occur, that is, the speed of the process. Then, the wider the window $\Delta t = j - (j - 1)$ within which the true durations are known to lie, the higher the relative bias. In other words, for a fixed mean duration, the larger the window within which

[7]Rounding down durations may in some surveys be as common as rounding up. The qualitative aspects of the discussion and advice in this paper apply to rounding down as well as up.

durations are known to fall, the larger the bias.[8] This can be seen by a simple argument. Suppose we have exact measurements of durations. If so, the estimator in (4) applies. In this estimator we are free to choose the time units in which to measure durations t_i, for example, years or months. If we measure durations in years rather than months, we just divide the monthly duration measures by 12. From (4) it then follows that the rate when durations are measured in years is 12 times larger than the rate when durations are measured in months, even though the speed of the process is the same in the two cases. For example, if the rate is .05 when durations are measured in months, the annual rate is .60. As shown above, the higher the rate per time unit, the higher the time-aggregation bias. Therefore, if we know only whether or not an event occurred within a given year, the time-aggregation bias in percentage terms is larger than if we know whether or not the event occurred within a given month. This is so because for a fixed speed of the process, the annual rate is 12 times larger than the monthly rate, and the larger the rate, given the time interval within which events are known to lie or not lie, the larger the bias.

Table 1 further illustrates how the relative bias in (17) depends on the rate. It gives the relative bias B_u of α_u for 25 different values of α. It also reports the values towards which α_u converges for each value of α. We see that for values of α above .10, the relative bias is substantial. For values of α less than .10, the relative bias is small, that is, less than 5 percent. Continuing the example in the preceeding paragraph, where the monthly rate is .05 and the annual rate is .60, we see that the time-aggregation bias is small when durations are measured up to the nearest month but that it is 25 percent when durations are measured up to only the nearest year.

I state this analysis in two conclusions.

Conclusion 1: For a fixed window Δt within which the true durations lie, the higher the rate α, the higher the relative bias of the estimator α_u that does not take account of the grouping of the duration measurements.

Conclusion 2: For a fixed speed of the process, the wider the window Δt within which the true durations lie, the higher the relative

---

[8]Galler (1986) reached the same conclusion using the less satisfactory Monte Carlo experiment, not analytic results, as here. See also Arminger (1984, p. 474).

TABLE 1

Asymptotic Values for Estimated Rates and for Relative Bias in Estimated
Rates, By Underlying True Rate (α) and Hence Expected Waiting Time,
When the Continuous-Time Estimators in (5) and (21) Are Applied to Data
That Are Aggregated Over Time

True Rate α	Asymptotic Value of $\alpha_u{}^a$	Relative Bias B_u of $\alpha_u{}^b$	Asymptotic Value of $\alpha_{u,.5}{}^c$	Relative Bias $B_{u,.5}$ of $\alpha_{u,.5}{}^d$	Expected Waiting Time^c
2.0	.864665	.567668	1.523188	.238406	0.50
1.5	.776870	.482087	1.270298	.153135	0.66
1.0	.632121	.367879	.924234	.075766	1.00
.9	.593430	.340633	.843798	.062447	1.11
.8	.550671	.311661	.759898	.050128	1.25
.7	.503415	.280836	.672751	.038927	1.43
.6	.451188	.248019	.582625	.039827	1.67
.5	.393469	.213061	.489837	.028958	2.00
.4	.329680	.175800	.394751	.020325	2.50
.3	.259182	.136061	.297770	.013123	3.33
.25	.221199	.115203	.248706	.007433	4.00
.20	.181269	.093654	.199336	.005176	5.00
.15	.139292	.071387	.149719	.003320	6.66
.10	.095163	.048374	.099917	.001871	10.0
.09	.086069	.043680	.089939	.000674	11.1
.08	.076884	.038954	.079957	.000533	12.5
.07	.067606	.034197	.069971	.000408	14.3
.06	.058235	.029409	.059982	.000300	16.6
.05	.048771	.024588	.049990	.000208	20.0
.04	.039211	.019736	.039995	.000133	25.0
.03	.029554	.014851	.029998	.000075	33.3
.02	.019801	.009934	.019999	.000033	50.0
.01	.009950	.004983	.010000	.000008	100.0
.005	.004988	.002496	.005000	.000002	200.0
.001	.001000	.000500	.001000	.000000	1,000

Note: See section 2.3 for discussion of the issues.

^{a}This is the value, from equation (12), towards which the estimator α_u in equation (5) converges.

^{b}This is the asymptotic bias B_u, from equation (17), of the estimator α_u in equation (5).

^{c}This is the value towards which the estimator $\alpha_{u,.5}$ converges almost surely, given the value of the true rate α. The estimator $\alpha_{u,.5}$ uses the midpoint adjustment for the durations. That is, if an event happened between $j - 1$ and j, the assigned duration is $j - .5$. See section 4, equation (21), for the value towards which $\alpha_{u,k}$ converges for a general choice of k.

$^d B_{u,.5}$ is the relative bias of the estimator $\alpha_{u,.5}$. That is, $B_{u,.5}$ is the value towards which $b_{u,.5} \equiv (\alpha_{u,.5} - \alpha)/\alpha$ converges almost surely.

^{e}This is given as $1/\alpha$.

bias of the estimator α_u that does not take account of the grouping of the duration measurements.

I illustrate these conclusions with data on the movements within and out of a large hierarchically organized insurance company in the U.S. (see Petersen and Spilerman 1990). The company is organized into salary grade levels, from grade 1 (the lowest) to grade 20 (the highest). I study the rate at which a salary grade level is left. A grade is left when a person is promoted or demoted or when he or she leaves the company. I focus on the rates at which each of grades 1–6 is left. These grades comprise lower-level clerical positions. The rate is given in equation (1) and is specific to each salary grade level.

To address conclusions 1 and 2, I use three different aggregation levels of durations. At the first level, I measure durations in days. I then convert the number of days into months and fractions of months. At this level, there is no time-aggregation bias, so the estimates based on these duration measures are unbiased. At the second aggregation level, I measure durations in weeks. I then convert the number of weeks into months and fractions of months. The aggregation rule is to round up to the nearest week. There is some time-aggregation bias in estimators using these duration measures. At the third aggregation level, I measure durations in months. The aggregation rule is to round up to the nearest month, a rule that is often used in empirical research.

Table 2 gives the parameter estimates. In column 1 we see that the rate of leaving a salary grade level declines with the grade level: The rate is highest in grade 1 and then declines as the grade increases. When we hold the salary grade level constant and then compare the estimates across the columns of the table, we see that the estimates in column 2 are lower than those in column 1 and that the estimates in column 3 are lower than those in column 2. This illustrates conclusion 2: For a fixed rate α, the wider the window within which the true durations are known to fall, the larger the time-aggregation bias. The window is largest in column 3, and so is the time-aggregation bias. The bias in column 2, where the window is narrower, is lower than that in column 3. Columns 4 and 5 give the ratios of the estimates in column 2 to the estimates in column 1 and the ratios of the estimates in column 3 to the estimates in column 1. The closer these ratios are to 1.0, the lower the time-aggregation

TABLE 2

Effects of Time Aggregation on Estimated Rates for Leaving a Salary Grade
Level, By Various Levels of Time Aggregation and For Various
Underlying Rates, That Is, Salary Grade Levels
(Estimated Standard Errors in Parentheses)

Salary Grade Level	Aggregation Level for Durations			Column 2 Column 1	Column 3 Column 1
	Measured in Months and Days[a] (1)	Measured in Months and Weeks[b] (2)	Measured in Months[c] (3)		
1	.091757 (.001571)	.090905 (.001570)	.087694 (.001567)	.990714	.955719
2	.064257 (.000946)	.063803 (.000946)	.062181 (.000944)	.992934	.967692
3	.050958 (.000705)	.050640 (.000704)	.049578 (.000702)	.993759	.972918
4	.042455 (.000715)	.042232 (.000714)	.041419 (.000712)	.994747	.975597
5	.033830 (.000762)	.033671 (.000761)	.033090 (.000758)	.995300	.978125
6	.029267 (.000796)	.029137 (.000795)	.028708 (.000791)	.995558	.980899

Note: The data are taken from the personnel records of a large U.S. insurance company, described in detail in Petersen and Spilerman (1990). The estimates are of the constant rate in equation (1), section 2.1. The rates are estimated separately for each salary grade level. The estimation routine is described in Petersen (1986, appendices). It is implemented in BMDP (1985). A lengthy discussion of the routine is found in Blossfeld, Hamerle, and Mayer (1989, chap. 6).

[a] There is no time-aggregation bias in these estimates.

[b] Durations are measured as follows. If an event happened in the time interval between week $w - 1$ and week w within the month, it is assumed that it happened at the end of the interval, that is, at week w. If censoring occurred between week $w - 1$ and week w within the month, it is assumed that it occurred at the end of the interval, that is, at week w.

[c] Durations are measured as follows. If an event happened in the time interval between, say, month $j - 1$ and month j, it is assumed that it happened at the end of the interval, that is, at month j. If censoring occurred between month $j - 1$ and month j, it is assumed that it occurred at the end of the interval, that is, at month j.

bias. We see that the time-aggregation bias is about 2–4 percent in column 3, but only about 1 percent in column 2.

We see further that as the rate declines—that is, when one goes from level 1 to level 6—the time-aggregation biases in the estimates in both columns 2 and 3 also decline, as can be seen from the ratios in columns 4 and 5. This illustrates the first conclusion, that for a fixed window within which durations are measured, the lower the rate, the lower the time-aggregation bias. Note here, however, that the time-aggregation bias for a fixed window (i.e., column 2 or 3) does not decline very much with the rate—only about 0.5 percent in column 2 and about 2.5 percent in column 3—whereas the rate itself declines quite dramatically.

3. OPTIMAL CHOICE OF ASSIGNED DURATIONS

The estimator studied so far uses the assigned duration j_i when the true duration lies between $j_i - 1$ and j_i. In this section I study an estimator that uses an assigned duration that lies between $j_i - 1$ and j_i. The duration assigned is $j_i - k$, where k is a number between 0 and 1. I also derive the optimal choice of k for a given value of α. For $k = 0$, the estimator α_u in (5) obtains, which we studied in section 2.

To assess the estimator based on the assigned duration $j_i - k$, we need to evaluate the expectation of $J_i - k$. Using (10), it is given as

$$E(J_i - k) = E(J_i) - k \qquad (19)$$
$$= 1/[1 - \exp(-\alpha)] - k.$$

By SLLN we then get

$$(1/N) \sum_{i=1}^{N} (j_i - k) \xrightarrow{\text{a.s.}} E(J_i - k) = 1/[1 - \exp(-\alpha)] - k \qquad (20)$$
$$= \{1 - k \times [1 - \exp(-\alpha)]\}/[1 - \exp(-\alpha)].$$

Call the estimator that uses the assigned duration $j_i - k$ for $\alpha_{u,k}$. It obtains by replacing j_i in (5) with $j_i - k$. From (20), we then get (by White 1984, prop. 2.11, p. 17)

$$\alpha_{u,k} = N/\sum_{i=1}^{N} (j_i - k) \xrightarrow{\text{a.s.}} [1 - \exp(-\alpha)]/\{1 - k \times [1 - \exp(-\alpha)]\}. \qquad (21)$$

In general, therefore, the estimator based on the assigned duration $j_i - k$ is inconsistent.[9] However, there are values of k for which the estimator is consistent.

I now consider the optimal choice of k. Optimality is defined as the choice of k that minimizes the bias of the estimator.[10] Clearly, the optimal choice of k is the value of k that equates the right-hand side of (21) with the true value of α. Call this value of k for k^*. By equating the right-hand side of (21) with α and then solving for k, we get k^*:

$$k^* = -(1/\alpha) + 1/[1 - \exp(-\alpha)]. \tag{22}$$

Thus, the optimal choice of k depends on α, that is, on how fast the process moves. When k is chosen as in (22), the estimator $\alpha_{u,k}$ is consistent.

Unfortunately, α is unknown; therefore, k^* is unknown. Hence, it is impractical to use k^* in research, although it may be estimated from the data.[11] Fortunately, we can obtain some bounds on k^*, and these are straightforward enough for research. Consider two limiting cases $\alpha \downarrow 0$ and $\alpha \to \infty$:

[9]Arminger (1984, pp. 474–75) establishes the inconsistency of $\alpha_{u,k}$ when $k = .5$.

[10]A different approach to assigning durations would be to assign the expected value of T within the interval in which the duration is known to fall, an approach that Thompson (1977, p. 464) used to deal with censored observations (see note 18 below). For the relevant expression for noncensored observations, see Arminger (1984, p. 474) and Galler (1986, p. 13, eq. (10)). However, this approach is as cumbersome as deriving the likelihood that adjusts totally for the grouped measurements of durations, and nothing is gained by using it instead of the latter likelihood (i.e., (6)). A better approach is to compute the expectation of the *likelihood* with respect to the unobserved part of the duration. This procedure is explicated in the discussion of censored cases in section 5, equation (31).

[11]We could compute k^* iteratively using the time-aggregated data. In the first iteration, we compute α, assuming durations to be exactly measured. In the second iteration, we use (22) to obtain an estimate of k^*, using the estimate of α from the first iteration. Then, from the estimated k^*, we assign optimal durations. In this manner, we switch between estimating α and k^* until convergence. In my experience, this routine works well. The final estimates get very close to the estimates based on data containing no time aggregation. The main drawback of the procedure is that it requires special programming efforts. Hence, one might as well implement the likelihood that adjusts totally for the grouping of the duration measurements. A similar approach is outlined in Arminger (1984, p. 475) using the expected value of the duration *within* the interval in which the event happened. His solution also requires special programming efforts.

$$\lim_{a \to \infty} k^* = 1, \tag{23}$$

$$\lim_{a \downarrow 0} k^* = .5. \tag{24}$$

Equations (23)–(24) show that the optimal k lies between .50 and 1.0. Those boundaries present the two limiting cases of very high and very low rates. The optimal assigned duration should hence lie in the first half of the interval within which the event happened. That is, if an event happened between $j - 1$ and j, the optimal assigned duration lies between $j - 1$ and $j - .5$.

We can also see how k^* changes with α. The partial derivative of (22) with respect to α yields

$$\partial k^*/\partial \alpha = (1/\alpha^2) + 1/[1 - \exp(-\alpha)] > 0 \qquad \text{for all } \alpha > 0, \tag{25}$$

from which we see that the optimal k increases with the rate α.

Figure 1 graphs k^* as a function of α, from equation (22). It shows that for almost all relevant values of α (i.e., $\alpha \le .5$), the value of k^* is close to .5, ranging from .508 when $\alpha = .1$ to .541 when $\alpha = .5$. In most applications, α is likely to be small; $\alpha = .5$ is a very high rate. Thus, assigning a duration that lies at the midpoint of the interval within which the true duration is known to lie will in most cases give good results, because assigning the duration $j - .5$ comes very close to using the optimal assigned duration based on (22). The latter assignment yields consistent estimates. As shown in column 4 of Table 1, using the midpoint adjustment yields an estimator with an asymptotic bias of less than 3 percent for most relevant values of the underlying rate (i.e., $\alpha \le .50$).[12]

The qualitative aspects of the conclusions above can also be obtained by a slightly different argument. For noncensored cases, assign the duration $j_i - c^*$ in such a manner that the density based on $j_i - c^*$ equals the likelihood that adjusts totally for the grouping of the measurements, that is, the grouped likelihood in (6). This yields

$$\alpha \times \exp[-\alpha(j_i - c^*)] = \exp[-\alpha(j_i - 1)] \times [1 - \exp(-\alpha)]. \tag{26}$$

[12]If α is very high, say, 1 or 2, the window within which durations are known to lie may be too wide to obtain good estimates of the underlying rate. In repeatable event processes, an individual may experience several transitions within a given time interval, but only one of those will be recorded. If $\alpha = .5$, approximately 39 percent of the cases at risk will, in a large sample, experience the event in question within the first time interval, and 63 percent will experience it within the first two time intervals. Thus, using an estimator based on the assumption that durations are exactly measured may not produce good estimates even with the type of adjustment considered in equation (22) (e.g., $k = .5$.)

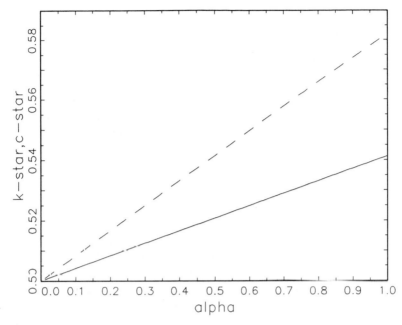

FIGURE 1. Graphs of k^* and c^* from equations (22) and (27) as functions of α (for α in the interval 0 to 1). The vertical axis gives the scale for k^* and c^* covering the interval .5 to .6. The horizontal axis gives the scale for α, covering the interval 0.0 to 1.0. The solid line gives the graph for k^* as a function of α from equation (22). The broken line gives the graph for c^* as a function of α from equation (27). The graph for ϵ^* as a function of α from equation (33) coincides with the graph for c^*.

Solving for c^* in (26) yields

$$c^* = 1 + \ln\{[1 - \exp(-\alpha)]/\alpha\}/\alpha. \qquad (27)$$

As in (22), the value of c^* depends on the unknown rate itself. But, also as in (22), we can derive the same qualitative conclusions as in (23)–(24), namely

$$\lim_{a \to \infty} c^* = 1, \qquad (28)$$

$$\lim_{a \downarrow 0} c^* = .5. \qquad (29)$$

As shown in Figure 1, c^* lies somewhat above k^*.

I state this analysis as conclusion 3.

Conclusion 3: The optimal assigned duration lies in the first half of the window or interval within which the true duration lies. That is, the optimal assigned duration lies between $j - 1$ and $j - .5$

when we know that the event happened between $j - 1$ and j. For most processes—that is, for processes with relatively low rates, say, .50 or less—the optimal assigned duration comes very close to $j - .5$, as shown in Figure 1. Hence, assigning the duration $j - .5$ will in most cases yield good estimates.

Table 3 illustrates these issues. It reports estimates of the same set of rates as in Table 2. Only one level of time aggregation is considered, namely, up to the nearest month—an aggregation often used in research. Three corrections for time-aggregation bias are reported. First, in column 1, the grouped likelihood is used. Non-censored observations contribute with equation (6) of section 2.1. This likelihood provides consistent estimates of the underlying pa-rameters, at least in the case with no censored observations. Observa-tions that were censored in the interval $j - 1$ to j contribute to the likelihood with equation (31), as justified in section 5. Second, in column 2, the optimal adjustment from this section, equation (22), is used for noncensored cases. Observations that were censored in the interval $j - 1$ to j were assigned the duration $j - c^*$, where c^* comes from (27) above, as justified in section 5. In computing both k^* and c^*, α is supplied from column 4 of Table 3, which is a reproduction of column 1 of Table 2. Third, in column 3 the midpoint adjustment for the durations is used: If an event happened between $j - 1$ and j, the assigned duration is $j - .5$. Cases that were censored between $j - 1$ and j were assigned the censoring time $j - .5$, as justified in section 5.

The results are simple. All three sets of estimates in Table 3, columns 1–3, do better than the estimates in column 3 of Table 2, where no attempt was made to adjust for time-aggregation bias. In fact, the estimates in columns 1–3 of Table 3 do very well: They come within 0.1 percent of the estimates using the exact durations (column 4 of Table 3), whereas the estimates in column 3 of Table 2 are off by about 2–5 percent. In conclusion, correcting for the time-aggregation bias improves the estimates considerably. Specifically, the simple mid-point correction gives very good estimates.

4. COVARIATES, DURATION DEPENDENCE, AND MULTIPLE STATES

So far I have considered the case of no explanatory variables, no duration dependence, and only one state. In this section I com-

TABLE 3
Estimates of Rates from Three Estimators That Adjust for Time Aggregation, for Various Underlying Rates, That Is, Salary Grade Levels
(Estimated Standard Errors in Parentheses)

| Salary Grade Level | Durations Measured Up to Nearest Month | | | |
	Grouped Likelihood[a] (1)	Optimal k Adjustment[b] (2)	Midpoint Adjustment[c] (3)	Exact Durations[d] (4)
1	.091820 (.001568)	.091820 (.001568)	.091755 (.001568)	.091757 (.001571)
2	.064288 (.000946)	.064287 (.000946)	.064264 (.000946)	.064257 (.000946)
3	.050969 (.000704)	.050968 (.000704)	.050957 (.000704)	.050958 (.000705)
4	.042464 (.000715)	.042464 (.000715)	.042457 (.000715)	.042455 (.000715)
5	.033833 (.000762)	.033833 (.000762)	.033829 (.000762)	.033830 (.000762)
6	.029268 (.000796)	.029268 (.000796)	.029265 (.000796)	.029267 (.000796)

Note: For description of the data and procedures, see the note to Table 2.

[a]In this likelihood, noncensored observations contribute with equation (6) of section 2.1. Censored observations contribute with equation (31) of section 5, where the censoring time is assumed to be uniformly distributed within the interval in which it is known to lie.

[b]Durations are measured as follows. If an event happened in the time interval between, say, month $j - 1$ and month j, the assigned duration is $j - k^*$, where k^* is computed according to equation (22) in section 3. For a censored case, we know only that censoring occurred between $j - 1$ and j, but not the exact time within that interval. The censoring time is then set equal to $j - c^*$, where c^* comes from equation (27), based on the assumption that the censoring time is uniformly distributed within the interval in which it is known to lie, as discussed in section 5. To compute k^* and c^*, I use the estimates of α given in column 4.

[c]If an event or censoring occurred between $j - 1$ and j, the assigned duration, for censored as well as noncensored cases, is the midpoint of the interval, $j - .5$.

[d]The estimates are taken from column 1 of Table 2, where the standard estimator based on exact durations is used. There is no time-aggregation bias in these estimates because the durations are measured in months and days.

ment briefly on these three complications. No analytic results are derived. In most cases, they cannot be derived.[13]

Consider first the case with covariates but no duration dependence and a single state. In that case the result of conclusion 3 applies with one minor modification: A separate value of k^* must be computed for each pattern of covariates. Again, since we do not know the parameters on which the optimal durations depend, all we can do is use the qualitative results from equations (23)–(24), as summarized in conclusion 3. In practice, therefore, one should follow a simple rule of thumb: Assign the duration that lies at the midpoint of the interval within which the true duration lies.

The case of duration dependence complicates the issue. Then, the optimal choice of k depends not only on the covariate values but also on the duration at which an event or censoring happened. If the duration dependence is negative, then the higher the duration, the closer the optimal k is to .5. That is, the optimal k decreases with the duration. If the duration dependence is positive, then the higher the duration, the closer the optimal k is to 1.0. That is, the optimal k increases with the duration.[14]

Again, it is cumbersome to assign the durations according to optimal rules. A reasonable rule of thumb, therefore, is to assign the midpoint of the interval.

Multistate processes complicate the issues even further. But the same formal apparatus as in equations (26)–(29) can be applied and the same qualitative conclusions will obtain: Assign the duration that lies at the midpoint of the interval within which the event happened.

5. ASSIGNMENT OF DURATIONS FOR CENSORED CASES

For right-censored cases the situation is more difficult. We usually know that censoring occurred between $j_i - 1$ and j_i but not the

[13]In a companion paper, Petersen and Koput (1990) derive an analytic expression for the bias of the parameters of an exponential model with a constant term and a single categorical covariate with several categories. The paper also presents a Monte Carlo study of the bias in several estimators, such as those based on the grouped likelihood and the midpoint adjustment.

[14]This can be shown by the following argument. Approximate a possibly very complicated duration dependence by a step function, that is, by a so-called piecewise constant rate, where the rate stays constant within, say, each month or time interval, but varies arbitrarily between months or time intervals. This approximation can be made exact and completely general by specifying sufficiently short intervals. With such a piecewise constant rate, one can apply the same type of reasoning as in the constant rate case, as in section 3.

true censoring time within that interval.[15] To deal properly with censored cases, we need to specify the process that creates censoring. Ideally, we should then estimate the parameters of this process along with the parameters of the failure-time process, as outlined in Cox and Oakes (1984, pp. 56–60). This is cumbersome in practice. Below, following Thompson (1977, p. 464) with one minor alteration, I present a procedure that yields a simple solution to the treatment of censored cases.

Let the exact but unknown censoring time be $j_i - \epsilon_i$, where ϵ_i lies in the interval 0 to 1. The survivor function based on the exact censoring time is

$$P(T_i \geq j_i - \epsilon_i) = \exp[-\alpha(j_i - \epsilon_i)]. \qquad (30)$$

It is now theoretically appealing to assume that the censoring time is uniformly distributed within the interval $j_t - 1$ to j_i.[16] That is, the distribution of ϵ_i is uniform with density $f(\epsilon_i) = 1$ within the interval 0 to 1.[17] Integrating out the unobservable ϵ_i from (30) yields

$$EP(T_i \geq j_i - \epsilon_i) = \int_0^1 \exp[-\alpha(j_i - \epsilon_i)]d\epsilon_i$$

$$= \exp(-\alpha j_i) \times [1 - \exp(-\alpha)] \times (1/\alpha). \qquad (31)$$

---

[15]In some data sets we know the exact date at which censoring occurred because observation terminates at that point. Even in such cases there will often be time aggregation with respect to the duration in the state at the time of censoring because we rarely know the exact date at which a state was entered, only that it was entered within a given time interval. If we know the exact date of entry into a state and the exact censoring date, no correction is needed for censored cases.

[16]There are several ways to informally justify a uniform distribution for ϵ_i. One such way is when observation terminates in a given time interval, say, a specific month. If all cases at risk in that interval are interviewed during the interval and interviews are distributed evenly on the days within the period, then a uniform distribution may be a good approximation for the distribution of ϵ_i.

[17]Cox and Oakes (1984, pp. 53–56) discuss an alternative and more rigorous approach. They specify a multistate process in which one rate governs transitions (e.g., α_1) and another the censoring of cases (e.g., α_2). Censored and noncensored cases will then contribute with equation (9), where the numerator in the last term on the right-hand side equals α_1 if the case experiences a transition and α_2 if the case is censored. This approach leads to the same conclusion as below. Cox and Oakes (1984, p. 54) note that "this estimator is in a sense equivalent to assuming that the deaths and censorings occur uniformly throughout the interval." One way to show this is to replicate the arguments in equations (26)–(29). Wu (1989, pp. 135–36) uses Cox and Oakes's approach.

We want to avoid (31) in research because it requires separate programming efforts. Instead, we want to assign a censoring time $j_i - \epsilon^*$ that is to be used in the survivor function based on exact measurements of durations. Using the same idea as in equation (26) of section 3, we can assign this censoring time as follows. Treat $j_i - \epsilon^*$ as the exact censoring time and insert it into the survivor function. This gives

$$P(T_i \geq j_i - \epsilon^*) = \exp[-\alpha(j_i - \epsilon^*)]. \tag{32}$$

Then choose ϵ^* so that the right-hand side of (32) gets equated with the survivor function where we have integrated out the unobserved censoring time within the interval $j_i - 1$ to j_i, that is, the right-hand side of (31). This yields

$$\exp[-\alpha(j_i - \epsilon^*)] = \exp[-\alpha(j_i - 1)] \times [1 - \exp(-\alpha)] \times (1/\alpha). \tag{33}$$

By multiplying both sides of (33) by α, we see that (33) is identical to (26). Hence, ϵ^* coincides with c^* in (27). The same qualitative conclusions obtained for c^*—in (28) and (29)—pertain to ϵ^*: When the process moves fast, the assigned censoring time should be close to the beginning of the interval within which the censoring occurred. When the process moves slowly, the assigned censoring time should be close to the midpoint of the interval within which censoring occurred. As we can see from Figure 1, for most relevant values of α—that is, values of α less than .5—the value of c^* and hence of ϵ^* is very close to .5. Therefore, assigning a censoring time that lies at the midpoint of the interval within which censoring occurred is likely to function fine.[18] I state this analysis as the fourth conclusion.

Conclusion 4: Assuming that the censoring time is uniformly distributed within the interval in which censoring is known to occur, the assigned duration for censored cases ought to lie in the first half of that window. That is, the assigned duration ought to lie between $j - 1$ and $j - .5$ when we know that censoring occurred between $j - 1$

---

[18]Thompson (1977, p. 464) reaches the same conclusion but by reasoning that does not appear to be entirely sound. From the fact that $E(j - \epsilon) = j - .5$ when ϵ is uniformly distributed, he seems to infer that $EP(T \geq j - \epsilon) = P(T \geq j - .5)$. But by Jensen's inequality (e.g., DeGroot 1970, sect. 7.6), $EP(T \geq j - \epsilon) > P(T \geq j - E\epsilon)$, as illustrated in Figure 1, where the value of ϵ^* is always greater than .5 in order to obtain the equality in equation (33).

and j. In practice, the assigned censoring time ought to be the mid-point of the interval within which the true censoring time is known to lie. This can be justified when the distribution of the censoring time within the time interval is uniform. It can also be justified by assigning a separate rate for the censoring process, as in Cox and Oakes (1984, pp. 53–56).

6. COMMENTS ON DISCRETE-TIME METHODS

The most popular solution to time-aggregation bias in sociological research is to abandon the use of a continuous-time hazard-rate model altogether. Instead, one specifies a discrete-time model in which the probability of a transition is defined for each time interval within which events are known to happen or not happen (see Allison 1982; Guilkey and Rindfuss 1987). This alternative solution is attractive and easy to implement. For continuous-time processes, its main drawback is that the coefficients estimated, say, from a logit or a probit model for each time interval need not be entirely comparable to coefficients obtained from a continuous-time hazard-rate model. However, if the probability of an event in each time interval is small, then the coefficients obtained from the discrete-time specification will for most models be quite close to those obtained from the continuous-time specification. For example, the coefficients from a logit model will approximate the coefficients from a proportional-hazards model (e.g., Weibull or Gompertz) quite well, as long as the probability of an event in each time interval is small. And only the constant term, which captures the rate for the baseline group, will depend strongly on the length of the time interval (see Arjas and Kangas 1988), whereas the other coefficients, which can be interpreted as relative risks, tend to be unaffected by changes in the time unit.[19]

[19]An often-used discrete-time specification is the complimentary log-log function available in GLIM (see Baker and Nelder 1978). It provides consistent estimates of the proportional-hazards parameters (e.g., a piecewise constant rate) regardless of the interval length or (equivalently) the size of the rate (see, e.g., Prentice and Gloeckler 1978, p. 58; Allison 1982, pp. 72–73; Arjas and Kangas 1988, p. 5). This property is not shared by the logistic model. If the objective is to obtain estimates of the parameters of an underlying continuous-time hazard-rate model, the complimentary log-log function has the advantage (see the discussion in Allison 1982, pp. 72–73).

To see this point, consider, without loss in generality, a single-state process. In the discrete-time framework, the probability of a transition in the next time interval, between, say, month $j - 1$ and month j, may be specified by a logit model:

$$P(j - 1 < T \leq j \mid T > j - 1, x_{j-1}) = 1/\{1 + \exp[-\beta x_{j-1} - g(j, \gamma)]\} \quad (34)$$
$$\equiv p(j \mid x_{j-1}),$$

where x_{j-1} are the covariates evaluated at entry into the period $j - 1$ to j, $g(j, \gamma)$ is the duration dependence term, and γ are the coefficients pertaining to j.

When $p(j \mid x_{j-1})$ is small, we easily get the approximation

$$\exp[\beta x_{j-1} + g(j, \gamma)] = p(j \mid x_{j-1})/[1 - p(j \mid x_{j-1})] \quad (35)$$
$$\approx p(j \mid x_{j-1}).$$

Hence, $\exp[\beta x_{j-1} + g(j, \gamma)]$ can be interpreted roughly as the probability of a transition in the duration interval $j - 1$ to j when that probability is small. But this term has the form of a proportional-hazards model, say, a Weibull, Gompertz, or piecewise constant rate. It is well known that the instantaneous rate of transition from a continuous-time model approximates well the probability of a transition in the next time unit, say, a week or a month, when that transition probability is small (see, e.g., Petersen 1990b, sects. 2–3). Therefore, for small transition probabilities per time unit, the parameters from a discrete-time logit and a continuous-time proportional-hazards specification are quite close.

7. SUMMARY

I have considered the problem of time-aggregation bias in continuous-time hazard-rate models. The most natural solution to this problem is to construct estimators that correct for the grouping of duration measurements. For many researchers, this may be too cumbersome. This paper shows how to minimize the time-aggregation bias without applying the estimator that adjusts totally for the grouping of the durations. I developed an explicit formula that yields consistent estimates for an exponential model with no covariates and no censoring. The formula depends on the unknown rate itself. However, this qualitative result obtains: The optimal assigned duration lies within the first half of the window within which the event happened.

The same type of conclusion can be derived for censored observations. The assigned duration should lie within the first half of the interval within which censoring occurred. This conclusion is based on a less general assumption than the conclusion regarding noncensored observations. In both cases—that is, censored and noncensored—the assigned durations based on the explicit formulas lie close to the midpoint of the interval within which the event or censoring time is known to lie, at least when the rate α is within the range found in most studies, say, less than .5.

In practice, models contain covariates, duration dependence, and sometimes multiple states. In those cases, computing optimal assigned durations must be done separately for each constellation of covariates, and given the constellation of covariates, the adjustment varies with the time interval within which the duration is known to lie and with the type of transition made. As before, the optimal assigned duration depends on the unknown parameters themselves. Thus, a good rule of thumb is to assign the duration that lies at the midpoint of the window within which the true duration lies—a rule used extensively in estimation routines based on the life table (see, e.g., Cox and Oakes 1984, pp. 53–59; Breslow and Crowley 1974).

APPENDIX: PROOF OF EQUATION (10) IN SECTION 2.3

To obtain the expectation of J_i, we must compute the probabilities of each of the possible outcomes of J_i. The density with respect to counting measure of the various values j_i of J_i is given as

$$P(J_i = 1) = [1 - \exp(-\alpha)],$$
$$P(J_i = 2) = [1 - \exp(-\alpha)] \times \exp[-\alpha],$$
$$P(J_i = 3) = [1 - \exp(-\alpha)] \times \exp[-\alpha 2], \tag{A1}$$
$$\vdots$$
$$P(J_i = j_i) = [1 - \exp(-\alpha)] \times \exp[-\alpha(j_i - 1)].$$

Therefore, the expectation of J_i is

$$E(J_i) = \sum_{j_i=1}^{\infty} j_i \times [1 - \exp(-\alpha)] \times \exp[-\alpha(j_i - 1)] \tag{A2}$$

$$= [1 - \exp(-\alpha)] \times \exp(\alpha) \times \left[\sum_{j_i=1}^{\infty} j_i \times \exp(-\alpha j_i) \right].$$

The expression in (A2) is an *infinite series* (see, e.g., Apostol 1967, chap. 10.5). In (A2), define $a_{j,i} \equiv j_i \times \exp(-\alpha j_i)$. The terms $a_{j,i}$ constitute an *infinite sequence* (see, e.g., Apostol 1967, p. 379). To compute the value of (A2), we must first check whether this infinite sequence converges. By using L'Hopital's rule (see, e.g., Apostol 1967, thm. 7.10, p. 298) twice, we can show that

$$\lim_{j_i \to \infty} j_i \times \exp(-\alpha j_i) = 0. \tag{A3}$$

From (A3), we see that the infinite sequence $a_{j,i}$ converges to zero (see, e.g., Apostol 1967, p. 379). We can then go on to the next test.

We must decide whether the series (A2) itself converges. Since $a_{j,i} > 0$ for all finite j_i, we can apply the ratio test for infinite sequences (see, e.g., Buck 1978, p. 232). This yields

$$
\begin{aligned}
L &\equiv \lim_{j \to \infty} \sup \ (a_{j+1,i})/(a_{j,i}) \\
&= \lim_{j_i \to \infty} \sup \ (j_i + 1) \times \exp[-\alpha(j_i + 1)]/j_i \times \exp(-\alpha j_i) \quad \text{(A4)} \\
&= \exp(-\alpha).
\end{aligned}
$$

Since $\alpha > 0$, by (1) we see that $L < 1$. Therefore, by the ratio test the infinite series converges.

It remains to compute the value towards which the series converges. To do this, set first $\exp(-\alpha) \equiv a$. The sum in (A2) can then be written

$$\sum_{j_i=1}^{\infty} j_i \times \exp(-\alpha j_i) = \sum_{j_i=1}^{\infty} j_i \times a^{j_i}. \tag{A5}$$

It is now straightforward, but tedious, to show that (A5) converges to

$$
\begin{aligned}
\sum_{j_i=1}^{\infty} j_i \times \exp(-\alpha j_i) &= \sum_{j_i=1}^{\infty} j_i \times a^{j_i} \\
&= \exp(-\alpha)/[1 - \exp(-\alpha)]^2
\end{aligned}
\tag{A6}
$$

(see Davis 1962, p. 104).

Hence, by inserting the right-hand side of the last equality in (A6) into (A2), we get the desired expression in (10):

$$E(J_i) = 1/[1 - \exp(-\alpha)]. \tag{A7}$$

This proves equation (10).

REFERENCES

Allison, P. D. 1982. "Discrete-Time Methods for the Analysis of Event Histories." Pp. 61–98 in *Sociological Methodology 1982*, edited by S. Leinhardt. San Francisco: Jossey-Bass.

Apostol, T. M. 1967. *Calculus*. Vol. 1, 2d ed. New York: Wiley.

Arjas, E., and P. Kangas. 1988. "A Discrete Time Method for the Analysis of Event Histories." Stockholm Research Reports in Demography No. 49. Stockholm: University of Stockholm.

Arminger, G. 1984. "Modelltheoretische und methodische Probleme bei der Analyse von Paneldaten mit qualitativen Variablen." *DIW-Vierteilsjahrshefte zur Wirtschaftsforschung* 4:470–80.

Baker, R. J., and J. A. Nelder. 1978. *The GLIM System. Release 3*. Oxford: Numerical Algorithms Group.

Blossfeld, H.-P., A. Hamerle, and K. U. Mayer. 1989. *Event History Analysis*. Hillsdale, NJ: Erlbaum.

BMDP Statistical Software. 1985. Berkeley: University of California Press.

Breslow, N. 1974. "Covariance Analysis of Censored Survival Data." *Biometrics* 30:89–99.

Breslow, N., and J. Crowley. 1974. "A Large Sample Study of the Life Table and Product Limit Estimates Under Random Censorship." *Annals of Statistics* 2:437–53.

Buck, R. C. 1978. *Advanced Calculus*. 3d ed. New York: McGraw-Hill.

Cox, D. R. 1975. "Partial Likelihood." *Biometrika* 62:262–76.

Cox, D. R., and D. Oakes. 1984. *Survival Analysis*. London: Chapman and Hall.

Davis, H. T. 1962. *The Summation of Series*. San Antonio: The Principia Press of Trinity University.

DeGroot, M. H. 1970. *Optimal Statistical Decisions*. New York: McGraw-Hill.

Elandt-Johnson, R. C., and N. L. Johnson. 1980. *Survival Models and Data Analysis*. New York: Wiley.

Galler, H. P. 1986. "Übergangsratenmodelle bei intervalldatierten Ereignissen." *Statistische Hefte* 27:1–22.

Guilkey, D. K., and R. R. Rindfuss. 1987. "Logistic Regression. Multivariate Lifetables. A Communicative Approach." *Sociological Methods and Research* 16:276–300.

Harris, T. E., P. Meier, and J. W. Tukey. 1950. "Timing of the Distribution of Events Between Observations. A Contribution to the Theory of Follow-Up Studies." *Human Biology* 22:249–70.

Heijtan, D. F. 1989. "Inference from Grouped Continuous Data: A Review." *Statistical Science* 4:164–83.

Holford, T. R. 1976. "Life Tables With Concomitant Information." *Biometrics* 32:587–97.

———. 1980. "The Analysis of Rates and Survivorships Using Log-linear Models." *Biometrics* 36:299–305.

Kalbfleisch, J. D., and R. L. Prentice. 1980. *The Statistical Analysis of Failure Time Data*. New York: Wiley.

Lawless, J. F. 1982. *Statistical Models and Methods For Lifetime Data.* New York: Wiley.

Petersen, T. 1983. "Time Aggregation Bias in Continuous Time Hazard Rate Models." Working Paper #83-45. Madison: University of Wisconsin, Center for Demography and Ecology.

———. 1986. "Estimating Fully Parametric Hazard Rate Models With Time-Dependent Covariates. Use of Maximum Likelihood." *Sociological Methods and Research* 14:219–46.

———. 1988. "Analyzing Change Over Time in a Continuous Dependent Variable: Specification and Estimation of Continuous State Space Hazard Rate Models." Pp. 137–64 in *Sociological Methodology 1988,* edited by C. C. Clogg. Washington, DC: American Sociological Association.

———. 1990a. "Analyzing Continuous State Space Failure Time Processes: Two Further Results." *Journal of Mathematical Sociology* 15:247–57.

———. 1990b. "Analyzing Event Histories." Pp. 259–88 in *New Statistical Methods in Longitudinal Research,* vol. 2, edited by A. von Eye. Orlando: Academic Press.

Petersen, T., and K. W. Koput. 1990. "Time Aggregation Bias in Hazard Rate Models With Covariates." Unpublished Manuscript.

Petersen, T., and S. Spilerman. 1990. "Job-Quits From an Internal Labor Market." Chap. 4 in *Event History Analysis in Life Course Research,* edited by K. U. Mayer and N. B. Tuma. Madison: University of Wisconsin Press.

Prentice, R. L., and L. A. Gloeckler. 1978. "Regression Analysis of Grouped Survival Data With Application to Breast Cancer Data." *Biometrics* 34:57–67.

Rao, C. R. 1973. *Linear Statistical Inference and Its Applications.* 2d ed. New York: McGraw-Hill.

Thompson, W. A., Jr. 1977. "On the Treatment of Grouped Observations in Life Studies." *Biometrics* 33:463–70.

White, H. 1984. *Asymptotic Theory for Econometricians.* Orlando: Academic Press.

Wu, L. L. 1989. "Issues in Smoothing Empirical Hazard Rates." Pp. 127–59 in *Sociological Methodology 1989,* edited by C. C. Clogg. Oxford: Blackwell.

❧ 10 ❧

STATISTICAL MODELS AND SHOE LEATHER

David A. Freedman*

Regression models have been used in the social sciences at least since 1899, when Yule published a paper on the causes of pauperism. Regression models are now used to make causal arguments in a wide variety of applications, and it is perhaps time to evaluate the results. No definitive answers can be given, but this paper takes a rather negative view. Snow's work on cholera is presented as a success story for scientific reasoning based on nonexperimental data. Failure stories are also discussed, and comparisons may provide some insight. In particular, this paper suggests that statistical technique can seldom be an adequate substitute for good design, relevant data, and testing predictions against reality in a variety of settings.

1. INTRODUCTION

Regression models have been used in the social sciences at least since 1899, when Yule published his paper on changes in "out-relief" as a cause of pauperism: He argued that providing income support outside the poorhouse increased the number of people on relief. At present, regression models are used to make causal argu-

This research was partially supported by NSF grant DMS 86-01634 and by the Miller Institute for Basic Research. Much help was provided by Richard Berk, John Cairns, David Collier, Persi Diaconis, Sander Greenland, Steve Klein, Jan de Leeuw, Thomas Rothenberg, and Amos Tversky. Special thanks go to Peter Marsden.
*University of California, Berkeley

291

ments in a wide variety of social science applications, and it is perhaps time to evaluate the results.

A crude four-point scale may be useful:

1. Regression usually works, although it is (like anything else) im-
    perfect and may sometimes go wrong.
2. Regression sometimes works in the hands of skillful practitio-
    ners, but it isn't suitable for routine use.
3. Regression might work, but it hasn't yet.
4. Regression can't work.

Textbooks, courtroom testimony, and newspaper interviews
seem to put regression into category 1. Category 4 seems too pessi-
mistic. My own view is bracketed by categories 2 and 3, although
good examples are quite hard to find.

Regression modeling is a dominant paradigm, and many investigators seem to consider that any piece of empirical research has to
be equivalent to a regression model. Questioning the value of regression is then tantamount to denying the value of data. Some declara-
tions of faith may therefore be necessary. Social science is possible,
and sound conclusions can be drawn from nonexperimental data.
(Experimental confirmation is always welcome, although some experiments have problems of their own.) Statistics can play a useful
role. With multidimensional data sets, regression may provide helpful summaries of the data.

However, I do not think that regression can carry much of the
burden in a causal argument. Nor do regression equations, by themselves, give much help in controlling for confounding variables. Arguments based on statistical significance of coefficients seem generally
suspect; so do causal interpretations of coefficients. More recent
developments, like two-stage least squares, latent-variable modeling, and specification tests, may be quite interesting. However, technical fixes do not solve the problems, which are at a deeper level. In
the end, I see many illustrations of technique but few real examples
with validation of the modeling assumptions.

Indeed, causal arguments based on significance tests and regression are almost necessarily circular. To derive a regression model, we
need an elaborate theory that specifies the variables in the system,
their causal interconnections, the functional form of the relationships,

and the statistical properties of the error terms—independence, exogeneity, etc. (The stochastics may not matter for descriptive purposes, but they are crucial for significance tests.) *Given the model,* least squares and its variants can be used to estimate parameters and to decide whether or not these are zero. However, the model cannot in general be regarded as given, because current social science theory does not provide the requisite level of technical detail for deriving specifications.

There is an alternative validation strategy, which is less dependent on prior theory: Take the model as a black box and test it against empirical reality. Does the model predict new phenomena? Does it predict the results of interventions? Are the predictions right? The usual statistical tests are poor substitutes because they rely on strong maintained hypotheses. Without the right kind of theory, or reasonable empirical validation, the conclusions drawn from the models must be quite suspect.

At this point, it may be natural to ask for some real examples of good empirical work and strategies for research that do not involve regression. Illustrations from epidemiology may be useful. The problems in that field are quite similar to those faced by contemporary workers in the social sciences. Snow's work on cholera will be reviewed as an example of real science based on observational data. Regression is not involved.

A comparison will be made with some current regression studies in epidemiology and social science. This may give some insight into the weaknesses of regression methods. The possibility of techni cal fixes for the models will be discussed, other literature will be reviewed, and then some tentative conclusions will be drawn.

2. SOME EXAMPLES FROM EPIDEMIOLOGY

Quantitative methods in the study of disease precede Yule and regression. In 1835, Pierre Louis published a landmark study on bleeding as a cure for pneumonia. He compared outcomes for groups of pneumonia patients who had been bled at different times, and found

> that bloodletting has a happy effect on the progress
> of pneumonitis; that it shortens its duration; and this

effect, however, is much less than has been commonly believed. (Louis [1835] 1986, p. 48)

The finding, and the statistical method, were roundly de-
nounced by contemporary physicians:

By invoking the inflexibility of arithmetic in order to
escape the encroachments of the imagination, one
commits an outrage upon good sense. (Louis [1835]
1986, p. 63)

Louis may have started a revolution in our thinking about
empirical research in medicine, or his book may only provide a convenient line of demarcation. But there is no doubt that within a few
decades, the "inflexibility of arithmetic" had helped identify the
causes of some major diseases and the means for their prevention.
Statistical modeling played almost no role in these developments.

In the 1850s, John Snow demonstrated that cholera was a
waterborne infectious disease (Snow [1855] 1965). A few years later,
Ignaz Semmelweiss discovered how to prevent puerperal fever (Semmelweiss [1861] 1941). Around 1914, Joseph Goldberger found the
cause of pellagra (Carpenter 1981; Terris 1964). Later epidemiolo-
gists have shown, at least on balance of argument, that most lung
cancer is caused by smoking (Lombard and Doering 1928; Mueller
1939; Cornfield et al. 1959; U.S. Public Health Service 1964). In
epidemiology, careful reasoning on observational data has led to
considerable progress. (For failure stories in that subject, see below.)

An explicit definition of good research methodology seems
elusive; but an implicit definition is possible, by pointing to examples. In that spirit, I give a brief account of Snow's work. To see his
achievement, I ask you to go back in time and forget that germs
cause disease. Microscopes are available but their resolution is poor.
Most human pathogens cannot be seen. The isolation of such micro-
organisms lies decades into the future. The infection theory has some
supporters, but the dominant idea is that disease results from "mias-
mas": minute, inanimate poison particles in the air. (Belief that
disease-causing poisons are in the ground comes later.)

Snow was studying cholera, which had arrived in Europe in
the early 1800s. Cholera came in epidemic waves, attacked its victims

suddenly, and was often fatal. Early symptoms were vomiting and acute diarrhea. Based on the clinical course of the disease, Snow conjectured that the active agent was a living organism that got into the alimentary canal with food or drink, multiplied in the body, and generated some poison that caused the body to expel water. The organism passed out of the body with these evacuations, got back into the water supply, and infected new victims.

Snow marshalled a series of persuasive arguments for this conjecture. For example, cholera spreads along the tracks of human commerce. If a ship goes from a cholera-free country to a cholera-stricken port, the sailors get the disease only after they land or take on supplies. The disease strikes hardest at the poor, who live in the most crowded housing with the worst hygiene. These facts are consistent with the infection theory and hard to explain with the miasma theory.

Snow also did a lot of scientific detective work. In one of the earliest epidemics in England, he was able to identify the first case, "a seaman named John Harnold, who had newly arrived by the *Elbe* steamer from Hamburgh, where the disease was prevailing" (p. 3). Snow also found the second case, a man who had taken the room in which Harnold had stayed. More evidence for the infection theory.

Snow found even better evidence in later epidemics. For example, he studied two adjacent apartment buildings, one heavily hit by cholera, the other not. He found that the water supply in the first building was contaminated by runoff from privies and that the water supply in the second building was much cleaner. He also made several "ecological" studies to demonstrate the influence of water supply on the incidence of cholera. In the London of the 1800s, there were many different water companies serving different areas of the city, and some areas were served by more than one company. Several companies took their water from the Thames, which was heavily polluted by sewage. The service areas of such companies had much higher rates of cholera. The Chelsea water company was an exception, but it had an exceptionally good filtration system.

In the epidemic of 1853–54, Snow made a spot map showing where the cases occurred and found that they clustered around the Broad Street pump. He identified the pump as a source of contaminated water and persuaded the public authorities to remove the handle. As the story goes, removing the handle stopped the epidemic and proved Snow's theory. In fact, he did get the handle removed and the epidemic did stop. However, as he demonstrated with some clarity, the epidemic was stopping anyway, and he attached little weight to the episode.

For our purposes, what Snow actually did in 1853–54 is even more interesting than the fable. For example, there was a large poorhouse in the Broad Street area with few cholera cases. Why? Snow found that the poorhouse had its own well and that the inmates did not take water from the pump. There was also a large brewery with no cases. The reason is obvious: The workers drank beer, not water. (But if any wanted water, there was a well on these premises too.)

To set up Snow's main argument, I have to back up just a bit. In 1849, the Lambeth water company had moved its intake point upstream along the Thames, above the main sewage discharge points, so that its water was fairly pure. The Southwark and Vauxhall water company, however, left its intake point downstream from the sewage discharges. An ecological analysis of the data for the epidemic of 1853–54 showed that cholera hit harder in the Southwark and Vauxhall service areas and largely spared the Lambeth areas. Now let Snow finish in his own words.

> Although the facts shown in the above table [the ecological data] afford very strong evidence of the powerful influence which the drinking of water containing the sewage of a town exerts over the spread of cholera, when that disease is present, yet the question does not end here; for the intermixing of the water supply of the Southwark and Vauxhall Company with that of the Lambeth Company, over an extensive part of London, admitted of the subject being sifted in such a way as to yield the most incontrovertible proof on one side or the other. In the subdistricts enumerated in the above table as being supplied by both Companies, the mixing of the supply is of the most intimate kind. The pipes of each Company go down all the streets, and into nearly all the courts and alleys. A few houses are supplied by

one Company and a few by the other, according to the decision of the owner or occupier at that time when the Water Companies were in active competition. In many cases a single house has a supply different from that on either side. Each company supplies both rich and poor, both large houses and small; there is no difference either in the condition or occupation of the persons receiving the water of the different Companies. Now it must be evident that, if the diminution of cholera, in the districts partly supplied with improved water, depended on this supply, the houses receiving it would be the houses enjoying the whole benefit of the diminution of the malady, whilst the houses supplied with the water from Battersea Fields would suffer the same mortality as they would if the improved supply did not exist at all. As there is no difference whatever in the houses or the people receiving the supply of the two Water Companies, or in any of the physical conditions with which they are surrounded, it is obvious that no experiment could have been devised which would more thoroughly test the effect of water supply on the progress of cholera than this, which circumstances placed ready made before the observer.

The experiment, too, was on the grandest scale. No fewer than three hundred thousand people of both sexes, of every age and occupation, and of every rank and station, from gentlefolks down to the very poor, were divided into two groups without their choice, and in most cases, without their knowledge; one group being supplied with water containing the sewage of London, and amongst it, whatever might have come from the cholera patients, the other group having water quite free from such impurity.

To turn this grand experiment to account, all that was required was to learn the supply of water to each individual house where a fatal attack of cholera might occur. (pp. 74–75)

TABLE 1
Snow's Table IX

	Number of Houses	Deaths from Cholera	Deaths Per 10,000 Houses
Southwark and Vauxhall	40,046	1,263	315
Lambeth	26,107	98	37
Rest of London	256,423	1,422	59

Snow identified the companies supplying water to the houses of cholera victims in his study area. This gave him the numerators in Table 1. (The denominators were taken from parliamentary records.)

Snow concluded that *if* the Southwark and Vauxhall company had moved their intake point as Lambeth did, about 1,000 lives would have been saved. He was very clear about quasi randomization as the control for potential confounding variables. He was equally clear about the differences between ecological correlations and individual correlations. And his counterfactual inference is compelling.

As a piece of statistical technology, Table 1 is by no means remarkable. But the story it tells is very persuasive. The force of the argument results from the clarity of the prior reasoning, the bringing together of many different lines of evidence, and the amount of shoe leather Snow was willing to use to get the data.

Later, there was to be more confirmation of Snow's conclusions. For example, the cholera epidemics of 1832 and 1849 in New York were handled by traditional methods: exhorting the population to temperance, bringing in pure water to wash the streets, treating the sick by bleeding and mercury. After the publication of Snow's book, the epidemic of 1866 was dealt with using the methods suggested by his theory: boiling the drinking water, isolating sick individuals, and disinfecting their evacuations. The death rate was cut by a factor of 10 or more (Rosenberg 1962).

In 1892, there was an epidemic in Hamburg. The leaders of Hamburg rejected Snow's arguments. They followed Max von Pettenkofer, who taught the miasma theory: Contamination of the ground caused cholera. Thus, Hamburg paid little attention to its water supply but spent a great deal of effort digging up and carting away carcasses buried by slaughterhouses. The results were disastrous (Evans 1987).

What about evidence from microbiology? In 1880, Pasteur created a sensation by showing that the cause of rabies was a microorganism. In 1884, Koch isolated the cholera *vibrio,* confirming all the essential features of Snow's account; Filipo Pacini may have discovered this organism even earlier (see Howard-Jones 1975). The *vibrio* is a water-borne bacterium that invades the human gut and causes cholera. Today, the molecular biology of cholera is reasonably well understood (Finlay, Heffron, and Falkow 1989; Miller, Mekalanos, and Falkow 1989). The *vibrio* makes protein enterotoxin, which affects the metabolism of human cells and causes them to expel water. The interaction of enterotoxin with the cell has been worked out, and so has the genetic mechanism used by the *vibrio* to manufacture this protein.

Snow did some brilliant detective work on nonexperimental data. What is impressive is not the statistical technique but the handling of the scientific issues. He made steady progress from shrewd observation through case studies to analysis of ecological data. In the end, he found and analyzed a natural experiment. (Of course, he also made his share of mistakes: For example, based on rather flimsy analogies, he concluded that plague and yellow fever were also propagated through the water (Snow [1855] 1965, pp. 125–27).

The next example is from modern epidemiology, which has adopted regression methods. The example shows how modeling can go off the rails. In 1980, Kanarek et al. published an article in the *American Journal of Epidemiology*—perhaps the leading journal in the field—which argued that asbestos fibers in the drinking water caused lung cancer. The study was based on 722 census tracts in the San Francisco Bay Area. There were huge variations in fiber concentrations from one tract to another; factors of 10 or more were commonplace.

Kanarek et al. examined cancer rates at 35 sites, for blacks and whites, men and women. They controlled for age by standardization and for sex and race by cross-tabulation. But the main tool was loglinear regression, to control for other covariates (marital status, education, income, occupation). Causation was inferred, as usual, if a coefficient was statistically significant after controlling for covariates.

Kanarek et al. did not discuss their stochastic assumptions, that outcomes are independent and identically distributed given covariates. The argument for the functional form was only that "theoretical construction of the probability of developing cancer by a certain time yields a function of the log form" (1980, p. 62). However, this model of cancer causation is open to serious objections (Freedman and Navidi 1989).

For lung cancer in white males, the asbestos fiber coefficient was highly significant ($P < .001$), so the effect was described as strong. Actually, the model predicts a risk multiplier of only about 1.05 for a 100-fold increase in fiber concentrations. There was no effect in women or blacks. Moreover, Kanarek et al. had no data on cigarette smoking, which affects lung cancer rates by factors of 10 or more. Thus, imperfect control over smoking could easily account for the observed effect, as could even minor errors in functional form. Finally, Kanarek et al. ran upwards of 200 equations; only one of the P values was below .001. So the real significance level may be closer to $200 \times .001 = .20$. The model-based argument is not a good one.

What is the difference between Kanarek et al.'s study and Snow's? Kanarek et al. ignored the ecological fallacy. Snow dealt with it. Kanarek et al. tried to control for covariates by modeling, using socioeconomic status as a proxy for smoking. Snow found a natural experiment and collected the data he needed. Kanarek et al.'s argument for causation rides on the statistical significance of a coefficient. Snow's argument used logic and shoe leather. Regression models make it all too easy to substitute technique for work.

3. SOME EXAMPLES FROM THE SOCIAL SCIENCES

If regression is a successful methodology, the routine paper in a good journal should be a modest success story. However, the situation is quite otherwise. I recently spent some time looking through leading American journals in quantitative social science: *American Journal of Sociology, American Sociological Review,* and *American Political Science Review.* These refereed journals accept perhaps 10 percent of their submissions. For analysis, I selected papers that were published in 1987–88, that posed reasonably clear research questions, and that used regression to answer them. I will discuss three of these papers. These papers may not be the best of their kind, but they are far from the worst. Indeed, one was later awarded a prize for the best article published in *American Political Science Review* in 1988. In sum, I believe these papers are quite typical of good current research practice.

Example 1. Bahry and Silver (1987) hypothesized that in Russia, perception of the KGB as efficient deterred political activism. Their study was based on questionnaires filled out by Russian emigres in New York. There was a lot of missing data and perhaps some confusion between response variables and control variables. Leave all that aside. In the end, the argument was that after adjustment for covariates, subjects who viewed the KGB as efficient were less likely to describe themselves as activists. And this negative correlation was statistically significant.

Of course, that could be evidence to support the research hypothesis of the paper: If you think the KGB is efficient, you don't demonstrate. Or the line of causality could run the other way: If you're an activist, you find out that the KGB is inefficient. Or the association could be driven by a third variable: People of certain personality types are more likely to describe themselves as activists and also more likely to describe the KGB as inefficient. Correlation is not the same as causation; statistical technique, alone, does not make the connection. The familiarity of this point should not be allowed to obscure its force.

Example 2. Erikson, McIver, and Wright (1987) argued that in the U.S., different states really do have different political cultures. After controlling for demographics and geographical region, adding state dummy variables increased R^2 for predicting party identification from .0898 to .0953. The F to enter the state dummies was about 8. The data base consisted of 55,000 questionnaires from CBS/*New York Times* opinion surveys. With 40 degrees of freedom in the numerator and 55,000 in the denominator, P is spectacular.

On the other hand, the R^2's are trivial—never mind the increase. The authors argued that the state dummies are not proxies for omitted variables. As proof, they put in trade union membership and found that the estimated state effects did not change much. This argument does support the specification, but it is weak.

Example 3. Gibson (1988) asked whether political intolerance during the McCarthy era was driven by mass opinion or elite

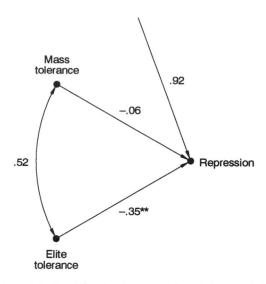

FIGURE 1. Path model of political intolerance. Adapted by permission from Gibson (1988).

opinion. The unit of analysis was the state. Legislation was coded on a tolerance/intolerance scale; there were questionnaire surveys of elite opinion and mass opinion. Then comes a path model; one coefficient is significant, one is not. Gibson concluded: "Generally it seems that elites, not masses, were responsible for the repression of the era" (p. 511).

Of the three papers, I thought Gibson's had the clearest question and the best summary data. However, the path diagram seems to be an extremely weak causal model. Moreover, even granting the model, the difference between the two path coefficients is not significant. The paper's conclusion does not follow from the data.

4. SUMMARY OF THE POSITION

In this set of papers, and in many papers outside the set, the adjustment for covariates is by regression; the argument for causality rides on the significance of a coefficient. But significance levels depend on specifications, especially of error structure. For example, if the errors are not correlated or heteroscedastic, the conventional formulas will give the wrong answers. And the stochastic specification is never argued in any detail. (Nor does modeling the covariances fix the problem, unless the model for the covariances can be validated; more about technical fixes, below.)

To sum up, each of the examples has these characteristics:

1. There is an interesting research question, which may or may not be sharp enough to be empirically testable.
2. Relevant data are collected, although there may be considerable difficulty in quantifying some of the concepts, and important data may be missing.
3. The research hypothesis is quickly translated into a regression equation, more specifically, into an assertion that certain coefficients are (or are not) statistically significant.
4. Some attention is paid to getting the right variables into the equation, although the choice of covariates is usually not compelling.
5. Little attention is paid to functional form or stochastic specification; textbook linear models are just taken for granted.

Clearly, evaluating the use of regression models in a whole field is a difficult business; there are no well-beaten paths to follow. Here, I have selected for review three papers that, in my opinion, are good of their kind and that fairly represent a large (but poorly delineated) class. These papers illustrate some basic obstacles in applying regression technology to make causal inferences.

In Freedman (1987), I took a different approach and reviewed a modern version of the classic model for status attainment. I tried to state the technical assumptions needed for drawing causal inferences from path diagrams—assumptions that seem to be very difficult to validate in applications. I also summarized previous work on these issues. Modelers had an extended opportunity to answer. The technical analysis was not in dispute, and serious examples were not forthcoming.

If the assumptions of a model are not derived from theory, and if predictions are not tested against reality, then deductions from the model must be quite shaky. However, without the model, the data cannot be used to answer the research question. Indeed, the research hypothesis may not really be translatable into an empirical claim except as a statement about nominal significance levels of coefficients in a model.

Two authorities may be worth quoting in this regard. Of course, both of them have said other things in other places.

> The aim . . . is to provide a clear and rigorous basis for determining when a causal ordering can be said to hold between two variables or groups of variables in a model. . . . *The concepts . . . all refer to a model—a system of equations—and not to the "real" world the model purports to describe.* (Simon 1957, p. 12 [emphasis added])

> If . . . we choose a group of social phenomena with no antecedent knowledge of the causation or absence of causation among them, then the calculation of correlation coefficients, total or partial, will not advance us a step toward evaluating the importance of the causes at work. (Fisher 1958, p. 190)

In my view, regression models are not a particularly good way of doing empirical work in the social sciences today, because the technique depends on knowledge that we do not have. Investigators who use the technique are not paying adequate attention to the connection—if any—between the models and the phenomena they are studying. Their conclusions may be valid for the computer code they have created, but the claims are hard to transfer from that microcosm to the larger world.

For me, Snow's work exemplifies one point on a continuum of research styles; the regression examples mark another. My judgment on the relative merits of the two styles will be clear—and with it, some implicit recommendations. Comparisons may be invidious, but I think Snow's research stayed much closer to reality than the modeling exercises. He was not interested in the properties of systems of equations but in ways of preventing a real disease. He formulated sharp, empirical questions that could be answered using data that could, with effort, be collected. At every turn, he anchored his argument in stubborn fact. And he exposed his theory to harsh tests in a variety of settings. That may explain how he discovered something extraordinarily important about cholera, and why his book is still worth reading more than a century later.

5. CAN TECHNICAL FIXES RESCUE THE MODELS?

Regression models often seem to be used to compensate for problems in measurement, data collection, and study design. By the time the models are deployed, the scientific position is nearly hopeless. Reliance on models in such cases is Panglossian. At any rate, that is my view. By contrast, some readers may be concerned to defend the technique of regression modeling: According to them, the technique is sound and only the applications are flawed. Other readers may think that the criticisms of regression modeling are merely technical, so that technical fixes—e.g., robust estimators, generalized least squares, and specification tests—will make the problems go away.

The mathematical basis for regression is well established. My question is whether the technique applies to present-day social science problems. In other words, are the assumptions valid? Moreover, technical fixes become relevant only when models are nearly right. For instance, robust estimators may be useful if the error terms are independent, identically distributed, and symmetric but long-tailed. If the error terms are neither independent nor identically distributed and there is no way to find out whether they are symmetric, robust estimators probably distract from the real issues.

This point is so uncongenial that another illustration may be in order. Suppose $y_i = \alpha + \epsilon_i$, the ϵ_i have mean 0, and the ϵ_i are *either* independent and identically distributed *or* autoregressive of order 1. Then the well-oiled statistics machine springs into action. However, if the ϵ_i are just a sequence of random variables, the situation is nearly hopeless—with respect to standard errors and hypothesis testing. So much the worse if the y_i have no stochastic pedigree. The last possibility seems to me the most realistic. Then formal statistical procedures are irrelevant, and we are reduced (or should be) to old-fashioned thinking.

A well-known discussion of technical fixes starts from the evaluation of manpower-training programs using nonexperimental data. LaLonde (1986) and Fraker and Maynard (1987) compare evaluation results from modeling with results from experiments. The idea is to see whether regression models fitted to observational data can predict the results of experimental interventions. Fraker and Maynard conclude:

> The results indicate that nonexperimental designs
> cannot be relied on to estimate the effectiveness of
> employment programs. Impact estimates tend to be
> sensitive both to the comparison group construction
> methodology and to the analytic model used. There
> is currently no way a priori to ensure that the results
> of comparison group studies will be valid indicators
> of the program impacts. (p. 194)

Heckman and Hotz (1989, pp. 862, 874) reply that specification tests
can be used to rule out models that give wrong predictions:

> A simple testing procedure eliminates the range of
> nonexperimental estimators at variance with the ex-
> perimental estimates of program impact. . . . Thus,
> while not definitive, our results are certainly encour-
> aging for the use of nonexperimental methods in
> social-program evaluation.

Heckman and Hotz have in hand (a) the experimental data,
(b) the nonexperimental data, and (c) LaLonde's results as well as
Fraker and Maynard's. Heckman and Hotz proceed by modeling the
selection bias in the nonexperimental comparison groups. There are
three types of models, each with two main variants. These are fitted
to several different time periods, with several sets of control variables. Averages of different models are allowed, and there is a
"slight extension" of one model.

By my count, 24 models are fitted to the nonexperimental data
on female AFDC recipients, and 32 are fitted to the data on high
school dropouts. *Ex post facto,* models that pass certain specification
tests can more or less reproduce the experimental results (up to very
large standard errors). However, the real question is what can be
done *ex ante,* before the right estimate is known. Heckman and Hotz
may have an argument, but it is not a strong one. It may even point
us in the wrong direction. Testing one model on 24 different data sets
could open a serious enquiry: Have we identified an empirical regularity that has some degree of invariance? Testing 24 models on one
data set is less serious.

Generally, replication and prediction of new results provide a harsher and more useful validation regime than statistical testing of many models on one data set. Fewer assumptions are needed, there is less chance of artifact, more kinds of variation can be explored, and alternative explanations can be ruled out. Indeed, taken to the extreme, developing a model by specification tests just comes back to curve fitting—with a complicated set of constraints on the residuals.

Given the limits to present knowledge, I doubt that models can be rescued by technical fixes. Arguments about the theoretical merit of regression or the asymptotic behavior of specification tests for picking one version of a model over another seem like arguments about how to build desalination plants with cold fusion as the energy source. The concept may be admirable, the technical details may be fascinating, but thirsty people should look elsewhere.

6. OTHER LITERATURE

The issues raised here are hardly new, and this section reviews some recent literature. No brief summary can do justice to Lieberson (1985), who presents a complicated and subtle critique of current empirical work in the social sciences. I offer a crude paraphrase of one important message: When there are significant differences between comparison groups in an observational study, it is extraordinarily difficult if not impossible to achieve balance by statistical adjustments. Arminger and Bohrnstedt (1987, p. 366) respond by describing this as a special case of "misspecification of the mean structure caused by the omission of relevant causal variables" and cite literature on that topic.

This trivializes the problem and almost endorses the idea of fixing misspecification by elaborating the model. However, that idea is unlikely to work. Current specification tests need independent, identically distributed observations, and lots of them; the relevant variables must be identified; some variables must be taken as exogenous; additive errors are needed; and a parametric or semiparametric form for the mean function is required. These ingredients are rarely found in the social sciences, except by assumption. To model a bias, we need to know what causes it, and how. In practice, this may be even more difficult than the original research question. Some empirical evidence is provided by the discussion of manpower-training program evaluations above (also see Stolzenberg and Relles 1990).

As Arminger and Bohrnstedt concede (1987, p. 370),

> There is no doubt that experimental data are to be
> preferred over nonexperimental data, which practi-
> cally demand that one knows the mean structure ex-
> cept for the parameters to be estimated.

In the physical or life sciences, there are some situations in which the
mean function is known, and regression models are correspondingly
useful. In the social sciences, I do not see this precondition for regression modeling as being met, even to a first approximation.

In commenting on Lieberson (1985), Singer and Marini (1987)
emphasize two points:

1. "It requires rather yeoman assumptions or unusual phenomena
   to conduct a comparative analysis of an observational study as
   though it represented conclusions (inferences) from an experiment." (p. 376)
2. "There seems to be an implicit view in much of social science
   that any question that might be asked about a society is answerable in principle." (p. 382)

In my view, point 1 says that in the current state of knowledge
in the social sciences, regression models are seldom if ever reliable
for causal inference. With respect to point 2, it is exactly the reliance
on models that makes all questions seem "answerable in principle"—
a great obstacle to the development of the subject. It is the beginning
of scientific wisdom to recognize that not all questions have answers.
For some discussion along these lines, see Lieberson (1988).

Marini and Singer (1988) continue the argument:

> Few would question that the use of "causal" models
> has improved our knowledge of causes and is likely
> to do so increasingly as the models are refined and
> become more attuned to the phenomena under inves-
> tigation. (p. 394)

However, much of the analysis in Marini and Singer contradicts this
presumed majority view:

> Causal analysis . . . is not a way of deducing causation but of quantifying already hypothesized relationships. . . . Information external to the model is needed to warrant the use of one specific representation as truly "structural." The information must come from the existing body of knowledge relevant to the domain under consideration. (pp. 388, 391)

As I read the current empirical research literature, causal arguments depend mainly on the statistical significance of regression coefficients. If so, Marini and Singer are pointing to the fundamental circularity in the regression strategy: The information needed for building regression models comes only from such models. Indeed, Marini and Singer continue:

> The relevance of causal models to empirical phenomena is often open to question because assumptions made for the purpose of model identification are arbitrary or patently false. The models take on an importance of their own, and convenience or elegance in the model building overrides faithfulness to the phenomena. (p. 392)

Holland (1988) raises similar points. Causal inferences from nonexperimental data using path models require assumptions that are quite close to the conclusions; so the analysis is driven by the model, not the data. In effect, given a set of covariates, the mean response over the "treatment group" minus the mean over the "controls" must be assumed to equal the causal effect being estimated (1988, p. 481).

> The effect . . . cannot be estimated by the usual regression methods of path analysis without making untestable assumptions about the counterfactual regression function. (p. 470)

Berk (1988, p. 161) discusses causal inferences based on path diagrams, including "unobservable disturbances meeting the usual (and sometimes heroic) assumptions." He considers the oft-recited arguments that biases will be small, or if large will tend to cancel, and concludes, "Unfortunately, it is difficult to find any evidence for these beliefs" (p. 163). He recommends quasi-experimental designs, which

> are terribly underutilized by sociologists despite their considerable potential. While they are certainly no substitute for random assignment, the stronger quasi-experimental designs can usually produce far more compelling causal inferences than conventional cross-sectional data sets. (p. 163)

He comments on model development by testing, including the use of specification tests:

> The results may well be misleading if there are *any* other statistical assumptions that are substantially violated. (p. 165)

I found little to disagree with in Berk's essay. Casual observation suggests that no dramatic change in research practice took place following publication of his essay; further discussion of the issues may be needed.

Of course, Paul Meehl (1978) already said most of what needs saying in 1978, in his article, "Theoretical Risks and Tabular Asterisks: Sir Karl, Sir Ronald, and the Slow Progress of Soft Psychology." In paraphrase, the good knight is Karl Popper, whose motto calls for subjecting scientific theories to grave danger of refutation. The bad knight is Ronald Fisher, whose significance tests are trampled in the dust:

> The almost universal reliance on merely refuting the null hypothesis as the standard method for corroborating substantive theories in the soft areas is . . . basically unsound. (p. 817)

Meehl is an eminent psychologist, and he has one of the best data sets available for demonstrating the predictive power of regression models. His judgment deserves some consideration.

7. CONCLUSION

One fairly common way to attack a problem involves collecting data and then making a set of statistical assumptions about the process that generated the data—for example, linear regression with normal errors, conditional independence of categorical data given covariates, random censoring of observations, independence of competing hazards.

Once the assumptions are in place, the model is fitted to the data, and quite intricate statistical calculations may come into play: three-stage least squares, penalized maximum likelihood, second-order efficiency, and so on. The statistical inferences sometimes lead to rather strong empirical claims about structure and causality.

Typically, the assumptions in a statistical model are quite hard to prove or disprove, and little effort is spent in that direction. The strength of empirical claims made on the basis of such modeling therefore does not derive from the solidity of the assumptions. Equally, these beliefs cannot be justified by the complexity of the calculations. Success in controlling observable phenomena is a relevant argument, but one that is seldom made.

These observations lead to uncomfortable questions. Are the models helpful? Is it possible to differentiate between successful and unsuccessful uses of the models? How can the models be tested and evaluated? Regression models have been used on social science data since Yule (1899), so it may be time to ask these questions; although definitive answers cannot be expected.

REFERENCES

Arminger, G., and G. W. Bohrnstedt. 1987. "Making it Count Even More: A Review and Critique of Stanley Lieberson's *Making It Count: The Improvement of Social Theory and Research.*" Pp. 363–72 in *Sociological Methodology 1987,* edited by C. C. Clogg. Washington, DC: American Sociological Association.

Bahry, D., and B. D. Silver. 1987. "Intimidation and the Symbolic Uses of Terror in the USSR." *American Political Science Review* 81:1065–98.

Berk, R. A. 1988. "Causal Inference for Sociological Data." Pp. 155–72 in *Handbook of Sociology,* edited by N. J. Smelser. Los Angeles: Sage.

Carpenter, K. J., ed. 1981. *Pellagra.* Stroudsberg, PA: Hutchinson Ross.

Cornfield, J., W. Haenszel, E. C. Hammond, A. M. Lilienfeld, M. B. Shimkin, and E. L. Wynder. 1959. "Smoking and Lung Cancer: Recent Evidence and a

Discussion of Some Questions." *Journal of the National Cancer Institute* 22:173–203.

Erikson, R. S., J. P. McIver, and G. C. Wright, Jr. 1987. "State Political Culture and Public Opinion." *American Political Science Review* 81:797–813.

Evans, R. J. 1987. *Death in Hamburg: Society and Politics in the Cholera Years, 1830–1910.* Oxford: Oxford University Press.

Finlay, B. B., F. Heffron, and S. Falkow. 1989. "Epithelial Cell Surfaces Induce Salmonella Proteins Required for Bacterial Adherence and Invasion." *Science* 243:940–42.

Fisher, R. A. 1958. *Statistical Methods for Research Workers.* 13th ed. Edinburgh: Oliver and Boyd.

Fraker, T., and R. Maynard. 1987. "The Adequacy of Comparison Group Designs for Evaluations of Employment-Related Programs." *Journal of Human Resources* 22:194–227.

Freedman, D. A. 1987. "As Others See Us: A Case Study in Path Analysis" (with discussion). *Journal of Educational Statistics* 12:101–223.

Freedman, D. A., and W. Navidi. 1989. "Multistage Models for Carcinogenesis." *Environmental Health Perspectives* 81:169–88.

Gibson, J. L. 1988. "Political Intolerance and Political Repression During the McCarthy Red Scare." *American Political Science Review* 82:511–29.

Heckman, J. J., and V. J. Hotz. 1989. "Choosing Among Alternative Nonexperimental Methods for Estimating the Impact of Social Programs: The Case of Manpower Training" (with discussion). *Journal of the American Statistical Association* 84:862–80.

Holland, P. 1988. "Causal Inference, Path Analysis, and Recursive Structural Equations Models." Pp. 449–84 in *Sociological Methodology 1988,* edited by C. C. Clogg. Oxford: Basil Blackwell.

Howard-Jones, N. 1975. *The Scientific Background of the International Sanitary Conferences 1851–1938.* Geneva: World Health Organization.

Kanarek, M. S., P. M. Conforti, L. A. Jackson, R. C. Cooper, and J. C. Murchio. 1980. "Asbestos in Drinking Water and Cancer Incidence in the San Francisco Bay Area." *American Journal of Epidemiology* 112:54–72.

LaLonde, R. J. 1986. "Evaluating the Econometric Evaluations of Training Programs with Experimental Data." *American Economic Review* 76:604–20.

Lieberson, S. 1985. *Making It Count: The Improvement of Social Theory and Research.* Berkeley: University of California Press.

———. 1988. "Asking Too Much, Expecting Too Little." *Sociological Perspectives* 31:379–97.

Lombard, H. L., and C. R. Doering. 1928. "Cancer Studies in Massachusetts, 2. Habits, Characteristics and Environment of Individuals With and Without Lung Cancer." *New England Journal of Medicine* 198:481–87.

Louis, Pierre. (1835) 1986. *Researches on the Effects of Bloodletting in Some Inflammatory Diseases, and the Influence of Emetics and Vesication in Pneumonitis.* Translated and reprinted. Birmingham, AL: Classics of Medicine Library.

Marini, M. M., and B. Singer. 1988. "Causality in the Social Sciences." Pp. 347–409 in *Sociological Methodology 1988,* edited by C. C. Clogg. Oxford: Basil Blackwell.

Meehl, P. E. 1978. "Theoretical Risks and Tabular Asterisks: Sir Karl, Sir Ronald, and the Slow Progress of Soft Psychology." *Journal of Consulting and Clinical Psychology* 46:806–34.

Miller, J. F., J. J. Mekalanos, and S. Falkow. 1989. "Coordinate Regulation and Sensory Transduction in the Control of Bacterial Virulence." *Science* 243: 916–22.

Mueller, F. H. 1939. "Tabakmissbrauch und Lungcarcinom" (Tobacco abuse and lung cancer). *Zeitschrift fur Krebsforsuch* 49:57–84.

Rosenberg, C. E. 1962. *The Cholera Years.* Chicago: University of Chicago Press.

Semmelweiss, Ignaz. (1861) 1941. "The Etiology, the Concept and the Prophylaxis of Childbed Fever." Translated and reprinted. *Medical Classics* 5:338–775.

Simon, H. 1957. *Models of Man.* New York: Wiley.

Singer, B., and M. M. Marini. 1987. "Advancing Social Research: An Essay Based on Stanley Lieberson's *Making It Count: The Improvement of Social Theory and Research.*" Pp. 373–91 in *Sociological Methodology 1987,* edited by C. C. Clogg. Washington, DC: American Sociological Association.

Snow, John. (1855) 1965. *On the Mode of Communication of Cholera.* Reprint ed. New York: Hafner.

Stolzenberg, R. M., and D. A. Relles. 1990. "Theory Testing in a World of Constrained Research Design." *Sociological Methods and Research* 18:395–415.

Terris, M., ed. 1964. *Goldberger on Pellagra.* Baton Rouge: Louisiana State University Press.

U.S. Public Health Service. 1964. *Smoking and Health. Report of the Advisory Committee to the Surgeon General.* Washington, DC: U.S. Government Printing Office.

Yule, G. U. 1899. "An Investigation into the Causes of Changes in Pauperism in England, Chiefly During the Last Two Intercensal Decades." *Journal of the Royal Statistical Society* 62:249–95.

❧11❧

TOWARD A METHODOLOGY FOR MERE MORTALS

*Richard A. Berk**

1. INTRODUCTION

"Statistical Models and Shoe Leather" will be very difficult for most quantitative sociologists to accept. It goes to the heart of their empirical enterprise and in so doing, puts entire professional careers in jeopardy. It also gives no comfort to thoughtful empirical sociologists who make little use of numbers, since the issues raised go well beyond the uncritical use of regression routines in SAS or SPSS. What is needed, therefore, is a brief series of clarifications and expansions that anticipate efforts to wriggle off Freedman's hook. It will also prove useful to suggest other issues for which a lot more thought is necessary.

2. SOME CLARIFICATIONS: WHERE DO THE PROBLEMS LIE?

The difficulties that Freedman ties to regression models are *not* inherent in the statistical foundation of regression analysis. Indeed, linear regression models are well understood and, in principle, useful tools for certain kinds of empirical work. Freedman is describing a broad failure of scientific understanding. Simply put, the knowledge that sociology (and the other social sciences) can bring to a regression analysis is likely to be grossly inadequate. Stated another way, given that the regression model whose parameters are to be estimated must

*University of California, Los Angeles

be, in Freedman's terms, "nearly right," we do not know enough about the *substantive* phenomena we study to decide how to properly formulate a particular regression model. Often we cannot even determine if a regression approach is sensible to begin with.

It cannot be overemphasized that the problems Freedman raises reach well beyond the old saw of omitted variables to include functional form and the properties of the disturbance term (see Berk 1983 for general discussion). With respect to functional form, it is useful to examine recent work on nonlinear regression models (Bates and Watts 1988).[1] With respect to the disturbance distribution, it is useful to ponder the implications of William Kruskal's (1988) presidential address to the American Statistical Association, which challenges "the casual assumption of independence." In both cases, there are a number of interesting and powerful technical options, but they depend first and fundamentally on a sound *substantive* rationale.

Also implied is that popular research designs used by sociologists are often fundamentally inadequate. One cannot repair a weak research design with a strong data analysis. Almost inevitably what seems too good to be true is, and one is simply substituting untestable assumptions for the information one does not have.

Furthermore, it is important to point out that while Freedman is focusing primarily on conventional linear regression analysis, his critique carries over to virtually all statistical tools used by sociologists for causal modeling. For example, logistic regression, probit analysis, and "loglinear" models for the analysis of count data in contingency tables (i.e., Poisson regression) are all subsumed, like linear regression, under the generalized linear model (McCullagh and Nelder 1989). Freedman's concerns, therefore, clearly apply, and if the problem is really a failure of science, *any* statistical model used to infer cause is highly suspect.

---

[1]On a conceptual level, I view non-linear regression analysis as an extension of conventional linear regression models, and consequently, Freedman's concerns apply. In contrast, procedures for describing non-linear regression surfaces (Friedman and Stuetzle, 1981) or for linearizing regression models (Breiman and Friedman, 1985) are essentially exploratory techniques resting on a rather different rationale. For example, statistical inference seems fundamentally problematic since the final models are produced by algorithms that essentially "fish" through a given dataset. In short, they have much in common with conventional stepwise regression procedures (Friedman and Stuetzle 1981, pp. 817–818).

Of course, statistical models can be used for a wide variety of purposes in which the mechanisms driving the phenomena in question are not being explicitly depicted: forecasting, missing-data imputation, parameter estimation, and others (Cox 1990). Freedman does not address these other uses of ("noncausal") regression models, although in sociological applications, he would probably take a skeptical stance and wonder if sociological knowledge was up to the task.

The important work by Little and Rubin (1988) on missing data, for example, rests heavily on the assumption that the data are missing at random or conditionally at random. In the first case, one must know exactly what the "at random" entails (e.g., by the equivalent of simple random sampling), but in the second case, one must also know which variables to condition on and one must have these variables in one's dataset (even though the mechanisms by which missing data were produced do not have to be represented). In other words, these sorts of noncausal models must be "nearly right" as well. Given current sociological knowledge, this is no small requirement.

Finally, Freedman mentions statistical inference only in passing. If one's causal model is wrong, one's statistical inference is likely to be wrong as well. But as Freedman has observed elsewhere (Freedman and Lane 1983), the problems go much deeper. For example, when one's data do not derive from a probability sample or from an experiment with random assignment (e.g., much historical and comparative data), the sources of stochastic variation are often obscure. Furthermore, even when the sources are known, the particular (stochastic) data-generating mechanisms cannot be specified with the information on hand.

On a more fundamental level, there continues to be a lively debate among statisticians about what one can learn from statistical inference and how it is best carried out (Barnett 1982). As a form of applied probability, statistical inference is on reasonably sound mathematical footing. However, it does not necessarily follow that statistical inference makes sense when applied to the observable social world. As Freedman has noted (personal communication), "The really deep question is whether statistics is really *about* anything at all."

To summarize, Freedman's critique of how linear regression is used in causal modeling is really a critique of the intellectual content of sociology; it is a long way from the methodological hand-wringing that has appeared in the journals from time to time over the past three decades. While there are no doubt many examples of technical errors in the sociological literature, the solution is not better technical training, more complicated models, or even better technical tools. In addition, I suspect that Freedman would be skeptical of *any* modeling done by sociologists and, in the absence of random sampling or random assignment, statistical inference as well. Finally, while I am necessarily focusing on Freedman's particular concerns, it should be noted that they are shared by many statisticians and by some social scientists (see Berk 1988 for a review).

3. SOME EXPANSIONS: WHERE TO FROM HERE?

"Statistical Models and Shoe Leather" is not the first paper in which Freedman raises his concerns about causal modeling in sociology and other substantive disciplines. What makes this paper distinctive is its effort to show, at least by example, how sociology (and social science more generally) may be done better. That is, it tries to determine how empirical work in sociology should best proceed in the face of widespread substantive immaturity.

Three kinds of related lessons can be extracted: the need for a reduction over the medium term in scientific aspirations, the use of stronger research designs, and the development and use of analysis-validation techniques relying on data beyond those on which the original analysis was done. An example of the first is attempting in-depth description rather than causal inference, which is perhaps more consistent with current developments within data-analytic traditions (e.g., Atkinson 1985; Weihs and Schmidli 1990). An example of the second is the use of regression-discontinuity or cross-over designs (Cook and Campbell 1979) in which researchers have considerable control over the key variables. An example of the third is cross-validation (Picard and Berk 1990). I have at least briefly discussed the first two alternatives elsewhere (Berk 1988), so I will focus here (also briefly) on the third.

3.1. *Validation With New Data*

Drawing substantive conclusions from a causal model developed from a single dataset has at least three generic problems. First, most modeling efforts in sociology are some unarticulated combination of ideas brought to the data and ideas developed in the process of examining the data (Lehmann 1990). As a result, one is all too easily seduced by particular features of the data that are, in fact, idiosyncratic. Overfitting is perhaps the most well known example, with stepwise (also known as unwise) regression a common means to that end (Hurvich and Tsai 1990).

Cross-validation is perhaps the best known technique for protecting researchers against capitalizing improperly on idiosyncratic features of a given dataset. The basic idea is to withhold part of one's data for future use in model validation. That is, part of the data is used for model development and part is used for model validation, with the split often undertaken by some form of random sampling. While there are some nontrivial technical problems still to be solved, one can formally determine, for example, how much the goodness of fit declines when the model developed on one part of the data is applied to the other part (Picard and Berk 1990). This can provide a useful antidote to overfitting.

While Snow did not formally undertake anything like cross-validation, the appearance of the same substantive conclusions in a number of different datasets was comforting. It would have been very hard to believe that Snow was capitalizing on the idiosyncratic features of any particular dataset.

A second problem is that any given "observational" dataset will likely provide a very incomplete means by which to rule out competing explanations for a particular set of proposed causal effects. Key variables may be effectively constants, colinearity may prevent the disentangling of competing causal effects, or critical variables may be unmeasured. But by piecing together a number of datasets with different mixes of strengths and weaknesses, it may well be possible to effectively address spurious causal interpretations. For example, the addition of ecological data (a weakness) in which Snow could identify specific water companies (a strength) helped to rule out causal explanations based on victims' backgrounds.

A third problem is that it is rare for one's substantive interest to be limited to the particular dataset on hand. Sociologists are presumably in the business of developing generalizations about the social world for which a given dataset is but a convenient and incomplete vehicle. Thus, if the general import of one's findings is the issue, achieving a good fit and undertaking a bevy of successful specification tests is unresponsive; those tools rely solely on the data employed to develop the causal model under consideration. The real question is how the model will perform on *new* data.

Replications have long been advocated as a means to address the generalizability of one's findings (Cook and Campbell 1979). A good theory and its implied causal model should be essentially reproducible in a wide variety of settings and with a wide variety of subjects. Thus, part of the appeal in Snow's work is its replicability. His explanation for the cause of cholera seemed to apply to whatever dataset he collected. It was especially compelling that this was precisely what his theory required; infected water should make people sick regardless of their other life circumstances.

To summarize, one of the major methodological lessons from Snow's work is the need to validate one's findings on additional datasets. Depending on the problem being addressed, these data may be a random subset of data already on hand or "new" data with rather different properties. In principle, validation procedures will provide some protection against overfitting, will help rule out competing causal explanations, and will empirically address generalizability.

3.2. *Moving from Principles to Practice*

It is one thing to suggest in general terms that validating one's findings with new data is a good idea, and quite another to describe exactly how to proceed. To begin, it may be important to distinguish between reproducing the values of key parameter estimates and reproducing a good fit. For the former, the important regression coefficients from the original and the validation datasets should be the same (within the bounds of sampling error). For the latter, mean square error or multiple correlation should be the same (within the bounds of sampling error).

Just like for a single dataset, however, regression coefficients and goodness-of-fit measures may suggest different conclusions. It is entirely possible to reproduce a sensible set of regression coefficients and not the goodness of fit (and the reverse). Moreover, with large samples, either kind of results may differ in two or more datasets, but not enough to alter the overall substantive story. In short, the judgment calls that surface within a single dataset resurface in attempts to validate findings across several datasets. There are no recipes.

Furthermore, replicating parameter estimates or goodness-of-fit statistics allows only cross-dataset comparisons of *aggregate* calculations. And rather different data patterns may lead to rather similar aggregate statistics. A more demanding test is trying to reproduce the actual *observations* in a new dataset using the model (and its parameter estimates) developed from the old dataset. In the case of regression models, one would use the regression coefficients from the original data and the values of the explanatory variables from the new data to produce a set of conditional expectations for the response variable. These are then compared, often using graphical techniques, to the observed values of the response variable in the new data. The goal is to see if key patterns are reproduced and if key observations are well predicted. Ideally, the conditional expectations should closely track the observed values.

Consider an example in which the goal was to understand variation in the number of reported cases of AIDS in Los Angeles census tracts (Berk 1990). The distribution of AIDS across tracts was highly skewed: Virtually all of the reported cases of AIDS were found in about 5 percent of over 1,600 tracts, and the majority of cases were found in less than 1 percent of the tracts. A good model, therefore, should not only distinguish between tracts with cases and tracts with no cases, but also identify the tracts on the long tail of the distribution. While these tracts are outliers in a formal sense, they are also the places where the epidemic was unfolding most dramatically.

Three kinds of explanatory variables were included in the (Poisson) regression analysis: proxies at the census-tract level for high concentrations of male homosexuals (e.g., the ratio of the number of adult males to the number of adult females), proxies at the census-tract level for high-risk activities (e.g., the number of drug offenses reported to the police), and the usual sorts of control variables (e.g., population size).

For reasons that need not concern us here, the analysis was first undertaken on census tracts patrolled by the Los Angeles Police Department. By and large, the explanatory variables operated as expected. There were, for example, more cases of AIDS in tracts with more drug offenses and in tracts where males tended to outnumber females.

An effort was made to validate the model by applying the model as estimated to the different tracts patrolled by the Los Angeles County Sheriff's Department. The good news was that the key regression coefficients estimated from the new dataset were much the same as for the old dataset; the same substantive story surfaced. The bad news was that the model failed the more demanding test of reproducing key observations. In general, the model did a pretty good job of distinguishing those tracts with AIDS cases from those tracts without AIDS cases (roughly a binary variable), but it could not effectively reproduce the observed data with its very long tail. The model captured rather well what put some census tracts at risk, but it captured rather poorly how much the risk was. Had the observed data been well reproduced, the model validation would have been powerful indeed.

Clearly, the second dataset was extremely useful in documenting the strengths and weaknesses of the model originally estimated. However, in the context of Freedman's concerns, two points need to be stressed. First, there was no simple or straightforward way to determine how well the model fared in the new dataset. Graphical procedures were the primary tool, and much rested on difficult judgment calls. This is a rich and important area for statistical research: How does one recognize a successful or unsuccessful replication?

Second, it is ironic that in a paper criticizing the use of regression techniques, a regression analysis is used as the starting point to illustrate constructive methodological alternatives. However, by sociological standards, biomedical understanding of how the AIDS virus is transmitted is quite advanced. Whatever power the model demonstrated was *not* due to new technical fixes or even to a validation dataset. It was due to good science. Even so, when the results were interpreted, they were not given any particular causal import. Rather, they were used to describe and summarize a set of conditional associations. The primary goal was to launch a set of more focused studies using better data from better research designs.

4. CONCLUSIONS

"Statistical Models and Shoe Leather" is an important addition to recent critiques of causal modeling in sociology. Especially useful are some initial steps toward constructive recommendations that may improve everyday practice. In Freedman's view, sociology is simply not ready for causal modeling prime time. The methodological challenge, therefore, is to develop and use research strategies appropriate for the current state of sociological knowledge. Examples drawn from Snow's research include realistic aspirations about what can be learned from a given dataset, a far greater concern with data collection and research design, and the creative use of multiple datasets. These should be viewed as a *package* of recommendations, since uncoupling them reduces their import. And as a package, the recommendations go well beyond technical fixes or more of the same done better.

REFERENCES

Atkinson, A. C. 1985. *Plots, Transformation, and Regression.* New York: Wiley.

Barnett, Vic. 1982. *Comparative Statistical Inference.* 2d ed. New York: Wiley.

Bates, Douglas M., and Donald G. Watts. 1988. *Nonlinear Regression Analysis and Its Applications.* New York: Wiley.

Berk, Richard A. 1983. "Applications of the General Linear Model to Survey Data." Pp. 495–546 in *Handbook of Survey Research,* edited by Peter H. Rossi, James D. Wright, and Andy B. Anderson. New York: Academic Press.

———. 1988. "Causal Inference for Sociological Data." Pp. 155–72 in *Handbook of Sociology,* edited by Neil Smelser. Los Angeles: Sage.

———. 1990. "Prostitution, Drug Use, and the Prevalence of AIDS: An Analysis Using Census Tracts." *Journal of Sex Research* 27:607–21.

Breiman, L., and J. H. Friedman. 1985. "Estimating Optimal Transformations for Multiple Regression and Correlation." *Journal of the American Statistical Association* 80:580–619.

Cook, Thomas D., and Donald T. Campbell. 1979. *Quasi-Experimentation.* Chicago: Rand McNally.

Cox, David R. 1990. "Role of Models in Statistical Analysis." *Statistical Science* 5:169–74.

Freedman, David A., and David Lane. 1983. "Significance Testing in a Nonstochastic Setting." Pp. 185–208 in *A Festschrift for Erich L. Lehmann,* edited by Peter J. Bickel, Kjell A. Doksum, and J. L. Hodges, Jr. Belmont, CA: Wadsworth.

Friedman, Jerome H., and Werner Stuetzle. 1981. "Projection Pursuit Regression." *Journal of the American Statistical Association* 76:817–23.

Hurvich, Clifford M., and Chih-Ling Tsai. 1990. "The Impact of Model Selection on Inference in Linear Regression." *American Statistician* 44:214–17.

Kruskal, William. 1988. "Miracles and Statistics: The Casual Assumption of Independence." *Journal of the American Statistical Association* 83:929–40.

Lehmann, Eric L. 1990. "Model Specification." *Statistical Science* 5:160–68.

Little, Roderick J. A., and Donald B. Rubin. 1987. *Statistical Analysis with Missing Data.* New York: Wiley.

McCullagh, P., and J. A. Nelder. 1989. *Generalized Linear Models*. 2d ed. New York: Chapman and Hall.

Picard, Richard R., and Kenneth N. Berk. 1990. "Data Splitting." *American Statistician* 44:140–47.

Weihs, Claus, and Heinz Schmidli. 1990. "Online Multivariate Exploratory Graphical Analysis." *Statistical Science* 5:175–208.

𝕏12𝕏

ARE THERE REALLY ANY *CONSTRUCTIVE* ALTERNATIVES TO CAUSAL MODELING?

Hubert M. Blalock, Jr. *

While I find myself in close agreement with much of what Freedman has to say about much of the empirical research using regression-type analyses, I find his comments contain nothing really new in comparison to the numerous cautionary warnings and detailed discussions of pitfalls and required assumptions that have appeared in the sociological literature as far back as the 1950s. Much the same applies to relatively recent critiques by Lieberson (1985) and by Marini and Singer (1988) cited by Freedman. Many of us have long been concerned about the same kinds of abuses by empirical investigators, and I always welcome such notes of caution. However, the basic problem has been with us for a very long time, and there have been extensive discussions that, apparently, have not come to Freedman's attention. And by the same token, neither have empirically inclined sociologists paid serious attention to the methodological literature, and I regard this as a much more serious problem that continually deserves our attention.

Let me begin by stressing the major points made by Freedman, and many others before him, with which I am in basic agreement. Certainly, statistical models cannot stand alone and must be supplemented by a series of assumptions, many of which cannot be tested with the data that one has in hand. Technical fixes alone, therefore, cannot be relied on to resolve one's theoretical problems,

*University of Washington

325

nor can inadequate or missing data be compensated for by a statistical *tour de force*. Of course, correlation does not prove causation, as has been pointed out over and over again in our own literature, at least as far back as Lazarsfeld's methodological works. It *is* true that many empirical investigators appear to jump into their research without adequate exploratory work or careful thinking about alternative research designs. Unfortunately, it is also often the case that users of secondary data merely take poor or inadequate measures for granted and select among the variables contained in the data sets without an adequate theory. They then often produce a highly simplistic causal model containing only five or six variables. None of these practices are methodologically excusable.

We are also in agreement that not all questions have answers, not simply because many pieces of data are lost in history, but more basically because a number of questions are not posed in such a way that they can be answered empirically (Lenski 1988). Though it is admittedly not acted upon by some investigators this fact has been stressed repeatedly in virtually all of the research methods texts with which I am familiar. It has also been stressed that mere statistical significance and small probabilities can result from huge samples and that explained variances can be trivial, as is the case in the third political science example provided by Freedman. And as Glenn (1989) has recently stressed, the empirical literature is filled with studies in which investigators' conclusions do not follow from their data and in which causal conclusions are stated in overly dogmatic and unqualified form. We must plead guilty to all these abuses.

The phenomena in question are not new, nor are they confined to those who use regression approaches. Soon after Guttman scaling became fashionable in sociology during the 1950s, empirical researchers were running around "doing Guttman scaling" on nearly everything, often relying mechanistically on the measures proposed by Guttman as magical diagnostic devices for assessing the fit between scaling assumptions and the data. Guttman himself was deeply concerned about the theoretical underpinnings of this and other scaling approaches, as was his "rival" Paul Lazarsfeld. Both men devoted considerable attention to efforts to explicate the philosophical underpinnings of their several approaches and were careful to spell out the nature of the assumptions required for their use. Practitioners, we must assume, ignored these writings in their efforts to scramble onto the scaling bandwagon. A later scaling theorist, Clyde Coombs, was similarly theoretically inclined, as his major work's title, *A Theory of Data* (1964), implies. Coombs' and other scaling theorists' work on "nonmetric" approaches to data analysis never took hold among sociologists, but had they done so it seems safe to imagine a similar outcome.

Those who invented or made major contributions to factor analysis were similarly cautious, but this did not prevent a major outburst of atheoretical attempts to use factor analysis techniques on nearly every imaginable problem during the 1940s and 1950s. Certainly, Harold Hotelling, a theoretical statistician and one of my teachers, would have been highly disturbed had he known of this extensive and atheoretical abuse of what, if properly used, could be a very sensible data-reduction technique useful in the process of empirically based theory development. Hotelling, for example, made several important contributions to economic theory.

Those who introduced causal modeling ideas also stressed the theoretical underpinnings of regression approaches. Although I am not familiar enough with population genetics to assess Sewell Wright's contributions to theory in that field, his obituary statement prepared by a fellow member of the NAS indicated that his scholarly reputation was based very heavily on such work, and Wright's papers on path analysis bear this out. Much the same can be said of the work of many of the economists who contributed important ideas to the so-called structural equation literature. Certainly this was true of Tjalling Koopmans, whose classic (theoretical) work on identifiability had a major impact on the methodological literature. It was also true of the work of the Swedish statistician Herman Wold, whose many papers in the philosophy of science literature and participation in early debates over how economic models should be specified attest to a deep concern with theory and the very nature of social causation.

The handful of us who introduced causal modeling, path analysis, and structural equation modeling into the sociological literature during the 1960s encountered a problem similar to that faced by Wold (personal communication) a decade or so earlier. At that time, regression analysis was being used atheoretically and *causation* was a dirty word. Therefore, one of our top priorities was to attempt to bridge the gap between sociological theory and statistical applications. Actually, at that time and continuing into the present, there was the totally misleading notion that (perfect) experimental designs could provide causal information (without untested theoretical assumptions), whereas (actual, imperfect) nonexperimental research could only provide correlational evidence. So much of our attention at the time was devoted to developing the rationale for employing statistical techniques *along with supplementary assumptions* as an aid for assessing the fit between empirical data and predictions made from causal *models* about covariations and temporal sequences. Much of the flavor of that earlier literature has now been lost from view, as it is presumably no longer read either by contemporary researchers or recent critics such as Freedman.

We also engaged in a learning process during the 1960s, as one complication after another came to our attention. Gordon (1968), for example, noted the kinds of complications that can arise when multicollinearity is combined with differential measurement errors. Toward the middle of the decade and spilling into the early 1970s, many of us also became aware of the numerous complications that occur as a result of random and nonrandom measurement errors. The approach we took involved the notion that *causal theories* of measurement, including sources of measurement bias, are often necessary as "auxiliary" measurement theories that must be combined with theories about so-called structural equation modeling (Blalock 1964, 1968; Costner 1969; Heise 1969; Hauser and Goldberger 1971). In turn, this literature spawned a series of critical papers on panel designs and, through Werts' and Linn's collaboration with the Swedish statistician Karl Jöreskog, ultimately led to the development of a series of LISREL programs now in common use. Unfortunately, again, those empirical investigators rushing to use the latest and most sophisticated statistical packages are usually unaware of this earlier literature, and so, apparently, are Freedman and several other recent critics. They may even be unaware of the fact that one of the major contributors to this literature, Herbert Costner, has continually stressed the "detective" role, as the titles to some of his papers suggest: "Using Causal Models to Discover Flaws in Experiments" (1971), "Diagnosing Indicator Ills in Multiple-Indicator Models" (Costner and Schoenberg 1973), and "Respecification in Multiple-Indicator Models" (Herting and Costner 1985).

During the 1970s, discussions of path analysis and causal modeling became more routine and began to find their way into standard statistics texts and applied statistics courses, where I assume they were given very brief and inadequate coverage. Three sociological "texts" all appeared in 1975 (Duncan 1975; Namboodiri, Carter, and Blalock, 1975 Parts III and IV; and Heise 1975). In all three sources there were, once more, rather extensive discussions of pitfalls and assumptions, but by this time causal modeling had become something of a fad among sociological users, and the numbers of empirical articles using path analysis increased substantially, although virtually all of these were confined to recursive models that did not allow for feedback loops or lag periods.

Meanwhile, methodologically sophisticated discussions of so-called cross-level analysis problems involving theory and data at different levels of aggregation began to surface (Hannan 1971; Hannan and Burstein 1974; Langbein and Lichtman 1978; Firebaugh 1978). My distinct impression is that sociological practitioners were totally unaware of this literature. Certainly it is rarely cited either by such investigators or by recent critics, including Freedman. Sociologists continue to ignore self-selection processes in making individual-level inferences (say about children's learning) on the basis of school-level aggregated data without even considering Hannan's or Langbein and Lichtman's warnings about aggregation biases and how these are affected by grouping or aggregating by dependent variables. The point is, again, that Freedman is basically correct in criticising current practice but also misleading in seeming to imply that problems of this sort are suddenly being discovered by recent critics. I pointed to problems involved in grouping by dependent variables as far back as 1964, for example, although I was not aware at that time of the vast literature on aggregation that existed in econometrics or the connections between problems of aggregation and disaggregation and the so-called contextual effects literature that was also developing during the 1960s.

Let me turn, next, to some of the points Freedman makes with which I disagree or where I believe his arguments to be misleading. First, he has selected, *ex post facto,* a single instance of a successful "detective story," namely Snow's investigations of the sources of cholera. One wonders if it would have been so easy, without benefit of hindsight, to distinguish, contemporaneously, between the tactics of the very few successful detectives and those of the presumably much greater number of failing detectives. Certainly, in sociology we have a few examples of very good detective work (e.g., Durkheim's classic study of suicide) but many, many others of so-called "exploratory" research that has gone nowhere.

Detectives in novels practically always search from among a large number of possible candidates for single killers (causes), or at most for several who are closely linked. Snow's problem was of a similar nature, and he indeed must have employed ingenious and carefully designed studies to uncover a single source. It is very different, however, in most social science applications, where multiple causation is the rule rather than the exception and where it is often the case that no five or six variables stand out as overwhelming favorites. Not only is there multiple causation, but delayed feedbacks occur, and economists have found distributed lag models appropriate in many instances. Nor can simple homogeneity assumptions, which are common in the physical sciences, be justified. The "constants" appearing in regression equations are more realistically considered as variables, particularly as one attempts to increase the scope of one's generalizations (Blalock 1982).

These and other complications—which I attempted to specify in a semi-popular discussion (Blalock 1984)—mean that detective work is far from simple. If one could do it as systematically as Freedman seems to imply, we could reach a deeper understanding of the causal forces most immediately affecting our own lives. We could understand why our two daughters turned out to be very different, why our son stubbornly refuses to do more homework, why our marriages break up, or why we cannot seem to overcome selected biases or the temptation to smoke one more cigarette. In short, if careful detective work can be successful in the social sciences, why cannot we apply it to our own lives?

In my judgment the answer lies in the fact that there are very large numbers of individually unimportant causal factors operating in all such instances, many of which occurred over a long period of time but which have had lagged effects that are difficult to specify. Furthermore, our earlier behaviors (and our present ones) feed back in nonrecursive fashion to affect many of the "independent" variables that experimentally inclined investigators are willing to assume cannot be so affected. And, of course, there are many pieces of empirical information that cannot be recovered or that are unknown to us.

So we remain very poor detectives in accounting for our own personal experiences, successes and failures alike.

Let me turn to what I consider to be the most misleading of Freedman's arguments, namely the suggestion that experimental or quasi-experimental designs are presumably almost automatically superior to nonexperimental designs and the related thesis that required assumptions needed for nonexperimental research are usually not met and are indeed implausible, leading to what he terms circular arguments. This is indeed the case if one compares the *ideal* experimental (or quasi-experimental) design with the far from imperfect *real* instances of nonexperimental research that appear in the literature. In the idealized quasi-experimental design, for instance, one finds a "matching" comparison group, or perhaps a dramatic shift in an interrupted time-series design. But in real life, one "matches" on only a very few characteristics and then makes the (untested) *assumption* that comparison and treatment groups are nearly similar in terms of the numerous uncontrolled factors that have not been examined.

In real-life experiments it is indeed possible to randomize and therefore control for those relatively constant properties of individuals who have been placed into one or another treatment group. As has been discussed in all methods texts with which I am familiar, however, neither manipulations (which are practically always multidimensional and poorly understood theoretically) nor "uncontrolled events" that occur during the experiment can be randomized. Therefore, untested assumptions must be made in all but the ideal experimental design. Often such assumptions are also highly implausible to those of us not in the experimental design tradition. For example, the usual assumption is that uncontrolled events do not interact statistically with whatever experimental variables are being manipulated in the "treatments" of concern. The extremely naive (and convenient) assumption practically always made is that dependent variables have been measured without error and that there is no slippage between manipulations and the theoretical variables they supposedly cause. No other latent variables are assumed to be affected by such manipulations.

Even more serious is the fact that in the real world, experiments can only be carried out on relatively weak or docile subjects: school children, college freshmen volunteers from introductory social science courses, patients, and (in the past) prisoners. Furthermore, treatments must be innocuous, of short duration, and implemented under highly artificial conditions in which subjects are well aware that they are being experimented upon. Only very short-term effects can be studied, and lag periods are assumed to be extremely short. Distributed lags resulting from continued applications of the treatments are also virtually always ruled out. In all such instances *untested* assumptions are being made, but usually only implicitly.

Imagine trying to experiment on political elites, say members of the U.S. Congress. Could we have experimented on savings and loans executives during the period of time with which we are (belatedly) concerned? Could we conduct experiments or use quasi-experimental designs to study peasant revolutions, political or economic development, impacts of deeply held religious beliefs, domestic violence, or even husband-wife interaction patterns or peer influences on teenagers? Perhaps Chairman Mao was in a position to carry out large-scale experiments during the 1950s and 1960s, but the rest of us were not. If we were to confine our analyses to experimental and quasi-experimental designs, virtually all of sociology and political science would have to go by the wayside. Certainly, my own field of race and ethnic relations would have to be confined to an extremely narrow range of problems, many of which no longer interest us. The field of comparative race relations, in particular, would have to be discarded. Perhaps all of the topics I mention here belong under the heading of Unanswerable Questions, but this indeed depends on how perfectionistic or rigid one chooses to be about accepting "questionable" assumptions.

My position is that we *must* make use of untested assumptions in all research, experimental or not. But this means that we must collectively make such assumptions explicit so that they can be readily challenged, and then rely on a cumulative process through which specific questionable assumptions are challenged, new data are collected to assess such assumptions, and models altered accordingly. No matter how complex the model becomes, however, there must always remain a series of untested assumptions regarding disturbance terms and the unmeasured and unknown variables that affect them. I therefore see no reasonable alternative to the development of much more complex causal models than we presently are accustomed to "testing." I will fully admit, however, that we are presently failing rather miserably in engaging in such a collective effort.

There are many reasons behind this failing effort, some of which I have tried to enumerate in my *Basic Dilemmas* book (1984) and others in my *ASR* critique (1989) of quantitative research. Here a mere listing of such factors is all that space permits:

1. Low standards and weak curricula in undergraduate programs, leading to low-quality graduate students as measured by GRE scores
2. Weak graduate training programs, containing few requirements and only very low-level required statistics courses that are not well integrated with more general methods courses
3. An American student body that has virtually no interest in philosophy of science or theoretical issues but that is far more oriented to immediate applied problems of fashionable interest
4. Compartmentalization of statistics/methods courses and theory courses, combined with inattention of "theorists" to matters of verification (Lenski 1988)
5. An extreme splintering of the field into tiny subspecializations, many with highly applied orientations
6. Continued nonproductive disputes between science-oriented and anti-science-oriented members of the profession, with the latter poised to take advantage of intellectual exchanges such as the present one
7. Publication pressures favoring quick research and the use of secondary data sources, creating a vested interest in looking the other way and failing to conduct proper preliminary investigations
8. Journal policies and professional norms that fail to discourage bad practices
9. Inadequate funding for research combined with a lack of organizations capable of producing multifaceted, large-scale data sets

Freedman, by implication, has hit upon many of these, and practicing members of the profession ought to be appreciative. But we have known of these problems for a long time and have failed to act upon them. I would like to believe that we will now do so, but my own experience suggests that such a wish will again fall on many deaf ears. Indeed, very few empirically inclined sociologists will ever read this volume.

REFERENCES

Blalock, H. M. 1964. *Causal Inferences in Nonexperimental Research.* Chapel Hill: University of North Carolina Press.

———. 1968. "The Measurement Problem: A Gap Between the Languages of Theory and Research." Chapter 1 in *Methodology in Social Research,* edited by H. M. Blalock and A. B. Blalock. New York: McGraw-Hill.

———. 1982. *Conceptualization and Measurement in the Social Sciences.* Beverly Hills, CA: Sage.

———. 1984. *Basic Dilemmas in the Social Sciences.* Beverly Hills, CA: Sage.

———. 1989. "The Real and Unrealized Contributions of Quantitative Sociology." *American Sociological Review* 54:447–60.

Coombs, C. H. 1964. *A Theory of Data.* New York: Wiley.

Costner, H. L. 1969. "Theory, Deduction, and Rules of Correspondence." *American Journal of Sociology* 75:245–63.

———. "Utilizing Causal Models to Discover Flaws in Experiments." *Sociometry* 34:398–410.

Costner, H. L., and R. Schoenberg. 1973. "Diagnosing Indicator Ills in Multiple-Indicator Models." Chapter 9 in *Structural Equation Models in the Social Sciences,* edited by A. S. Goldberger and O. D. Duncan. New York: Seminar Press.

Duncan, O. D. 1975. *Introduction to Structural Equation Models.* New York: Academic Press.

Firebaugh, G. 1978. "A Rule for Inferring Individual-Level Relationships from Aggregate Data." *American Sociological Review* 43:557–72.

Glenn, N. D. 1989. "What We Know, What We Say We Know: Discrepancies between Warranted and Unwarranted Conclusions." Chapter 4 in *Crossroads of Social Science,* edited by H. Eulau. New York: Agathon Press.

Gordon, R. A. 1968. "Issues in Multiple Regression." *American Journal of Sociology* 73:592–616.

Hannan, M. T. 1971. *Aggregation and Disaggregation in Sociology.* Lexington, MA: Lexington Books.

Hannan, M. T., and L. Burstein. 1974. "Estimation from Grouped Observations." *American Sociological Review* 39:374–92.

Hauser, R. M., and A. S. Goldberger. 1971. "The Treatment of Unobservable Variables in Path Analysis." Chapter 4 in *Sociological Methodology 1971,* edited by H. L. Costner. San Francisco: Jossey-Bass.

Heise, D. R. 1969. "Separating Reliability and Stability in Test-Retest Correlation." *American Sociological Review* 34:93–101.

———. 1975. *Causal Analysis.* New York: Wiley.

Herting, J. R., and H. L. Costner. 1985. "Respecification in Multiple-Indicator Models." Chapter 15 in *Causal Models in the Social Sciences,* edited by H. M. Blalock. New York: Aldine.

Langbein, L. I., and A. J. Lichtman. 1978. *Ecological Inference.* Beverly Hills, CA: Sage.

Lenski, G. E. 1988. "Rethinking Macrosociological Theory." *American Sociological Review* 53:163–71.

Lieberson, S. 1985. *Making it Count: The Improvement of Social Theory and Research.* Berkeley: University of California Press.

Marini, M. M., and B. Singer. 1988. "Causality in the Social Sciences." Pp. 347–409 in *Sociological Methodology 1988,* edited by C. C. Clogg. Washington, DC: American Sociological Association.

Namboodiri, N. K., L. F. Carter, and H. M. Blalock. *Applied Multivariate Analysis and Experimental Designs.* New York: McGraw-Hill.

13

FREEDMAN IS RIGHT AS FAR AS HE GOES, BUT THERE IS MORE, AND IT'S WORSE. STATISTICIANS COULD HELP

*William M. Mason**

1. INTRODUCTION

There is an accumulation of about 10 years of David Freedman's compelling case studies of statistical practice in nonexperimental research, most of it in the social sciences (Freedman 1981; Freedman, Rothenberg, and Sutch 1983; Freedman and Peters 1984*a;* Freedman and Peters 1984*b;* Freedman 1983; Daggett and Freedman 1985; Freedman and Navidi 1986; Freedman 1987; Freedman and Zeisel 1988). On a sentence-by-sentence basis I agree with Freedman the vast majority of the time. This is clearly scholarship and logic of the highest order and integrity, and it deserves our ultimate compliment, which is careful study.

In what follows, I do not comment on Freedman's articles as such. Instead, after summarizing the view I attribute to Freedman and like-minded people, I ruminate on practice and training in "quantitative sociology" and fantasize about what I would like from statisticians.

David Freedman is one of the most important philosophers of

This is a slight revision of comments presented in response to David Freedman's "Statistical Models and Shoe Leather" at the Annual Meetings of the American Sociological Association, San Francisco, 1989.

*University of California, Los Angeles

science to focus on quantitative research in the social sciences. He takes the time to master what we write. His purpose is to assess our implicit framework, the unspoken rules that allow us to think that we are communicating with each other. This is traditionally a philosopher's job. However, I have rarely been satisfied with the results of philosophical discourse on the social sciences because the philosophers have not convinced me that they understand our trade. David Freedman does. He knows the statistics better than we do, he is a quick study when it comes to substance, his range is remarkable, and he carries out his own investigations on our work. His response to it is nonignorable.

2. THE FREEDMAN POSITION

A decade of criticisms of social science research and several discussions with Freedman can be summarized as follows:

1. The true experiment is strongly preferred to any other design if the purpose is to establish causality between X and Y and strength of relationship.
2. Absent a true experiment, one should aim for a quasi-experimental design.
3. Prospective, longitudinal studies can be revealing.
4. Time-series analysis, whether structural equation modeling, ARIMA, or what have you, is exceedingly difficult to defend.
5. Cross-sectional designs are perhaps slightly less difficult to defend but are highly tendentious nevertheless.
6. Simple tools should be used extensively. More complex tools should be used rarely, if at all. Thus, we should be doing more graphical analyses and computing fewer regressions, correlations, survival models, structural equation models, and so on.
7. Virtually all social science modeling efforts (and here I include social science experiments, though I'm not sure Freedman would) fail to satisfy reasonable criteria for justification of the stochastic assumptions. Why is Y, conditional on X, Gaussian i.i.d. or some other distributional form, or why do any other

such assumptions hold?[1] Social scientists rarely, if ever, have theory for the stochastic parts of the specification. In effect we engage in curve fitting as far as that part of our modeling effort is concerned. Sure, some Y may be normal, or normal under transformation, or some other catalogued distribution. But so what? We don't have theory that suggests normality or that accounts for normality or other functional forms. This is the best case. The worst case doesn't even check to see if normality is satisfied. I am guilty of some of this; most of us are—at least occasionally. Some of us argue that normality doesn't matter, as long as we satisfy symmetry, and so on. This means that current practice is indifferent to the stochastic assumptions of our analytic efforts: We tend not to check or satisfy our stochastic assumptions, and even if we do, we rarely, if ever, have a theoretical rationale for distributional form A, as opposed to forms B and C. I claim this is true for experimental as well as nonexperimental research in the social sciences.

8. Much reputable work pays inadequate attention to the assumptions and defense of the *deterministic* parts of our models. With regard to structural equation models, this includes the assumptions involving which variables are regressors and which are regressands. This criticism also refers to the nature of the "act" surrounding estimation of a structural equation model. We have *estimated* a "structure." We haven't tested the conception behind that structural concept except, possibly, in the trivial sense that we have used a procedure to restrict some coefficients to zero— using either a priori reasoning to identify simultaneity or some kind of test to exclude a variable from a list of regressors. Fundamentally, this enterprise does not distinguish right from wrong. It provides an "account" that may or may not be generalizable or sustain comparisons with other such accounts computed for other data. Maybe the whole works is nonlinear. Maybe some kind of threshold model is more appropriate. There is a general failure to try other accounts to see if they fit the data better.

[1]Freedman singles out regression with Gaussian errors, but he would be equally comfortable making the same point, suitably modified, about applications of loglinear models, survival models, bivariate probit specifications, and so on.

These eight points amount to an indictment of current practice. We do relatively few experiments. We do a lot of analysis of cross-sectional and time-series data. We rarely consider the validity of the underlying stochastic assumptions or their sense in relation to the problem of interest. Our deterministic specifications are rarely checked against meaningful alternatives—and here I am not talking about what passes conventionally for sensitivity analysis.

3. REACTIONS

Where do we go from here? Here is a bit of counterpoint and a prediction:

1. We can and will do more experiments. However, as Smith (1990) argues, as we continue to gain experience with experimentation, some of us will discover that theory is no less necessary. Omitted variables can *interact* with included variables, in which case randomization does not suffice. Further, as Berk et al. have noted, uncontrolled intervention can occur *between* experimental manipulation and experimental outcome (Berk, Lenihan, and Rossi 1980; Rossi, Berk, and Lenihan 1982). Smith expands upon this point to argue that experimentation does not necessarily yield a single dominant, preferred answer in such a case. None of this is to say that experimentation is bad. It is merely to point out that randomization and experimental manipulation don't solve all of our problems, whether these are statistical or philosophical in nature. In any case, we will do more.

2. I doubt we are going to give up on "observational" data. If anything, we are going to see more of it, and more of it analyzed. Why? For the reasons we know so well already. A lot of what we think about is in the past. It is macro. It is comparative. It is not readily manipulated.

3. As social scientists, we think about lots of problems that we are just not going to do experiments on. And if we do experiments, then there will be problems of external validity. Neither Freedman nor anybody else in relatively free societies seriously argues that sociologists and historians, commentators and journalists should stop observing, collecting "data," conceptualizing

how and why things fit together the way they do, and assessing how well their ideas conform to the reality they attempt to describe. But where do we go from there? We are back to the question of whether our work can cumulate. Like many others before me, I think it can, in the sense that hypotheses and arguments can be rejected by the marshalling of evidence.

4. It is perhaps a fair summary to say that, at least since Durkheim and Weber, social scientists have debated whether quantification can be used to assess theories, models, ideas, views. In these debates, the difference between the evidence provided by experiments and nonexperiments that Freedman has concentrated on has played a minor role. Much more important have been issues of measurement, conceptualization, comparability, and validity. A major benefit of the debate is that it has sharpened ideas on both sides, if sides there be. The *attempt* to quantify, even if it is judged inadequate in a given instance, is beneficial, or can be.

5. An example of what I am talking about is to be found in Somers's (1971) neglected (but superb) essay bearing the forbidding title, "Applications of an Expanded Survey Research Model to Comparative Institutional Studies." In this essay, Somers goes to considerable length to translate into a quantitative representation Barrington Moore's masterpiece, *Social Origins of Dictatorship and Democracy: Lord and Peasant in the Making of the Modern World.* He does not "test" Moore's thesis. Rather, among other things, he elucidates Moore's argument. This is important. Work of this kind can lead to actual quantification and to a form of testing. The next steps seem never to be perfect, but they also seem to represent progress.

6. A related point here is that multivariate, or multivariable, analysis with nonexperimental data may not be able to rule out all *additive* competitors to the argument at hand, but the gain from being able to consider *any* alternative to an argument (even just one alternative) is real. This does not always, or perhaps even frequently, happen. But the possibility exists. Moreover, there is emerging work on tests for specification error—in particular, those errors involving the assumption that the omitted variables of the regression are uncorrelated with the included regressors. This line of attack will not solve all the problems of analysis

with nonexperimental data, but if it provides any help at all, that is progress.

7. The randomized assignment of a controlled experiment allows us to test a substantive hypothesis about a single effect even if the list of (additive) determinants is long. But our universe of discourse is usually limited. Borrowing from Somers' (1971) essay, Charles Beard argued that it was possible to determine whether support for adoption of the U.S. Constitution was due to diffuse support for the ideals it embodied, and he contrasted that possibility with one other—namely, economic class. Beard's work received much scrutiny, but his critics have not thought up an infinity of alternative explanations, whether in an omitted variable framework or from a nonnested competing hypothesis perspective. One alternative might be that ethnicity played a role in people's positions. The point here is that alternatives are focussed: If Beard provides the usual keys to scrupulous scholarship, and he was thought to do just this in his day, then his readers accept his conclusion *conditionally*. If someone else is able to marshall data for a competing idea and to demonstrate nonexperimentally that the competing idea "dominates" the prior idea, then we switch allegiance, or we fight back. That is progress. Because conceptions of science are now quite diverse, I don't know if it is science. I do think that this form of argumentation with data involves a clear element of falsifiability, and that differentiates us from poetry and other humanistic pursuits. It also differentiates us within the social sciences from those who are self-admittedly interested in providing accounts, yet who have relatively implicit or nonexistent rules of evidence.

8. Now let us turn to assumptions about the stochastic portions of the specifications we use. It is rare that we have theories or knowledge about underlying choice of distribution. We engage in a form of curve fitting, in which the curve is rarely seen. As I noted earlier, some would argue that this does not much matter. After all, if distributional characteristics such as symmetry are satisfied, then OLS or something like it will perform reasonably well. There is an emerging literature on asymptotics that provides a kind of escape mechanism to Normality, and so on. Have statisticians made so much progress that we no longer

have to worry much about the underlying stochastic assumptions? Or are we simply using inappropriate technical machinery? Freedman would argue the latter. Perhaps he is right. This is a subject that requires directed, formal scrutiny.

When I began graduate school, unit record data processing equipment was still in common use for social science research. This meant that much of what we did involved crosstabular data, subject to the truly Procrustean Bed of the Hollerith card. In this context, if memory serves, Ed Borgatta was an innovator. He knew how to make an IBM collator (a device to merge two sets of IBM cards) obtain a centroid solution factor analysis. That was a stunning technocratic achievement. Computing a regression was hard in those days. We didn't worry much about satisfying Normality, and so on, back then. We were thinking about social reality and trying to come up with reasonable quantifications of concepts. A quarter century later, our conceptualizations still do not have much to say in defense of our chosen stochastics; meanwhile, statistical technique and computing have burgeoned. The microcomputer that sits on my desk is probably faster than the IBM 7094 that occupied a ballroom-size space and served the entire University of Chicago during much of the 1960s. The software on my PC is enormously powerful. Recognition of this imbalance, this hypertrophy, should be cautionary. Whether it should lead us into alliance with statisticians to develop a new form of quantitative analysis, or lead us to simpler forms of analysis, I don't know.

9. Much, perhaps most, use of statistical inference in the social sciences is ritualistic and even irrelevant. In many applications, analysts don't know the universe to which they wish to make inferences, and they don't know how to compute estimates of variability given that they can specify their universe. Moreover, they don't actually make inferences for their readers to react to. In addition, in many applications, even if the universe is specified, it is uninteresting. We should be explicit about this. Those asterisks that adorn the tables of our manuscripts are the product of ritual and little, if anything, more than that.

My recommendation is to address this head-on in our writing and teaching. Has major progress in the social sciences been aided by the notion of statistical significance, or confidence intervals, or standard errors? Show me. And even if there is some, how much of what we do really depends on that apparatus? Many people agree with what I am saying, but they continue to report standard errors and asterisks—business as usual. In our publications policies, we need to reassess the value of inference. Perhaps we will conclude that we can do with less of it.

As a partial antidote to ritualistic reliance on statistical significance, we should heed Leamer (1983). We need a variety of different *kinds* of studies on the same topic—a sort of meta-version of the multitrait-multimethod matrix. We already do this to some extent in sociology, but not enough. Instead, we divide into camps: hard vs. soft, Marxist vs. non-Marxist, for example. And we don't talk much across camp boundaries. The political economy of departmental life reinforces this posture, and it's not healthy. We need at least a partial truce so we can get those differing kinds of studies of the same subject in greater abundance.

10. I turn next to professional recruitment and socialization. Most sociologists come into the field from undergraduate majors in sociology or related fields. Many have studied little or no mathematics in college. They typically have not had a year of calculus and a semester or quarter of matrix algebra. Nor do they get it as graduate students. As undergraduates, they may have had a course in research methods and an introductory course in statistics. If they were lucky, their instructor used Freedman, Pisani, and Purves's (1978) *Statistics,* but they have probably forgotten the first author's name, they were probably exposed to no more than two thirds of the text, and they probably understood little of it or have forgotten most of it.

As graduate students, what do these people experience? The University of Michigan Sociology Department's model is fairly intensive and in that sense is a current best case. Unless students test out of the required sequence, they take a year of statistics, which is divided into a semester of introductory topics (e.g., hypothesis testing and confidence intervals) and a semester on the linear model that somehow manages to squeeze in a section on maximum likelihood estimation of the logistic response model. However, no calculus is used, and maximum likelihood itself receives no more than a fleeting glance. This does not define the extreme. At least one other program in the U.S. manages to pack in an introduction to structural equation modeling in its mandatory year of statistics. Michigan also offers a third-semester topics course, the substance of which depends on the instructor. It might include survival models or research design, for example.

There is also a substantial commitment to methodology, as distinguished from statistics. Students can choose to participate in the Detroit Area Study (DAS), which is an annual sample survey of metropolitan Detroit. It is both a teaching survey and a research tool for the principal investigator. It takes three semesters and part of a summer for a student to make it through the DAS. It has been criticized for packing a semester's worth of work into three, but nobody has succeeded in redesigning this experience—and many sociology departments look upon it as a model to emulate.

If a student is disinclined toward surveys, a sequence in field work is available. It takes two semesters and involves a lot of hard work. Alternatively, if a student leans toward history, a self-designed methods curriculum for learning historiography is available, as well as work with some truly gifted social historians.

Of course, budding quantitative methodologists in sociology don't settle for this curriculum, and they don't have wholly nonmathematical backgrounds. But they are atypical of the field, and their contributions do not make up the bulk of quantitative research. Instead, we too often encounter students and colleagues with questions like these:

1. "I need your help with this two-stage least squares *model. . . .*" This person doesn't understand the difference between model, estimation principle, and computational procedure.
2. "I want to prove that X causes Y, but not vice versa . . ." This person has a structural equation model in which the simultaneity cannot reasonably be identified.
3. "Why are all these numbers .999?" This person is staring at a page of LISREL output that contains the standardized estimated covariance matrix of the parameter estimates and has no idea how to use these numbers. There are several difficulties, and the entire problem needs to be rethought.

How do we improve quantitative sensitivities? We can modify the graduate curriculum, but that alone is not going to do the job. We need to start at the undergraduate level. You can't pack much more than Michigan does into the graduate curriculum. There are not enough hours in the day to teach all that is needed in the short time available in graduate school. Current practice born of expedience also has great momentum. Even our best researchers often use incorrect standard errors generated by the major computer packages. We rarely do experiments or discover natural experiments. Our measures are imperfect. We ignore Schumann and Presser's (1981) findings on question construction and questionnaire design.

And even if, someday, the most popular computer packages catch up with the statistical profession and include state-of-the-art interactive analytic graphics, jackknifing, bootstrapping, and robust estimation, we are still going to have to find time in the curriculum to teach it. And when we do, some people will use and teach it well, others will not. A future David Freedman will point this out.

But suppose we all became virtuosic at bootstrapping and graphical analysis of residuals. What then? Our modal design is nonexperimental. Our hope must be that, if we improve the internal logic of our statistical practice, we will also improve our substantive thinking and in the process produce more compelling research.

Muthén (1987) has proposed revisions in the curriculum. This would help, but there is a lot of material pouring out of statistics departments. Exploratory data analysis á la Tukey, graphics á la Cleveland, the jackknife, bootstrapping, frontal attacks on sampling errors for complex sample designs, survival models with or without heterogeneity, and so on. What's best? What do we keep and what do we set aside? We can't all be statisticians, and even if we could, we don't all want to be. What comes next is better cooperation between statisticians and social scientists and leadership from statisticians in those spheres in which we have a right to expect it.

4. WHAT I WANT FROM THE STATISTICS PROFESSION

How will better cooperation emerge? It would help if statisticians got their house in order on the following topics. In mentioning them, I should note that when I listed them for David Freedman, he found them of secondary importance. He's usually right, but he could also be reflecting his own more intimate knowledge of his own field. As a sociologist, there is a lot in the world of statistics that I wish were in better order.

1. Bayesian vs. non-Bayesian inference: What are nonstatisticians supposed to do about this fundamental debate? If it is so important for us to be Bayesians, then I want the Bayesians to tell me how to really do Bayesian statistics and give me computer programs that I can use without investing the rest of my life in them. What's out there is quite inadequate. Bayesians, many of whom tell us that theirs is the only logically consistent framework in statistics, need to take responsibility for the development of tools that substantive researchers can use conveniently.

2. I'd appreciate recognition from some of our best statisticians that a rejection of and condescension toward so-called off-the-shelf statistics is in fact a mistake. If we have to invent new statistics every time we do substantive research, we are in trouble—and not just in sociology.

3. I'd like somebody to tell me how to make meaningful statistical inferences in the social sciences. When do I really have a population? Or what is my superpopulation, and should I care?

4. In a related vein, please resolve the debate on what to do with sample weights. And when you do, please modify all pertinent computer programs, and please extend the solution beyond regression.

5. I'd like statisticians to stop propagating bad *substantive research,* as I think they often do when they work on research projects as hired guns. You see this especially in the biomedical areas. The doctors do the substance, and the statisticians do the statistics with little understanding of the substance. The result is often disappointing. What is needed is a more genuine interaction between subject matter researchers and statisticians.

6. Now what about textbooks? Freedman, Pisani, and Purves's *Statistics* is as good as they come. In it you will see much that is fully consistent with what Freedman has been telling the profession for the past decade. It cannot and does not go far enough with a program for what researchers should do with statistics. I can't find any other books that do. It's easy to find material that extolls the virtues of experiments, but that's not good enough

when I'm trying to work with people who are doing historical analyses or macro-comparative analyses. Similarly, it is inadequate to describe graphical procedures, resistant methods, and so on, without also facing the *real* problem, which is the integration of statistics with reasoning about substance.

7. The statistics profession needs to recognize that there is a division of labor between statisticians and nonstatisticians. It's okay for a Jay Kadane to write his own computer program to adjust the census for undercount. It's okay for a David Freedman to write his own programs for bootstrapping. It's not so okay for sociologists to do this. We usually don't have the skills or knowledge, and we can't be expected to assess the value of innovative statistical techniques. The statistics profession should be pressuring the keepers of the major statistical packages to include the features they think we need. There is a substantial lag here, and the lag concerns apparently important tools.

8. It's time for the statistics profession to come to terms with its disdain of the social sciences, especially sociology. Even if the level of practice is not high, the subject itself is difficult. The kind of statistics courses that are routinely offered to those who want to actually use statistics are very narrow. The graduate curriculum for professional statisticians, with exceptions, does little to prepare statisticians for working with social scientists. For example, most professional statisticians don't know much about structural equation estimation with or without latent variables, though in my experience, an expression of prejudice is not hard to elicit. If statisticians made more of an effort to find out what we are up to, and *why* we do what we do, maybe we could make a little more progress. I have frequently tried to talk to world famous statisticians who just didn't know enough to be useful to me (as well as those who did!). Statistics has definitely evolved into a field in which people can do their work without actually seeing and doing applications. Again, David Freedman is an exception.

9. How about comparative evaluation of nonnested models? This is an abstruse specialists' topic that has not been brought into the public domain, as it were. It needs a lot of attention. The

big fights in the substantive core of sociology are about competing ways of viewing social reality, not about omitted variables.

10. Analyses based on "all" the data are paradoxical. I once spent
a lot of time trying to do an analysis of tuberculosis mortality
(Mason and Smith 1985). My analysis was based on population
counts. I used maximum likelihood to estimate logistic regressions. There's a problem here. If I've got all the data, why do
I need a statistical procedure? If I've got a sample, what do I
have a sample of, and how do I figure out what the standard
errors are? For that matter, how do I figure out what the right
estimation procedure is? My answer at the time was that it was
convenient to do what I would have done had I been working
with a sample in the usual sense. I am not satisfied with this.
Neither are Freedman et al. (1978), who warn their readers to
watch out for circumstances like these. Statisticians need to
give us more instructive and concrete advice for cases of this
kind.

11. Not too long ago I attempted a careful look at what I considered to be a fundamental question (Kahn and Mason 1987). To
wit, do we need to think of the secular trend in political alienation as a cohort phenomenon, which is complicated, or can
we think of it as a period phenomenon, which is relatively
simple? I worked with pooled cross-sectional sample surveys
to test the Easterlin hypothesis that relative cohort size, especially for young adults, drives a lot of phenomena (including
political alienation) that, when aggregated, fluctuate over
time. In passing, note the contest here: *one* good idea pitted
against another.

What kind of estimation is best for this sort of quasi-historical
problem? Is this an estimation problem? Does the answer depend on
whether we think we are doing history or whether we think we are
doing science? If estimation is appropriate, how do we assess variability? Is this an off-the-shelf problem? Some critics, including a good
statistician, said that it was and that I didn't even know which shelf to
look on, though I was standing in front of it. Well, maybe. But show
me. I continue to think that I had a sample of *one* cycle, not a sample
of N (O'Brien and Gwartney-Gibbs 1989; Mason and Kahn 1989).

5. CONCLUSION

I've been all over the ball park. Where do I end up? I agree with David Freedman's criticisms, and I've tried to tell you where I think this leaves us. The fundamental points are that we need to shed the cloak of inappropriate statistical machinery and that we must improve all facets of our standards of discourse and training. This is not a "back to the basics" message (Berk 1988). It is a demand for greater rigor.

REFERENCES

Berk, Richard A. 1988. "Causal Inference for Sociological Data." Pp. 155–72 in *Handbook of Sociology,* edited by N. J. Smelser. Beverly Hills, CA: Sage.

Berk, Richard A., Kenneth J. Lenihan, and Peter H. Rossi. 1980. "Crime and Poverty: Some Experimental Evidence from Ex-offenders." *American Sociological Review* 54:447–60.

Daggett, R. S., and D. A. Freedman. 1985. "Econometrics and the Law: A Case Study in the Proof of Antitrust Damages." Pp. 123–73 in *Proceedings of the Berkeley Conference in Honor of Jerzy Neyman and Jack Kiefer,* vol. 1, edited by Lucien M. Le Cam and Richard A. Olshen. Belmont, CA: Wadsworth.

Freedman, David A. 1981. "Some Pitfalls in Large Econometric Models: A Case Study." *Journal of Business* 54:479–500.

––––––. 1985. "Statistics and the Scientific Method." Pp. 345–90 in *Cohort Analysis in Social Research: Beyond the Identification Problem,* edited by W. M. Mason and S. E. Fienberg. New York: Springer-Verlag.

––––––. 1987. "As Others See Us: A Case Study in Path Analysis" (with discussion). *Journal of Educational Statistics* 12:101–223.

Freedman, David A., and W. C. Navidi. 1986. "Regression Models for Adjusting the 1980 Census" (with discussion). *Statistical Science* 1:3–29.

Freedman, David A., and Stephen C. Peters. 1984a. "Bootstrapping an Econometric Model: Some Empirical Results." *Journal of Business and Economic Statistics* 2:150–58.

––––––. 1984b. "Bootstrapping a Regression Equation: Some Empirical Results." *Journal of the American Statistical Association* 79:97–106.

Freedman, David A., Robert Pisani, and Roger Purves. 1978. *Statistics.* New York: W. W. Norton.

Freedman, David A., Thomas Rothenberg, and Richard Sutch. 1983. "On Energy Policy Models" (with discussion). *The Journal of Business and Economic Statistics* 1:24–36 .

Kahn, Joan, and William M. Mason. 1987. "Political Alienation, Cohort Size, and the Easterlin Hypothesis." *American Sociological Review* 52:155–69.

Leamer, Edward. 1983. "Taking the Con out of Econometrics." *American Economic Review* 73:31–43.

Mason, William M., and Joan R. Kahn. 1989. "Political Alienation and Cohort Size Reconsidered: A Reply to O'Brien and Gwartney-Gibbs." *American Sociological Review* 54:480–84.

Mason, William M., and Herbert L. Smith. 1985. "Age-Period-Cohort Analysis and the Study of Deaths from Pulmonary Tuberculosis." Pp. 151–227 in *Cohort Analysis in Social Research: Beyond the Identification Problem,* edited by W. M. Mason and S. E. Fienberg. New York: Springer-Verlag.

Muthén, Bengt O. 1987. "Response to Freedman's Critique of Path Analysis: Improve Credibility by Better Methodological Training." *Journal of Educational Statistics* 12:178–84.

O'Brien, Robert M., and Patricia A. Gwartney-Gibbs. 1989. "Relative Cohort Size and Political Alienation: Three Methodological Issues and a Replication Supporting the Easterlin Hypothesis." *American Sociological Review* 54:476–80.

Rossi, Peter H., Richard A. Berk, and Kenneth J. Lenihan. 1980. "Saying it Wrong with Figures: A Comment on Zeisel." *American Journal of Sociology* 88:390–93.

Schuman, Howard, and Stanley Presser. 1981. *Questions and Answers and Attitude Surveys.* New York: Academic Press.

Smith, Herbert L. 1990. "Problems of Specification in Experimental and Nonexperimental Social Research." Pp. 59–92 in *Sociological Methodology 1990,* edited by Clifford C. Clogg. Oxford: Basil Blackwell.

Somers, Robert H. 1971. "Applications of an Expanded Survey Research Model to Comparative Institutional Studies." Pp. 357–420 in *Comparative Methods in Sociology,* edited by Ivan Vallier. Berkeley: University of California Press.

14

A REJOINDER TO BERK, BLALOCK, AND MASON

David A. Freedman*

We are all in Peter Marsden's debt for organizing this discussion of important (and thorny) topics. Berk, Blalock, and Mason also deserve thanks for thoughtful contributions from different perspectives. There is substantial agreement among us on the state of empirical research in the social sciences. The disagreements—at least on diagnosis—seem relatively minor.

1. BERK

Berk and I see things the same way. Other than approval, I cannot add much to his comments. As is customary, my rejoinder will focus on points at issue.

2. BLALOCK

Blalock was the most critical. His position, if I understand him, can be summarized as follows:

1. The problems I discuss are very well known.
2. These problems are not confined to regression analysis.
3. Most empirical workers ignore such problems and are not doing a serious job of testing theory against reality.

This research was partially supported by NSF grant DMS 86-01634 and by the Miller Institute for Basic Research.
*University of California, Berkeley

4.   Potentially useful statistical procedures quickly get converted to recipes and are then used quite thoughtlessly.

5.   It is misleading for me to suggest "that experimental or quasi-experimental designs are presumably almost automatically superior to nonexperimental designs."

6.   I should be kinder to sociologists because they are plagued by individual differences.

7.   It is easier to pick the winners after the race has been run.

8.   "We *must* make use of untested assumptions in all research, experimental or not."

I will respond to each point in turn.

1.   Blalock may well have priority, but the state of the social science literature suggests that critical discussion of modeling issues is still in order.

2.   Points 2, 3, and 4 are common ground.

5.   Very little in our line of work is automatic. I don't agree with the details of his critique, but the bottom line is right: There are a lot of bad studies based on experiments and quasi experiments, just as Blalock says. On the other hand, there are a lot of good examples. My essay summarized one, and cited several others. With causal modeling in the social sciences, the situation is altogether different. Where are the real gains from the activity, practical or intellectual? There have been many public exchanges on the topic, and the one thing modelers do not provide is a bibliography of solid accomplishments. This omission is a strong signal.

6.   I should be kinder, for other reasons. Individual differences are endemic, even in physics. A single molecule in a gas is quite unpredictable, and thermodynamic laws are statistical in nature. Epidemiology is more relevant; two examples illustrate the pervasive role of individual differences. First, as Snow's data show, most people who were exposed to contaminated water survived; some who drank clean water died. Still, cholera is an infectious, water-borne disease. Second, most smokers do not get lung cancer; some nonsmokers do. This was once an argument to show that cigarettes did not cause cancer. Even today, we cannot ex-

plain individual differences in susceptibility. Still, the evidence against cigarettes is rather strong.

7. Hindsight is 20-20, but this principle seems ungenerous when applied to Snow. An empirical test is almost possible: Spend an hour reading Snow's book. You will see that he was a great scientific detective, and you will be richer for the experience.

8. Blalock and I seem to part company on the value of untestable assumptions. In my opinion, and others', you're not doing science unless you can test your theory. Path models were developed in part to make social science theories more testable, which lends considerable irony to the present discussion. However, I do not believe that modeling has advanced us very far towards the goal: t tests on regression coefficients don't count for much. There seems to be considerable agreement on this point, and on the reasons.

In the end, of course, Blalock's position on untestable assumptions comes close to mine. What is untestable with one data structure can be tested with another. He recommends (as I would)

> that we must collectively make such assumptions explicit so that they can be readily challenged, and then rely on a cumulative process through which specific questionable assumptions are challenged, new data are collected to assess such assumptions, and models altered accordingly. (p. 332)

He goes on to say:

> I therefore see no reasonable alternative to the development of much more complex causal models than we presently are accustomed to "testing." I will fully admit, however, that we are presently failing rather miserably in engaging in such a collective effort. (pp. 332–33)

As to current use of regression models, Blalock is less forgiving than I am, and the two sentences just quoted are at the core of the issue. The similarity of his position to mine outweighs the differences. However, the optimism about complex models seems misplaced. We don't test the current ones, and the next crop will be even more loosely connected to reality. The social science literature, viewed as a historical record, makes this point rather clearly.

Blalock's explanation for our collective failure, in terms of the nine roadblocks to testing, is convincing. Our professional ethic rewards methodological innovation and technical elaboration. Institutionally, we are less appreciative of scholarship or the development of substantive knowledge. The consequences for our enterprise are bitter.

3. MASON

Mason's points sound right to me, with one caveat. He writes:

> At least since Durkheim and Weber, social scientists have debated whether quantification can be used to assess theories, models, ideas, views. In these debates, the difference between the evidence provided by experiments and nonexperiments . . . has played a minor role. Much more important have been issues of measurement, conceptualization, comparability, and validity. (p. 341)

Of course, the issues he cites are central. But so, I think, is the difference between experiments and nonexperiments. In crude but useful shorthand, regression models are popular because they seem to convert nonexperiments to experiments. That is how models derive cause from correlation. However, the derivation is legitimate only if the model's assumptions about cause and effect are right. For additional discussion and references, see Lieberson (1985) or Freedman (1987) or the papers cited by Blalock.

The difficulty is a famous one. And it is handled as famous difficulties often are: acknowledged in a footnote and then ignored. But I think the issue is better faced now than later, and Mason agrees.

Mason has a series of hard questions for statisticians. I can respond only to the first one: Is the Bayesian approach likely to save the day for causal modeling? I think not. For thirty years, I have found Bayesian statistics to be a rich source of mathematical questions. However, I no longer see it as the preferred way to do applied statistics, because I find that uncertainty can rarely be quantified as probability. The Reverend Thomas Bayes had his doubts too, which is why he allowed his essay to be published only after his death; and the matter has been debated ever since.

Mason goes on to say, "Statistics has definitely evolved into a field in which people can do their work without actually seeing and doing applications." If anything, he is being tactful. Some members of the profession are trying hard to make changes, by teaching courses in which substantive questions come first and technique is introduced to find answers. Of course, all too often, technique comes first; data come in as purely decorative illustrations—a practice that is not confined to statistics departments.

4. CONCLUSION

Science grows out of the confrontation between theory and reality. Regression models seemed to offer good testing grounds for social science theory; but that promise has proved largely illusory. There is a surprising degree of agreement on this central point and on the reasons for the failure. It is much less clear, and naturally so, where we go from there.

Berk suggests a reduction in the level of aspirations, better designs, and cross-validation (including testing models on new data). This seems like good advice.

Blalock advocates more complex models and more rigorous testing. I wish him well, but I am not optimistic. If I am right, playing the game harder will not help. It is the rules that we need to change.

Mason recommends more use of experiments; although, as he notes, he will be using nonexperimental data for a long time to come. He writes, "Much, perhaps most, use of statistical inference in the social sciences is ritualistic and even irrelevant" (p. 343), and he recommends a change in journal editorial policies. Finally, he argues for better methodological training, with some help (to which he is surely entitled) from the statistics profession.

Where do I think we should go from here? My answer is fragmentary. Our situation is difficult but far from hopeless. We can retrieve it only by a long succession of small steps: Few can be taken on auto-pilot, and some may turn out in the end to have been misdirected. We should adopt the habit of making empirical claims that are more sharply focused and perhaps more modest. We need to take more seriously the job of comparing theory to reality. And we need to build the requisite tools: reality tests instead of t tests. It is not complexity that will help us, but simplicity.

At any given time, most interesting questions will not have empirical answers. Some do, however, and we have to identify them. Then, different questions demand different kinds of answers. For some issues, anecdotal evidence is the best that can be brought to bear. For others, case studies are appropriate. At times, descriptive statistics will help: 2×2 tables, or even a regression equation. A formal statistical model with significance tests may be just the right approach, on occasion. At present, such distinctions are seldom made. And typical empirical papers, even the good ones, drift off into fantasy. Yet the real world, with all its frustrations, is where we belong.

REFERENCES

Freedman, D. A. 1987. "As Others See Us: A Case Study in Path Analysis" (with discussion). *Journal of Educational Statistics* 12:101–223.
Lieberson, S. 1985. *Making It Count: The Improvement of Social Theory and Research.* Berkeley: University of California Press.

NAME INDEX

SUBJECT INDEX

365